International Trade Theory and Competitive Models

Features, Values, and Criticisms

World Scientific Studies in International Economics
(ISSN: 1793-3641)

World Scientific Studies in International Economics includes works dealing with the theory, empirical analysis, and evaluation of international economic policies and institutions, with topics covering international macroeconomics and finance, international trade theory and policy, as well as international legal and political economy. Monographs and edited volumes will comprise the core of the publications.

The complete list of the published volumes in the series can be found at
http://www.worldscientific.com/series/wssie

65 World Scientific
Studies in
International
Economics

International Trade Theory and Competitive Models

Features, Values, and Criticisms

Ronald W Jones

University of Rochester, USA

 World Scientific

NEW JERSEY · LONDON · SINGAPORE · BEIJING · SHANGHAI · HONG KONG · TAIPEI · CHENNAI · TOKYO

Published by

World Scientific Publishing Co. Pte. Ltd.

5 Toh Tuck Link, Singapore 596224

USA office: 27 Warren Street, Suite 401-402, Hackensack, NJ 07601

UK office: 57 Shelton Street, Covent Garden, London WC2H 9HE

Library of Congress Cataloging-in-Publication Data

Names: Jones, Ronald Winthrop, 1931– author.

Title: International trade theory and competitive models : features, values, and criticisms /
    Ronald W. Jones (University of Rochester, USA).

Description: New Jersey : World Scientific, [2017] | Series: World Scientific studies in
    international economics ; volume 65 | Includes bibliographical references.

Identifiers: LCCN 2017017758| ISBN 9789813200661 (hardcover) |
    ISBN 9813200669 (hardcover)

Subjects: LCSH: International trade.

Classification: LCC HF1379 .J6643 2017 | DDC 382.01--dc23

LC record available at https://lccn.loc.gov/2017017758

British Library Cataloguing-in-Publication Data

A catalogue record for this book is available from the British Library.

For any available supplementary material, please visit
http://www.worldscientific.com/worldscibooks/10.1142/10297#t=suppl

Desk Editor: Alisha Nguyen

Typeset by Stallion Press
Email: enquiries@stallionpress.com

Printed in Singapore

To my grand Grands:

Kenneth
Christopher
Nicholas
William
Helen
Alistair
Laila
Oscar
Rowan

About the Author

Ronald W. Jones has just finished a 58 year period as Professor at the University of Rochester. His field of research and focus of teaching, both to undergraduate and graduate classes, has been International Trade Theory. He has had a number of visiting appointments, e.g. at Kobe University, the University of Geneva, Monash University (and many others). He is a Fellow of the Econometric Society, the American Academy of Arts and Sciences and the National Academy of Sciences. He was a co-author with Richard Caves (and, for the last 6 editions, Jeffrey Frankel), of the textbook, *World Trade and Payments*. He has also published around 180 articles and a couple of books. The focus has usually been on General Equilibrium features of international trade models. He has been the recipient of six honorary doctorates.

Contents

Foreword

More than 50 years ago, early in his career, and not long after work on the existence of competitive equilibrium by Kenneth Arrow, Gerard Debreu, and Lionel McKenzie, Ronald Jones made the wager that simple versions of such models would be a most useful approach for comparative statics and thus to understand how market economies work. Considering two factors of production located in each of two countries that trade two goods, he was able to show how wages and outputs could be explained in terms of technology, ability of factors to move between sectors, and income shares. Surprisingly, he was able to do so without assuming specific functional forms. In subsequent work, some of it recent, Jones has applied this elegant and illuminating approach to other economic situations and questions by varying assumptions on the mobility of factors of production, on whether goods are consumables or used as inputs in further production, and on the use and trade of services, to list a few.

Some of the 19 papers in this terrific volume consider classic questions — among them, the assignment problem: who should produce what? Other papers investigate novel questions — for example, how does international fragmentation of production, an increasingly important phenomenon, affect wages? In all of them, and with his trademark display of mastery and enthusiasm, Jones takes advantage of the low dimensionality to present not only equations, but also detailed verbal explanations and, when possible, diagrams to further illuminate the analysis.

The result is a menu of general equilibrium models of multiple competitive markets — models that are transparent and simple and yet are able to address such vastly important concerns as the wages and employment of labor and other productive factors. These models, being multi-market, also offer a more intuitive approach to economic analysis than does partial

International Trade Theory and Competitive Models

equilibrium analysis, which assumes that the one market under consideration has no economic significance for the overall economy. "But if it is not important for others than the buyers and sellers in that market, why should anyone else have any interest?" the reader might ask. With general equilibrium analysis this conundrum no longer exists.

At this time of questioning of international trade and the associated policies and institutions, there is a great need for the kind of cool and powerful economic analysis that Jones offers. The timing of publication of this volume is indeed fortuitous.

Carsten Kowalczyk
The Fletcher School of Law and Diplomacy
Tufts University

Preface

This book is the outcome of an invitation from Keith Maskus, a professor from the University of Colorado, speaking for World Scientific Publishing, to write a book containing a selection of some of my research that had appeared in various journals or parts of books. My field of research has throughout been in the discipline of international trade, with emphasis on trade theoretical research in the micro-economics area. I had, decades earlier, produced such a book for the North-Holland Publishing Company, *International Trade: Essays in Theory*, (1979). But of course much time has passed since then, and in my research and teaching obligations (both for undergraduates and graduate students) at the University of Rochester I continued to produce papers in professional journals and books. My overall average for papers has been around three a year, so that there was enough fodder from which to choose without raiding material from the 1979 book. In this book, there is one exception, my 1965 paper, "*The Structure of Simple General Equilibrium Models*," which appeared in the *Journal of Political Economy* and seems to be my most popular article in the 60 years since my first publication. I decided also to select that paper now (as Chapter 4) because many of the other chapters of this new book make use of the material found there.

I must admit that trying to select a relatively small number of papers from a considerably higher pile is not easy. Is it because they are all so terrific? No. (They may not even *be* terrific, especially after the passage of so much time.) I wanted to bring together especially those articles that had interesting remarks to make about a small selection of *model* types. In almost every discipline (including economics), theoretical arguments take place based on assumptions made as to the *form* of a model. Let me now indulge myself briefly in talking about an incident that involved me in the early 1960s. At that time in the economics profession, one of the important developments was taking place in the field of economic history. There was a small group of economists (mostly of the younger generation) who wanted to make use of some of the mathematical tools that had recently found their way into economics. An especially eager member was Robert Fogel, who at that time was finishing his graduate work at Johns Hopkins University (along with Stanley Engerman, who also would end up at Rochester). The Rochester economics department, under the guiding hand of their recently acquired chairman, Lionel McKenzie, was especially focused on hiring bright young recruits who, in their more applied fields of interest such as labor economics or international trade, would desire to make use of basic economic theory to help guide their research. McKenzie had heard that Fogel was looking for a job, and quickly invited him to give a recruiting seminar at Rochester. We were so impressed by his talk (I believe on the importance of the railroad in opening up the American West in the early 19th century) that he received (and accepted) our offer before the day was out. (Things like that were done more quickly in those days.) After he joined our department, he made clear to Lionel that he wished to learn more about general equilibrium theory to help him in his research. McKenzie then turned to me to provide him with some useful information because he knew that I was particularly interested in the role GE was playing in international trade theory. This request led eventually to my aforementioned 1965 paper. I had an especially strong incentive to make the mathematical (and economic) reasoning *easier* than typically found — not just for Fogel's benefit, but so that *I* finally understood the material better. (I hope the readers of the chapters in this book find value in my desire to make reasoning found in GE-types of models used in trade theory more simple.) Let me finish this diatribe of mine with a remark that Robert Fogel made to me about the attitude held by many historians concerning the *new* economic history emerging from people like himself. They would sneer at him because he had *models* to explain historical events. His response: "You also have a model; you just don't know it."

The models discussed here in the various chapters of the book are assumed to be competitive. There are, of course, markets that are not perfectly competitive, such as the Chamberlin model of monopolistic competition or more general models of imperfect competition such as monopoly or oligopoly models. (Models that are based on "game theory" fundamentals are also not pursued in these chapters.) However, there is a particular distinction found in most perfectly competitive models used in international trade theory since the work on the important concept of comparative advantage by David Ricardo 200 years ago: Although some markets are considered as "world markets," other markets are strictly "country markets" (or perhaps markets that are even more local). In many general equilibrium models not concerned with international trade, there might be many different commodity or factor markets that are each highly competitive, so that prices and costs are strongly (equally) matched in market equilibria. In international trade models, by contrast, it is never thought that there are *only* world markets. Rather, even if many (if not all) commodity markets are world markets, generally *factor* markets are *country* markets. There indeed may be many world markets, but countries are countries for a reason — even if they are interested in receiving gains from international trade in some markets, in other markets they may insist on keeping exchanges to remain only for their own country.

This assumption of a distinction between world markets and country markets has, not surprisingly, a long history, going as far back at least to the book by David Ricardo *On the Principles of Political Economy and Taxation* (1817). Perhaps the most celebrated idea in Ricardo's work concerns the concept of comparative advantage, which he used in discussing patterns of international trade among countries. If countries were initially not having contact with other countries, there would nonetheless be a variety of markets within countries, where buyers and sellers could exchange commodities, workers with the same skill-sets get the same wage rates in equilibrium, and lands of the same quality get the same returns. (Ricardo had a four-letter word to describe differences in remuneration for lands of different qualities — it is called *rent*.) Ricardo realized that if there were a pair of countries contemplating free trade with each other and each country had an absolute advantage over the other country in producing one commodity but an absolute disadvantage in producing the other commodity, both countries would obviously want to exchange one commodity for the other. No one ever doubted that. But if one country was better than the other in producing *both* commodities there seemed no point in contemplating mutual gains from trade. But that is the wrong conclusion, argued Ricardo. It is not absolute advantage for each country that is required, only *comparative* advantage! That is a huge distinction, one not only that

International Trade Theory and Competitive Models

is central in international trade theory but also in any scenario where two individuals, say, are contemplating an exchange in two different jobs that need to be done. One individual might be better at both jobs, but more so in one than in the other. So they both should be willing to accept this split according to comparative advantage as long as the more skilled individual gets a higher pay. This is the analog to trade between two countries when one country has an absolute advantage over the other in making both goods. If there is no world market in workers, a trade equilibrium involving commodities can be reached without requiring that the wage rates in both countries are equalized, since labor markets are country markets, not world markets. Ricardo's concept of comparative advantage is, in my view, one of the most important concepts in all of economics that deals with competitive markets.

In Part I of the book, the model named after Ricardo makes a very simple assumption about the way commodities are produced: The *only* input required is labor. In Part II, a pair of other models is discussed: The Heckscher–Ohlin model is the name used to capture the important work of Eli Heckscher and Bertil Ohlin, both Swedes. Heckscher was the teacher and Ohlin the student. The model deliberately makes a different assumption as to *how* commodities are produced: Each requires not only labor but either land or capital as well. To help distinguish the Heckscher–Ohlin model from that of Ricardo, they often assumed that *technology* of production in one country was the same as that used in production in the other country (whereas country technologies were different in the Ricardian model). In Heckscher–Ohlin what matters are two basic elements: (i) How does the ratio of labor to land (or to capital) that is required in production differ between commodities? and (ii) How do the relative endowment ratios of labor and capital differ between countries?

Each model has a different kind of explanation as to the source of comparative advantage in production between countries. But it still is comparative advantage that underlies trade patterns.

The third kind of model I focus on in this book is (what I called) the Specific-Factors model, or (what Paul Samuelson called) the Ricardo-Viner model. The ideas of this model were used by many an economist even prior to the Heckscher–Ohlin model, but the more formal expositions were provided only in 1971.[1] The Specific-Factors model in the simple form (the so-called [3 × 2] version) has three different factors of production rather than only two, as in the Heckscher–Ohlin (2 × 2) model. However, its greater simplicity is based on the fact that in Heckscher–Ohlin both factors are mobile between industries, while the word "specific" in the Specific-Factors model refers to the fact that two of the factors are each "specific" to a particular industry, leaving only a single factor that is mobile between sectors. Sometimes this model assumes only two factors of production, but one factor is mobile in the sense that it can move from industry to industry whereas the other (e.g., capital in some models) cannot, at least in the "short run." Chapter 8 has a more fulsome answer to the question as to how similar or different the two models are.

In using this pair of models, the most typical question asked is how sensitive are wage rates and capital (or land) rents to any given change either in (i) commodity prices or, instead, a given change in (ii) factor endowments (assuming commodity prices are kept fixed). As is shown in many chapters of this book, the answers to such questions are *strikingly different* in the two models. In the first scenario, the surprising answer in the (2 × 2) Heckscher–Ohlin model is that if it is only the price of the more labor-intensive commodity that is raised, the country's wage rate will increase, not only in "nominal" terms but also in "real" terms. Furthermore, this claim (the increase in the real wage) does not depend upon a close inspection of taste patterns on the part of laborers. Why not? Because the wage rate increases relatively more than does the price of the labor-intensive commodity (with the other price constant or even rising by a smaller relative amount). This is what I have called the "magnification effect," and it is based on an assumption that is so basic it often is not even mentioned — each *single* commodity is produced by the *pair* of two factors. That is, there is no *joint production*. If the same question (i) is asked in the Specific-Factors model, the answer as to the wage rate change is very different. If either commodity price is raised while the other price remains constant, in relative terms the wage rate must increase, but not as much as the single price increase. Instead, the return to the type of capital used *only* in producing the commodity whose price has increased will itself increase

---

[1] The Jones and Samuelson (1971) papers are referenced in Chapter 8.

relatively by *more* than the commodity price and the return to the type of capital used in the industry in which price is constant will actually fall. The relative change in the wage rate is trapped between the relative price changes.

   These two models give different answers to question (ii) as well. In the Heckscher–Ohlin model, if commodity prices are kept constant, any change in factor endowments has no effect on factor prices. If that result sounds too surprising, it is partly because it is generally assumed that the pattern of production is not changed by the change in factor endowments. If, say, the capital/labor endowment rises enough, the country will specialize completely in producing the more capital-intensive commodity. If so, the Heckscher–Ohlin model no longer applies. With only a single commodity produced, it is as if a kind of degenerative form of the Specific-Factors model takes over — a (2 × 1) form instead of the (3 × 2) form. If only one commodity is produced the increase in the capital/labor endowment ratio must *raise* the wage/rent ratio, and, if the capital/labor endowment ratio rises even further, the country might in addition start to produce another even more capital intensive commodity, and once again the *model* that is appropriate changes, from the (2 × 1) form of the Specific-Factors model to the (2 × 2) Heckscher–Ohlin model. The difference between this and the earlier version of the Heckscher–Ohlin model is that the *two commodities* bundle is different. The more labor-intensive commodity in the earlier version is no longer produced, and instead a much more capital-intensive commodity is produced. The other commodity is produced in both cases, but changes from being a relatively capital-intensive commodity to becoming the new more labor-intensive commodity. Note that with international trade, a country need not produce more than a pair of commodities, even though consumers might consume a greater number of commodities. This should remind you of the difference between the Heckscher–Ohlin model and the Ricardian model. In Chapter 1, the many-commodity case of the Ricardian model is also discussed, and that model emphasizes that an important difference between a country being in autarky as opposed to being allowed to trade commodities with other countries is that with trade a country can continue to consume many commodities, but typically will need to produce a smaller number, even only one — the commodity in which it has its greatest comparative advantage. The small-scaled version of the Heckscher–Ohlin model focuses on which commodity is exported and which imported. However, if the scenario allows a trading economy that uses only two factors of production to experience growth in capital/labor endowment ratios, it may continue to consume many commodities but produce no more than a pair of commodities or even only one. Chapter 19 provides a full discussion of a scenario that by allowing growth there may emerge situations in which there is a *blending* of these trade models.

To conclude this discussion, what can be said of the way in which the Specific-Factors model behaves if there are changes in factor endowments but not in commodity prices? As discussed in Chapter 18 and in some earlier chapters (e.g. Chapter 12), if, say, there are many commodities produced, each with a different specific kind of capital used in production with labor that is used in all sectors, and in one of the sectors (commodity j) there is an increase in the endowment only of the specific form of capital used there, K_j, the return to this type of capital *does* change even if commodity prices remain fixed. Furthermore, the wage rate increases, by the same amount in all sectors, which also implies that the return to capital in *every* sector of the economy falls, but not by the same amount in all sectors. However, as discussed in Chapter 12, the return to a specific capital in some industry *other* than industry j may fall by a greater relative amount than the return to the type of capital used in the jth- sector.

The chapters in Part III are concerned with another kind of question. Assume that typically each final commodity that reaches consumers in a trading world may make use of a number of *parts* or *components* in its production. If so, need all such parts be produced in the same country as the one producing (and exporting) the final commodity? Not if the costs of the service links required to allow such parts to join other parts in the final production process are low enough. If they are too expensive for some part, the producer will not bother to fragment the production process by using that country to produce the part. If such service link costs are low enough, a relatively large number of parts *will* be produced in those countries that have the greatest comparative advantage in producing them. Well, if such service link costs have been falling as much as they have in the past few decades, we might expect that there is allowed a large reduction in final consumer prices because of the finer degree of *fragmentation* that results in various parts being assigned to the countries having the highest comparative advantage in producing that part. Even if laborers or land or capital may not be traded on world markets, it may become possible to trade some of the parts they produce that are then used with other parts to produce the final commodity. Gains are linked to the finer application of the concept of comparative advantage. Ricardo strikes yet again!

The material found in the pair of articles in Part IV is quite readable and is indeed meant to unite the material found in other parts of the book. It is time to end here so that you may proceed to whichever articles you wish to read. This has only been a *Preface*, because each article may be discussed in the remarks made in the (lower case) preface found in the assigned *Part* in which the article is found. I wish you well.

Acknowledgements

To my many co-authors and to my son, Brenn, for great help in connecting with those who put things together.

Part I

An Old Favorite: The Ricardian Model

The Ricardian Model is named after David Ricardo, who, in his book, *The Principles of Political Economy and Taxation*, (1817), discussed the concept of comparative advantage, a concept that has been fundamental for 200 years in the developments in international trade theory. Chapter 1 is taken from the Supplement to Chapter 5 of the third edition of the textbook, *World Trade and Payments*, (Richard Caves and Ronald Jones). The supplement was based on my 1961 article, *"Comparative Advantage and the Theory of Tariffs: A Multi-Commodity, Multi-Country Model,"* published in *The Review of Economic Studies*, June 1961, (and also appears as Chapter 3 in my 1979 book *International Trade: Essays in Theory*). The chapter begins by mentioning how the famous concept of comparative advantage was originally formulated in a simple model based on the gains from international trade taking place between two countries, each of them capable of producing two commodities, but with the required labor inputs relatively different between the countries. If each country was better at producing one of the commodities but not the other, it seemed obvious to many that international free trade based upon these assumptions clearly would result in benefits to each country. The Ricardian argument that has been so fundamental to trade theory is that such benefits could be shared by both countries even if labor in one country was better in producing both commodities than the other country. The only requirements for such

1

a mutual gain are that each country would export the commodity in which it possessed a comparative advantage and that goods have a global market but labor (the only input in production) has only a national market (i.e., is not mobile between countries so that wage rates can differ between countries).

In Chapter 1, the display of labor costs in countries A, B, and C are considered for the three commodities corn, linen, and cloth. Suppose countries B and C produce only linen and cloth. Country C has an *absolute advantage* in producing both of these commodities compared with country B, since 3 is lower than 7 and 2 is lower than 3. However, the degree of superiority by country C is more pronounced in linen then it is in cloth. That is, country B has a *comparative advantage* in producing cloth since 3/2 is smaller than 7/3. Could these two countries both gain from trade with each other? Yes, but only if the wage rate in country B is somewhat lower than in country C. In Ricardo's scenario, having the two countries engage in free trade does not mean all items are traded in world markets. The major factor of production, labor, is assumed to be mobile only in country markets. This is what makes comparative advantage so important in international trade. Countries are countries for a reason, and this entails that whereas some commodity markets may be traded on world markets, other markets, such as labor, may have only country markets, with wage rates differing between countries.

Turn now to the simpler scenario of just corn and linen and only two countries, A and B. There are only three classes of complete specialization whereby each country produces only a single commodity: Both could produce just corn, or both could produce just linen, or one country could be specialized in corn and the other specialized in linen. It is the latter class of complete specialization that has a pair of possibilities. Given the numbers in the table for this class, country A has a comparative advantage in producing linen (relative to corn) compared with country B in these two commodities. With a_j^i denoting the quantity of labor required to produce a unit of commodity i in the jth country, country A's comparative advantage in linen is usually written as $a_{Lin}^A / a_{Co}^A < a_{Lin}^B / a_{Co}^B$. An alternative way of expressing this is by cross-multiplying, $a_{Lin}^A a_{Co}^B < a_{Co}^A a_{Lin}^B$. This alternative obviously becomes more attractive if the number of firms and countries goes from 2 to 3 (or even higher). Consider, now, the case of three countries (A, B, and C) and three commodities (corn, linen, and cloth). In the class of complete specializations where one country is specialized to linen, one to corn, and the third to cloth, and markets are purely competitive, there are 6 possibilities. The winner is given by the allocation that minimizes the product of assignments according to comparative advantage, just as in the 2 × 2 case: Country A produces corn, country B produces cloth, and country C produces linen. Of course, the pattern of demand conditions is also important. The role of comparative advantage is reflected in the assignments shown on the world transformation surface. For example, if demand is shown by point "*x*," country A produces both linen and corn, and country C produces both linen and cloth. Country B is specialized to producing cloth. Relative prices of commodities are completely determined at point "x." The role of comparative advantage is not (by itself) to determine what goods a country produces. But it does show what production combinations are *not* possible.

Note that the diagram (Figure 1.4) that illustrates what countries would produce along a world transformation surface has 10 different points in which each country is specialized to producing only a single commodity. The three corner points each have all three countries producing the same commodity. If this should be corn, note that if only two countries would be specialized in producing corn and one country completely specialized in cloth, this would be country C. There are three classes of complete specialization in which only one country produces one commodity, while the other two countries produce the same other commodity. A final class of complete specializations has a different single commodity produced by each country, and there are six possible contenders for this outcome. One such contender has country A producing linen, country B producing corn, and country C producing cloth. This contender does indeed satisfy each *bilateral* pair of comparative advantages. However, the *trilateral* product of assignments is 100, which is larger than the alternative assignment, A producing corn, B producing cloth, and country C producing linen, with a product of 90. As Chapter 1 emphasizes, there is a limited set of commodity prices that would encourage production of this second assignment, but there is *no* set of prices that would allow the first set of assignments to be selected in a purely competitive set of markets.

Chapter 2 shows how the concept of comparative advantage can be utilized in scenarios not involved with issues in international trade. This chapter is the result of a telephone call I received in the late 1980s from Prof.

Alan Deardorff (a former student of mine when I taught a graduate trade class at Cornell University in 1967). Alan told me that they were planning a conference at the University of Michigan, and wanted all attendants to write a paper in a field different from the one he or she normally worked on. (So much for comparative advantage!) I was tempted to find out the dates of the conference so that I might claim that unfortunately I had a conflict when Alan added that the conference would take place in over a year. At least I suspected that others would probably "cheat." So I accepted, and got in touch with a former Japanese student of mine (Michihiro Ohyama from Keio University in Japan) to join me. This led to the joint paper that is Chapter 2. The focus is on decision-making made by a couple of heterogeneous firms in a particular industry. The "leader" firm is more productive because it has been in the industry longer than the "follower" firm and there is "learning by doing" and they both use a particular *type* of technology (called the θ type). However, there are many other industries in the economy, and they use other types of technologies. A question being pondered by both the leader and follower in the particular industry of interest is whether some parts of a different type of technology, say the β type, should replace some parts in the θ type. There are three possible answers: Both may say "no," both may say "yes," or one might say "no" and the other wish to switch to the β-type. If the responses differ, is there any presumption about which firm wants to switch? The leader is presumed to have a comparative advantage in the use of the θ-type, so we argued for a presumption that it would be the follower who then changes to the β-technology, even if the leader might have an absolute advantage in the new technology. Furthermore, the decision to stick to the old technology might be made by the leader even if he or she had perfect knowledge that the current follower would overtake the current leader in the next period. The concept of comparative advantage is shown to have relevance in other areas of economics.

In international trade models, questions that are quite simple may yet lead to surprising answers. Chapter 3 illustrates such an outcome. Suppose that in a two-country Ricardian model (with labor the only factor of production), there are many commodities, but that the "Home" country has an absolute advantage in producing all commodities, with the greatest advantage in commodity 1, the second in commodity two, and the least in commodity n, in which "Foreign" has its greatest comparative advantage, but Home still has an absolute advantage. Now suppose that Foreign steals Home's technology for producing commodity 1, with no payment of any sort to Home. Question: Could Home nonetheless (paradoxically) end up better off? Yes, but not necessarily. Perhaps surprisingly, Home cannot be made better off unless Home no longer produces any of the first commodity. Consumers at Home would benefit from a lower price for the first commodity. However, Foreign gains and the resulting increase in the foreign wage rate will cause an increase in price for all commodities imported by Home. Chapter 3 makes use of a simple set of diagrams to illustrate how Foreign's wage rate may not rise very much (or perhaps not at all) so that on net Home still gains from the fall in the price of the first commodity.

CHAPTER 1

Comparative Advantage
and the Assignment Problem*

Ronald W. Jones

Because the Ricardian trade model has such a simple production structure — each commodity produced only with labor at fixed coefficients —
it is ideally suited to the analysis of production assignments in a world with
many countries and commodities. The concept of the world transformation schedule provides the focus for our discussion here of comparative
advantage in the more general case.

It is useful to consider a concrete example. Suppose the world consists
of three countries: A (America), B (Britain), and C (Continental Europe).
Furthermore suppose only three commodities can be produced and consumed: corn (Co), linen (Lin), and cloth (Cl). Let the numbers in the
following table show the invariant labor input–output coefficients in each
country to produce a unit of each commodity[1]:

	A	B	C
Corn	10	10	10
Linen	5	7	3
Cloth	4	3	2

*Originally published in Richard Caves and Ronald Jones, *World Trade and Payments*,
Edition 3, (1981).
[1]This example, and much of the subsequent analysis, is found in R. W. Jones (1961).
"Comparative Advantage and the Theory of Tariffs: A Multi-Commodity, Multi-Country
Model," *Review of Economic Studies*, June 1961, pp. 161–75, and reprinted as Chapter 3
in *International Trade: Essays in Theory*. Amsterdam: North-Holland, 1979. See also *ibid.*,
Chapter 18.

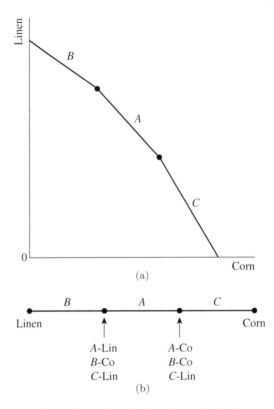

Figure 1.1.   The World Transformation Schedule: Three Countries
The world transformation schedule in the three-country, two-commodity version is a three-segment linear schedule bowed out from the origin. Information as to the pattern of specialization for countries A, B, C in linen and corn can be summarized in the one-dimensional Line in panel (b).

If only corn and linen are produced, Fig. 1.1 would show that the relatively most efficient producer of corn is Britain, followed by America and, last, Continental Europe, despite the fact that all three countries have the same absolute costs. In drawing Fig. 1.1, I have arbitrarily assumed all countries have the same size labor force, an assumption that does not interfere with our analysis of *patterns* of specialization in production.

Panel (b) in Fig. 1.1 summarizes much of what the two-dimensional transformation schedule in panel (a) shows. All countries produce linen at the left-hand linen origin. The lettering reveals that country B is the first country to release labor to produce corn, since it has the greatest comparative advantage in producing corn *relative to linen*. Country A is next in the

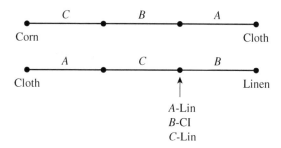

Figure 1.2. Bilateral Cost Rankings
Patterns of comparative advantage taking two commodities at a time are summarized below as in Figure 1.1(b).

line of comparative advantage so that two-thirds across to the corn origin countries A and B are completely specialized in corn and C in linen.

It is clear that adding one more country to a two-commodity analysis introduces no fresh difficulties. And a similar kind of ranking could display separately positions of comparative advantage in linen and cloth on the one hand and corn and cloth on the other. The information on bilateral cost ratios is computed from the table and summarized graphically in Fig. 1.2. For example, if only cloth and linen are to be produced, and if two countries are to be assigned to produce linen and only one country to produce cloth, country B is selected as the cloth producer because its relative cost, $\frac{3}{7}$, is lower than either $\frac{2}{3}$ or $\frac{4}{5}$. Note that there are potentially three possible assignments that put one country in cloth and two in linen. Think of a *class* of assignments as a specification of the number of countries assigned to each commodity. In this example it was zero countries in corn, one in cloth, and two in linen. (There are five other classes of this type, e.g., zero countries in cloth, one in corn, and two in linen.) The doctrine of comparative advantage singles out the *efficient* assignment in each class.

But suppose all three commodities are to be produced. If each country were to be assigned a different commodity, which assignment pattern reflects comparative advantage? Turn back to the table of cost figures. If only corn and linen were to be produced and only countries A and B involved, clearly B has a comparative advantage in corn and A in linen. Now add country C and the new commodity, cloth. Country C is in absolute terms the lowest-cost cloth producer. Therefore, suppose we consider the assignment: A in linen, B in corn, and C in cloth. As just noted, A has a comparative advantage in linen relative to corn compared with country B. Likewise C has a comparative advantage in cloth relative to corn compared with B($\frac{2}{10}$ is less than $\frac{3}{10}$). Finally, a bilateral comparison between countries A and C in linen and cloth shows that linen is produced relatively cheaply in A($\frac{5}{4}$ is smaller than $\frac{3}{2}$). And yet this pattern of specialization is inefficient! There are six possible assignments in which all three commodities are produced and the efficient one has corn produced by country A, cloth by country B, and linen by country C.

To check out that this alternative assignment is indeed efficient, recall that the force of competition in world markets rules out inefficient production patterns. In a competitive equilibrium, any commodity that is actively produced in a country must have unit labor costs equal to price so that profits are bid away. Furthermore, if a country does not produce a commodity, it must not be the case that unit labor costs are actually less than the world price of that commodity. As we now show, there is a range of world prices at which, simultaneously, country A can produce corn, country B cloth, and country C linen.

Since only relative prices matter, let us arbitrarily set the price of corn at unity. If country A is to produce corn, the wage rate in country A must equal $\frac{1}{10}$. This, in turn, reveals that *if* country A were to attempt to produce linen, unit costs would equal $\frac{1}{2}$. Therefore, a competitive equilibrium in which country A does not produce linen must be one in which the world price of linen, p_{Lin}, is less than or equal to $\frac{1}{2}$. Figure 1.3 shows possible ranges for the world prices of linen and cloth (given our assumption that the price of corn is unity). Any value of p_{Lin} greater than $\frac{1}{2}$ is thus ruled out. Also, with a wage rate of $\frac{1}{10}$ the unit cost of producing cloth in A would be $\frac{2}{5}$, and this cannot fall short of the world price of cloth.

Now consider country B, which has been assigned to cloth production. The wage rate in country B depends on the price of cloth, and will equal one-third times p_{Cl}. Therefore, if B were to attempt to produce corn, the cost per unit would be 10 times the wage rate, which must not fall short of the price of corn (which equals unity by assumption). That is, $\frac{10}{3}p_{Cl}$ must be ≥ 1, which puts a lower bound on the price of cloth. Similarly, unit costs in B for linen production would equal $(\frac{7}{3})p_{Cl}$, which must be greater than or equal to the world price of linen. That is, any acceptable p_{Lin} must lie below the ray from the origin whose equation is $p_{Lin} = \frac{7}{3}p_{Cl}$. Finally, consider the required comparison in country C between the unit costs of corn and cloth

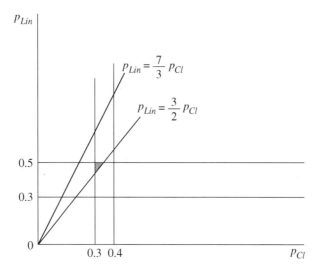

Figure 1.3. Price Possibilities
If the price of corn is unity, any price combination for linen and cloth in the shaded area satisfies the competitive profit conditions when *A* produces corn, *B* cloth, and *C* linen.

and world prices. *C* is assigned to linen, so that the wage rate in *C* equals one-third the world price of linen. Its unit costs in corn would then be $\frac{10}{3}$ times the price of linen so that $\frac{10}{3}p_{Lin}$ must exceed unity to avoid *C* being a potentially profitable location for corn production. Finally, unit costs for cloth in *C* would be two times the wage rate in *C* or $\frac{2}{3}$ times the price of linen. This cost figure must not fall short of the price of cloth, which means p_{Lin} must exceed $\frac{3}{2}$ times the price of cloth.

The shaded area in Fig. 1.3 shows combinations of prices of linen and cloth, relative to a unit price for corn, at which competition allows America to produce corn, Britain to produce cloth, and, simultaneously, Continental Europe to produce linen. Of the six assignments in the *class* for which each country produces a commodity distinct from the other two, this one is the only efficient one. There is *no* set of free-trade prices that would tolerate the others (e.g., *A* in linen, *B* in corn, and *C* in cloth as we originally suggested). This information is necessary in drawing the full world transformation surface. Such a surface would be three-dimensional, but a two-dimensional representation of the assignments can be made, just as panel (b) of Fig. 1.1 contained in one dimension the information about assignments captured in panel (a)'s transformation locus.

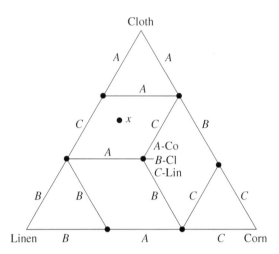

Figure 1.4.   Assignments Along the World Transformation Surface
Along the ridges one country's labor force is being reallocated between two of the three commodities.

Figure 1.4 shows the efficient assignment pattern along the world transformation surface.[2] The bottom edge of the triangle corresponds to panel (b) of Fig. 1.1, while the side edges replicate the assignment patterns in Fig. 1.2. In constructing the shape of the surface it was necessary to go through our previous analysis in search of the efficient assignment for the interior point where all three commodities are produced and each country is specialized. Figure 1.4 suggests that the transformation surface is made up of planar elements, ridges, and points. Points correspond to positions in which all countries are completely specialized, and once the efficient assignment in each class of complete specialization is determined, the entire surface can be mapped out. Suppose we start at the linen corner, where all countries are producing linen. The cost figures suggest that country B has a strong comparative **dis**advantage in linen production, so that should the world wish to consume small amounts of either cloth or corn (or both), it is country B's labor that is first freed up from its assignment to linen. Indeed, relative commodity prices in the lower left-hand triangle in Fig. 1.4

_____

[2] The technique of reducing a three-dimensional surface to a two-dimensional pattern of assignments was pioneered by Lionel McKenzie in "Specialization and Efficiency in World Production," *Review of Economic Studies*, June 1954.

are given solely by comparative labor costs in country B. Thus if the price of corn is unity, the price of linen would be $\frac{7}{10}$ and of cloth $\frac{3}{10}$. The lower left-hand triangle exactly replicates country B's planar transformation surface. At a point such as x, country B is completely specialized in cloth, while country A produces both linen and corn and country C produces linen and cloth. Thus country A's technology determines the linen/corn relative price ($\frac{1}{2}$) and country C's labor costs determine that the relative price of linen to cloth is $\frac{3}{2}$. Along a ridge just one country is incompletely specialized to two commodities, so that one relative price is fixed and the other free to vary (within bounds). At the interior point showing complete specializations, both relative prices are free to vary within the bounds set by the three adjacent planes; this corresponds to relative prices in the shaded area of Fig. 1.3.

There is a simple general rule for locating the assignment that is efficient in its *class*. Reconsider the interior class in which each country is specialized completely to a different commodity. In the efficient specialization A was assigned corn, B cloth, and C linen so that in symbols,

$$w^A a^A_{Co} = p_{Co}$$
$$w^B a^B_{Cl} = p_{Cl}$$
$$w^C a^C_{Lin} = p_{Lin},$$

where w^i is country i's wage rate and a^i_j is country i's labor cost of producing a unit of commodity j. It is also the case that

$$w^A a^A_{Lin} \geq p_{Lin}$$
$$w^B a^B_{Co} \geq p_{Co}$$
$$w^C a^C_{Cl} \geq p_{Cl}$$

since otherwise some country would have an unexploited profitable production possibility. Multiply the three equalities to get:

$$w^A w^B w^C a^A_{Co} a^B_{Cl} a^C_{Lin} = p_{Co} p_{Cl} p_{Lin}.$$

Multiply the three inequalities, with at least one strict inequality, to obtain:

$$w^A w^B w^C a^A_{Lin} a^B_{Co} a^C_{Cl} > p_{Co} p_{Cl} p_{Lin}.$$

A comparison now reveals that if the assignment A-Co, B-Cl, C-Lin was the efficient member of its class, the product $a^A_{Co} a^B_{Cl} a^C_{Lin}$ must not exceed

a_{Lin}^A a_{Co}^B a_{Cl}^C. According to the table, the first product is 90 while the second is 100. The general rule is that the assignment pattern that *minimizes the product of labor coefficients* among all assignments in its class is the efficient optimal assignment. No other assignment patterns in that class can ever be supported in a free-trade equilibrium. This is the generalization of the Ricardian law of comparative advantage that in the two-commodity, two-country case was cast in terms of cost ratios.

As a final observation note that the doctrine of comparative advantage does not state what a country *will* produce. The actual production pattern depends largely upon demand. Instead, it points out production patterns that are *ruled out* by free trade. In our 3 × 3 numerical example there are 3^3 or 27 possible complete specialization assignments of countries to commodities. Of these 17 are inefficient and would never be observed in a free-trade world. The remaining 10 are the ones shown in Fig. 1.4. The fraction of inefficient production patterns ruled out by the austere pressures of competition and free trade rises drastically as the number of countries and commodities expands.[3]

---

[3] For further discussion see R. W. Jones, *International Trade: Essays in Theory* (Amsterdam: North-Holland, 1979), Chapter 18.

CHAPTER 2

Technology Choice, Overtaking, and Comparative Advantage*

Michihiro Ohyama and Ronald W. Jones

Abstract

This paper argues that the basic concept of comparative advantage, used in inter-national trade theory to establish choices of commodities exported, can also be used to explain choice of technology by a firm. A firm with a current leading position in a given technology may spurn a new technology, which is developed by a currently lagging firm, leading to future overtaking.

> The bell of the Gion Temple tolls into every man's heart to warn him that all is vanity and evanescence. The faded flowers of the sala trees by the Buddha's death-bed bear witness to the truth that all who flourish are destined to decay.
> — *Tale of the Heike*

2.1   Introduction

World history seems replete with tales of overtaking — of success followed by failure for individuals, firms, and nations. At the individual level certain attributes often attend a rise to fame or fortune that turns sour — laziness, corruption, inflexibility, and a tendency to cling to the forms of behavior

*Originally published in *Review of International Economics*, 3(2), (1995), pp. 224–234.
We wish to thank Robert Barro, Stanley Engerman, JoAnne Feeney, Sergio Rebelo, Alasdair Smith, Edward Sieper and Scott Taylor for helpful comments. A longer version of this paper, which also analyzes technology choice in a context of imperfect competition, was presented to the conference New Issues in Trade Theory run by Alan Deardorff and Robert Stern in October, 1993.

15

which seem to accompany success. So also firms may cease to pay sufficient attention to changing market conditions or major alterations in technological possibilities. Newcomers, challengers, and those who presently lag behind often claim, as in the Avis advertisement, that "we try harder." And such efforts frequently pay off — the leading firm may find its advantage eroded in the face of challenges from others. As well as firms, whole nations seem to go into relative eclipse — the Roman Empire, China ten to five centuries ago, Great Britain at the end of the nineteenth century, not to mention, as some would claim, the United States at the end of the twentieth.

Much attention has recently been paid by economists to the central importance of technological progress in the phenomenon of growth. If such progress can be endogenously explained and justified as an ongoing phenomenon, theory holds open the possibility of smooth, long-run sustained improvements in per capita incomes. Such a vision, however, does little justice to the possibility of persistent epicycles wherein individuals, firms, or nations are constantly in the process of changing places in the ranking among leaders and laggards. Is there a basic economic rationale in the dynamics of change to suggest that, as in the *Tale of the Heike*, such overtaking or "leapfrogging" represents a natural outcome of forces working on rational agents? In this paper we put forth an affirmative answer which reflects a basic concept in the field of international economics: comparative advantage.

The doctrine of comparative advantage provides the cornerstone for the theory of international trade. As long as a country contains factors or resources which are immobile behind national boundaries, it can engage in a mutually profitable exchange of commodities with other countries even if these factors would suffer absolutely in any head-to-head productivity comparison with comparable factors abroad. It is a comparison of relative productivities that matters. This paper argues that this basic concept has an even wider range of applicability: a new technology may be embraced by one firm and eschewed by another even if the former firm's resources are absolutely less adept at exploiting the new technology. Such an outcome depends upon a comparison of old and new productivities. Thus it may emerge that a firm surrenders a current position of leadership in an industry and is overtaken by a currently laggard firm because the leader's absolute superiority in an existing technology grants the laggard a comparative advantage in a new technology. And such a phenomenon of "overtaking" or "leapfrogging" need not imply any myopia or irrational behavior on the part of either firm. Thus the concept of comparative advantage may be of primary relevance in explaining the oft-observed phenomenon whereby the growth process is accompanied by epicyclical behavior in which firms and perhaps countries trade places as new products and technologies are developed.

2.2   The Core Model

The relevance of the concept of comparative advantage to the phenomenon of overtaking can most easily be illustrated in a core model with two firms in a given industry. To simplify further, we start by assuming away the international ramifications of having the two firms in different countries, with the attendant likelihood that wages and other input prices may differ to a degree which affects relative industry success. Instead, these two firms are part of a large national industry. The two firms are asymmetrically placed: one firm has established over time a technological leadership; the other firm lags behind and forms part of a competitive fringe. Further simplification follows if we suppose that the price of the commodity which both produce is set on world markets. The question dealt with here is that of choice of technology for price-taking firms which are thus freed up from concerns which a firm may have as to the repercussions of technology decisions on market prices or, indeed, on the type of market which will emerge.

The advantages of having a head start and the concept of learning by doing provide the key explanations for the technological superiority of the leading firm in the initial setting. This firm started earlier, and its production and research team has developed techniques which lead to quasi rents or profits compared with the rival lagging firm. Firms are nonetheless assumed to be of the same size so as to put aside notions of scale economies which are not dependent upon the learning experience. Each firm has associated with it the skilled labor which has the acquired knowledge, and this labor is not mobile.

The economy supports many different types of economic activities, and this is an important feature of the model. Although final outputs produced may differ substantially in form or use from industry to industry, technologies developed for some industries may prove to be applicable, perhaps in modified form, to others. That is, there are technological spillovers possible which may prove of use in the industry with which we are concerned. These spillovers include the possibility that new capital goods or other inputs will become available. In the initial setting all such possible profitable externalities have been incorporated into the techniques used by the "leading" firm as well as (perhaps to a lesser extent) by the "laggard." But this is a situation which can change in the future. The research team in the leading firm presumably has developed a superior set of skills that allows it better to incorporate technological developments as they emerge in other areas of the economy as long as these developments are in some sense "close" to previously developed technology. However, spillovers may also prove applicable from technologies that are quite foreign to those currently employed by either the leading or the laggard firm, and any advantage the leading firm has from its previous learning experience does not extend, at least to as great an extent, to these new techniques.

These ideas can be captured in the following simple core setting. There are two time periods, current and future. There is an existing technology, whose net productivity in the current period is denoted by θ_1 for the leading firm and θ_1^* for the laggard. (Although at this stage we assume that both firms are located in the same country, we adopt the notation used in trade theory and will think of the leading firm as the "home" firm and the laggard as the "foreign" firm). Technological superiority of the leading firm implies that θ_1 is greater than θ_1^*. Looking towards the future, the θ technology will yield to improvements by a learning process in production for each of these firms, by the development efforts of their research labs, and by an assimilation of knowledge stemming from technological spillovers of other industries whose methods of production contain elements which are "near" to those used by these firms. Thus future net productivities, θ_2 and θ_2^*, are respectively higher than θ_1 and θ_1^*. Nonetheless, as long as the θ technology forms the primary source for productive techniques, the leading firm maintains its acquired technological dominance and θ_i exceeds θ_i^* for $i = 1, 2$. These θs represent productivities net of costs of labor or other inputs acquired on open markets.

The current value to the firm of its resource base, V_θ or V_θ^*, depends on the factor by which future productivity is discounted. Denote such a discount factor by δ and δ^* for the two firms, although in most of what follows these two firms are assumed to discount the future at the same rate, leading to the same discount factor, δ. Thus

$$V_\theta = \theta_1 + \delta\theta_2; \quad V_\theta^* = \theta_1^* + \delta^*\theta_2^*.$$

Unless these discount factors differ markedly between firms, and we assume they do not, the leading firm's technological superiority in both periods guarantees that V_θ exceeds V_θ^*.

The presumed rich variety of productive activity throughout the economy eventuates in a set of technological breakthroughs in a number of areas. Some of these are close to the θ technology, and are absorbed by these two firms, with the leading firm doing a better job of assimilation. Other improvements represent greater departures, which nonetheless may have relevance in the production of the commodity in which these two firms are involved. (We abstract in this description from an extremely important feature of actual change — the product itself may improve in quality or, indeed, be superseded by a new product which satisfies many of the needs of the demanders of the old.) Let β denote one such new technology that emerges from the activities of firms in other industries. Some new possibilities would unquestionably be attractive to the laggard; e.g., if future net productivity, β_2^*, exceeds future expected θ_2^* and, as well, current productivity of the new technology, β_1^*, exceeds θ_1^*. Given the distance separating current technology of the two firms, such a new possibility could nonetheless be dominated by the old for the leading firm, both in current and future productivities. In such a case the laggard would switch to the new β^* technology, but would succeed only in narrowing the gap between firms, rather than in overtaking the leading firm, which would stick with the old.

To highlight the phenomenon of overtaking when the new technology is potentially attractive for both firms, but would require a current sacrifice in order to obtain future productivity enhancement, assume that β_1 and β_1^*, the current productivities for the new technology, fall short even of θ_1^*, but learning by doing with the new technology holds out the promise of sufficient productivity enhancement in the future for both β_2 and β_2^* actually to exceed the leading firm's expected value of θ_2.

Each firm appraises the new β technology in terms that encompass both present and future net productivities. Thus the laggard firm switches to the new technology if $V_\beta^* > V_\theta^*$ or $\beta_1^* + \delta^*\beta_2^* > \theta_1^* + \delta^*\theta_2^*$. However, the leading firm would retain its old technology if $\beta_1 + \delta\beta_2 < \theta_1 + \delta\theta_2$. Alternatively phrased, the current lagging firm overtakes the leader in commandeering the new technology if

$$\delta^* > (\theta_1^* - \beta_1^*)/(\beta_2^* - \theta_2^*) \quad \text{and} \quad \delta < (\theta_1 - \beta_1)/(\beta_2 - \theta_2).$$

The numerators express the current losses or opportunity costs of switching to the new technology, whereas the denominators capture the excesses in future period 2 of the productivity in the new over the old technology. Both numerator and denominator are assumed to be positive, so that the inequality for the lagging firm requires a sufficiently high value for δ^*. Similarly, the leader finds the new technology less attractive than the old if it discounts future benefits at too high a rate. Suppose both firms share the same discount factor, δ. A necessary condition for the β technology to be adopted by the lagging firm but not by the leader is that

$$(\theta_1 - \beta_1)/(\beta_2 - \theta_2) > (\theta_1^* - \beta_1^*)/(\beta_2^* - \theta_2^*).$$

This is a statement of the *comparative advantage* which the leading firm possesses in the old technology, which implies a *comparative disadvantage* in the new.

Figure 2.1 illustrates how such an overtaking (or leapfrogging) in technology may take place even if the current leading firm's skills impart to it an *absolute advantage* in the new technology. The vertical axis represents the *current* net productivity of the new β technology, but points θ_1 and θ_1^* are also depicted, showing comparable firm values for the older θ technology. The horizontal axis shows *future* possibilities for the new β technology, along with expected values for θ_2 and θ_2^*. Thus points θ and θ^* represent current and future net productivities for the two firms if they stick with the old θ productivities but by learning develop them further in period 2. The fact that both θ and θ^* lie to the right of a 45° ray expresses such learning. Points θ and θ^* have been drawn so that they both lie on the same ray from the origin. This is a neutral assumption, suggesting that the learning curve for the θ technology is linear. The alternative assumption that there are diminishing marginal returns to the learning process would serve to position point θ on a steeper ray from the origin than θ^*, although dominating it.

As for the new β technology, we have assumed that it is potentially of relevance to both firms. In more detail, we restrict attention to a possible

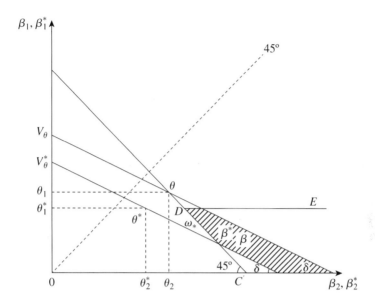

Figure 2.1. The Overtaking Zone

β technology that lies in the cone CDE, ensuring that (1) in the current period both β_1 and β_1^* reflect diminished net productivity, even relative to low θ_1^*. These values of β_1 and β_1^* are assumed to be positive in Figure 2.1, although high learning costs could make them negative; (2) in the future period both β_2 and β_2^* reflect superior technology even compared with the leading firm's θ_2; and (3) the β technology would be adopted by both firms if the (assumed common) discount factor, δ, is sufficiently large. (That is, consider a value of δ equal to unity. Line DC has slope-1, so that $[\beta_1 + \beta_2]$ and $[\beta_1^* + \beta_2^*]$ both exceed $[\theta_1 + \theta_2]$.)[1]

In addition, we assume that the leading firm would have a higher net productivity than the laggard with the new technology in each period of time. That is, β dominates β^*. This latter assumption is made in order to emphasize that the current laggard may in some cases surpass the current leader by being the only firm to switch to the new technology, even if the current leader should possess an absolute advantage in the new technology.

---

[1] This leaves out of account possible β technologies such as point ω (Figure 2.1). For such a technology, the laggard firm would switch and the leading firm would obviously not. Thus the phenomenon of overtaking is not constrained to the shaded area.

The negatively sloped lines drawn through θ and θ^* have slope $-\delta$, implying a common positive interest rate and vertical intercepts equal to V_θ and V_θ^*. The shaded region indicates the set of possible β technologies (of those restricted to cone CDE satisfying these specified properties) that lead to a switch to the new technology by the current lagging firm and an adherence to the old technology by the current leading firm. (Discounting β_2 and β_2^* leads to a value of V_β less than V_θ and of V_β^* greater than V_θ^*.) Line segment $\theta\beta$, not drawn, would be steeper than $\theta^*\beta^*$. The absolute value of the slope of the former is $(\theta_1 - \beta_1)/(\beta_2 - \theta_2)$, and of the latter, $(\theta_1^* - \beta_1^*)/(\beta_2^* - \theta_2^*)$, Overtaking reflects a relatively low-opportunity cost in the present period of adopting the new technology for the laggard, and a relatively large increase in future productivity. The leading firm's absolute superiority in the old technology encourages such comparisons. Actual overtaking requires both that the laggard firm has a comparative advantage in the new technology (despite the leading firm's absolute advantage in each technology) and that the common rate at which future benefits are discounted leads to an increase in profitability of the laggard firm but not for the leader.

Also shown in cone CDE are two other possible triangular regions for β and β^*. In the lower of these the ratios of future benefits to present costs are so low that neither firm would switch; in the upper triangle these ratios are sufficiently high that both firms abandon the θ technology in favor of the new β technology. The analogy here is to a many-country version of comparative-advantage theory with trade in commodities: one country may have a comparative advantage in producing a certain good relative to costs in another country. However, both countries may produce the same commodity if the relative price of the other is too low, with such a price a reflection of costs in myriads of other countries. So here discount rates, a reflection of many other activities in the economy, may dissuade both firms from adopting the new, or, alternatively, may encourage both to switch. It is the two-country version of comparative advantage that portrays countries (or firms) producing different goods (or adopting different techniques). The shaded area lies in between these two triangles. Thus the laggard's comparative advantage in the new technology, derived primarily from the laggard firm's absolute disadvantage in the old technology, is a necessary, but by no means sufficient, condition for overtaking. The leading firm would protect its lead if both firms adopt the new technology despite the leading firm's comparative advantage in the old.

2.3 Choice in Resource Allocation

The preceding analysis has a stark all-or-nothing flavor in contrasting the choice between the old θ and new β technologies. Firms are frequently more cautious. It is not typical for firms abruptly to abandon old technologies and wholeheartedly to embrace new. Instead, they may go through a period in which the new is tried, absorbing some of the firm's resources, but still leaving in place productive activity using the old technology. If the new technology is initially inferior, as assumed, such a strategy helps to maintain current levels of productivity. However, it also entails a cost in that the fewer resources currently devoted to learning by using the new technology, the smaller will be the future benefits flowing from its adoption. Here we provide a simple model designed to highlight the optimal allocation of the firm's resources between the two technologies. We start with the analysis for the leading firm. By comparing this with the position of the lagging firm we are able to establish that if both firms should channel some resources into the new technology, the lagging firm, with a comparative advantage in new techniques, always devotes a greater fraction of its resources in the current period to the new technology. This leads to overtaking in the following period.

Let $0 \leq \lambda \leq 1$ denote the fraction of the firm's resources devoted to production using the new technology, with productivity in the present period given by β_1 (a constant assumed to be smaller than θ_1 or θ_1^*). If we assume the two technologies do not interfere with each other, the actual net productivity this period will be a weighted average of the new (β_1) and the old (θ_1): $\lambda\beta_1 + (1-\lambda)\theta_1$. The net productivity of the new technology in future period 2 depends upon λ:

$$\beta_2 = \beta_2(\lambda), \quad \text{where } \beta_2(0) = \beta_1, \quad \beta_2' > 0, \quad \beta_2'' < 0.$$

That is, the future productivity of the new technology depends upon the extent to which current resources are engaged in its use, but there are diminishing returns to this allocation. The older θ technology will also improve as more resources, $(1-\lambda)$ of the total, are devoted to it in the present period. Of special relevance, however, is the value of θ_2 (or θ_2^*) if $\lambda = 0$, that is, if the firm maximizes its profits by sticking with the old technology. If the firm chooses to put current resources into the new technology, it must be the case that $\beta_2(\lambda)$ will exceed this maximum value of θ_2.

If the leading firm engages at all in the new technology, it wishes to maximize

$$\{\lambda\beta_1 + (1 - \lambda)\theta_1\} + \delta\beta_2(\lambda)$$

with respect to λ. The optimal value for λ, λ^*, satisfies the first-order conditions for optimization:

$$\delta\beta_2'(\lambda^*) = (\theta_1 - \beta_1).$$

It may turn out, however, that the leading firm wishes to stay with the old technology. This reluctance to invest in the new will prove a superior policy if

$$\{\lambda^*\beta_1 + (1 - \lambda^*)\theta_1\} + \delta\beta_2(\lambda^*) < (\theta_1 + \delta\theta_2),$$

where θ_2 is the benefit in period 2 if the firm devotes all its current resources to improving the θ technology.

Figure 2.2 illustrates the possibilities for the leading firm. The ray from the origin, $(\theta_1 - \beta_1)\lambda$, shows the opportunity costs in this current period of allocating resources to production using the new technology, in the form of foregone rents earned using old techniques. The rising curve shows the discounted value ($\delta < 1$, assumed to be the same for both firms) of the excess of future benefits with the β technology over the benefits with the θ technology if the maximum value, θ_2, is attained in the future period. The diagram reveals that future productivity of the new techniques, $\beta_2(\lambda)$, would actually fall short of the future productivity of the old, θ_2, if insufficient resources are currently devoted to learning the new. Indeed the vertical intercept is the negative value, $(\beta_1 - \theta_2)\delta$. Furthermore, Figure 2.2 illustrates the case in which the allocation of resources, λ^*, that is optimal if the new techniques are to some extent employed, indeed proves to be a superior strategy to maintaining the old, since $\delta[\beta_2(\lambda^*) - \theta_2)$, the present discounted value of the relative superiority of the new technology in the future, exceeds the current opportunity costs, $(\theta_1 - \beta_1)\lambda^*$. This comparison favoring some use of the new technology, however, does not warrant a complete switch in the present period away from the old (contrast the relative values at $\lambda = 1$).

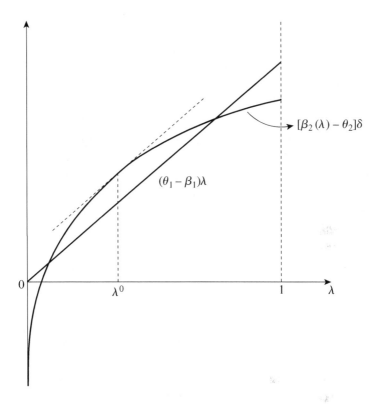

$$[\beta_2(\lambda) - \theta_2]\delta$$

$$(\theta_1 - \beta_1)\lambda$$

Figure 2.2.   Allocation of Resources Between Technologies

Of special interest is the comparison that can be made with the situation of the laggard firm. For this purpose we now suppose that the superior knowledge acquired by the leading firm by virtue of its greater familiarity with the θ type technology does not carry over any benefits with the new β type technology. Instead, let β_1^* equal β_1, and let the $\beta_2(\lambda)$ function be identical for both firms. In Figure 2.2 the present discounted value of the excess of future benefits, $\delta[\beta_2(\lambda^*) - \theta_2^*]$, is shown by a curve that is everywhere higher than that for the leading firm by the amount $\delta(\theta_2 - \theta_2^*)$. Therefore the slopes are equal for comparable values of the fraction of resources devoted to the new technology. By contrast, the ray showing the current-opportunity costs of the switch to the new is flatter than for the leading firm, since θ_1^* falls short of θ_1. Two consequences are immediately apparent: (1) if the leading firm finds it profitable to begin exploiting the new technology, the laggard must also find it profitable to devote some resources to the new. However, the converse need not be the case. The leading firm may find its optimal strategy is to adhere to the old technology while the laggard channels some resources to the new; and (2) if both firms devote some resources to the new technology, the fraction of resources thus devoted is higher for the laggard firm.

It is still possible to get the kind of overtaking result illustrated in the previous section whereby the laggard firm ends up in the future period using the superior technology (but perhaps being low on the learning curve, depending upon its optimal value of λ^*), and the current leading firm sticks completely to the old technology. (In Figure 2.2 the $\delta[\beta_2(\lambda) - \theta_2]$ curve would lie strictly below the $(\theta_1 - \beta_1)\lambda$ ray.) But even if both firms are attracted to the new β technology, optimal resource allocation finds the current lagging firm leapfrogging into technological leadership in the future. It is important to note the asymmetric role played by the absolute advantage of the leading firm in both periods in the old technology. Its advantage in period 2, $\theta_2 > \theta_2^*$, affects the position of the future excess benefits curve (discounted) but not its shape. Thus its advantage may dissuade the leading firm from switching at all; but if both firms do decide to invest in the new technology, the *marginal* gain to each from choosing a higher λ is the same. By contrast, the leading firm's advantage with the old technology in the current period, $\theta_1 > \theta_1^*$, implies a higher opportunity cost for the leading firm to make the switch, and this cost discrepancy gets higher the greater the fraction of resources devoted to the new. It is for this reason that, should both invest in the new, the current lagging firm will emerge in the future as the technological leader.

2.4   Overtaking and International Trade

In order to highlight the importance of a new technology and the possible asymmetry in choice of adoption, we have confined the comparison to two firms which face a similar set of factor prices for inputs not specific to the firm. What difference does it make if these firms are in different countries? For a given technology, and assuming away the advantages that come from a head start and learning by doing, these firms would not necessarily face the same θ profile, because wage rates and other factor prices could be different between the countries. These differences, in turn, often reflect characteristics of technology in other sectors of the economy.

For example, a firm producing cotton textiles in Great Britain may even have a technological superiority over a rival firm in India, but lose out in the world marketplace because technological advances in other industries in Great Britain have resulted in higher wage rates. The phenomenon of "Dutch Disease" is ubiquitous, and the overtaking of one firm by another in a different country need not reflect different choices made as to technology by these two firms.

In the international setting with firms located in different countries, it becomes less defensible to assume that discount factors are the same. If δ differs from δ^*, it is clear which way the comparison must run in order to enhance the possibility of overtaking. A common new β technology has been assumed to offer future benefits (from learning) at the expense of current sacrifice (before learning the new can progress). The present leader would face a bigger current sacrifice in exchange for smaller increase in future net benefits. If these future returns are more severely discounted by the leading firm, future overtaking becomes more likely. Such discounting could also take the form of a shorter time horizon. For example, the investment strategy of Japanese firms is often favorably compared with those of American firms in that a longer time horizon is allowed for future returns. If Japanese firms originally lagged in technology, such a difference would encourage technological overtaking.

A recent paper by Brezis, Krugman, and Tsiddon (1993) analyses the phenomenon of overtaking (or leapfrogging) in an international context by considering an explicit two-sector international trade model with a Ricardian structure. The English manufacturing firm has progressed further along a learning curve than has its American rival, and this absolute advantage gets translated into a comparative advantage in producing manufactured goods for England because both countries are assumed to possess the same technology in food (and this technology remains stagnant). A new technology for the manufacturing sector becomes available, but learning is also necessary in order to improve this technology. However, the lagging American firm finds the new technology appealing immediately, while the English firm, with myopic ignorance of the development possibilities of the new technology, sticks with the old. Such myopia leads to the American firm leapfrogging its English rival. By contrast, in our model both firms are aware of the learning possibilities, but the firm with the current technological lead spurns the new technology in full awareness of the over-taking that will occur in the future.[2] The present sacrifice of output in order to develop the new is not worth the future gains, but such a switch is appealing to the currently lagging firm.

The doctrine of comparative advantage can certainly be used in the Brezis, Krugman, and Tsiddon setting to establish which country produces and exports manufactures. The point of our analysis is to reveal that the same doctrine can be used to establish which firm will adopt the new technology. And such a choice helps to establish that current trade patterns can be changed in the future as a consequence of the asymmetry in the firms' choices of technologies.

2.5   Concluding Remarks

An extremely important type of overtaking has not received explicit attention in our discussion. One firm may introduce a type of product which differs in a quality dimension from existing brands. Every year firms introduce new automobiles, higher powered computers, new forms of sporting equipment utilizing newly developed materials. More significant is the introduction of radically different goods which prove to be good substitutes for the old. A classic case would be the development of steamships in the nineteenth century. This led to a decades-long competition with sail, during which some parts of the market (shorter hauls in earlier days) were served by the new steam vessels whereas others (lumber and other bulk cargoes, where speed was less essential) stuck with sail until early in the twentieth century (Harley, 1971). Transportation provides other famous examples: rail vs. canals, cars, buses, and trucks vs. horse-drawn conveyances; airplanes vs. ships. The field of communication as well is in a current state of transition as computers are utilized to provide cheaper and speedier transmissions than ordinary postal methods.

The type of competition explicitly considered in this paper is more prosaic: firms may utilize different technologies in their competition to

---

[2] In the longer version of this paper we consider firms in a duopoly setting in which choice of technique takes into account the effect of one's own decision, as well as the rival's decision, on future prices.

produce a product of standard quality. The concept of learning by doing provides the connective tissue whereby asymmetric past experience carries on to affect current and future costs and productivities. But one firm's advantage in the utilization of a standard technology, making it a current leader in its industry, lends a presumption as to its comparative disadvantage in adapting to a new technique where experience and learning are required to improve productivity. The doctrine of comparative advantage, of such profound significance in explaining trade patterns among countries, sheds light as well on the phenomenon whereby a current industry laggard may be first off the mark in gaining experience with a new technology, precisely because the leader's absolute advantage in mastering the old technology implies a comparative disadvantage in the new. Such overtaking or leapfrogging may take time, since new technologies may not be forthcoming that frequently or, when they do appear, may be adopted by leaders as well as laggards on the one hand or neglected by both on the other. But comparative advantage nonetheless provides an opening in which the discounting of net productivity benefits in the future with the opportunity costs of currently switching away from a more established technology may encourage the lagging firm rationally to opt for the new, whereas optimizing behavior on the part of the leader entails a pursuit of the older technology.

If the industry has a global basis, the overtaking firm may be located in one country and the present leader in another, with consequent repercussions on the pattern of international trade. However, the phenomenon whereby one country overtakes another depends as well on features of the economy not prominent in our analysis of leapfrogging by firms. Thus the Dutch Disease phenomenon may adversely affect all firms in one country's industry but not in another country's. Or government industrial policy might be utilized to promote one country's industry at the expense of other industries in that country, with mixed chances of success in encouraging overtaking. These possibilities raise an important question — do such policies, even if successful in leading to overtaking, serve as well to raise welfare? In this paper we have not answered this question, focusing instead on the mechanism whereby overtaking may be a natural reflection of comparative advantage.

References

Brezis, Elise, Paul Krugman, and Daniel Tsiddon, "Leapfrogging: A Theory of Cycles in National Technological Leadership," *American Economic Review* 83 (1993):1211–19.
Harley and Charles K., "The Shift from Sailing Ships to Steamships, 1850–1890: A Study in Technological Change and its Diffusion," ch. 6 in D. McCloskey (ed.), *Essays on a Mature Economy,* London: Methuen, 1971.

CHAPTER 3

The Technology Transfer Paradox*

Ronald W. Jones and Roy J. Ruffin

Abstract

This chapter examines whether a country that enjoys a superior technology in all commodities in a two-country, multi-commodity Ricardian setting could actually gain if its technology in which it possesses its greatest comparative advantage is stolen or transferred to the other country without any compensation. Such a paradoxical possibility is shown always to exist with a finite number of commodities and equal-shared Cobb–Douglas demand conditions for certain ranges of relative country size.

3.1 Introduction

One aspect of globalization concerns the increased ease of the transfer of technology among countries. This may take the form of outright sales in arms-length market transactions or of transfer activities within a multinational firm. Alternatively, there may be an illegal transfer, where in technological knowledge possessed by a firm in one country is transferred to another without any payment for the superior information. This latter kind of uncompensated technology transfer raises a critical question: Could the real income of the country originally the only possessor of the superior technology actually be *raised* by such "outsourcing"? A positive answer

---

*Originally published in *Journal of International Economics* 75, (2008), pp. 321–328.
We wish to thank Jonathan Eaton, two referees, Gokhan Akay, Paul Gregory, Peter Mieszkowski, and Costas Syropoulos for helpful comments.

would seem especially problematic in the case in which the technology that is stolen or given away is for a commodity the advanced country is exporting. And how could such a paradoxical result be reconciled with the *negative* effects on an advanced country's real income if by innovation a less developed country obtains a *small* improvement in its existing production of a commodity being exported by the advanced country? That is the setting and the conclusion reached in the article by Paul Samuelson (2004), in which a country such as China gets somewhat better at producing a commodity being exported by an advanced country such as the United States.[1] Without disagreeing with Samuelson's findings, in this chapter, we show how the advanced country may nonetheless *gain* by an uncompensated technology transfer sufficiently great to drive the advanced country out of producing its best export commodity. We label this outcome *The Technology Transfer Paradox.*

Ruffin and Jones (2007) illustrated this paradoxical outcome for the two-commodity case, but the many-commodity case is more compelling because it reveals more clearly the fundamental economics that is involved, allowing us to discuss an important case in which an advanced country is incipiently producing an import without, at the same time, being a large country. In the large country Ricardian case with only two commodities, a transfer that creates specialization must result in gain for the advanced country because it is producing all commodities prior to the transfer (no gain). Thus, Sec. 3.2 describes possible Ricardian equilibria in the two-country, many-commodity case, followed, in Sec. 3.3, by a discussion of the effect on an advanced country's real income of an uncompensated transfer of technology of producing that country's commodity that is highest on its list of comparative advantage. Section 3.4 provides some extensions and Sec. 3.5 some concluding remarks.

3.2   Before Technology Transfer

In a two-country (Home and Foreign), many-commodity Ricardian setting, relative country size is important. If Foreign is relatively large, it must

---

[1] This leads to a deterioration in the advanced country's terms of trade. For popular discussion and controversy see the *New York Times* (September 9, 2004). Gomory and Baumol (2000) present a similar argument, but put stress on the role of economies of scale.

produce a large fraction of commodities in world markets, and in order to compete successfully, its wage rate must be sufficiently low. Thus if a diagram were drawn with the vertical axis showing Foreign's wage rate relative to Home's wage rate, w^*/w, and a horizontal axis showing the relative size of Foreign's labor supply, L^*/L, the relationship between the two would be downward sloping. In the continuum model this negative slope would literally be correct.[2] With a finite number of commodities, the model we select as more appropriate to the issue, such a locus would be downward sloping only in regions in which no commodity is produced in common in the two countries — each is specialized to a different group of commodities. However, for regions of relative country size in which they have a commodity produced in common, the relative wage rate between countries is fixed by the relative productivities of labor in producing the common commodity in the two countries.

In what follows we make a completely innocent assumption that serves to simplify the exposition. Let commodities 1 through n be producible in both countries using only labor, and let all commodity units be selected so that firms in Home take only a single unit of labor to produce one unit of each commodity. Furthermore, let the *numeraire* be selected as Home labor. Therefore Home's nominal wage rate is always unity, as is the price of any commodity produced by Home. This convenient assumption allows us to deduce real income from an ideal price index. To highlight the purpose of the chapter in showing the consequences of a transfer without compensation of the technology for producing a commodity at Home to Foreign, we also assume that Home has a technological superiority in every commodity, so that all unit labor requirements in Foreign exceed unity. Assume that commodities are numbered such that

$$a_1^* > a_2^* > \cdots > a_n^* > 1 \tag{3.1}$$

That is, Foreign's greatest comparative advantage before transfer is in producing the nth commodity, and its lowest is in producing the first, where a_1^* indicates the absolute labor costs per unit production of the ith commodity in Foreign.

---

[2]This statement *assumes* that the set of goods with a particular productivity ratio between the countries is always of measure zero, which need not be the case.

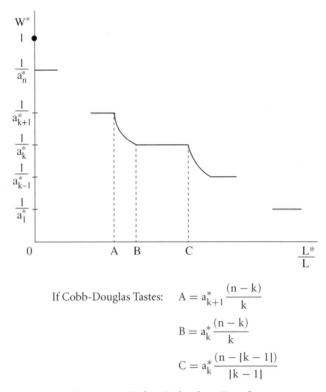

If Cobb-Douglas Tastes: $A = a_{k+1}^* \dfrac{(n-k)}{k}$

$B = a_k^* \dfrac{(n-k)}{k}$

$C = a_k^* \dfrac{(n - |k-1|)}{|k-1|}$

Figure 3.1.   Before Technology Transfer

With Home's nominal wage rate always unity, the relationship between the ratio of wage rates to relative country size is, for selected parts of the range, illustrated in the well-known Fig. 3.1, with w^* on the vertical axis. With Home having unit productivity in all commodities, the ratio of Foreign to Home Productivity is measured by the reciprocals $1/a_n^*, \ldots, 1/a_1^*$ on the vertical axis. Consider, first, the pair of cases in which one of the countries is relatively so small that it cannot supply the entire world market even for the commodity in which it has its greatest comparative advantage. If this is Foreign, with both countries producing commodity n in order to satisfy world demand, their wage rates are locked together by their productivities, with Foreign's wage rate at $1/a_n^*$. At the other extreme, if it is Home that is relatively so small that Foreign must use some of its labor as well to produce the commodity in which Home has the greatest comparative advantage, Foreign's wage rate must be at the minimum level of $1/a_1^*$.

In Fig. 3.1's middle range, suppose relative country size, L^*/L, lies strictly between A and B, with Home producing commodities 1 through k and Foreign the remaining $(n - k)$ commodities. In this range Foreign's wage rate must be less than $1/a^*_{(k+1)}$ so that it can be the only producer of commodities $(k + 1)$ and higher, but greater than $1/a^*_k$, so that Foreign is not able to compete in the market for commodity k. A slight increase in Foreign's relative size increases its production of commodities $(k + 1)$ through n, and this can be accommodated in world markets only by a reduction in all their prices, and, with them, Foreign's wage rate. This continues if L^*/L grows until point B is reached, at which point Foreign's wage rate has been reduced to $1/a^*_k$, and further increases in L^*/L will see Foreign taking over increasing shares of world production of the kth commodity until Foreign becomes the only producer of the kth commodity (when L^*/L reaches point C), after which the cycle repeats itself.

So far nothing has been said about taste patterns. We start by adopting a popular assumption of a very "neutral" kind (Samuelson, 2004; Ruffin and Jones, 2007): Tastes are of the Cobb–Douglas variety, the same for both Home and Foreign, and (until later) of the same expenditure share for every commodity. What this implies is that if each country is specialized in producing a subset of commodities, say 1 through k for Home and $(k + 1)$ through n for Foreign, the ratio of the number of commodities produced in Foreign to those produced in Home corresponds to the ratio of their national incomes as reflected in total payments to labor. Thus:

$$w^*(L^*/L) = (n - k)/k \qquad (3.2)$$

Referring back to Fig. 3.1, relationship (3.2) allows us to identify the relative labor supplies corresponding to points A, B, and C. If the (relative) size of Foreign's labor force reaches point A, the assignment of commodities to countries shown in Eq. (3.2) is satisfied because Foreign has just become the world's sole supplier of commodity $(k + 1)$, as well as all higher numbered commodities. At point A, Home is an *incipient* producer of commodity $(k + 1)$. The journey from A to B is down a rectangular hyperbola as Foreign increases its production of commodities $(k + 1)$ through n, encouraging a proportional fall in prices and a drop in Foreign's wage rate, w^*, until, at point B, Foreign can just begin to produce some of the kth commodity. Although each country's specialization pattern at B is the same as at A, the fact that Foreign's wage rate is lower at B leads to the value for

B compared with *A* shown in Fig. 3.1. Foreign's wage rate is now linked to the unit wage rate at Home by technology; and when L^*/L increases to point *C*, Foreign takes over the world's entire production of commodity *k*.

Summary: All that we said above can be summarized by locating L^*/L somewhere in the following sequence.

$$[(n - k)/k]a^*_{k+1} < [(n - k)/k]a^*_k < \{[n - (k - 1)]/(k - 1)\}a^*_k \qquad (3.3)$$

When L^*/L is in the first interval, Home produces commodities $1, \ldots, k$, and Foreign commodities $k + 1, \ldots, n$ with $w^* = L(n - k)/L^*k$; and when L^*/L is in the second interval, $w^* = 1/a^*_k$ with Foreign incipiently specialized when $L^*/L = [(n - k)/k]a^*_k$ and Home incipiently specialized when $L^*/L = \{[(n - (k - 1)]/(k - 1)\}a^*_k$.

3.3   A Transfer of Technology

The details of technology transfer in the real world involve the movement of factors of production, the sharing of patents, royalty and/or profit sharing agreements, training of foreign workers, branch plants, and so forth. Technology differs between countries because of climate, the human capital of the workforce, the available machinery, and the infrastructure of rail, highway, and river transportation. But the bottom line is that productivity of labor differs between countries.

In our many-country Ricardian setting it is supposed that the absolute advantage that Home possesses in producing all commodities compared with Foreign is based entirely on superior blueprints at Home. Furthermore, it is assumed that Foreign obtains the blueprints for one of the commodities in the list of exports for Home, and that absolutely no payment is made for such transfer.[3] If there is uniform demand for all exports, it makes no difference which commodity is transferred because Foreign is not producing the commodity in any case, and so the degree of superiority is irrelevant. For convenience, we will usually think of the transferred commodity as the first or best commodity. We now show that even when the

---

[3] Any Home firms possessing such blueprints will of course lose. The question is whether Home as a country is necessarily worse off, where in the model all income is in the form of wages.

advanced country is not large prior to the transfer, there must be multiple relative country sizes in which such transfers are beneficial to that country.

Earlier a simplifying (and entirely innocent) assumption was made that fixed Home's nominal wage rate at unity. As a consequence the question of the effect of transfer on Home real incomes depends entirely on what happens to the price level.[4] Such a transfer of technology to Foreign with its lower nominal wage rate server to reduce the world price of the commodity (and wipe out Home's entire production). If this new acquisition of better technology serves to increase Foreign's wage rate, the prices of all commodities produced only abroad (except for the first commodity) would also increase. Could the effect on the price index of the price reduction for the first commodity outweigh any increases in commodity prices for Home's imports? This depends upon the effect of the transfer on Foreign's wage rate, and, as our analysis shows, the change in w^* depends upon the relative size of the two countries' labor forces.

Imagine that before the transfer we are at point A in Fig. 3.1. Foreign wages are $w^* = 1/a_{k+1}^*$ but Home is incipiently producing commodity $k + 1$ while Foreign supplies the entire world market. Prices are $p_1 = \cdots p_{k+1} = 1$, and $p_{k+j} = a_{k+j}^*/a_{k+1}^* < 1$ for $j > 1$. Pre-transfer trade is then beneficial to the Home country. The transfer of commodity 1's technology simply reduces the price of that good to $p_1 = 1/a_{k+1}^*$ (or any transferred export), with Home shifting its resources out of commodity 1 into commodity $k + 1$ and Foreign doing the exact reverse along horizontal supply curves. All other prices remain the same so that Home must be better off. We refer to such a position as a *turning point*. At turning points there is a seamless change, with no pressure exerted on w^*, resulting in Home gaining because it can now purchase its former export at a lower price and pay the same prices for all other commodities. The key here is not much the uniform demand assumption, but that the share of income devoted to commodity $k + 1$ be the same as the share of income devoted to the transferred commodity. This implies that the resources released from the contracting former export industry are exactly absorbed by the expanding industry. Notice as long as we make the assumption of uniform Cobb–Douglas

---

[4]Technically, the uniform Cobb–Douglas assumptions made imply that the price index is the geometric mean of all commodity prices. This will decrease if and only if the product of all prices itself falls.

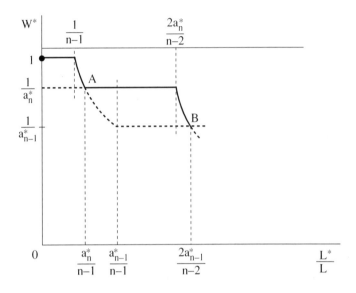

Figure 3.2.   Technology Transfer and Turning Points

preferences it makes no difference whether the technology of commodity 1 or that of any of the others is transferred.

The effect of a transfer on the Foreign wage profile is pursued in Fig. 3.2. We concentrate on the scenario in which Foreign's labor supply is relatively small in order to see the initial shift in the wage profile, but all the other shifts are similar. The dashed locus depicts the situation before the technology transfer, and shows that until the relative size of Foreign's labor force reaches $a_n^*/(n-1)$ both countries are required to share production of commodity n, the commodity representing Foreign's greatest comparative advantage. After the technology transfer, Foreign's best commodity becomes commodity 1, which formerly was Home's best. The solid post-transfer locus reveals that if Foreign's labor force is sufficiently small its wage rate will be at the Home level of unity since both produce a new commodity (Eq. (3.1)) in common. This improvement in productivity for Foreign's workers implies not only a higher wage rate, but that Foreign can supply the entire market for the first commodity at a lower relative labor supply, $\{1/(n-1)\}$, than it previously took to produce all the world's demand for commodity n. If (L^*/L) were to increase from this level, the world price of the first commodity would fall and w^* would be driven down until eventually, when (L^*/L) reaches $\{a_n^*/(n-1)\}$, Foreign's wage rate falls to $1/a_n^*$.

Note the significance of point A in Fig. 3.2: If (L^*/L) were equal to $\{a_n^*/(n-1)\}$, the technology transfer would leave the Foreign wage rate precisely at its previous level. This is a guaranteed consequence of the uniform Cobb–Douglas assumption that leads to Eq. (3.2). At point A originally Foreign had just *completed* its provision for the entire world market's demand for commodity n, which was originally its best. After transfer, at this size labor force it would just *begin* to produce commodity n, which has now slipped to second best in its ranking by comparative advantage. Whether it has just satisfied the world market for n or is just about to enter that market, Foreign's wage rate relative to Home's unitary wage must reflect its relative productivity, $1/a_n^*$. The after-transfer Foreign wage schedule in Fig. 3.2 is *not* just an upward-shifted locus of the original wage schedule; there is a leftward shift as well, expressing Foreign's productivity gain in having acquired Home's better technology for producing the first commodity.

Home gains from this technology transfer are not constrained just to the turning points; Home would also gain for nearby levels of Foreign's relative labor supply. If being in the neighborhood of turning points ensures that technology transfer actually benefits Home, Fig. 3.2 suggests that the greatest danger to Home real incomes comes from situations in which w^* is raised by the maximal amount, and this occurs when both before and after transfer Home and Foreign produce a commodity in common, a different commodity after the transfer. The reason? The before-and-after Foreign wage rate disparity is greatest when w^* corresponds to the productivity of Foreign's labor force in two neighboring commodities instead of being partway between them. And it is this disparity that hurts Home by causing an increase in the price of all commodities not produced by Home. In contrast, Home's real wage is helped by the drop in the price of the commodity whose technology has been transferred. Such a price fall-caused by the *difference* between Home and Foreign wage rates–will be greater the larger, relatively, is Foreign's labor force. Whereas Home's nominal wage rate is unity, that ruling in Foreign monotonically decreases the higher the value of L^*/L.

An explicit formulation of the comparison between the product of commodity prices before and after transfer when w^* increases by the maximal amount can be obtained by assuming that initially the two countries share in the production of commodity k (with L^*/L in the BC range of Fig. 3.1). This implies that the prices of commodities 1 through k are all unity. Foreign's wage rate must be $1/a_k^*$, making the sequence of prices for commodities $(k+1)$ through n equal to:

$$a_{k+1}^*/a_k^*, a_{k+2}^*/a_k^*, \ldots, a_n^*/a_k^*$$

Let Π_O represent the product of commodity prices in this initial situation:

$$\Pi_O = \{a_{(k+1)}^* a_{(k+2)}^* \cdots a_n^*\}/(a_k^*)^{(n-k)} \tag{3.4}$$

Note that this product is less than unity because all Foreign-produced commodities except for commodity k have prices less than unity. In the after-transfer situation Foreign becomes sole producer of the first commodity and shares production of commodity $(k+1)$ with Home. Letting Π_A denote the after-transfer product of commodity prices,

$$\Pi_A = \{a_{(k+2)}^* a_{(k+3)}^* \cdots a_n^*\}/(a_{(k+1)}^*)^{(n-k)} \tag{3.5}$$

(Foreign still produces $(n-k)$ commodities because it also produces the first commodity after transfer). Comparing Eq. (3.4) with Eq. (3.5) it is clear that Π_A is smaller than Π_O, and thus Home gains by the technology transfer, if and only if condition (3.6) is satisfied:

$$\Pi_A/\Pi_O = \{1/a_{(k+1)}^*\}\{a_k^*/a_{(k+1)}^*\}^{(n-k)} < 1 \tag{3.6}$$

The first term, less than unity, reveals the *discrepancy* between Home and Foreign wage rates, which helps Home, while the second term is greater than unity, reflecting the *rise* in w^* and thus the price of every commodity (save the first) produced in Foreign.[5]

What happens to this ratio of price products in Eq. (3.6) if Foreign's relative size increases until initially both countries produce commodity $(k-1)$ and, after transfer, produce commodity k in common? Would there be any reason to expect this ratio to decline with relative Foreign size? On the one hand the drop in the price of the commodity whose technology has been transferred tends to be greater the higher is L^*/L; successive turning points are at ever lower levels of Foreign's wage rate, so that the first term in Eq. (3.6)'s inequality becomes smaller the lower is k, the number of

---

[5] In Ruffin and Jones (2007), this condition for Home gain for two commodities reduces to $(a_2^*)^2 > a_1^*$.

commodities produced at Home. On the other hand, a lower value for k (for given n) implies that a larger number of commodities is produced in Foreign and imported by Home. This is what is captured by the second term in Eq. (3.6), with every such commodity price multiplied upwards by the term $\{a_k^*/a_{(k+1)}^*\}$, the ratio of post transfer Foreign wage to pre-transfer w^*.

We pointed out earlier that with uniform tastes turning points do not depend on which export commodity is transferred. Condition (3.6) provides the criterion for Home gain in the worst-case scenario in which before and after Foreign wage rates are at their maximal spread (between a pair of turning points).[6] Note that the condition does not refer to the commodity whose technology has been transferred, but only to the characteristics of the profile of comparative and absolute advantage near the break point between Home and Foreign production.

Further insight into this question can be obtained by comparing the expression in Eq. (3.6), illustrated by point A in Fig. 3.3, with the size of

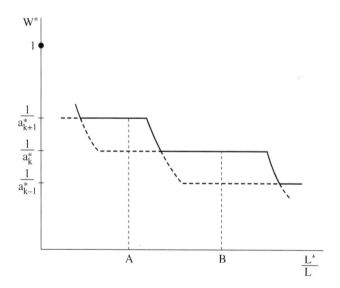

Figure 3.3. Shared Production: A Comparison

---

[6]Depending upon the technology, there may not be any points such as A or B in Fig. 3.3 in which the two countries share production of a (different) commodity in common both before and after transfer. But a comparison of the two situations that would occur if w^* changed by this maximal amount provides sufficient conditions for Home gain.

Π_A / Π_O for a larger value of L^*/L (illustrated by point B in Fig. 3.3) in which initially the two countries produce commodity $(k-1)$ in common and, after transfer, commodity k in common. Call this new value $(\Pi_A / \Pi_O)'$:

$$(\Pi_A / \Pi_O)' = \{1/a_k^*\}\{a_{(k-1)}^*/a_k^*\}^{(n-k+1)} \tag{3.7}$$

To compare with Eq. (3.6) multiply both Eqs. (3.6) and (3.7) by a_k^*. This reveals that

$$(\Pi_A / \Pi_O)' \leq (\Pi_A / \Pi_O) \quad \text{iff} \quad a_{(k-1)}^*/a_k^* \leq a_k^*/a_{(k+1)}^* \tag{3.8}$$

Comparisons between terms such as $a_k^*/a_{(k+1)}^*$ and $\{a_{(k-1)}^*/a_k^*\}$ refer to the *rate of increase* in Home's absolute advantage as production moves towards Home's best commodity. If this rate of increase remains constant, so also will the change in the consumer price index as Foreign gets larger.

3.4   Extensions

These results, showing the possibility of Home gains with technology transfer, can be extended[7]:

(i) Suppose instead of the uniform array of Cobb–Douglas taste patterns the world has a *lower* spending share on commodity 1 (or just the transferred commodity) and higher relative shares on the other commodities. Assume as before that Home is incipiently producing commodity $k + 1$ before the transfer. When an export technology is transferred, Foreign need not shift all of its resources out of commodity $k+1$ into the transferred commodity. Thus turning points become, instead, turning regions in which all prices remain the same but for the falling price of the transferred commodity. If, instead, the share devoted to the first commodity *exceeds* that for others, there will be no turning points, although it is still quite possible that Home can gain. Foreign must shift resources out of commodity $k + 1$ and others into the transferred commodity. While turning regions are lost, the cheaper transferred commodity looms more important in the price index.

---

[7] But note: If Home transfers its superior technology in *all* commodities, Home must lose with no gains from trade. In the Ricardian case, literature also shows how Home can gain if it transfers its superior technology for the commodity or commodities that it imports. See Kemp and Shimomura (1988) and Beladi, Jones, and Marjit (1997).

(ii) The issue of the share of income devoted to the transferred commodity or commodities is related to the issue of the optimum technology transfer from the standpoint of the advanced country. Note that any number of commodities can be transferred. As is usually the case in economics, a necessary condition for an optimum requires that a marginal change in the number of commodities transferred has no effect on the cost of living. A transfer is gainful if the cost of living falls. It is possible that there may be no profitable transfer, as in the case of two commodities, and the failure of condition (3.6) above. But one advantage of the assumption of many commodities is that even if condition (3.6) is not satisfied for the transfer of a single commodity, the transfer of another commodity might prove, on net, to be beneficial because of a favorable impact on the cost of living.

(iii) What kind of paradox is represented by a technology transfer that is unrequited, but leads to an improvement in Home's real wage rate? The theory of international trade, of course, contains a number of paradoxes, and it is appropriate to ask how this one fits into the pantheon comprised of the others. The transfer welfare paradox (for gifts of commodities) depends on countries exhibiting different taste patterns, whereas here tastes are similar between countries. The immiserizing growth paradox entails an outward shift in Home's transformation surface. Here the transformation surface is not affected. The technology transfer paradox differs in requiring that the shock to the original equilibrium be sufficiently large that production patterns change. Consider, for example, a situation such as that described by Samuelson (2004). Both Home (say the United States) and Foreign (say China) produce a commodity in common (i.e., equilibrium is on a flat in the w^*-locus). If China gets a bit better at producing the commonly produced commodity but US production gets reduced only by 10 percent or so, Home (the US) must lose.[8] But if the productivity change in producing this commodity in China is so large that the US industry gets completely wiped out, the US *may* gain. That is, this paradox displays the property that results appropriate when

[8]This loss does not depend upon whether the US is an importer or exporter of this commodity. For a general analysis of technology changes that do not disrupt the pattern of production see Jones (1979).

shocks are small may prove to have nonmonotonic effects on welfare if shocks are large enough to alter production patterns.[9]

(iv) Now consider the case of a continuum. It is easy to show that that there can be no turning points. A measure zero cannot be transferred, so Home can only transfer a subset of its exports to Foreign. The prices of these goods fall, but Foreign wages must rise. The reason: if Foreign wages remained the same, Home exports would fall and Home imports rise by the value of the transferred commodities — an untenable disequilibrium. Unlike the case of a finite number of goods, the common commodity is of infinitesimal measure and so the transfer cannot simply expand or contract production of that commodity to maintain equilibrium — new commodities must be produced. Since turning points make economic sense (the ability to expand or contract production in a commodity), we consider the continuum to be less appropriate for studying technology transfers. However, in studying optimal transfers, the continuum case might be useful because one can then look at strictly marginal changes in the number of commodities transferred. We leave this subject for future analysis.

3.5 Concluding Remarks

Most developed countries have experienced changes in their patterns of production and international trade over time. By their own investment activities new positions of comparative advantage are acquired, accompanied by their losing their comparative advantage in other commodities. This loss is an inescapable consequence of success in new ventures raising their real wage rates and of less developed countries acquiring new technology and skills in producing commodities such as textiles, steel, or automobiles. Years ago Ray Vernon (1966) sketched out a *product cycle* theory describing this evolution of production and trading patterns.

It has been emphasized by Samuelson (2004) and Gomory and Baumol (2000) (and Jones [1979]) that if foreign countries develop increased expertise in commodities that a Home developed country *continues to produce,*

---

[9]For a discussion of other nonmonotonic results, e.g., to the Stolper–Samuelson theorem, see Jones (2008).

Home real incomes will fall with a deterioration in Home's terms of trade. Thus increasing degrees of globalization that are characterized by Foreign technological advances rather than those at Home can do damage to income levels at Home. In this chapter, we consider improvements in Foreign technology that *surpass,* in scope, those considered either by Samuelson or by critics of globalization. We stack the deck in asking whether an advanced country can actually *gain* by an uncompensated transfer to a foreign country of its advanced technology in producing the export commodity in which it possesses its *greatest* comparative advantage. The answer we give in this case of technology transfer is it depends, but if Cobb–Douglas demand shares are all alike, the advanced home country *must* gain by such unrequited transfer near the so-called *turning points*.

A crucial question concerns the effect of such transfer on the relative wage rates of Home and Foreign (i.e., the *double factoral terms of trade*). At the critical turning points relative wage rates are not affected by the transfer, whereas for other values of relative country size the technology transfer raises Foreign's wage rate, which serves as well to increase the prices faced by Home labor for all commodities (except the first) produced by Foreign and imported by Home. If Foreign's wage rate does increase as a consequence of transfer, there emerge two conflicting effects on the consumer price index facing Home's workers, *viz.* a falling price for the commodity whose technology has been transferred, on the one hand, and an increase in prices of other goods imported by Home on the other. Our normalization assumption, whereby all input–output labor coefficients for Home are set at unity, leading as well to a unit value for Home's wage rate, coupled with strong Cobb–Douglas assumptions regarding taste patterns, simplifies the proof to show that if the product of world commodity prices falls, Home laborers must experience an increase in real income (real wages).

What is striking in our scenario is that it is precisely the *complete loss* of Home's original best industry that allows a reduction in its world price and thus works in favor of the increase in real wages at Home. In many advanced countries workers have benefited, as consumers, from lower priced and better quality TV sets, cameras, automobiles and electronic goods after Foreign has taken over their production. Without denying the importance of new technological developments in advanced countries, of the type envisaged by Vernon (1966), what we have argued is that even *without* such advances, pure improvements abroad, such as represented by stealth or uncompensated acquisition of some of our better technology, may serve to raise real wages and incomes in the advanced home country. Trade patterns are altered, and the subtle mechanisms of comparative advantage can yield net gains to the advanced country.

There is a *cyclical* pattern of gains and losses to Home that depends on Foreign's relative size. With strong demand assumptions there are repeated neighborhoods of such relative size in which technology transfer without compensation *must* yield net gains to Home.

References

Beladi, H., Jones, R.W., and Marjit, S. (1997). Technology for Sale. *Pacific Economic Review*, 2, 187–196.

Gomory, R. and Baumol, W. (2000). *Global Trade and Conflicting National Interests*. Cambridge, MA: MIT Press.

Jones, R.W. (1979). Technical Progress and Real Incomes in a Ricardian Trade Model. In: R.W. Jones (Ed.), *International Trade: Essays in Theory* (Ch. 17). Amsterdam: North-Holland.

Jones, R.W. (2008). Key International Trade Theorems and Large Shocks. *International Review of Economics and Finance*, 17, 103–112.

Kemp, M. and Shimomura, K. (1988). The Impossibility of Global Absolute Advantage in the Heckscher–Ohlin Model of Trade. *Oxford Economic Papers*, 40, 575–576.

New York Times (2004). *An Elder Challenges Outsourcing's Orthodoxy*, 9 September.

Ruffin, R.J. and Jones, R.W. (2007). International Technology Transfer: Who Gains and Who Loses? *Review of International Economics*, 15, 209–222.

Samuelson, P.A. (2004). Where Ricardo and Mill Rebut and Confirm Arguments of Mainstream Economists Supporting Globalization. *Journal of Economic Perspectives*, 18, 135–146.

Vernon, R. (1966). International Investment and International Trade in the Product Cycle. *Quarterly Journal of Economics*, 80, 190–207.

Part II

More General Equilibrium Models: Heckscher–Ohlin and Specific-Factor Models

The Ricardian model is especially simple in that production of commodities had a requirement of only a single factor of production, labor. The next major step in international trade theory was to allow more than a single factor, perhaps land, capital, or both, to join labor in theoretical attempts at explaining the wide variety in trade patterns among countries. Eli Heckscher in 1919 and one of his students in Sweden, Bertil Ohlin, in 1933, worked on what became known as the Heckscher–Ohlin model.

The two-country, two-commodity version of the Heckscher–Ohlin model had a formal presentation provided in my paper for the *Journal of Political Economy* (1965), which is reprinted here as Chapter 4. (This also appears as Chapter 4 in my 1979 book *International Trade: Essays in Theory.*) This may well be my most cited paper (and did receive a 50th anniversary celebration at the University of Calcutta in 2015). Some details will occasionally be made in subsequent remarks. The basic eight equations of competitive equilibrium in the (2 × 2) model are the pair of full employment equations, the pair of equations of commodity price with average costs of production for each commodity, and the four equations that state that the input-output fractions (four of them) each depend on the wage/rent ratio (of labor either to land or to capital). It is easy to use the differential calculus to obtain eight equations of change if small changes are found in commodity prices or in factor endowments. This formulation of the eight-equation system can easily be solved since it only takes a pair of equations at a time to solve for the eight unknowns. What I labeled as the "magnification effect" is reflected in the pair of solutions in the case of relative changes in factor endowments. In Chapter 4, the two commodities are M and F (manufactured goods and food). The two factors of production are labor, L, and land, T. The departure from the assumption of a single input, labor (as in the Ricardian model), to the assumption of a *pair* of inputs in the Heckscher–Ohlin model is fundamental. Patterns of trade among countries can depend upon the difference in relative factor endowments used in the two industries as well as (or instead of) differences in technologies linking input requirement per unit of output in order to suggest which commodity gets exported and which imported with free trade. Furthermore, commodities can differ in the land/labor ratio used in production.

Let me assume (for now) that although input ratios are sensitive to changes in wage/rent ratios, manufactures, M, are generally *labor-intensive*, in the sense of being produced using a higher L/T ratio than does F. As can simply be observed, if the labor endowment should increase relative to any change in the endowment of land, and if commodity prices are constant, the relative change in the output of M exceeds the relative change in either factor endowment and the relative change in the production of F is negative (if there is no change in the endowment of land), or at least the relative change is lower than in that of T. Letting a "hat" over a variable imply a relative change in that variable (e.g., $\hat{x}$ is defined as dx/x), the changes can be shown by the ranking:

$$\hat{M} > \hat{L} > \hat{T} > \hat{F}$$

A "dual" ranking links relative factor price changes to commodity price changes, not even assuming there is no change in the economy's factor endowments. If $\hat{p}_M > \hat{p}_F$, then

$$\hat{w} > \hat{p}_M > \hat{p}_F > \hat{r}$$

This latter ranking of factor price responses to changes in commodity prices was the most important relation stressed in the 1941 famous article by Wolfgang Stolper and Paul Samuelson, "Protection and Real Wages" in the *Review of Economic Studies*. In Chapter 4, I referred to this ranking as the "Magnification Effect." The Stolper–Samuelson setting was one in which a country that imports its more labor-intensive commodity (clothing) protects its production by imposing a tariff on imports. The tariff is assumed to raise the *domestic* price of clothing, causing the wage rate to rise, not only in nominal terms but in *real* terms as well (i.e., by a greater relative amount than either commodity price regardless of the taste pattern of laborers).[1] This Magnification Effect is based on a most commonly (although rarely mentioned) assumption: To produce either commodity, it takes *two* inputs (not just a single input, e.g., labor, as in the Ricardian model). Equations of change (1b)–(4b) in Chapter 4 show that if commodity prices are constant, so will be factor prices. If commodity prices do change, each commodity price change is (in the calculus) a *weighted average* of the (relative) factor price changes, where the weights (the θ_{ij}'s) refer to the *factor shares* in production of each commodity (and add up to 1). If commodity prices do not change, relative changes in factor endowments are absorbed by a weighted average of output changes, in this case, the weights are the fractions of the factor inputs used in producing each commodity (the λ_{ij}'s), which also add to unity.

There is an interesting question that can be raised in the Stolper–Samuelson proof of the magnification effect. Their proof: They use an original variation of the concept of a consumption box diagram that was traditionally used by economists when analyzing the effects on commodity price ratios when aggregate quantities of two commodities (measured along the sides of the box) are fixed and each country's taste patterns are revealed by a set of indifference curves rising from opposite corners of the box. The concept of a *contract curve*, everywhere along which an indifference curve

---

[1] Lloyd Metzler, in a famous article, "Tariffs, the Terms of Trade, and the Distribution of National Income," *The Journal of Political Economy*, (1949) suggested that a tariff imposed by a large country might cause the domestic price of imports to *fall*, thus contradicting the Stolper–Samuelson result. As a consequence, in future years, the Stolper–Samuelson theorem was interpreted as the type of ranking between changes in domestic factor prices and domestic commodity prices, as in our current ranking stated above.

for one country is tangent to an indifference curve for the other country, is utilized to reveal how the commodity price ratio (revealed by the common slopes of tangent isoquants) changes as the real income (along the contract curve) of one country is raised and that of the other country is reduced. Their reinterpreted analogy of the box diagram has the sides of the box (now called a *production box*) represent the amounts of labor and capital (in the Stolper–Samuelson article capital is the other factor, not land) used to produce each of the commodities and the "contract curve" now shows where two isoquants, each rising from a different opposite origin, are tangent so that the slope of the tangent line reveals the factor price ratio. As the domestic price of the import commodity increases, so does output in this sector as the capital-intensive export sector contracts, and both factors leave to work in the labor-intensive import sector, which causes capital/labor ratios to rise in *both* sectors, thus unambiguously causing the *real* wage rate increase.

This is the simple but important proof of the Stolper–Samuelson theorem. It also leads to perhaps an interesting question: If technology is rigid in the sense of there being only a single technique for production in either sector (which means no capital/labor change in either sector), does that destroy the Stolper–Samuelson theorem? No. Go back to the kind of argument using calculus in the equilibrium price = average cost equations of change. They state that the two commodity price changes are flanked by the two relative changes in factor prices. If the input–output factors are frozen, the argument that an increase in the relative price of the labor-intensive commodity leads to an increase in the real wage rate still holds. Perhaps this is even more transparent when realizing that the real wage *must* increase in a competitive equilibrium, even if an argument based on changes in techniques leading to increasing the returns to labor will not suffice. The Stolper–Samuelson theorem was indeed very clearly proved by using the movements along the contract curve in a production box. That does not imply that this argument is necessary even in more simple scenarios (in which input/output techniques cannot be changed).

Chapter 6 was written (in 2006) to offer some remarks on the history of trade theory *after* the Stolper–Samuelson article appeared 65 years previously. The Stolper–Samuelson article did reveal in a more formal manner some of the relationships that are to be found in the Heckscher and Ohlin papers (1919 and 1933). Furthermore, an article written in 1948 by

Samuelson argued that two economies in a free trade setting that shared the same technology for the production of a pair of commodities could, as a consequence of trade, share the *same* factor prices even though factor endowment ratios happened to be *different.* This could only occur because it is only commodities that engage in world trade, not factors of production.[2] The surprise this article created made Samuelson follow up the next year with his article, "International Factor-Price Equalization Once Again," also appearing in the same journal (the *Economic Journal*).

The history of ideas over time discussed in Chapter 6 also concerns a question that applies to *any* of the small-scale competitive models used in international trade theory: As the dimensionalities get larger, the obvious question is whether the results from the small-scale model still hold. One feature of such an enquiry is that it may be too much to ask for a price rise for a *single* commodity, say, to result in an increase in the real wage for labor in a *many*-commodity setting. However, as Chapter 6 discusses, perhaps the most general question, one that should be of main importance to students of Political Science, is whether in an economy in which many commodities are produced and exchanged in perfectly competitive markets, governments can, *in a nontransparent fashion*, raise the real income of *any* group by interfering in markets (by altering demand patterns that affect prices, for example). The general answer is, yes. However, it may be too much to ask if it would be sufficient to change only a *single* commodity price, as in the original Stolper–Samuelson model.

The material in Chapter 7 suggests a reappraisal of the reasoning appearing in the famous 1953 article by Wassily Leontief, published, surprisingly, not in an economics journal but in *The Proceedings of the American Philosophical Society*, v. 97.[3] His argument was rapidly referred to as the *Leontief Paradox.* Leontief found that in the United States, assumed everywhere to be a relatively capital-abundant country, the capital/labor ratios found in import-competing industries were greater than those in American export sectors. This seemed to contradict Heckscher–Ohlin arguments

---

[2]Just as in the Ricardian model, commodities are exchanged between countries whereas the (single) factor input, labor, is only mobile between sectors within a country, not between countries.

[3]The article was subsequently reprinted in *Economia Internazionale*, v. 3, (1954).

that relatively capital abundant countries would export relatively capital-intensive commodities.

Let the typical 2×2 setting be somewhat enlarged to one in which there are *many* commodities that could be produced. This does not imply that many commodities are produced at the same time in any country. Rather, with only two factor inputs international trade implies that any country need not produce more than two commodities, and may even be specialized to one. The well-known concept of the "Hicksian Composite Unit Value Isoquant," with Capital (K) (or Land, T, if preferred) on the vertical axis and Labor (L) on the horizontal in Fig. 6.1 of Chapter 6 proves to be very useful if, as the country develops, its capital/labor ratio increases over time, causing the country to change the *pattern* of production. An initially very labor-abundant country might produce only commodity 1 (Fig. 6.1), but with growth may start to produce the more capital-intensive commodity 2 as well, and, with more growth, go through a period of producing only commodity 2 until it can start to produce commodity 3 as well. Figure 6.2 illustrates how, as a country grows and becomes more capital abundant, its production pattern is one in which the country is completely specialized to one commodity, and then shares production with another as well until it is specialized again to an even more capital-intensive commodity.

As Chapter 7 then explains, the growing country that is producing two commodities will, in the early stage, export only its more labor-intensive commodity, while in time (but still producing the same pair of commodities) its pattern changes to exporting the commodity that is the more capital-intensive. This is followed by a period in which it is producing *only* its (previously) more capital-intensive commodity and then starts to produce an even more capital-intensive one as well. At any given time, in which it produces a pair of commodities, it may indeed be exporting its capital-intensive commodity; however, this will change. With further growth, the country will then be importing this same commodity, which then has become its more labor-intensive commodity because it is also producing small amounts of a more capital-intensive commodity (that it must be importing as well — from a more capital-abundant country). In any case, if all countries share the same technologies, any country that is more capital-abundant than another must be producing one or two commodities that are both more capital-intensive than any commodity produced by the more labor-abundant country. *That* comparison *does* link capital-abundance with capital-intensity. The comparison that counts is not between commodities produced within a country but rather between countries, a remark that hopefully explains the so-called *Leontief Paradox*.

The *Specific-Factors model* makes its appearance in Chapter 8, and the focus is on a comparison with the Heckscher–Ohlin model. Furthermore, this comparison can be made either in a scenario in which an initial trading equilibrium is disturbed by an infinitesimal change in a commodity price (or perhaps in a factor endowment), in which case calculus tools can be used, or the disturbance could be finite in size. Both types of scenarios are worth discussing, especially because the views held by trade economists are different from those typically held by labor economists if differential calculus is the appropriate tool. The Specific-Factors model is older than the Heckscher–Ohlin model, and rather more simple even though, in the typical two-commodity case, the Heckscher–Ohlin model has only two factor inputs while the Specific-Factors model has three.[4] One input, say labor, is mobile between the two sectors whereas capital is not moveable from one sector to another, it is *specific* in its use. (Alternatively, the other two factors might be completely different, like capital and land.)

Focus on the effect of a price increase, say in commodity 1, on the wage rate. If x_1 is the labor-intensive commodity in a Heckscher–Ohlin model, the price increase raises the wage rate relatively more than the price rise. In the Specific-Factors model, the wage rate also increases, but by a smaller relative amount. That is, the ranking is: $\hat{r}_1 > \hat{p}_1 > \hat{w} > \hat{p}_2$ $(= 0) > \hat{r}_2$. Using the techniques found in Chapter 8 [see equations (11) and (12)], the relative change in the wage rate if only the price of the first commodity rises (with no changes in factor endowments), is $\hat{w} = \theta_1\{i_1 s_1\}\hat{p}_1$, where θ_1 refers to the fraction of national income represented by the output of industry 1. The two terms in parentheses refer to two aspects of technology: i_1 refers to the *labor-intensity* of the first industry and s_1 to the relative *flexibility* of technology in the first industry. Note this very different solution for the wage change in the two models: In the Heckscher–Ohlin model, only relative labor-intensities matter, whereas in the (more simple) Specific-Factors model the importance of the industry

---

[4]The formal model was discussed in Jones (1971) and Samuelson (1971). (References are found in Chapter 7.)

in which the price has increased as well as the relative degree of *flexibility* in that industry also matter. The reason for the difference in the models is that the Specific-Factors model has two industries and three factors of production, so that knowledge of commodity price changes is *not* sufficient to determine what happens to the returns to the three factor prices. As illustrated in Eq. (16), in the Heckscher–Ohlin model changes in factor prices depend *only* on changes in the commodity price ratio and $|\theta|$, the *determinant of coefficients*, i.e., the difference between labor shares in the two sectors.

The figures in Chapter 8 when changes to equilibrium take place reveal how the calculus results can differ from those found with finite changes. Perhaps the discussion about technical progress shown in Fig. 8.4 helps to illustrate. The three upwardly sloping curves illustrate how changes in wage/rent ratios affect capital/labor ratios used in production. The dark locus reveals how factor prices are themselves affected by changes in endowments, with the horizontal portions showing that factor prices are completely determined by given commodity prices if growth takes place while a pair of commodities are produced. When commodity prices do change, such as an increase in the price of commodity 2, the horizontal section when the second commodity is the relatively capital-intensive commodity shifts downwards while at higher K/L endowments, it is shifted upwards because there, if two commodities are produced, the second commodity is labor-intensive. If the shifts are only a response to price changes, the original upwardly sloped sections would not shift. However, if it is technical progress that takes place in the second industry, the upwardly sloping industry 2 curve will only stay in place if technical progress is *Hicksian neutral*, meaning that the capital/labor ratio chosen for production would be the same after progress as before, for any given factor price ratio. By contrast, in Fig. 8.4, the portion of the after-progress curve for the second commodity shifts to the *left* if progress is *Hicksian capital-saving*. The resultant effect on the wage/rent ratio thus depends upon where the *initial K/L* ratio was if commodity 1 and commodity 2 were being produced. The remarks made about this figure in Chapter 8 may be more surprising to trade theorists than to Labor economists. Why? Because if the change is small, as in the calculus examples that are familiar to trade theorists, the weighted average of relative changes in the a_{ij} input/output fractions vanishes (because firms in the initial equilibrium are minimizing costs), so that the change in the wage rate depends *only* on which industry gets a price increase. Bias does not matter. But it will matter if technical progress takes place and the progress is finite, as many Labor economists might assume. (Furthermore, note that in the scenario such as shown in Fig. 8.4, the Specific-Factors model illustrated is *not* the (3 × 2) version, but rather a kind of (2 × 1) version in which a factor is "specific" only because there is no other industry in which to go since the economy is completely specialized).

Chapter 9 may seem to have a strange title in featuring "*Bubble Diagrams.*" The "bubbles" do not indicate malfunctions in macroeconomic models. Instead, the chapter makes use of simple diagrams in which each bubble refers to a particular commodity. For example, Fig. 9.5(a) illustrates a country (Foreign, with a $*$) that produces two commodities: Y^* uses inputs of specific capital, K_Y^*, and L^*, which is used both in Y^* and in an *enclave* (X^E) using some of Home's specific factor, K_x^E that is specific to the industry but mobile between countries. Home is the owner of X-type capital used both in X^E in Foreign and in X at Home, which is also the only user of Home labor, L. This is the scenario used in a paper I wrote with a former student, Fumio Dei, in 1983 (see references in Chapter 9). A question we pondered had to do with the direction between countries of a possible flow of K_X if the world price of X should increase. This turns out to be a very easy question to answer by taking it in two parts. First, ask about the change in the rate of return to X-type capital in each country if no further change in country location is allowed. In Home, both the rate of return to capital and the wage rate would increase by the same relative amount as the increase in p_X. Of course the same outcome would be seen in the Foreign Enclave if no labor movements are allowed. But if labor is allowed to move between sectors in Foreign some labor will move to the Enclave. With no change in the price of commodity Y^*, the Foreign wage rate will rise, but not by as relatively great an amount as p_X because the rate of return to capital in the Enclave will rise relatively by more than does p_X. Once the constraint on capital flows between countries is lifted this will encourage a capital flow towards the Enclave and away from Home. Why? Foreign has a *hinterland* (in the Y^* sector) and Home does not. (Fig. 9.6 in Chapter 9 allows a hinterland in both countries.)

This example of international capital flows (in Fig. 9.5a) is *structurally* very similar to a model (as in Fig. 9.5b) in which land and unskilled labor are used to produce an agricultural product, unskilled labor and capital produce a low-technology commodity (N), and capital is also used to produce a high-technology manufacturing commodity (M) along with skilled labor specific to that sector. Bubble diagrams are useful for showing how similarities can be found in specific factor models used in different disciplines and, when the specific factor is allowed to move either between sectors or between countries in the same sector, the similarities between disciplines can be observed.

Chapter 9 also briefly speaks of a model used by Fred Gruen and Max Corden in a (1970) publication. Theirs is a model in which there are two sectors, agriculture and manufacturing. Manufacturing is a sector that has only one industry, using *capital* and labor. The agricultural sector has two industries, grain and wool, both using *land* and labor. Thus, whereas manufacturing makes use of a specific-factors 2×1 model, Agriculture is a Heckscher–Ohlin 2×2 nugget and both are embedded in a larger 3×3 Heckscher–Ohlin model. This idea leads to a very useful and simple higher dimensional model, one in which an economy has n sectors, each of which makes use of a type of capital used *only* in that sector. All but one of the sectors produce a single unique commodity (such as manufacturing in the Gruen/Corden paper). The remaining sector produces two commodities, making it a Heckscher–Ohlin nugget.[5] Although this model has a large number of factors, no industry uses more than two. This avoids dealing with models in which more than two factors are used in producing a commodity (in which case a pair of factors may be complements instead of substitutes, which greatly complicates the analysis).

In Chapter 10, diagrams are quite unusual in revealing how a collection of countries that have different *relative* factor endowments will experience different effects on their *real* wage rates when the price of a particular commodity is reduced or if there is technical progress in a particular commodity. For example, Fig. 10.4 assumes that commodities 1 through 4 are produced somewhere in the world of countries engaged in free trade (and

---

[5]A discussion of this $(n+1) \times (n+1)$ Heckscher–Ohlin model can be found in R. Jones and S. Marjit, "International Trade and Endogenous Production Structures" in W. Neuefeind and R. Riezman (eds.): *Economic Theory and International Trade: Essays in Memoriam J. Trout Rader*, (Springer-Verlag), 1992.

ignoring transport costs, etc., so that they all face the similar array of commodity prices). Technology for producing each commodity is shared by all countries, but each country has a different endowment of capital and labor, the two inputs involved in all production. Commodity 1 is produced by more labor-intensive techniques than is commodity 2, which, in turn, is produced with more labor-intensive techniques than commodity 3, and commodity 4 is the commodity that is produced with the highest capital/labor ratio. For a given set of commodity prices, a *Hicksian composite unit value isoquant* reveals that very labor-abundant countries will produce only commodity 1, countries with slightly higher capital/labor endowment (K/L) ratios can produce both commodities 1 and 2. And in similar fashion, countries with various higher K/L endowments may become specialized in producing only commodity 2, or, further on, might produce both commodities 2 and 3 or (going further) just commodity 3, or (even further) commodities 3 and 4, and, for those with even higher capital/labor endowment proportions, be specialized in producing commodity 4. Now assume that in world markets there is a drop in the price of commodity 2. What happens to the real wage rate in these countries? The answer depends upon *which* commodity (or pair of commodities) each produces. For example, those who do not produce commodity 2 (i.e., those with very low K/L ratios) or those at the other end of the distribution (with much higher K/L endowment ratios) will have their real wage rates be improved because the price of a commodity not produced (but still consumed) goes down and their monetary wage rate has not been changed. For those countries that are completely specialized in producing *only* commodity 2, there is a drop in the real wage rate because their nominal wage rate has dropped by the same relative amount as the drop in the price of the second commodity but all other commodity prices are assumed to be unchanged.

To continue: Nothing yet has been said about those countries that produce commodity 2 *and* either commodity 1 or commodity 3. The production model that explains their real income change is the Heckscher–Ohlin 2×2 model (but with consumption of all four commodities as well). For those countries producing commodity 1 as well as commodity 2, there has been a price drop in their more *capital-intensive* commodity, and that means that their real wage will rise relatively more than it would if they produced only commodity 1. By contrast, for those countries producing both commodity 2 and commodity 3, the price drop is for their more *labor-intensive* of the two commodities produced. Therefore, their wage rate falls by more than it would if it produced only the second commodity. If either of these countries produced only the second commodity, their real wage will either rise less, or fall less, than if they produce another commodity as well, because the 2×1 Specific-Factors model does not exhibit the *magnification effects* on factor prices in the same manner that is a feature of the 2×2 Heckscher–Ohlin model.

Chapter 10 also discusses the interesting different outcomes possible if instead of a price change there is technical progress in the way a particular commodity is produced. As Chapter 8 has already argued, whether technical progress in an industry is labor-saving or is capital-saving makes no difference *unless* the progress is *finite* instead of being infinitesimal so that the calculus techniques make bias unimportant. As well, Chapter 10 also talks about technical progress (of a finite amount) in certain service sector activities that leads to a *fragmentation* in the production process. This is an issue that will be discussed in detail in Part III.

The title of Chapter 11 suggests that even more can be said about factor bias and technical progress. Here I will only propose that you take a peek at the four diagrams in order to agree that the arguments put forward there are probably fairly simple, but nonetheless important enough to read. For example, Fig. 11.4 shows a case in which an economy with a fixed K/L endowment ratio at point A and initially producing commodities 2 and 3 is blessed by technical progress in producing the second commodity, which is the *labor-intensive good* (compared with commodity 3). A trade economist might assume that of course the wage will go up, but the diagram shows the wage rate falling (because the progress is *biased* in being purely labor-saving). A labor economist might smile and say "of course."

Chapter 12 is a paper focused on economic models used in international trade theory, as in most of the previous chapters. It tries to point out that even very simple, low-dimensional models can both appeal to common sense so strongly that one might wonder why a model is necessary, and yet also be capable of revealing outcomes that may seem unusual, or even paradoxical. Consider a simple sector-specific model where there are many commodities produced, and in each sector there is a kind of capital that is used only there, along with labor (which is mobile between sectors). Suppose there is an increase in the market price of the first commodity, but all other commodity prices stay constant. What would happen to all the factor prices in a competitive market? Clearly, the wage rate will be driven up, but only by a small amount. The rate of return to the kind of capital used in the first commodity will rise in relative terms by more than the commodity price increase, but the return to (specific) capital in every other sector will fall. No surprises there. Suppose that instead of a price rise in the first commodity there is an increase in the endowment of the capital used *specifically* in the first sector. Then, of course, the return to capital used specifically in that sector falls because the wage rate for labor will increase, and this will as well lower the rates of return in all other sectors. Keep in mind that I assume all commodity prices are fixed. Question: Must the fall in the return to capital in the sector in which the endowment amount of the specific factor used there has been increased fall *more* than the return to (specific) capitals in other sectors? As economists love to say, "it all depends." On what? Only on the labor shares in production in each and every commodity! In the commodity that is the most "labor-intensive," the return to capital will fall by the greatest relative amount, regardless of whether or not that is the commodity in which the specific capital endowment has increased. It's that simple. And Chapter 12 has several other examples in which there may be changes that seem surprising but the reasoning is simple. This should be expected for many of these *surprising* examples that appear in competitive trade models. Enjoy!

CHAPTER 4

The Structure of Simple General Equilibrium Models*

Ronald W. Jones

4.1 Introduction

It is difficult to find any major branch of applied economics that has not made some use of the simple general equilibrium model of production. For years, this model has served as the work-horse for most of the developments in the pure theory of international trade. It has been used to study the effects of taxation on the distribution of income and the impact of technological change on the composition of outputs and the structure of prices. Perhaps the most prominent of its recent uses is to be found in the neoclassical theory of economic growth.

Such intensive use of the simple two-sector model of production suggests that a few properties are being retranslated in such diverse areas as public finance, international trade, and economic growth. The unity provided by a common theoretical structure is further emphasized by the dual relationship that exists between sets of variables in the model itself. Traditional formulations of the model tend to obscure this feature. My purpose in this chapter is to analyze the structure of the simple competitive model of production in a manner designed to highlight both the dual relationship

*Originally published in *Journal of Political Economy*, 73, (1965), pp. 557–572.
I am indebted to the National Science Foundation for support of this research in 1962–1964. I have benefited from discussions with Hugh Rose, Robert Fogel, Rudolph Penner, and Emmanuel Drandakis. My greatest debt is to Akihiro Amano (1963), whose dissertation was a stimulus to my own work.

and the similarity that exists among a number of traditional problems in comparative statics and economic growth.

The model is described in Secs. 4.2 and 4.3. In Sec. 4.4, I discuss the dual nature of two theorems in the theory of international trade associated with the names of Stolper and Samuelson on the one hand and Rybczynski on the other. A simple demand relationship is added in Sec. 4.5, and a problem in public finance is analyzed — the effect of excise subsidies or taxes on relative commodity and factor prices. The static model of production is then reinterpreted as a neo-classical model of economic growth by letting one of the outputs serve as the capital good. The dual of the "incidence" problem in public finance in the static model is shown to have direct relevance to the problem of the stability of the balanced growth path in the neoclassical growth model. In the concluding section of the chapter, I show how these results can be applied to the analysis of technological progress. Any improvement in technology or in the quality of factors of production can be simply viewed as a composite of two effects, which I shall term the "differential industry" effect and the "differential factor" effect. Each effect has its counter-part in the dual problems discussed in the earlier part of the chapter.

4.2 The Model

Assume a perfectly competitive economy in which firms (indefinite in number) maximize profits, which are driven to the zero level in equilibrium. Consistent with this, technology in each of two sectors exhibits constant returns to scale. Two primary factors, labor (L) and land (T), are used in producing two distinct commodities, manufactured goods (M) and food (F). Wages (w) and rents (r) denote the returns earned by the factors for use of services, whereas p_M and p_F denote the competitive market prices of the two commodities.

If technology is given and factor endowments and commodity prices are treated as parameters, the model serves to determine eight unknowns: The level of commodity outputs (two), the factor allocations to each industry (four), and factor prices (two). The equations of the model could be given by the production functions (two), the requirement that each factor receive the value of its marginal product (four), and that each factor be fully employed (two). This is the format most frequently used in the theory of international trade and the neoclassical theory of growth.[1] I consider, instead, the formulation of the model suggested by activity analysis.

The technology is described by the columns of the A matrix,

$$A = \begin{pmatrix} a_{LM} & a_{LF} \\ a_{TM} & a_{TF} \end{pmatrix},$$

where a_{ij} denotes the quantity of factor i required to produce a unit of commodity j. With constant returns to scale total factor demands are given by the product of the a's and the levels of output. The requirement that both factors be fully employed is thus given by Eqs. (4.1) and (4.2). Similarly, unit costs of production in each industry are given by the columns of A multiplied by the factor prices. In a competitive equilibrium with both goods being produced, these unit costs must reflect market prices, as in Eqs. (4.3) and (4.4).[2]

$$a_{LM} M + a_{LF} F = L, \tag{4.1}$$

$$a_{TM} M + a_{TF} F = T, \tag{4.2}$$

$$a_{LM} w + a_{TM} r = p_M, \tag{4.3}$$

$$a_{LF} w + a_{TF} r = p_F. \tag{4.4}$$

This formulation serves to emphasize the dual relationship between factor endowments and commodity outputs on the one hand (Eqs. [4.1] and [4.2]) and commodity prices and factor prices on the other (Eqs. [4.3] and [4.4]).

In the general case of variable coefficients, the relationships shown in Eqs. (4.1)–(4.4) must be supplemented by four additional relationships determining the input coefficients. These are provided by the requirement that in a competitive equilibrium each a_{ij} depends solely upon the ratio of factor prices.

---

[1] As an example in each field see Kemp (1964) and Meade (1961).

[2] These basic relationships are usually presented as inequalities to allow for the existence of resource(s) in excess supply even at a zero price or for the possibility that losses would be incurred in certain industries if production were positive. I assume throughout that resources are fully employed, and production at zero profits with positive factor and commodity prices is possible. For a discussion of the inequalities, see, for example, Dorfman *et al.* (1958) or Hicks (1960).

4.3   The Equations of Change

The comparative statics properties of the model described in Sec. 4.2 are developed by considering the effect of a change in the parameters on the unknowns of the problem. With unchanged technology the parameters are the factor endowments (L and T) and the commodity prices (P_M and P_F), the right-hand side of Eqs. (4.1)–(4.4).

Let a hat ($^\wedge$) indicate the relative change in a variable or parameter. Thus, $\hat{p}_F$ denotes dp_F/p_F and $\hat{L}$ denotes dL/L.[3] The four equations in the rates of change are shown in Eqs. (4.1a)–(4.4a):

$$\lambda_{LM}\hat{M} + \lambda_{LF}\hat{F} = \hat{L} - [\lambda_{LM}\hat{a}_{LM} + \lambda_{LF}\hat{a}_{LF}], \qquad (4.1a)$$

$$\lambda_{TM}\hat{M} + \lambda_{TF}\hat{F} = \hat{T} - [\lambda_{TM}\hat{a}_{TM} + \lambda_{TF}\hat{a}_{TF}], \qquad (4.2a)$$

$$\theta_{LM}\hat{w} + \theta_{TM}\hat{r} = \hat{p}_M - [\theta_{LM}\hat{a}_{LM} + \theta_{TM}\hat{a}_{TM}], \qquad (4.3a)$$

$$\theta_{LF}\hat{w} + \theta_{TF}\hat{r} = \hat{p}_F - [\theta_{LF}\hat{a}_{LF} + \theta_{TF}\hat{a}_{TF}]. \qquad (4.4a)$$

The λ's and θ's are the transforms of the a's that appear when relative changes are shown. A fraction of the labor force is used in manufacturing (λ_{LM}), and this plus the fraction of the labor force used in food production (λ_{LF}) must add to unity by the full-employment assumption (shown by Eq. (4.1)). Similarly λ_{TM} and λ_{TF}. The θ's, by contrast, refer to the factor shares in each industry. Thus, θ_{LM}, labor's share in manufacturing, is given by $a_{LM}w/p_M$. By the zero profit conditions, θ_{LJ} and θ_{TJ} must add to unity.

In this section, I assume that manufacturing is labor-intensive. It follows that labor's share in manufacturing must be greater than labor's share in food, and that the percentage of the labor force used in manufacturing must exceed the percentage of total land that is used in manufacturing. Let λ and θ be the notations for the matrices of coefficients shown in ([4.1a], [4.2a]) and ([4.3a], [4.4a]).

$$\lambda = \begin{pmatrix} \lambda_{LM} & \lambda_{LF} \\ \lambda_{TM} & \lambda_{TF} \end{pmatrix}; \quad \theta = \begin{pmatrix} \theta_{LM} & \theta_{TM} \\ \theta_{LF} & \theta_{TF} \end{pmatrix}.$$

---

[3] This is the procedure used by Meade (1961). The λ and θ notation has been used by Amano (1963). Expressing small changes in relative or percentage terms is a natural procedure when technology exhibits constant returns to scale.

Since each row sum in λ and θ is unity, the determinants $|\lambda|$ and $|\theta|$ are given by

$$|\lambda| = \lambda_{LM} - \lambda_{TM} \quad \text{and} \quad |\theta| = \theta_{LM} - \theta_{LF},$$

and both $|\lambda|$ and $|\theta|$ are positive by the factor-intensity assumption.[4]

If coefficients of production are fixed, Eqs. (4.1a)–(4.4a) are greatly simplified as every a_{ij} and, therefore, the λ and θ weighted sums of the $\hat{a}_{ij}$'s reduce to zero. In the case of variable coefficients, sufficient extra conditions to determine the $\hat{a}$'s are easily derived. Consider, first, the maximizing role of the typical competitive entrepreneur. For any given level of output he attempts to minimize costs; that is, he minimizes unit costs. In the manufacturing industry these are given by $(a_{LM}w + a_{TM}r)$. The entrepreneur treats factor prices as fixed, and varies the a's so as to set the derivative of costs equal to zero. Dividing by p_M and expressing changes in relative terms leads to Eq. (4.6). Equation (4.7) shows the corresponding relationship for the food industry:

$$\theta_{LM}\hat{a}_{LM} + \theta_{TM}\hat{a}_{TM} = 0, \qquad (4.6)$$

$$\theta_{LF}\hat{a}_{LF} + \theta_{TF}\hat{a}_{TF} = 0. \qquad (4.7)$$

With no technological change, alterations in factor proportions must balance out such that the θ-weighted average of the changes in input coefficients in each industry is zero.

This implies directly that the relationship between changes in factor prices and changes in commodity prices is *identical* in the variable and fixed coefficients cases, an example of the Wong–Viner envelope theorem. With costs per unit of output being minimized, the change in costs resulting from

---

[4]Let P and W represent the diagonal matrices,

$$\begin{pmatrix} p_M & 0 \\ 0 & p_F \end{pmatrix} \quad \text{and} \quad \begin{pmatrix} w & 0 \\ 0 & r \end{pmatrix},$$

respectively, and E and X represent the diagonal matrices of factor endowments and commodity outputs. Then $\lambda = E^{-1}AX$ and $\theta = P^{-1}A'W$. Since $|A| > 0$ and the determinants of the four diagonal matrices are all positive, $|\lambda|$ and $|\theta|$ must be positive. This relation among the signs of $|\lambda|$, $|\theta|$, and $|A|$ is proved by Amano (1963) and Takayama (1963).

a small change in factor prices is the same whether or not factor proportions are altered. The saving in cost from such alterations is a second-order small.[5]

A similar kind of argument definitely does *not* apply to the λ-weighted average of the $\hat{a}$'s for each factor that appears in the factor market-clearing relationships. For example $(\lambda_{LM}\hat{a}_{LM}+\lambda_{LF}\hat{a}_{LF})$ shows the percentage change in the total quantity of labor required by the economy as a result of changing factor proportions in each industry at unchanged outputs. The crucial feature here is that if factor prices change, factor proportions alter in the same direction in both industries. The extent of this change obviously depends upon the elasticities of substitution between factors in each industry. In a competitive equilibrium (and with the internal tangencies implicit in earlier assumptions), the slope of the isoquant in each industry is equal to the ratio of factor prices. Therefore the elasticities of substitution can be defined as in (4.8) and (4.9):

$$\sigma_M = \frac{\hat{a}_{TM} - \hat{a}_{LM}}{\hat{w} - \hat{r}}, \tag{4.8}$$

$$\sigma_F = \frac{\hat{a}_{TF} - \hat{a}_{LF}}{\hat{w} - \hat{r}}, \tag{4.9}$$

Together with (4.5) and (4.6) a subset of four equations relating the $\hat{a}$'s to the change in the relative factor prices is obtained. They can be solved in pairs; for example (4.5) and (4.7) yield solutions for the $\hat{a}$'s of the M industry. In general,

$$\hat{a}_{Lj} = -\theta_{Tj}\sigma_j(\hat{w} - \hat{r}); \quad j = M, F,$$
$$\hat{a}_{Tj} = \theta_{Lj}\sigma_j(\hat{w} - \hat{r}); \quad j = M, F.$$

These solutions for the $\hat{a}$'s can then be substituted into Eqs. (4.1a)–(4.4a) to obtain:

$$\lambda_{LM}\hat{M} + \lambda_{LF}\hat{F} = \hat{L} + \delta_L(\hat{w} - \hat{r}), \tag{4.1b}$$

$$\lambda_{TM}\hat{M} + \lambda_{TF}\hat{F} = \hat{T} - \delta_T(\hat{w} - \hat{r}), \tag{4.2b}$$

---

[5]For another example of the Wong–Viner theorem, for changes in real income along a transformation schedule, see Jones (1961).

$$\theta_{LM}\hat{w} + \theta_{TM}\hat{r} = \hat{p}_M, \tag{4.3b}$$

$$\theta_{LF}\hat{w} + \theta_{TF}\hat{r} = \hat{p}_F, \tag{4.4b}$$

where

$$\delta_L = \lambda_{LM}\theta_{TM}\sigma_M + \lambda_{LF}\theta_{TF}\sigma_F,$$

$$\delta_T = \lambda_{TM}\theta_{LM}\sigma_M + \lambda_{TF}\theta_{LF}\sigma_F.$$

In the fixed-coefficients case, δ_L and δ_T are zero. In general, δ_L is the aggregate percentage saving in labor inputs at unchanged outputs associated with a 1 percent rise in the relative wage rate, the saving resulting from the adjustment to less labor-intensive techniques in both industries as relative wages rise.

The structure of the production model with variable coefficients is exhibited in Eqs. (4.1b)–(4.4b). The latter pair states that factor prices are dependent only upon commodity prices, which is the factor-price equalization theorem.[6] If commodity prices are unchanged, factor prices are constant and Eqs. (4.1b) and (4.2b) state that changes in commodity outputs are linked to changes in factor endowments via the λ, matrix in precisely the same way as θ links factor price changes. This is the basic duality feature of the production model.[7]

4.4 The Magnification Effect

The nature of the link provided by λ or θ is revealed by examining the solution for $\hat{M}$ and $\hat{F}$ at constant commodity prices in Eqs. (4.1b) and (4.2b) and for $\hat{w}$ and $\hat{r}$ in Eqs. (4.3b) and (4.4b).[8] If both endowments expand at the same rate, both commodity outputs expand at identical rates. But if factor endowments expand at different rates, the commodity

---

[6] Factor endowments come into their own in influencing factor prices if complete specialization is allowed (or if the number of factors exceeds the number of commodities). See Samuelson (1953–1954) for a detailed discussion of this issue.

[7] The reciprocal relationship between the effect of a rise in the price of commodity i on the return to factor j and the effect of an increase in the endowment of factor j on the output of commodity i is discussed briefly by Samuelson (1953–1954).

[8] The solutions, of course, are given by the elements of λ^{-1} and θ^{-1}. If M is labor-intensive, the diagonal elements of λ^{-1} and θ^{-1} are positive and exceed unity, while off-diagonal elements are negative.

intensive in the use of the fastest growing factor expands at a greater rate than either factor, and the other commodity grows (if at all) at a slower rate than either factor. For example, suppose labor expands more rapidly than land. With M labor-intensive,

$$\hat{M} > \hat{L} > \hat{T} > \hat{F}.$$

This *magnification effect* of factor endowments on commodity outputs at unchanged commodity prices is also a feature of the dual link between commodity and factor prices. In the absence of technological change or excise taxes or subsidies, if the price of M grows more rapidly than the price of F,

$$\hat{w} > \hat{p}_M > \hat{p}_F > \hat{r}.$$

Turned the other way around, the source of magnification effect is easy to detect. For example, since the relative change in the price of either commodity is a positive weighted average of factor-price changes, it must be bounded by these changes. Similarly, if input coefficients are fixed (as a consequence of assuming constant factor and commodity prices), any disparity in the growth of outputs is reduced when considering the consequent changes in the economy's demand for factors. The reason, of course, is that each good requires both factors of production.

Two special cases have been especially significant in the theory of international trade. Suppose the endowment of only one factor (say labor) rises. With $\hat{L}$ positive and $\hat{T}$ zero, $\hat{M}$ exceeds $\hat{L}$ and $\hat{F}$ is negative. This is the Rybczynzki theorem in the theory of international trade: At unchanged commodity prices an expansion in one factor results in an absolute decline in the commodity intensive in the use of the other factor. (See Rybczynski [1955] and also Chapter 1.) Its dual underlies the Stolper–Samuelson (1941) tariff theorem.[9] Suppose $\hat{p}_F$ is zero (for example, F could be taken as numeraire). Then an increase in the price of M (brought about, say, by a tariff on imports of M) raises the return to the factor used intensively in M by an even greater relative amount (and lowers the return to the other factor). In the case illustrated, the *real* return to labor has unambiguously risen.

---

[9]A graphical analysis of the dual relationship between the Rybczynski theorem and the Stolper–Samuelson theorem is presented in "Duality in International Trade: A Geometrical Note," in *Canadian Journal of Economics & Political Science*, 1965, pp. 390–393.

For some purposes it is convenient to consider a slight variation of the Stolper–Samuelson theorem. Let p_j stand for the *market* price of j as before, but introduce a set of domestic excise taxes or subsidies so that $s_j p_j$ represents the price received by producers in industry j; s_j is one plus the *ad valorem* rate of subsidy to the industry.[10] The effect on factor prices of an imposition of subsidies on commodities is derived from Eqs. (4.3c) and (4.4c):

$$\theta_{LM}\hat{w} + \theta_{TM}\hat{r} = \hat{p}_M + \hat{s}_M, \tag{4.3c}$$

$$\theta_{LF}\hat{w} + \theta_{TF}\hat{r} = \hat{p}_F + \hat{s}_F. \tag{4.4c}$$

At fixed commodity prices, what impact does a set of subsidies have on factor prices? The answer is that all the subsidies are "shifted backward" to affect returns to factors in a *magnified* fashion. Thus, if M is labor-intensive and if the M industry should be especially favored by the subsidy,

$$\hat{w} > \hat{s}_M > \hat{s}_F > \hat{r}.$$

The *magnification* effect in this problem and its dual reflects the basic structure of the model with fixed commodity prices. However, if a demand relationship is introduced, prices are determined within the model and can be expected to adjust to a change in factor endowments or, in the dual problem, to a change in excise subsidies (or taxes). In the next section, I discuss the feedback effect of these induced price changes on the composition of output and relative factor prices. The crucial question to be considered concerns the extent to which commodity price changes can dampen the initial magnification effects that are produced at constant prices.

4.5 The Extended Model: Demand Endogenous

To close the production model, I assume that community taste patterns are homothetic and ignore any differences between the taste patterns of laborers and landlords. Thus, the ratio of the quantities consumed of M

---

[10]I restrict the discussion to the case of excise subsidies because of the resemblance it bears to some aspects of technological change, which I discuss later. In the case of taxes, $s_i = 1/(1 + t_i)$, where t_i represents the *ad valorem* rate of excise tax.

and F depends only upon the relative commodity price ratio, as in Eq. (4.5):

$$\frac{M}{F} = f\left(\frac{p_M}{p_F}\right). \tag{4.5}$$

In terms of the rates of change, (4.5a) serves to define the elasticity of substitution between the two commodities on the demand side, σ_D:

$$(\hat{M} - \hat{F}) = -\sigma_D(\hat{p}_M - \hat{p}_F). \tag{4.5a}$$

The effect of a change in factor endowments at constant commodity prices was considered in the previous section. With the model closed by the demand relationship, commodity prices adjust so as to clear the commodity markets. Equation (4.5a) shows directly the change in the ratio of outputs consumed. Subtracting (4.2b) from (4.1b) yields the change in the ratio of outputs produced:

$$(\hat{M} - \hat{F}) = \frac{1}{|\lambda|}(\hat{L} - \hat{T}) + \frac{\delta_L + \delta_T}{|\lambda|}(\hat{w} - \hat{r}).$$

The change in the factor-price ratio (with no subsidies or taxes) is given by

$$(\hat{w} - \hat{r}) = \frac{1}{|\theta|}(\hat{p}_M - \hat{p}_F),$$

so that, by substitution,

$$(\hat{M} - \hat{F}) = \frac{1}{|\lambda|}(\hat{L} - \hat{T}) + \sigma_S\left(\hat{p}_M - \hat{p}_F\right),$$

where

$$\sigma_S \equiv \frac{1}{|\lambda||\theta|}(\delta_L + \delta_T).$$

σ_S represents the elasticity of substitution between commodities on the *supply* side (along the transformation schedule).[11] The change in the

---

[11]I have bypassed the solution for $\hat{M}$ and $\hat{F}$ separately given from (4.1b) and (4.2b). After substituting for the factor-price ratio in terms of the commodity-price ratio the expression for $\hat{M}$ a could be written as

$$\hat{M} = \frac{1}{|\lambda|}|\lambda_{TF}\hat{L} - \lambda_{LF}\hat{T}| + e_M(\hat{p}_M - \hat{p}_F),$$

where, e_M, the shorthand expression for $\{1/|\lambda||\theta|\}(\lambda_{TF}\delta_L + \lambda_{LF}\delta_T)$, shows the percentage change in M that would be associated with a 1 percent rise in M's relative price along a given transformation schedule. It is a "general equilibrium" elasticity of supply, as discussed commodity-price ratio is then given by the mutual interaction of demand and supply:

$$(\hat{p}_M - \hat{p}_F) = -\frac{1}{|\lambda|(\sigma_S + \sigma_D)}(\hat{L} - \hat{T}). \qquad (4.10)$$

Therefore the resulting change in the ratio of commodities produced is

$$(\hat{M} - \hat{F}) = \frac{1}{|\lambda|}\frac{\sigma_D}{(\sigma_S + \sigma_D)}(\hat{L} - \hat{T}). \qquad (4.11)$$

With commodity prices adjusting to the initial output changes brought about by the change in factor endowments, the composition of outputs may, in the end, not change by as much, relatively, as the factor endowments. This clearly depends upon whether the "elasticity" expression, $\sigma_D/(\sigma_S + \sigma_D)$, is smaller than the "factor-intensity" expression, $|\lambda|$. Although it is *large* values of σ_S (and the underlying elasticities of factor substitution in each industry, σ_M and σ_F) that serve to dampen the spread of outputs, it is *small* values of σ_D that accomplish the same end. This comparison between elasticities on the demand and supply side is familiar to students of public finance concerned with questions of tax (or subsidy) incidence and shifting. I turn now to this problem.

The relationship between the change in factor prices and subsidies is given by (4.3c) and (4.4c). Solving for the change in the ratio of factor prices,

$$(\hat{w} - \hat{r}) = \frac{1}{|\theta|}\{(\hat{p}_M - \hat{p}_F) + (\hat{s}_M - \hat{s}_F)\}. \qquad (4.12)$$

Consider factor endowments to be fixed. Any change in factor prices will nonetheless induce a readjustment of commodity outputs. On the supply side,

$$(\hat{M} - \hat{F}) = \sigma_S\{(\hat{p}_M - \hat{p}_F) + (\hat{s}_M - \hat{s}_F)\}.$$

The relative commodity price change that equates supply and demand is

$$(\hat{p}_M - \hat{p}_F) = -\frac{\sigma_S}{\sigma_S + \sigma_D}(\hat{s}_M - \hat{s}_F). \qquad (4.13)$$

---

in Jones (1961). It is readily seen that $\sigma_S = e_M + e_F$. Furthermore, $\theta_M e_M = \theta_F e_F$, where θ_M and θ_F denote the share of each good in the national income.

Substituting back into the expression for the change in the factor-price ratio yields

$$(\hat{w} - \hat{r}) = \frac{1}{|\theta|} \frac{\sigma_D}{\sigma_S + \sigma_D}(\hat{s}_M - \hat{s}_F). \qquad (4.14)$$

This is a familiar result. Suppose M is subsidized more heavily than F. Part of the subsidy is shifted backward, affecting relatively favorably the factor used intensively in the M-industry (labor). Whether labor's relative return expands by a greater proportion than the spread in subsidies depends upon how much of the subsidy has been passed forward to consumers in the form of a relatively lower price for M. And this, of course, depends upon the relative sizes of σ_S and σ_D.

Notice the similarity between expressions (4.11) and (4.14). Factors produce commodities, and a change in endowments must result in an altered composition of production, by a magnified amount at unchanged prices. By analogy, subsidies "produce" returns to factors, and a change in the pattern of subsidies alters the distribution of income. In each case, of course, the extent of readjustment required is eased if commodity prices change, by a factor depending upon the relative sizes of demand and supply elasticities of substitution.

4.6   The Aggregate Elasticity of Substitution

The analysis of a change in factor endowments leading up to Eq. (4.11) has a direct bearing on a recent issue in the neoclassical theory of economic growth. Before describing this issue it is useful to introduce yet another elasticity concept — that of an economy-wide elasticity of substitution between factors.[12] With no subsidies, the relationship between the change in the factor price ratio and the change in endowments can be derived from (4.10). Thus,

$$(\hat{w} - \hat{r}) = -\frac{1}{|\lambda||\theta|(\sigma_S + \sigma_D)}(\hat{L} - \hat{T}). \qquad (4.15)$$

By analogy with the elasticity of substitution in a particular sector, define σ as the percentage rise in the land/labor endowment ratio required to raise

---

[12] For previous uses see Amano (1964) and Drandakis (1963).

the wage/rent ratio by 1 percent. Directly from (4.15),

$$\sigma = |\lambda||\theta|(\sigma_S + \sigma_D).$$

But recall that σ_s is itself a composite of the two elasticities of substitution in each industry, σ_M and σ_F. Thus, σ can be expressed in terms of the three *primary* elasticities of substitution in this model:

$$\sigma = Q_M\sigma_M + Q_F\sigma_F + Q_D\sigma_D,$$

where

$$Q_M = \theta_{LM}\lambda_{TM} + \theta_{TM}\lambda_{LM},$$
$$Q_F = \theta_{LF}\lambda_{TF} + \theta_{TF}\lambda_{LF},$$
$$Q_D = |\lambda| \cdot |\theta|.$$

Note that σ is not just a linear expression in σ_M, σ_F, and σ_D — it is a weighted average of these three elasticities as $\Sigma Q_i = 1$. Note also that σ can be positive even if the elasticity of substitution in each industry is zero, for it incorporates the effect of intercommodity substitution by consumers as well as direct intracommodity substitution between factors.

Finally, introduce the concept, σ, into expression (4.11) for output changes:

$$(\hat{M} - \hat{F}) = \frac{|\theta|\sigma_D}{\sigma}(\hat{L} - \hat{T}), \tag{4.11a}$$

and into expression (4.14) for the change in factor prices in the subsidy case:

$$(\hat{w} - \hat{r}) = \frac{|\lambda|\sigma_D}{\sigma}(\hat{s}_M - \hat{s}_F). \tag{4.14a}$$

One consequence is immediately apparent: If the elasticity of substitution between commodities on the part of consumers is no greater than the overall elasticity of substitution between factors, the *magnification* effects discussed in Sec. 4.4 are more than compensated for by the dampening effect of price changes.

4.7   Convergence to Balanced Growth

The two-sector model of production described in Secs. 4.1–4.6 can be used to analyze the process of economic growth. Already I have spoken of increases in factor endowments and the consequent "growth" of outputs. But a more satisfactory growth model would allow for the growth of at least one factor of production to be determined by the system rather than given parametrically. Let the factor "capital" replace "land" as the second factor in the two-sector model (replace T by K). And let M stand for machines rather than manufacturing goods. To simplify, I assume capital does not depreciate. The new feedback element in the system is that the rate of increase of the capital stock, $\hat{K}$, depends on the current output of machines, M. Thus $\hat{K} = M/K$. The "demand" for M now represents savings.

Suppose the rate of growth of the labor force, $\hat{L}$, is constant. At any moment of time the rate of capital accumulation, $\hat{K}$, either exceeds, equals, or falls short of $\hat{L}$. Of special interest in the neoclassical theory of growth (with no technological progress) is the case of balanced growth where $\hat{L} = \hat{K}$. Balance in the growth of factors will, as we have seen, result in balanced growth as between the two commodities (at the same rate). But if $\hat{L}$ and $\hat{K}$ are not equal, it becomes necessary to inquire whether they tend toward equality (balanced growth) asymptotically or tend to diverge even further.

If machines are produced by labor-intensive techniques, the rate of growth of machines exceeds that of capital if labor is growing faster than capital, or falls short of capital if capital is growing faster than labor. (This is the result in Sec. 4.4, which is dampened, but not reversed, by the price changes discussed in Sec. 4.5.) Thus, the rate of capital accumulation, if different from the rate of growth of the labor supply, falls or rises toward it. The economy tends toward the balanced-growth path.

The difficulty arises if machines are capital intensive. If there is no price change, the change in the composition of outputs must be a magnified reflection of the spread in the growth rates of factors. Thus, if capital is growing more rapidly than labor, machine output will expand at a greater rate than either factor, and this only serves to widen the spread between the rates of growth of capital and labor even further.[13] Once account is taken of price changes, however, the change in the composition of outputs may

---

[13] See Shinkai (1960) for a discussion of the fixed-coefficients case. At constant commodity prices the impact of endowment changes on the composition of output is the same

be sufficiently dampened to allow convergence to balanced growth despite the fact that machines are capital intensive.

Re-examine Eq. (4.11a), replacing by $\hat{T}$ and $\hat{K}$ recognizing that $|\theta|$ is negative if machines are capital intensive. If σ exceeds $-|\theta|\sigma_D$, on balance a dampening of the ratio of outputs as compared to factor endowments takes place. This suggests the critical condition that must be satisfied by σ, as compared with σ_D and $|\theta|$, in order to insure stability. But this is not precisely the condition required. Rather, stability hinges upon the *sign* of $(\hat{M} - \hat{K})$ being opposite to that of $(\hat{K} - \hat{L})$. There is a presumption that when $(\hat{M} - \hat{F})$ is smaller than $(\hat{K} - \hat{L})$ (assuming both are positive) the output of the machine sector is growing less rapidly than is the capital stock. But the corresponding is not exact.

To derive the relationship between $(\hat{M} - \hat{K})$ and $(\hat{M} - \hat{F})$ consider the two ways of expressing changes in the national income (Y). It can be viewed as the sum of returns to factors or the sum of the values of output in the two sectors. Let θ_i refer to the share of factor i or commodity i in the national income. In terms of rates of change,

$$\hat{Y} = \theta_L(\hat{w} + \hat{L}) + \theta_K(\hat{r} + \hat{K}) = \theta_M(\hat{p}_M + \hat{M}) + \theta_F(\hat{p}_F + \hat{F}).$$

But the share of a factor in the national income must be an average of its share in each sector, with the weights given by the share of that sector in the national income. This, and Eqs. (4.3b) and (4.4b), guarantee that

$$\theta_L\hat{w} + \theta_K\hat{r} = \theta_M\hat{p}_M + \theta_F\hat{p}_F.$$

That is, the rates of change of the financial components in the two expressions for $\hat{Y}$ balance, leaving an equality between the physical terms:

$$\theta_L\hat{L} + \theta_K\hat{K} = \theta_M\hat{M} + \theta_F\hat{F}.$$

The desired relationship is obtained by observing that θ_K equals $(1 - \theta_L)$ and θ_M is $(1 - \theta_F)$. Thus,

$$(\hat{M} - \hat{K}) = \theta_F(\hat{M} - \hat{K}) - \theta_L(\hat{K} - \hat{L}).$$

---

regardless of elasticities of substitution in production. Thus, a necessary and sufficient condition in Shinkai's case is the factor-intensity condition. For the variable coefficients case the factor-intensity condition was first discussed by Uzawa (1961).

With this in hand it is easy to see that (from [11a]) $(\hat{M} - \hat{K})$ is given by

$$(\hat{M} - \hat{K}) = \frac{\theta_L}{\sigma} \left\{ -\frac{\theta_F |\theta|}{\theta_L} \sigma_D - \sigma \right\} (\hat{K} - \hat{L}). \qquad (4.16)$$

It is not enough for σ to exceed $-|\theta|\sigma_D$, it must exceed $-(\theta_F/\theta_L)|\theta|\sigma_D$ for convergence to balanced growth.[14] It nonetheless remains the case that σ greater than σ_D is sufficient to insure that the expression in brackets in (4.16) is negative. For (4.16) can be rewritten as (4.16a):

$$(\hat{M} - \hat{K}) = -\frac{\theta_L}{\sigma} \left\{ \sigma - \left[1 - \frac{\theta_{LM}}{\theta_L} \right] \sigma_D \right\} (\hat{K} - \hat{L}). \qquad (4.16a)$$

Thus, it is overly strong to require that σ exceed σ_D.[15]

4.8 Savings Behavior

A popular assumption about savings behavior in the literature on growth theory is that aggregate savings form a constant percentage of the national income. (See, for example, Solow [1956]) This, of course, implies that σ_D is unity. In this case it becomes legitimate to inquire as to the values of σ or σ_M and σ_F as compared with unity. For example, if each sector's production function is Cobb–Douglas (σ_M and σ_F each unity), stability is guaranteed. But the value "unity" that has a crucial role in this comparison only serves as a proxy for σ_D. With high σ_D even greater values for σ_M and σ_F (and σ) would be required.

If σ_D is unity when the savings ratio is constant, is its value higher or lower than unity when the savings ratio depends positively on the rate of profit? It turns out that this depends upon the technology in such a way as to encourage convergence to balanced growth precisely in those cases where factor intensities are such as to leave it in doubt.

The capital goods, machines, are demanded not for the utility they yield directly, but for the stream of additional future consumption they allow.

---

[14]The two requirements are equivalent if $\theta_F = \theta_L$, i.e., if total consumption ($p_F F$) is matched exactly by the total wages (wL). This equality is made a basic assumption as to savings behavior in some models where laborers consume all and capitalists save all. For example, see Uzawa (1964).

[15]A condition similar to (4.16a), with the assumption that $\sigma_D = 1$, is presented by Amano (unpublished).

This is represented by the rate of return (or profit), which is linked by the technology to the relative price of machines according to the magnification effects implicit in the Stolper–Samuelson theorem. The assumption that the savings ratio (the fraction of income devoted to new machines) rises as the rate of profit rises implies that the savings ratio rises as the relative price of machines rises (and thus that σ_D is less than unity) if and only if machines are capital intensive. Of course the savings assumption also implies that σ_D exceeds unity (that is, that the savings ratio falls as the relative price of machines rises) if machines are labor intensive, but convergence to balanced growth is already assured in this case.[16]

4.9   The Analysis of Technological Change

The preceding sections have dealt with the structure of the two-sector model of production with a given technology. They nonetheless contain the ingredients necessary for an analysis of the effects of technological progress. In this concluding section, I examine this problem and simplify by assuming that factor endowments remain unchanged and subsidies are zero. I concentrate on the impact of a change in production conditions on relative prices. The effect on outputs is considered implicitly in deriving the price changes.

Consider a typical input coefficient, a_{ij}, as depending both upon relative factor prices and the state of technology:

$$a_{ij} = a_{ij}(w/r, t).$$

In terms of the relative rates of change, $\hat{a}_{ij}$ may be decomposed as

$$\hat{a}_{ij} = \hat{c}_{ij} - \hat{b}_{ij}.$$

$\hat{c}_{ij}$ denotes the relative change in the input–output coefficient that is called forth by a change in factor prices as of a given technology. The $\hat{b}_{ij}$ is a measure of technological change that shows the alteration in a_{ij} that would take place at constant factor prices. Since technological progress usually involves a *reduction* in the input requirements, I define $\hat{b}_{ij}$ as $-\,(1/\hat{a}_{ij})\partial a_{ij}/\partial t$.

---

[16]For a more complete discussion of savings behavior as related to the rate of profit, see Uzawa (1963) and Inada (1965).

The $\hat{b}_{ij}$ are the basic expressions of technological change. After the discussion in Sec. 4.3 it is not surprising that it is the λ and θ weighted averages of the $\hat{b}_{ij}$ that turn out to be important. These are defined by the following set of π's:

$$\pi_j = \theta_{Lj}\hat{b}_{Lj} + \theta_{Tj}\hat{b}_{Tj} \quad (j = M, F),$$
$$\pi_i = \lambda_{iM}\hat{b}_{iM} + \lambda_{iF}\hat{b}_{iF} \quad (i = L, T).$$

If a $\hat{B}$ matrix is defined in a manner similar to the original A matrix, π_M and π_F are the sums of the elements in each column weighted by the relative factor shares, and π_L and π_T are sums of the elements in each row of $\hat{B}$ weighted by the fractions of the total factor supplies used in each industry. Thus, π_M, assumed nonnegative, is a measure of the rate of technological advance in the M-industry and π_L, also assumed nonnegative, reflects the overall labor-saving feature of technological change.

Turn now to the equations of change. The $\hat{c}_{ij}$ are precisely the $\hat{a}_{ij}$ used in Eqs. (4.6)–(4.9) of the model without technological change. This subset can be solved, just as before, for the response of input coefficients to factor price changes. After substitution, the first four equations of change (Eqs. [4.1a]–[4.4a]) become

$$\lambda_{LM}\hat{M} + \lambda_{LF}\hat{F} = \pi_L + \delta_L(\hat{w} - \hat{r}), \tag{4.1d}$$

$$\lambda_{TM}\hat{M} + \lambda_{TF}\hat{F} = \pi_T - \delta_T(\hat{w} - \hat{r}), \tag{4.2d}$$

$$\theta_{LM}\hat{w} + \theta_{TM}\hat{r} = \hat{p}_M + \pi_M, \tag{4.3d}$$

$$\theta_{LF}\hat{w} + \theta_{TF}\hat{r} = \hat{p}_F + \pi_F. \tag{4.4d}$$

The parameters of technological change appear only in the first four relationships and enter there in a particularly simple form. In the first two equations it is readily seen that, in part, technological change, through its impact in reducing input coefficients, has precisely the same effects on the system as would a change in factor endowments. π_L and π_T replace $\hat{L}$ and $\hat{T}$, respectively. In the second pair of equations, the improvements in industry outputs attributable to technological progress enter the model precisely as do industry subsidies in Eqs. (4.3c) and (4.4c) of Sec. 4.4. Any general change in technology or in the quality of factors (that gets translated into a change in input coefficiencies) has an impact on prices and outputs that can be decomposed into the two kinds of parametric changes analyzed in the preceding sections.

Consider the effect of progress upon relative commodity and factor prices. The relationship between the changes in the two sets of prices is the same as in the subsidy case (see Eq. (4.12)):

$$(\hat{w} - \hat{r}) = \frac{1}{|\theta|}\{(\hat{p}_M - \hat{p}_F) + (\pi_M - \pi_F)\}. \qquad (4.17)$$

Solving separately for each relative price change,

$$(\hat{p}_M - \hat{p}_F) = -\frac{|\theta|}{\sigma}\{(\pi_L - \pi_T) + |\lambda|\sigma_S(\pi_M - \pi_F)\}, \qquad (4.18)$$

$$(\hat{w} - \hat{r}) = -\frac{1}{\sigma}\{(\pi_L - \pi_T) - |\lambda|\sigma_D(\pi_M - \pi_F)\}. \qquad (4.19)$$

For convenience I refer to $(\pi_L - \pi_T)$ as the "differential factor effect" and $(\pi_M - \pi_F)$ as the "differential industry effect."[17]

Define a change in technology as "regular" if the differential factor and industry effects have the same sign.[18] For example, a change in technology that is relatively "labor-saving" for the economy as a whole ($[\pi_L - \pi_T]$ positive) is considered "regular" if it also reflects a relatively greater improvement in productivity in the labor-intensive industry. Suppose this to be the case. Both effects tend to depress the relative price of commodity M: The "labor-saving" feature of the change works exactly as would a relative increase in the labor endowment to reduce the relative price of the labor-intensive commodity (M). And part of the differential industry effect, like a relative subsidy to M, is shifted forward in a lower price for M.

Whereas the two components of "regular" technological change reinforce each other in their effect on the commodity price ratio, they pull the factor price ratio in opposite directions. The differential factor effect in the above case serves to depress the wage/rent ratio. But part of the relatively greater improvement in the labor-intensive M industry is shifted backward

---

[17] The suggestion that a change in technology in a particular industry has both "factor-saving" and "cost-reducing" aspects has been made before. See, for example, Bhagwati and Johnson (1960) and Meier (1963). Contrary to what is usually implied, I point out that a Hicksian "neutral" technology change in one or more industries has, nonetheless, a "factor-saving" or "differential factor" effect. The problem of technological change has been analyzed in numerous articles; perhaps those by Johnson (1955) and Findlay and Grubert (1959) should especially be mentioned.

[18] Strictly speaking, I want to allow for the possibility that one or both effects are zero. Thus, technological change is "regular" if and only if $(\pi_L - \pi_T)(\pi_M - \pi_F) \geqq 0$.

to increase, relatively, the return to labor. This "backward" shift is more pronounced the greater is the elasticity of substitution on the demand side. There will be some "critical" value of σ_D, above which relative wages will rise despite the downward pull of the differential factor effect:

$$(\hat{w} - \hat{r}) > 0 \quad \text{if and only if} \quad \sigma_D > \frac{(\pi_L - \pi_T)}{|\lambda|(\pi_M - \pi_F)}.$$

If technological progress is not "regular" these conclusions are reversed. Suppose $(\pi_L - \pi_T) > 0$, but nonetheless $(\pi_M - \pi_F) < 0$. This might be the result, say, of technological change where the primary impact is to reduce labor requirements in food production. Labor is now affected relatively adversely on both counts, the differential factor effect serving to depress wages as before, and the differential industry effect working to the relative advantage of the factor used intensively in food production — land. On the other hand, the change in relative commodity prices is now less predictable. The differential factor effect, in tending to reduce M's relative price, is working counter to the differential industry effect, whereby the F industry is experiencing more rapid technological advance. The differential industry effect will, in this case, dominate if the elasticity of substitution between goods on the supply side is high enough:

$$(\hat{p}_M - \hat{p}_F) > 0 \quad \text{if and only if} \quad \sigma_S > -\frac{\pi_L - \pi_T}{|\lambda|(\pi_M - \pi_F)}.$$

The differential factor and industry effects are not independent of each other. Some insight into the nature of the relationship between the two can be obtained by considering two special cases of "neutrality."

Suppose, first, that technological change is "Hicksian neutral" in each industry, implying that, at unchanged factor prices, factor proportions used in that industry do not change (see Hicks [1932]). In terms of the $\hat{B}$ matrix, the rows are identical ($\hat{b}_{Lj} = \hat{b}_{Tj}$). As can easily be verified from the definition of the π's, in this case

$$(\pi_L - \pi_T) = |\lambda|(\pi_M - \pi_F),$$

and technological change must be "regular." If, overall, technological change is "labor-saving" (and note that this can happen even if it is Hicksian neutral in each industry), the price of the relatively labor-intensive commodity must fall. Relative wages will, nonetheless, rise if σ_D exceeds the critical value shown earlier, which in this case reduces to unity.

The symmetrical nature of this approach to technological change suggests an alternative definition of neutrality, in which the columns of the $\hat{B}$ matrix are equal. This type of neutrality indicates that input requirements for any factor, i, have been reduced by the same relative amount in every industry. The relationship between the differential factor and industry effects is given by

$$(\pi_M - \pi_F) = |\theta|(\pi_L - \pi_T).$$

Again, technological change must be "regular." If the reduction in labor coefficients in each industry exceeds the reduction in land coefficients, this must filter through (in dampened form unless each industry uses just one factor) to affect relatively favorably the labor-intensive industry. The remarks made in the case of Hicksian neutrality carry over to this case, except for the fact that the critical value which σ_D must exceed in order for the differential industry effect to outweigh the factor effect on relative wages now becomes higher. Specifically, σ_D must exceed $1/|\lambda||\theta|$, which may be considerably greater than unity. This reflects the fact that in the case of Hicksian neutrality $(\pi_L - \pi_T)$ is smaller than $(\pi_M - \pi_F)$, whereas the reverse is true in the present case.

With Hicksian neutrality the paramount feature is the difference between rates of technological advance in each industry. This spills over into a differential factor effect only because the industries require the two factors in differing proportions. With the other kind of neutrality the basic change is that the input requirements of one factor are cut more than for the other factor. As we have just seen, this is transformed into a differential industry effect only in dampened form.

These cases of neutrality are special cases of "regular" technological progress. The general relationship between the differential factor and industry effects can be derived from the definitions to yield

$$(\pi_L - \pi_T) = Q_M\beta_M + Q_F\beta_F + |\lambda|(\pi_M - \pi_F) \qquad (4.20)$$

and

$$(\pi_M - \pi_F) = Q_L\beta_L + Q_T\beta_T + |\theta|(\pi_L - \pi_T). \qquad (4.21)$$

In the first equation, the differential factor effect is broken down into three components; the labor-saving bias of technical change in each industry (β_j

is defined as $\hat{b}_{Lj} - \hat{b}_{Tj}$) and the differential industry effect.[19] In the second expression, the differential industry effect is shown as a combination of the relatively greater saving in each factor in the M industry (β_L, for example, is $\hat{b}_{LM} - \hat{b}_{LF}$) and the differential factor effect.[20] With these relationships at hand it is easy to see how it is the possible asymmetry between the row elements and/or the column elements of the $\hat{B}$ matrix that could disrupt the "regularity" feature of technical progress.[21]

For some purposes it is useful to make the substitution from either (4.20) or (4.21) into the expressions for the changes in relative factor and commodity prices shown by (4.17)–(4.19). For example, if technological change is "neutral" in the sense described earlier, where the reduction in the input coefficient is the same in each industry (although different for each factor), β_L and β_T are zero in (4.21) and the relationship in (4.17) can be rewritten as

$$(\hat{w} - \hat{r}) = \frac{1}{|\theta|}(\hat{p}_M - \hat{p}_F) + (\pi_L - \pi_T).$$

To make things simple, suppose π_T is zero. The uniform reduction in labor input coefficients across industries might reflect, say, an improvement in labor quality attributable to education. Aside from the effect of any change in commodity prices on factor prices (of the Stolper–Samuelson variety), relative wages are directly increased by the improvement in labor quality.

Alternatively, consider substituting (4.20) into (4.19), to yield (4.19a):

$$(\hat{w} - \hat{r}) = -\frac{1}{\sigma}\left\{ Q_M\beta_M + Q_F\beta_F + Q_D(1 - \sigma_D)\frac{\pi_M - \pi_F}{|\theta|} \right\}. \quad (4.19a)$$

Will technological change that is Hicks neutral in every industry leave the factor-price ratio unaltered at a given ratio of factor endowments?

---

[19]Note that Q_M and Q_F are the same weights as those defined in Section 4.6. The analogy between the composition of σ and that of $(\pi_L - \pi_T)$ becomes more apparent if $|\lambda|(\pi_M - \pi_F)$ is rewritten as $\sigma_D\{(\pi_M - \pi_F)/|\theta|\}$. The differential factor effect is weighted average of the Hicksian factor biases in each industry and a magnified $(1/|\theta|)$ differential industry effect.
[20]Q_L equals $\lambda_{LF}\theta_{LM} + \lambda_{LM}\theta_{LF}$, and Q_T is $(\lambda_{TF}\theta_{TM} + \lambda_{TM}\theta_{TF})$. Note that $Q_L + Q_T$ equals $Q_M + Q_F$.
[21]These relationships involve the *difference* between π_L and π_T, on the one hand, and π_M and π_F on the other. Another relationship involving *sums* of these terms is suggested by the national income relationship, as discussed in Section 4.7. With technical progress, $\theta_M\pi_M + \theta_F\pi_F$ equals $\theta_L\pi_L + \theta_T\pi_T$.

Eq. (4.19a) suggests a negative answer to this query unless progress is at the same rate in the two industries ($\pi_M = \pi_F$) or unless σ_D is unity.[22]

There exists an extensive literature in the theory of international trade concerned with (a) the effects of differences in production functions on pre-trade factor and commodity price ratios (and thus on positions of comparative advantage), and (b) the impact of growth (in factor supplies) or changes in technological knowledge in one or more countries on the world terms of trade.[23] The analysis of this chapter is well suited to the discussion of these problems. The connection between (a) and expressions (4.17)–(4.19) is obvious. For (b) it is helpful to observe that the impact of any of these changes on world terms of trade depends upon the effect in each country separately of these changes on production and consumption at constant commodity prices. The production effects can be derived from the four equations of change for the production sector (Eqs. [4.1a]–[4.4a] or later versions) and the consumption changes from equation (4.5a).[24] The purpose of this chapter is not to reproduce the results in detail but rather to expose those features of the model which bear upon all of these questions.

References

Amano, A. (1963). *Neo-Classical Models of International Trade and Economic Growth.* New York: University of Rochester.

Amano, A. (1964). Determinants of Comparative Costs: A Theoretic Approach. *Oxford Economic Papers*, 16(3), 389–400.

Amano, A. (unpublished). A Two-Sector Model of Economic Growth Involving Technical Progress.

---

[22] Recalling n. 19, consider the following question: If the elasticity of substitution between factors is unity in every sector, will a change in the ratio of factor endowments result in an equal percentage change in the factor price ratio? From Sec. 4.6, it is seen that this result can be expected only if σ_D is unity.

[23] See Johnson (1962) and the extensive bibliography there listed. The most complete treatment of the effects of various differences in production conditions on positions of comparative advantage is given by Amano (1964) who also discusses special cases of Harrod neutrality. For a recent analysis of the impact of endowment and technology changes on the terms of trade see Takayama (1964).

[24] Account must be taken, however, of the fact that with trade the quantities of M and F produced differ from the amounts consumed by the quantity of exports and imports.

Bhagwati, J. and Johnson, H. (1960). Notes on Some Controversies in the Theory of International Trade. *Economic Journal*, 71, 427–430.

Dorfman, R., Samuelson, P.A., and Solow, R.M. (1958). *Linear Programming and Economic Analysis*. New York: McGraw-Hill.

Drandakis, E. (1963). Factor Substitution in the Two-Sector Growth Model. *Review of Economic Studies*, 30(3), 217–228.

Findlay, R. and Grubert, H. (1959). Factor Intensities, Technological Progress and the Terms of Trade. *Oxford Economic Papers*, 11(1), 111–121.

Hicks, J.R. (1932). *The Theory of Wages*. New York: Macmillan.

Hicks, J.R. (1960). Linear Theory. *Economic Journal*, 70(280), 671–709.

Inada, K.-I. (1965). On Neoclassical Models of Economic Growth. *Review of Economic Studies*, 32(2), 151–160.

Johnson, H. (1955). Economic Expansion and International Trade. *Manchester School of Economic and Social Studies*, 23, 95–112.

Johnson, H. (1962). Economic Development and International Trade. In: G. Allen and Unwin (Eds.), *Money, Trade, and Economic Growth* (Ch. 4). New York: Macmillan.

Jones, R.W. (1961). Stability Conditions in International Trade: A General Equilibrium Analysis. *International Economic Review*, 2(2), 199–209.

Kemp, C.M. (1964). *The Pure Theory of International Trade* (pp. 10–11). Englewood Cliffs: Prentice-Hall.

Meade, J.E. (1961). *A Neo-Classical Theory of Economic Growth* (pp. 84–86). London: Allen and Unwin.

Meier, G.M. (1963). *International Trade and Development* (Ch. 1). New York: Harper and Row.

Rybczynski, T.M. (1955). Factor Endowments and Relative Commodity Prices. *Economica*, 22(88), 336–341.

Samuelson, P.A. (1953–1954). Prices of Factors and Goods in General Equilibrium. *Review of Economic Studies*, 21(1), 1–20.

Shinkai, Y. (1960). On Equilibrium Growth of Capital and Labor. *International Economic Review*, 1(2), 107–111.

Solow, R. (1956). A Contribution to the Theory of Economic Growth. *Quarterly Journal of Economics*, 70(1), 65–94.

Stolper, W.F. and Samuelson, P.A. (1941). Protection and Real Wages. *Review of Economic Studies*, 9(1), 58–73.

Takayama, A. (1963). On a Two-Sector Model of Economic Growth: A Comparative Statics Analysis. *Review of Economic Studies*, 30(2), 95–104.

Takayama, A. (1964). Economic Growth and International Trade. *Review of Economic Studies*, 31(3), 207–220.

Uzawa, H. (1961). On a Two-Sector Model of Economic Growth. *Review of Economic Studies*, 29(1), 47–70.

Uzawa, H. (1963). On a Two-Sector Model of Economic Growth-II. *Review of Economic Studies*, 30(2), 105–118.

CHAPTER 5

The Golden Anniversary: Stolper–Samuelson at 50*

Ronald W. Jones

It is a pleasure for me to lead off the panel discussion, a pleasure made double by the fact that it honors two of my former professors — Wolfgang Stolper for my first course in economics at Swarthmore in 1948 and Paul Samuelson at MIT four years later. We are here today to celebrate the 50th anniversary of the appearance of their joint paper, a celebration which by rights should have taken place earlier, and would have if this country's official house organ, the *American Economic Review*, had not rejected the piece. It all turned out well in the end, and I frequently cite this rejection to my students to prepare them for the real world.

Why has this paper attained such an important place in the literature? There are, I think, several strands to the answer. Initially, perhaps, because on its appearance it ran directly counter to received wisdom. Proponents of free trade, and at the occasion of the Smoot–Hawley tariff the number in the economics profession ran to over a thousand, were willing to concede that special interest groups might gain from protection, but hardly such an important group as labor. It also took general equilibrium theory off its lofty, pristine shelf and revealed how small-scale versions can usefully be harnessed in comparative statics to reveal, in this case, firm answers to the question of the effects of commercial policy on the distribution of

---

*Originally published in "The Stolper Samuelson Theorem: A Golden Jubilee," Chapter 15, eds. Alan Deardorff and Robert M. Stern, The University of Michigan Press (1994).

income. In doing so it introduced the applicability of the box diagram, already familiar to some for its uses in consumption and exchange models by Edgeworth and Bowley, to the allocation of resources for productive purposes. Readers could glance at this diagram and confirm for themselves the surprising conclusion that the ratio of land to labor used in every sector of the economy could rise even though the economy's overall endowment ratio did not change. This was the key to understanding the Stolper–Samuelson theorem that protection would unambiguously improve the real wage, regardless of taste patterns.[1] As well, a fuse was lit which in time would lead to a criticism directed at the small-scale dimensions of what became the standard trade model. Could the Stolper–Samuelson theorem survive in a world of many commodities and factors? Let me pick up this theme now.

In the late sixties and early seventies, several key papers on the issue of dimensionality were published. As sometimes happens, major contributions by John Chipman, on the one hand, and Murray Kemp and Leon Wegge, on the other, appeared back-to-back in the International Economic Review in 1969. Although the particular form of the query differed in the two cases, these two pieces shared a common frustration in that a result that could be obtained when the number of commodities and factors was raised from two to three succumbed to a counter example when *n* equals four.

Kemp and Wegge asked about what came to be known as the *strong* form of the theorem, while Chipman focused on the *weak* form. The strong form obtains if each sector can be associated with a unique factor of production (the "intensive" factor) such that an increase in any single commodity price raises the return to the associated factor relatively more and lowers the return to all other factors. The weak form is so called because it does not require that all "unintensive" factors lose. These results, of course, could not be expected to hold for any technology — even ones characterized by a lack of joint production, constant returns to scale, and a balance between the number of factors and commodities. Kemp and Wegge assumed that for each factor *i* and commodity *j*, sector *i* used factor *i* intensively in the

---

[1] I recall being asked by Kermit Gordon on the occasion of an oral exam at Swarthmore how the Stolper–Samuelson result would fare if the foreign country retaliated with a tariff of its own. My knee-jerk reaction that retaliation always undoes the initial response was caught just in time. Real wages would rise even further.

sense that factor i's distributive share in industry i was "large" — relative to any factor's (k) share in industry i, compared with the analogous ratio of shares of factors i and k in any other industry. That is, if θ_{ij} denotes the distributive share of factor i in industry j, the Kemp–Wegge assumption is

$$\frac{\theta_{ii}}{\theta_{ki}} > \frac{\theta_{ij}}{\theta_{kj}} \quad \text{for all } i, \quad k \neq i, \quad j \neq i,$$

(Chipman makes a somewhat weaker assumption, that $\theta_{ii} > \theta_{ij}$). Although a counter-example proved the insufficiency of this condition for $n \geq 4$, Kemp and Wegge did establish that theirs was a necessary condition.

An example of a production structure that satisfies the Kemp–Wegge conditions and is even strong enough to guarantee the strong form of the Stolper–Samuelson theorem illustrates the close connection between this theorem and the Specific-Factors model of production (see Jones, 1971; Samuelson, 1971). These two models, often portrayed as staunchly different in small-scale versions (2×2 and 3×2), actually have much in common. In the Specific-Factors model when there are many goods, each produced by using a unique factor combined with a mobile factor, the rise in any commodity price unambiguously improves the real return (or rent) to the factor of production only used in that sector, and reduces the real return to all other specific factors. These results accord with strong Stolper–Samuelson. The difference in the income distribution fallout of a price rise is found in the return to the mobile factor — it rises, but not as much, relatively, as the increase in the commodity price. But, as illustrated in Jones and Marjit (1985, 1991), if the mobile factor is itself produced by all the "specific" factors, in any manner that involves them all, the resulting $n \times n$ production structure must exhibit strong Stolper–Samuelson properties. Mathematically this corresponds to the result that the inverse of the sum of a positive matrix of rank one and a positive diagonal matrix must exhibit a positive diagonal and negative off-diagonal elements. Each final commodity is produced by mixing some amount of the "produced mobile factor" with some amount of a unique factor which, when counting direct and indirect inputs, is thus seen to be used intensively in producing the commodity.

The strong form of the Stolper–Samuelson theorem posits three results. First, it establishes that a change in a commodity price causes factor prices to change by relatively *more*, so that *real* factor returns change unambiguously. The asymmetric assumption that productive activities each combine

many inputs to produce a single output (non-joint production) is the key
to this asymmetry in the spread of factor returns relative to commodity
prices. Secondly, the Kemp–Wegge condition pinpoints for each commodity price rise which factor will be the unambiguous winner, the intensively
used factor. But a third aspect is involved as well — a symmetry in the fate
of the unintensive factors — they all lose. This symmetry in result reflects
a symmetry in productive structure. Roughly speaking, such symmetry is
provided if the ratios of shares of the unintensive factors cannot differ by
very much from industry to industry. As established in Jones, Marjit, and
Mitra (1991), a *sufficient* condition for the strong form of the Stolper–
Samuelson theorem to hold is that the difference $\{\frac{\theta_{ii}}{\theta_{ki}} - \frac{\theta_{ij}}{\theta_{kj}}\}$ not only be
positive, but that it exceed the expression $\sum_{r\neq i,k,j} |\frac{\theta_{ri}}{\theta_{ki}} - \frac{\theta_{rj}}{\theta_{kj}}|$, and this hold
for all i, j. In a special case — the so-called Produced-Mobile-Factor struc-
ture of Jones and Marjit discussed above, each discrepancy in the ratio of
shares of unintensive factors in this sum vanishes, so that the Kemp–Wegge
conditions are sufficient. These extra conditions limiting the discrepancy
between ratios of unintensive factor shares are vacuous unless the number
of factors and commodities equals at least four, helping to explain why
Kemp and Wegge's counterexample was reached only at this count.

The strong or weak forms of the Stolper–Samuelson theorem are not the
only candidates which could be considered as the appropriate generalization to higher dimensions. For example, note that the original 2×2 version
specified a balance between the numbers of winners and losers consequent
to a price rise, whereas the strong version of the $n \times n$ case posits an
extreme asymmetry in income distribution: A single price rise awards the
intensive factor an increase in its real reward and causes $(n - 1)$ factors to
lose.[2] An alternative productive structure, the "neighborhood" structure of
Jones and Kierzkowski (1986), attempts to highlight a feature which, if at
all present, destroys the strong version of the Stolper–Samuelson theorem
in higher dimensions: Factors of production have limited job opportunities.[3] We take this almost to the extreme, avoiding complete specificity, by

---

[2] Ken-ichi Inada (1971) described a production structure at the opposite end of the spectrum: Any price rise causes a single factor to lose (big) and all other factors to gain, at least
in nominal terms.

[3] The existence of a single zero θ_{ij} disallows the strong version.

assuming each industry employs only two of n factor types and each factor has access to only two of the n industries (its "neighbors" in a regional interpretation of the model). A rise in a single commodity price increases the returns to half the factor groups and lowers them for the remaining factors.[4] Of course, if $n = 2$, the 2×2 version of the Stolper–Samuelson model re-emerges. Such a structure perhaps should have equal claim to represent the general version.

My own preference for the appropriate higher-dimensional generaliza-tion of the Stolper–Samuelson theorem is none of the above. Descending from the lofty plain of these highly stylized models one might ask a weaker question: What limitations on productive activity and dimensionality suf-fice to ensure that any productive factor can unambiguously gain in real terms by the indirect route of a change in relative commodity prices, engi-neered perhaps by commercial policy or other forms of public taxes or expenditures? The reference to the indirect route confirms that no account is taken of tax or tariff revenues raised by such a policy — just as this direct form of subsidy was ignored in the original Stolper–Samuelson contribu-tion. The answer to this question is that the restrictions on technology are much weaker than provided in Kemp and Wegge. As shown in Jones (1985), the lack of joint production and the existence of at least as many actively produced commodities as factors suffice to guarantee that *any* fac-tor can rely on some simple set of commodity price changes to create an unambiguous improvement in its real earnings. Some other factors might gain also, and it may take more than a rise in a single commodity price, but from a political economy point of view these features seem not to matter. Indeed, any particular factor might well prefer to pursue a policy in which it did not stand out nakedly as the only beneficiary. This is the stuff of politics.

The absence of joint production is important. Suppose n independent activities are undertaken, all of which yield outputs in the same proportions. A rise in any commodity price will increase the value of all activities in the same proportion and, as well, the returns to all factors. There would be no change in income distribution. More generally, even with elements of joint production, changes in relative commodity prices cause alterations

---

[4]If n is odd, a price increase raises the rewards for $(n + 1)/2$ factors.

in relative factor prices and these could be ranked relative to each other. The change in any factor price could be compared with the average, which is the same as the average of changes in all producer prices. If tastes are the same from group to group, statements as to changes in *real* incomes of individual factors could be attempted, depending on whether the terms of trade have been improved or worsened. Of course, one advantage of the original Stolper–Samuelson scenario is precisely that it dispenses with such assertions about tastes.

Questions concerning the effects of government policies on the distribution of income are, if anything, more prominent today than half a century ago. This is the age of suspicion — of awareness that government measures such as commercial policy may be undertaken not because the national interest warrants, but because special interests are involved in rent seeking. The Stolper–Samuelson analysis of the effects of tariffs provides a solid foundation for the pursuit of these vital questions in political economy.

A year before Bertil Ohlin died I had a conversation with him in Stockholm about his contribution to trade theory. He seemed somewhat annoyed at the tendency to think of Heckscher–Ohlin Theory in terms of the simple 2×2 model launched by the Stolper–Samuelson article, inasmuch as his book had so much more. My own attitude, expressed with reservations, was that many grand visions in economics end up rather neglected unless the central ideas can be conveyed in a clean, stripped-down version of a model. With the aid of Stolper–Samuelson and the work subsequently launched, Ohlin's ideas did get conveyed, and his future reward was assured.

References

Chipman, J. (1969). Factor Price Equalization and the Stolper–Samuelson Theorem. *International Economic Review*, 10, 399–406.

Inada, K-I. (1971). The Production Coefficient Matrix and the Stolper–Samuelson Condition. *Econometrica*, 39, 219–240.

Jones, R. (1971). A Three-Factor Model in Theory, Trade, and History. In: Bhagwati, Jones, Mundell and Vanek (Eds.), *Trade, Balance of Payments and Growth* (Ch. 1). Amsterdam: North Holland.

Jones, R. (1985). Relative Prices and Real Factor Rewards: A Reinterpretation. *Economic Letters*, 19, 47–49.

Jones, R. and Kierzkowski, H. (1986). Neighborhood Production Structures with an Application to the Theory of International Trade. *Oxford Economic Papers*, 38, 59–76.

Jones, R. and Marjit, S. (1985). A Simple Production Model with Stolper–Samuelson Properties. *International Economic Review*, 19, 565–567.

Jones, R. and Marjit, S. (1991). The Stolper–Samuelson Theorem, The Leamer Triangle and the Produced Mobile Factor Structure. In: Takayama, Ohyama, and Ohta (Eds.), *Trade, Policy and International Adjustments* (Ch. 6). New York: Academic Press.

Jones, R., Marjit, S., and Mitra, T. (1991). The Stolper–Samuelson Theorem: Links to Dominant Diagonals. (unpublished).

Kemp, M. and Wegge, L. (1969). On the Relation between Commodity Prices and Factor Rewards. *International Economic Review*, 10, 407–413.

Samuelson, P. (1971). Ohlin was Right. *Swedish Journal of Economics*, 73, 365–384.

Stolper, W. and Samuelson, P. (1941). Protection and Real Wages. *Review of Economic Studies*, 9, 58–73.

CHAPTER 6

"Protection and Real Wages": The History of an Idea*

Ronald W. Jones

Abstract

Few economics articles have achieved the celebrity that still attaches to the paper, "Protection and Real Wages," by Wolfgang Stolper and Paul Samuelson in (1941). In this chapter, I discuss how the Stolper–Samuelson theorem has been re-interpreted over subsequent decades, and how attempts to generalize the theorem to higher dimensions have met with qualified results. The theorem leads to a simple proposition in political economy: In competitive models any productive factor can have its real return increased by a nontransparent policy whereby relative commodity prices are altered if there are enough commodities and joint production is not too severe.

Few contributions to economics have attained as much prominence as the 1941 article by Wolfgang Stolper and Paul Samuelson that bore the title "Protection and Real Wages." It suffered the same birthing pains experienced by some other famous articles — initial rejection by a major journal, in this case the *American Economic Review*, until finding a home in the *Review of Economic Studies*. Its success is reflected in its golden jubilee celebration at the University of Michigan in 1991 (see Deardorff and Stern, 1994). The volume of the proceedings of the conference contains a Selected Annotated Bibliography of 144 items, a fraction of the number of articles making reference to this important theorem. In recent years, in which the impact of increasing globalization and trade on real wages has commanded attention in the popular press, the theorem is even explicitly mentioned,

---

*Originally published in *The Japanese Economic Review*, 57(4), (2006).

although it is sometimes confused with the related but separate "Factor-Price Equalization Theorem."

The message of the original Stolper–Samuelson theorem is simple and powerful: A country producing two commodities in perfectly competitive conditions, with two productive inputs (call them capital and labor)[1] and importing its labor-intensive commodity, could *unambiguously* improve the *real wage* of its workers by levying a tariff on imports. More explicitly, such protection would serve to increase the nominal wage rate by a greater percentage than that of the price of the import good. The theorem remains as a benchmark against which most discussions of the effect on wages of protection or international trade is measured. The purpose of the present article is to describe how the interpretation of the theorem has altered in succeeding decades. Scores of critics have argued that the theorem is basically flawed because of the difficulties in establishing results in the case of many commodities and productive factors — results that match the elegance found in the original setting. As I hope to reveal, there is a simple, quite general result, easily obtainable, that requires a reinterpretation of the original proposition. Such a re-interpretation avoids the difficulties that have bedevilled the efforts faced by mathematical economists to generalize the theorem and yields a result that is of direct relevance not only to the theory of international trade but, more widely, to the newly expanding field of political economy.

The original Stolper–Samuelson result was proved and illustrated by an early use of the production box diagram, which for decades has become standard fare in most microtheory textbooks. The dimensions of the box reveal the quantities of the two productive factors, say capital and labor, available in fixed amounts to the economy.[2] Assuming smooth substitution possibilities between factors and the standard linear homogenous production technology typically found in competitive models, there exists a set of efficient factor allocations where the ratio of marginal products of the two factors in one industry matches the ratio in the other. Graphically

---

[1] Note that later Samuelson (1948) substituted land for capital, thus avoiding the many difficulties associated with the concept of "capital," difficulties that would lead to such argumentation in the professional journals in subsequent decades.

[2] The fixity of factor endowments is not a crucial ingredient in the proof of the Stolper–Samuelson theorem.

these allocations make up the contract curve in the box diagram. Suppose, now, that a tariff is levied that increases the relative price of the (assumed) labor-intensive import competing commodity. The production of this commodity increases, and the resulting move along the contract curve raises the capital/labor ratio used in both industries.[3] In their 1941 article, it is clear that Stolper and Samuelson realized that such a result, in which capital/labor ratios rise in *both* sectors and yet total supplies of capital and labor are assumed fixed, might seem counter-intuitive. With the overall ratio of capital to labor fixed, both sectors can adopt more capital-intensive techniques only if the weights attached to outputs in the two sectors change, as they will in a manner favoring output of the labor-intensive import commodity. Thus, with both sectors using more capital-intensive techniques, the real marginal product of labor must increase. That is, the *real* wage rate must rise. This way of describing things is like putting the cart before the horse. It is in fact the increase in the relative price of the labor-intensive commodity that forces an increase in the real wage, and this, in turn, will lead to a more intensive use of the now relatively cheaper capital in each sector. Not only could the capital/labor ratio move in the same direction in both sectors, it must do so if techniques can change at all, because each sector economizes on labor as it faces the same increase in the wage/rental rate as does the other sector.

The basic logic of the Stolper–Samuelson result emerges more clearly if techniques of production are actually rigid in each sector, with no alteration in output levels as prices change.[4] Consider the competitive profit conditions of equilibrium in each sector: Unit costs must be matched by commodity prices. Keep the price of exportables constant and raise the price of the labor-intensive import competing good. Unit costs must rise in this latter sector, and to accomplish this one of the factor returns must rise by more than the price of the import competing good (unless both factor returns were to increase by the same relative amount). By itself this would raise costs of producing exportables, and to keep these unit costs constant, the return to the other factor must actually fall. This is the

---

[3] The declining capital-intensive export sector is releasing more capital per unit of labor than is required, at initial factor prices, by the expanding labor-intensive import competing sector.

[4] That is, the economy is at a kink along its transformation schedule.

magnification result (Jones, 1965), whereby with two commodities being produced, each using the same pair of factor inputs, any change in commodity prices must result in the relative change in each such price; this is flanked by the relative change in the two factor returns because the percentage change in unit costs must be a positive weighted average of percentage changes in these factor returns. With protection raising the relative price of labor-intensive imports, it is the wage rate that must rise by relatively more than either commodity price, and the return to capital by less than either commodity price. (With the export price kept constant, the return to capital must fall.) The asymmetry between factor returns and commodity prices embodied in the magnification effect is directly a consequence of an assumption about production made by Stolper and Samuelson as well as in most work in production theory, namely that it takes both factors to produce each commodity, in a separate production process. That is, there is no joint production. I will comment in more detail on this later.

Before proceeding with an account of the development of the Stolper–Samuelson idea, it is important to stress that their paper was one of the first attempts to use general equilibrium theory to achieve comparative statics results. This was accomplished by dealing with a model of low dimensionality, albeit one in which factor allocations and factor returns respond to alterations in relative commodity prices.

The late 1940s witnessed two research results that served to highlight and alter the framework for the Stolper–Samuelson findings. The first result was the "Factor-Price Equalization Theorem," proved by Samuelson in the first of two articles in the *Economic Journal*, 1948.[5] This result, based on the same model as the earlier Stolper–Samuelson article, asked not what a tariff would do to factor returns, but instead asked about the effect of free trade on wage rates and rents in one country compared with those in another country that shared the same technology. If the two countries were identical, it would not be surprising to find factor prices equalized between countries once free trade led them to face the same commodity prices. Samuelson showed that this equalization result might hold even if

---

[5]This result seemed so surprising that Samuelson wrote a follow-up explanatory piece one year later in the same journal.

countries differed in the relative supplies of capital and labor. Factors were assumed to be internationally immobile, so that there was no international labor market or capital market. Despite this fact, Samuelson showed that if relative factor supplies were not too different between countries, free trade would bring about an equality in wages and rents. I shall say more about this result later.

The second result was developed by Metzler in (1949). What Metzler showed was that a country large enough to alter world commodity prices by its protectionist policy might not succeed in raising the relative domestic price of its import competing commodity by levying a tariff. Why not? A tariff serves to reduce domestic demand for importables at their initial world price. If elasticities of demand are sufficiently low in world markets,[6] the tariff might improve the home country's terms of trade by more than the amount of the tariff. That is, the relative domestic price of importables could fall, so that the Stolper–Samuelson result, whereby a tariff on a country's labor-intensive imports would raise the real wage rate, would be violated. To salvage the theorem, the Stolper–Samuelson result was re-interpreted to focus on the relationship between factor returns and domestic commodity prices. This helped to separate the Stolper–Samuelson theorem from the effects of international trade policy. The theorem directly links the real wage to the relative price of the labor-intensive commodity, regardless of whether protection would raise the relative price of imports if the domestic import competing commodity were labor-intensive. Such a separation of the theorem from trade policy sets the stage for a much wider application of the theorem, dealing with the effects of any policy aimed at commodity markets and its effect on another set of markets — factor markets.

In the subsequent development of the Stolper–Samuelson idea special attention should be paid to the 1953 *Review of Economic Studies* article by Samuelson in which, inter alia, he developed the reciprocity theorem, whereby the consequences of a commodity price change on factor returns are closely linked to the consequences of a change in a country's factor supplies to commodity outputs (assuming commodity prices are given, as

---

[6]The more precise condition for a tariff not to be protective is that foreign demand elasticity for imports be smaller than the home country's marginal propensity to consume its export commodity.

they would be for a small country with commodities traded internationally). Literally, suppose that the price of commodity j increases by one unit. What effect would this have on the return to factor i? Obviously this depends on technological details — the ith factor return might go up, or go down, or not change at all. Now ask a completely different question: What would be the consequence of a unit change in the economy's supply of factor i on the output of the jth commodity if commodity prices are held constant? Perhaps not surprisingly, the signs of the answer to these two queries are the same. Samuelson showed that this duality result is even stronger — the two answers are numerically identical! The timing of this result proved to be auspicious because 1953 was the same year that Wassily Leontief's paradoxical result concerning trade patterns in the United States appeared: The USA's trade pattern seemed to suggest that its import competing sectors were capital intensive relative to its export sectors (Leontief, 1953). This surprising result — surprising because it was assumed that the USA was indeed a relatively capital-abundant country which, by standard trade theory associated with Heckscher (1919) and Ohlin (1933), would suggest its exports would be *more* capital-intensive — led to an avalanche of dissertations and articles based both on Heckscher–Ohlin's theory and the work of Stolper and Samuelson.[7] As well, the Samuelson reciprocity relationship was proven in the very general framework of many productive factors and many commodities. The Stolper–Samuelson result was limited dimensionally to the case of two factors and two commodities, the so-called 2×2 model. The question could then be put: Does the Stolper–Samuelson result survive in higher dimensions?

The early 1970s were a particular time in which harsh criticisms were leveled at the Stolper–Samuelson theorem, the factor-price equalization result, and the Heckscher–Ohlin proposition about the direction of trade flows because all were embedded in a 2×2 framework. Consider a sample of such criticism.[8] Frank Hahn (1973) was particularly severe: "It is well known that an economy with only two goods has a number of important properties which do not carry over to the general case." (p. 297). Earlier, Pearce (1970), maintained that "... many textbooks of *International Trade*

---

[7] My own dissertation at M.I.T. was part of this group. See Jones (1956).

[8] These are cited in Jones and Scheinkman (1977).

Theory (even the most advanced) lay a great deal too much emphasis upon propositions which are true *only* for models with two commodities and two factors of production." (p. 320, italics added). Attempts have been made to generalize the Stolper–Samuelson result to higher dimensions. As I cite below, early efforts did have some success, but only for minor extensions of dimensionality. Equally as important for this discussion is the fact that extensions of the 2 × 2 result require a statement of precisely what the proposition states in higher dimension, because there is no unique general statement. This is pointedly revealed in two efforts to expand the Stolper–Samuelson theorem in two independent articles that happened to appear in published form next to each other in the same journal.

Kemp and Wegge (1969) in the *International Economic Review* realized that to generalize the Stolper–Samuelson theorem to higher dimensions required not only a specification of what the theorem states, but also a stricter set of assumptions regarding production structures than are required in the 2 × 2 model. They searched for conditions sufficient to yield the following changes subsequent to an increase in the price of some commodity, j, with all other commodities held constant: Some factor return rises by a greater relative amount than j's commodity price, and all other factors lose. Additionally, for each factor there is a unique commodity with which it is associated in this "real winner" association. They restricted themselves (as is common, e.g., in the 2 × 2 case) to the "even" case in which the number of produced commodities exactly balances the number of productive factors, so that without any loss of generality the favored factor for any given commodity price increase can be assigned the same number as that commodity. What restrictions on the productive structure do they impose? They assume that if you compare the ratio of factor i's usage in producing the ith commodity to that of any other factor used there, the ratio would exceed the comparable ratio of factor i to that other factor in all other commodities. This indeed is a strong version of the 2 × 2 requirement that one of the two goods utilizes a higher labor/capital ratio than does the other, and these conditions would not be satisfied for many production structures. However, suppose they are. Are these sufficient to ensure the result they desire, whereby for any factor there will be a unique commodity such that an increase in that commodity price alone suffices to raise that factor's real return — with all other factors losing? Yes — certainly in the

3×3 case, but not necessarily in higher dimensions. They even provide a counter-example for the case of four factors and four commodities.

Chipman (1969), in the same issue of the *International Economic Review*, asked for conditions sufficient to yield an alternative, and weaker, set of factor price changes given a commodity price change. Raise the price (alone) of any commodity. Suppose the real return to a unique associated factor increases, but no restrictions are placed on the fate of other factors — they may rise, fall or remain unchanged. What assumptions are required to guarantee that this result holds with a unique correspondence of factors to commodities, numbered as above so that commodity i is "intensive" in its use of factor i? Only that the distributive factor share of factor i in industry i exceeds factor i's share in any other industry (and for all i). However, just as in the Kemp–Wegge case, this condition proves insufficient in the 4×4 case, as shown once again by a counter-example.

The choice that Kemp and Wegge (1969) selected as the generalization of Stolper–Samuelson is known as the "strong form" because it specified that with each commodity price change there would be one winner, with every other factor losing, whereas Chipman (1969) considers the "weak form," that allows for the possibility that some of the nonintensive factors might nonetheless also gain. Note that in the 2×2 version there is only a single winner when one commodity price changes, but there is also only a single loser, so that it is possible to consider a production structure that would, in higher dimensions yield roughly as many winners as losers accompanying a commodity price rise. Such a structure would seem to have as much claim to represent a generalization of Stolper–Samuelson as the Kemp–Wegge strong form. An example leading to such a balanced outcome of factor winners and losers was provided by Jones and Kierzkowski (1986). Their structure highlights the possibility that any factor of production has limited access to industries in which they may find employment. Suppose there are a number of commodities produced in a country. Furthermore, suppose each commodity uses only two inputs and that each factor input is employed in only two commodities.[9] A price rise only in a single commodity will cause one or both of its input returns to increase. In the neighboring industry one

---

[9] In the article a circular location of "neighboring" industries is suggested, with each factor situated between two such industries and employed only in its two "neighbors."

factor's return rises, causing the other factor employed there to fall since that industry's price is constant. The next industry thus employs one factor whose return has fallen, causing its other factor to experience a rise in its return. There ensues a kind of "ripple effect" leading to a balance between the number of gainers and losers.[10]

The kinds of negative results in higher dimensions associated with the Kemp–Wegge and Chipman contributions cast a pall for many years on attempts at generalization.[11] There is one extension, however, that is quite simple and yields an interesting variation on the Stolper–Samuelson theorem. Maintain the two-factor assumption, but let there be a number of different commodities that can be produced. A basic feature of international trade in this context is that a country need not produce all commodities on its own — trade allows a high degree of concentration. Indeed, assuming there are many countries, two countries that share the same technology might each produce just one or a pair of commodities, and these could be different from those produced in the other country. At the other extreme, if the two countries have factor endowment proportions that are very similar, they may produce, say, the same pair of commodities.

Suppose that endowment proportions are not that similar, so that with international trade the two countries produce a single, overlapping good in common but also another commodity that differs between countries. In the more capital-abundant country that other commodity will be produced by more capital-intensive techniques than the commodity produced in common, while in the more labor-abundant country the "other" commodity will be its labor-intensive commodity. Suppose as well that the commodity that is produced in common is nonetheless exported by the more labor-abundant country and imported by the capital-abundant country, and that initially there is free trade. If the importing, capital-abundant country levies a tariff (on its imports of its labor-intensive good), its real wage rate will increase a la Stolper and Samuelson (assuming away the Metzler paradox).

---

[10]Suppose there are *n* commodities and *n* factors. If *n* is an even number (such as in the 2 × 2 case), there is exactly the same number of winners as losers, and in the favored sector (where the price rises) there is one winner and one loser. If *n* is an odd number, there is one more winner than loser; in the favored sector both factor inputs are nominal winners.
[11]This is not to say that attempts were not made. See Ethier (1984) for a useful discussion of many of the formal results derived for higher dimensional cases.

Such a tariff serves to lower the price of the commonly produced commodity in the labor-abundant country, but this commodity is produced by relatively capital-intensive techniques there, so that the other country's tariff raises the real wage in that country as well. This parallel movement in the two countries' wage rates is a consequence of a kind of factor-intensity reversal that must occur if the two countries have endowments fairly close but not close enough to result in identical production patterns. In the framework of the original Stolper–Samuelson theorem, the 2 × 2 case, a tariff would raise the real wage in one country and lower it in the other. The fact that instead there could be a common upward or downward movement of real wages in both exporting and importing countries does not contradict Heckscher–Ohlin (or Stolper–Samuelson) theory; it merely illustrates that such theory is more robust in its predictions in the many-commodity case.

   Earlier, mention was made of the Factor Price Equalization theorem, whereby free trade in commodities between a pair of countries that shared common knowledge of technology and factor skills could result in factor prices brought to equality between countries despite the lack of international factor mobility if their endowment proportions were not too different. This latter proviso is important, because with international trade a country need not produce more commodities than the number of its employed factors of production, so that if endowment differences are sufficiently different, the set of commodities produced in the two countries could differ (even if overlapping). (In the 2 × 2 discussion one of the countries, or both, could become specialized.) Does such an equalization result hold in higher dimensions (where the number of possible commodities exceeds the number of factors)? When mathematical economists turned to this issue, they ended up asking a different question: If an economy produces the same number of commodities as it has factors of production, are factor returns uniquely determined by a given set of commodity prices? This depends upon properties of the array (or matrix) of distributive factor shares, since these are the weights that represent the importance of any factor in unit costs (which, in equilibrium, are equal to commodity prices). Without going into the mathematical details of this literature, note how the focus of the question has changed. There is no mention of similarity or difference of factor endowments between countries, or that countries' technologies are assumed to be identical. Instead, the original query about factor-price equalization with trade is converted into a query about the mathematical properties of the distributive share matrix.[12]

It is possible to argue that the literature about extending the Stolper–Samuelson result also re-routed a question that initially was of interest to economists into one of more interest to mathematicians. Without stating things in a formal fashion, suppose that a country produces n commodities with the use of an "even" number of productive factors, n, with unit costs equal, in equilibrium, to the set of commodity prices. If factor prices change, so will unit costs, and in any industry the percentage change in unit costs will be a positive weighted average of the percentage changes in all the factor returns. The weights will depict the distributive factor shares. Each element of the inverse of the matrix of distributive shares answers the following question: If a particular commodity goes up in price, all other commodity prices constant, what will be the effect on one of the factor returns? In the 2×2 case, if factor i is intensively used to produce commodity i, the inverse of the factor share matrix must have a diagonal whose elements are positive and exceed unity, and negative off-diagonal elements. The kind of question posed by Kemp and Wegge (1969) for the higher-dimensional $n \times n$ case, is what conditions on technology suffice to ensure that again the inverse exhibits diagonal elements all exceeding unity and negative off-diagonal elements. Such an inverse matrix satisfies the *strong* Stolper–Samuelson condition whereby each commodity is associated with a unique factor (different for each commodity) such that an increase in that commodity's price alone results in the *real* return to the associated productive factor to rise, with all other factor returns falling. The conditions they

---

[12] In Jones (1995), I have argued that a variation of the factor price equalization theorem may be more fundamental than the question of whether trade equalizes factor prices between countries. This variation asks about factor-price dependence — the extent to which producing commodities for the world market at given world prices lessens the control that can be maintained by a country over returns to its nontraded factors. If the country produces as many commodities for the world market as it has factors, its factor returns are completely determined by world commodity prices, regardless of whether other countries produce the same commodities or have the same technology. As Neary (1985) has shown, as the number of commodities produced by a country approaches the number of its factors, the degree of dependence monotonically increases. For a country that puts value on its ability to control returns in its own factor markets, it may be willing to forego some of the gains from trade in commodities in order to preserve some control over factor prices.

supplied, as narrow as they are, prove to be sufficient in the 3×3 case, but not in higher than three dimensions.[13]

A more interesting version of the Stolper–Samuelson theorem was suggested in Jones (1985). Suppose an arbitrarily selected factor of production knocks on the door of its government representative and says, "Help — can you do something that will serve to increase my real factor reward?" The representative reaches into its desk drawer to pull out a checkbook. "No," replies the factor, "the media would pounce on me if they found out about such a direct intervention. Instead, can you use a technique that is less transparent, can you change taxes, regulations, the pattern of government spending, or some other device that serves to alter relative commodity prices in a manner that will increase my real return? If taxes are levied, I cannot be seen to partake of the tax revenue, or of tariff revenue if tariffs are imposed. Does there exist a change in relative commodity prices that will result in my real factor return unambiguously rising?" The answer, not surprisingly, is "perhaps." That is, certain conditions must be satisfied. Are these conditions of the type that lead to inverse matrices with positive diagonals and negative off-diagonal elements? No — they are much weaker. First, suppose that technology does not exhibit joint production —, i.e., each commodity is produced in a separate production process utilizing all productive factors. Secondly, if alterations in commodity prices are to do the "heavy lifting," there must be enough weapons — the number of produced commodities must be at least as large as the number of factors. Anything more? No. This pair of conditions suffices to ensure that the real return to any productive factor can be improved by the appropriate change in relative commodity prices. The proof is simple, and makes use of Samuelson's reciprocity theorem described earlier.[14]

---

[13] In Jones *et al.* (1993), sufficient conditions are provided for this result. These conditions are more strict than, but are related to, the Kemp–Wegge conditions. In order for a commodity price increase to result in all factors save one to be losers, the difference in their intensity ratios relative to the use of the winning factor cannot be very large from factor to factor. That is, a similarity in outcome (all the losers have a fall in factor return) must be reflected in fairly similar factor intensities for these factors, compared with the intensity of the winning factor. Related conditions for the weak theorem of Chipman are provided in Mitra and Jones (1999).

[14] Suppose factor i pleads for such support. Consider the following scenario. If all commodity prices are constant, suppose the endowment of factor i increases (alone). Techniques

The assumption of lack of joint production can be weakened somewhat. In a sense what is required is that the array of factors used in any process be less diverse than the array of outputs emerging from the activity.[15] After all, the statement of the *magnification* effect, whereby for any commodity price change the alterations in some factor returns are greater, points to an asymmetry between factor price changes and commodity price changes, and such an asymmetry must reflect an asymmetry between inputs and outputs in the production structure. This is what a lack of joint production entails — it takes many inputs to make a single output.

The focus on individual elements of the inverse of the matrix of distributive shares is natural for mathematicians. But it is of little relevance to the political-economy issue posed in the form of asking if changes in relative commodity prices can ensure an increase in the real return to any pre-assigned factor. After all, it may be the case that an increase in a single commodity price may not be sufficient to raise the selected real factor return. So what? It is easy to show that the desired result can be achieved by raising a subset of commodity prices by the same relative amount, and keep all other prices constant. And, of course, nothing has been said about all other factor prices falling. Indeed, it would be of great convenience to the factor seeking this kind of help if some other factor returns go up as well. In this day and age of concern with income distribution, the factor that seeks indirect help would welcome other gainers… "they did it for them."

It is easy to see why it is stipulated that there be enough commodities — at least as many as the number of factors. The Specific-Factors model (Jones, 1971; Samuelson, 1971) provides an example to illustrate how having more factors than goods obviates the Stolper–Samuelson result. In the simple 3×2 case, a pair of commodities is produced, with one type of capital and labor used in one sector and a different type of capital and labor used in the other. Labor is freely mobile from sector to sector. An increase

---

are unchanged because factor prices (in this $n \times n$ case) are determined by the commodity prices and thus remain constant. Since all other endowments are constant, not all commodity outputs can increase. Suppose the output of commodity j falls. The reciprocity results then ensure that a decrease in the price of commodity j, all other prices constant, must raise the return to factor i. Such a price change must increase the real return to factor i — the generalized Stolper–Samuelson result. For further details see Jones (1985).

[15]This is really too loose a statement. Basically the cone of outputs should contain the cone of inputs into the process.

in either commodity price raises the nominal wage rate, but only by a fraction of the price rise. The real winner for any price change is the specific factor used in that sector. No change in relative commodity prices can succeed in raising the nominal wage rate for mobile labor by more than any commodity price.

Is it possible to conceive of even weaker statements that suggest that the indirect use of policies that change relative commodity prices can effectively improve the real return of any preselected factor? Yes, but at the expense of giving up the magnification effect associated with the original statement of the Stolper–Samuelson theorem. A given factor's real return improves if its nominal return increases relatively more than that factor's cost of living, even if its nominal return might not increase relative to all commodity price changes. With this in mind, note that for given factor endowments and technology, the proportional change in any factor return is a weighted average of the proportional changes in all commodity prices.[16] Of course some of the weights can be negative, and some might exceed unity. Now consider the change in the cost of living. If the factor consumes something of all items, the proportional increase in the cost of living is a positive weighted average of all commodity price changes.[17] As long as the weights used for the cost of living index are not identical to those for the change in the nominal factor return, the proposition can be obtained: That is, regardless of the number of factors and commodities and whether or not there is joint production in some activities, any factor's real return can be improved by policies that alter relative commodity prices. My own preference is for the previous result that relied on having a sufficient number of commodities and the relative absence of joint production; using this result, no reference need be made of taste patterns; this was one of the key and surprising features of the original Stolper–Samuelson theorem. However, the more general remarks serve to emphasize the power of altering prices in one set of markets in order to facilitate a significant change of real returns in other markets. This, surely, is an important characteristic of competitive economies that has a central role to play in discussions of political

---

[16]Imagine a 10 percent increase in all commodity prices. This should lead to a uniform 10 percent change in every factor return if there is no "money illusion."

[17]If some commodity is not consumed, its weight would be zero.

economy. It also owes much to the pioneering work of Wolfgang Stolper and Paul Samuelson more than 60 years ago.

References

Chipman, J. (1969). Factor Price Equalization and the Stolper-Samuelson Theorem. *International Economic Review*, 10, 399–406.

Deardorff, A. and Stern, R. (1994). *The Stolper-Samuelson Theorem: A Golden Jubilee.* Ann Arbor, MI: University of Michigan Press.

Ethier, W. (1984). Higher Dimensional Issues in Trade Theory. In: R. W. Jones and P. B. Kenen (Eds.), *Handbook of International Economics* (Vol. 1), Amsterdam: North-Holland.

Hahn, F. (1973). General Equilibrium Theory and International Trade: Takashi Negishi. *Journal of International Economics*, 3, 297–298.

Heckscher, E. (1919). The Effect of Foreign Trade on the Distribution of Income. *Ekonomisk Tidskrift*, 21, pp. 497–512.

Jones, R.W. (1956). Factor Proportions and the Heckscher-Ohlin Theorem. *Review of Economic Studies*, 24, 1–10.

Jones, R.W. (1965). The Structure of Simple General Equilibrium Models. *Journal of Political Economy*, 73, 557–572.

Jones, R.W. (1971). A Three Factor Model in Theory, Trade and History. In: R. Jones, R. Mundell and J. Vanek (Eds.), *Trade, Balance of Payment and Growth*, Amsterdam: North Holland.

Jones, R.W. (1985). Relative Prices and Real Factor Rewards: A Re-interpretation. *Economics Letters*, 19, 47–49.

Jones, R.W. (1995). The Discipline of International Trade. *Swiss Journal of Economics and Statistics*, 131, 273–288.

Jones, R.W. and Kierzkowski, H. (1986). Neighborhood Production Structures with an Application to the Theory of International Trade. *Oxford Economic Papers*, 38, 59–76.

Jones, R.W. and Scheinkman, J. (1977). The Relevance of the Two-Sector Production Model in Trade Theory. *Journal of Political Economy*, 85, 909–936.

Jones, R.W., Marjit, S., and Mitra, T. (1993). The Stolper-Samuelson Theorem: Links to Dominant Diagonals. In: Becker, Boldrin, Jones and Thomson (Eds.), *General Equilibrium, Growth and Trade II* (pp. 429–441). New York: Academic Press

Kemp, M. and Wegge, L. (1969). On the Relation between Commodity Prices and Factor Rewards. *International Economic Review*, 10, 407–413.

Leontief, W. (1953). Domestic Production and Foreign Trade: The American Capital Position Re-examined. *Proceedings of the American Philosophical Society*, 97, 332–349.

Metzler, L. (1949). Tariffs, the Terms of Trade and the Distribution of National Income. *Journal of Political Economy*, 57, 1–29.

Mitra, T. and Jones. R.W. (1999). Factor Shares and the Chipman Condition. In: J. Moore. R. Riezman and J. Melvin (Eds.), *Trade, Theory and Econometrics: Essays in Honor of John S. Chipman* (pp. 125–133). London: Routledge.

Neary, J.P. (1985). International Factor Mobility, Minimum Wage Rates and Factor-Price Equalization: A Synthesis. *Quarterly Journal of Economics*, 100(3), 551–570.

Ohlin, B. (1933). *Interregional and International Trade.* Cambridge, MA: Harvard University Press.

Pearce, I.F. (1970). *International Trade.* New York: Norton.

Samuelson, P.A. (1948). International Trade and the Equalisation of Factor Prices. *Economic Journal,* 58, 163–184.

Samuelson, P.A. (1949). International Factor-Price Equalization Once Again. *Economic Journal,* 59, 181–197.

Samuelson, P.A. (1953). Prices of Factors and Goods in General Equilibrium. *Review of Economic Studies,* 21, 1–20.

Samuelson, P.A. (1971). Ohlin was Right. *Swedish Journal of Economics,* 73, 365–384.

Stolper, W. and Samuelson, P.A. (1941). Protection and Real Wages. *Review of Economic Studies,* 9, 58–73.

CHAPTER 7

Heckscher–Ohlin Trade Flows: A Re-appraisal*

Ronald W. Jones

Abstract

The famous Leontief paradox compared the factor proportions used in a country's export sectors with those used in that country's import-competing sectors in order to conclude whether a country was relatively capital abundant (in a two-factor, labor, and capital setting). When examined in a two-factor, many commodity setting, this procedure reveals the troubling conclusion that as a country's relative capital endowment rises, its export sector relative to its import-competing sector cycles from being labor-intensive to being capital-intensive, to being labor-intensive, etc., which serves to invalidate the Leontief procedure.

Few economics articles have had the impact created by Wassily Leontief's finding in 1953 that the United States international trade pattern seemed at variance with predictions supported by the models based on the work of Eli Heckscher (1919) and Bertil Ohlin (1933). According to his input–output data, United States exports were produced by more labor-intensive techniques than those used in American production activities that competed with imports, a comparison that seemed distinctly at odds with the pre-conceived notion that the United States was more capital abundant than almost all of its trading partners. Such a finding was bound to encourage many articles, both theoretical and empirical, that, in the words of

---

*Originally published in *Trade and Development Review*, 1(1), (2008), pp. 1–6.

Wilfred Ethier (1974), greatly enhanced our understanding of the relationship between factor endowments and the pattern of trade (formally, the Heckscher–Ohlin theorem), which was one of the four basic theorems of Heckscher–Ohlin theory, the others being the Factor-Price Equalization theorem, the Stolper–Samuelson theorem (both antedating Leontief) and the Rybczynski theorem (1955).

Early work that more carefully analyzed the link between factor endowments and technology admittedly was based on the two-country, two-factor, two-commodity setting explored by Samuelson in his two factor-price equalization papers (1948, 1949). Subsequent analyses revealed the simplicity of the many-commodity, two-factor setting because with international trade the number of commodities a country might have to produce would not exceed the number of its productive factors. If factors were limited to capital and labor, a country's technology and the set of commodity prices ruling in world markets would yield a Hicksian composite unit-value isoquant, more colloquially described as the isoquant for "producing a buck" on world markets. Depending upon a country's factor endowment capital/labor ratio, such an isoquant would reveal either which single commodity would be the best to produce or, alternatively, which pair of commodities would be observed in a competitive trade equilibrium. It is this setting I will use in criticizing the standard interpretation of the Heckscher–Ohlin theorem whereby a ranking of factor intensities in export and import-competing activities within a country reveals evidence of capital/labor endowment rankings.

Figure 7.1 illustrates a Hicksian composite unit-value isoquant in the four-commodity case in which the country's technology would allow production of any of the four commodities at the given commodity prices if factor endowment proportions were appropriate. Factor endowment rays that would intersect the tangent chords, AB, CD, or EF correspond to situations in which the country produces a pair of commodities. It proves convenient to transcribe this information into Fig. 7.2. Given the country's technology, the rising curve for each commodity depicts the capital-labor ratio (on the horizontal axis) that would be employed for various levels of the ratio of wages to capital rentals (on the vertical axis).

The pattern of production for any factor endowment proportions depends upon world prices, and in Fig. 7.2 the set of given prices determines the heavier locus that combines the possibility that complete

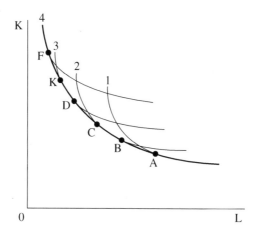

Figure 7.1.   The Hicksian Composite Unit Value Isoquant

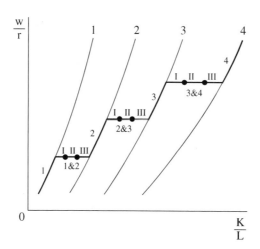

Figure 7.2.   Factor Endowments and Factor Prices

specialization occurs (along a rising curve for a single commodity) with "flats" connecting a pair of such curves, and along which production of a pair of commodities takes place and the factor price ratio is completely determined. Thus if a country with a given technology should develop as the capital/labor endowment ratio grows, its production pattern would systematically alternate between producing a single commodity and producing a pair, and the composition of production would change as long as commodity prices remain the same. Alternatively, comparisons could be made between a pair of countries that differ in their endowment ratios but face the same world prices. It was this latter question that revealed that factor prices could be equilibrated between two such economies if their endowment proportions were not too far apart.

For each "flat" in Fig. 7.2 three regions have been identified. For illustrative purposes concentrate on the middle flat along which the country produces commodities 2 and 3. Regions II are those in which production of each commodity (2 or 3 for the middle flat) is sufficiently great that both commodities are exported. However, in such Regions there is no "import-competing" activity — with imports consisting only of commodities (1 and 4 in the middle flat) that are consumed but obtained in full by imports from the rest of the world. Similarly, if only a single commodity is produced, there is obviously no import-competing local activity. Such is not the case, however, in Regions I and III. For the middle flat in Region I, i.e., for a country whose capital/labor endowment proportions allow only small levels of production of the third commodity, local consumption requires as well some imports of the third commodity from the rest of the world (with commodity 2 being exported). For higher capital/labor endowment ratios, such that production takes place in its Region III, the asymmetries in production and trade are reversed. For Region III of the middle flat the country exports the third commodity and imports the second, along with the first and fourth commodity that is does not produce.

Now consider a pair of countries (call them Home and Foreign) that share the same technology and face the same commodity prices, but have different factor endowment proportions. Suppose Home is relatively labor abundant, and producing in Region III in the first flat, i.e., producing and exporting commodity 2 and importing (and also producing) commodity 1. By contrast, Foreign is sufficiently capital abundant that it produces commodities 3 and 4 in Region I of the highest flat. The relatively labor-abundant Home country exports commodity 2, which is relatively capital intensive compared with its import-competing commodity 1. Compare this with the relatively capital-abundant Foreign country, a country that exports its relatively labor-intensive commodity (3) whereas its more capital-intensive commodity produced (4) must be imported because local production is too limited. To summarize: The relatively labor-abundant Home country exports its relatively capital-intensive commodity and the relatively capital-abundant Foreign country exports its relatively labor-intensive commodity. This would violate the form of the Heckscher–Ohlin theorem that predicts a comparison of techniques within a country between its exporting and import-competing sectors from the ranking of relative factor endowments.

Earlier literature (e.g., Jones, 1956) pointed out a pair of possibilities that could explain the failure of the Heckscher–Ohlin theorem. The first is the case of technological "factor-intensity reversal" that, in Fig. 7.2, would be illustrated if a pair of the rising curves indicating factor intensities selected at various factor prices, intersected. Here I have explicitly avoided that technological reversal phenomenon. The second is the case in which demand patterns are strongly asymmetrical in the two countries, with, say, the labor-abundant country having such a biased demand in favor of its labor-intensive commodity that it makes use of trading possibilities to import this commodity. Here demand conditions could be the same between countries and balanced among commodities (say equal shares in a Cobb–Douglas setting).

Note that as a country is placed in a growth context, with increases in its capital/labor endowment proportions, it systematically switches from exporting its labor-intensive commodity to exporting its capital-intensive commodity and then switching back to exporting its labor-intensive commodity, with each switch interrupted by periods of growth in which there is no import-competing production (either both produced goods are exported or the country is completely specialized). Imagine a set of countries with different factor endowments but sharing access to the same technology and facing the same commodity prices. It would be natural *not* to find a consistent positive ranking between capital/labor endowment proportions on the one hand, and intra-country factor intensity rankings, on the other. In this multi-commodity setting, the use of intra-country intensity rankings to deduce relative factor abundance is inappropriate.

Notwithstanding the questionable Leontief intra-country ranking, there are two observations that do serve to connect a country's factor endowments to the relative capital intensity of its exports. First of all, a country will tend to produce commodities that require for their production factor intensities fairly similar to those found in its endowment bundle, and tend to import commodities which, if produced at home, would reflect both higher and lower capital/labor ratios than the commodities actually produced at home (Jones, 1974). Secondly, a comparison of two countries that share the same technology but do not produce exactly the same bundle of commodities reveals that every commodity produced by the capital-abundant country uses techniques that are more capital intensive than those used by the labor-abundant country in any commodity.

Given the duality in trade theory between relationships involving factor endowments and commodity outputs on the one hand and factor prices and commodity prices on the other (e.g., Jones, 1965a, 1965b), it is instructive to consider a case such as would be illustrated in Fig. 7.2 by considering Home producing in the middle flat, with Foreign producing in the highest flat. Both countries produce a commodity (3) in common. However, it is *not* a violation of Heckscher–Ohlin theory to observe that an increase in the price of the commonly produced commodity (3) would raise the relative wage in one country and lower it in the other. Perhaps more surprising is that the country in which the wage rate would increase is the relatively capital abundant Foreign country. If the relatively labor-abundant Home country produces in Region I (of the middle flat), and has imposed a tariff on imports of commodity 3 from the capital-abundant Foreign country (producing in Region I of the highest flat), a movement towards freer trade (in commodity 3) would serve to raise the wage rate in both countries. In a multi-country version these results do not contradict Heckscher–Ohlin theory.

References

Ethier, W. (1974). Some of the Theorems of International Trade with Many Goods and Factors. *Journal of International Economics*, 4, 199–206.

Heckscher, E. (1919). The Effect of Foreign Trade on the Distribution of Income. *Ekonomisk*, Reprinted as Chapter 13 in A.E.A. (1949). *Readings in the Theory of International Trade* 272–300 (Philadelphia: Blakiston) with a Translation in H. Flam and M. J. Flanders (Eds.). 1991. *Heckscher-Ohlin Trade Theory*, 43–69. Cambridge, MA: MIT Press.

Jones, R.W. (1956). Factor Proportions and the Heckscher-Ohlin Theorem. *Review of Economic Studies*, 24, 1–10.

Jones, R.W. (1965a). Duality in International Trade: A Geometrical Note. *Canadian Journal of Economics and Political Science*, 390–393.

Jones, R.W. (1965b). The Structure of Simple General Equilibrium Models. *Journal of Political Economy*, 73, 557–572.

Jones, R.W. (1974). The Small Country in a Many-Commodity World. *Australian Economic Papers*, 13, 225–236.

Leontief, W.W. (1953). Domestic Production and Foreign Trade: The American Capital Position Re-examined. *Proceedings of the American Philosophical Society*, 97, 332–349.

Ohlin, B. (1933). *Interregional and International Trade.* Cambridge, MA: Harvard University Press.

Rybczynski, T.M. (1955). Factor Endowments and Relative Commodity Prices. *Economica*, 22, 336–341.

Samuelson, P.A. (1948). International Trade and the Equalization of Factor Prices. *Economic Journal*, 58, 163–184.

Samuelson, P.A. (1949). International Factor-Price Equalization Once Again. *Economic Journal*, 59, 181–197.

CHAPTER 8

Heckscher–Ohlin and Specific-Factors Trade Models for Finite Changes: How Different Are They?*

Ronald W. Jones

Abstract

In competitive international trade theory, two of the basic models are the Specific-Factors model and the Heckscher–Ohlin model, with dimensionality 3×2 and 2×2, respectively. A surprising result in Heckscher–Ohlin is that the effect on factor prices of an infinitesimal change in a commodity price depends neither on the importance of the industry nor on the differences between sectors in the flexibility of technology. For finite price changes, this need no longer be the case, and the model form itself may change endogenously as production patterns get altered. Furthermore, the extent of the response of the wage rate to a price increase in the more labor-intensive commodity becomes less severe the greater is the discrepancy between the degree of labor-intensity difference between sectors in the Heckscher–Ohlin model but more severe in the Specific-Factors model.

8.1 Introduction

The Heckscher–Ohlin and the Specific-Factors models represent the pair of competitive international trade models most frequently used in multifactor competitive settings to obtain comparative static results when equilibrium positions are disturbed by small changes in commodity prices (e.g., when a pair of countries are price takers in world markets), for changes in factor endowments, or for shocks reflecting improvements in technological

---

*Originally published in *International Review of Economics and Finance*, 29 (2014), pp. 650–659.

knowledge.[1] These questions have been typically analyzed using calculus techniques, and attention has often been directed to the *differences* found between these two trade models. A more realistic analysis would focus on scenarios in which shocks are of finite size, and conclusions obtained in such a setting may well differ from those obtained from using calculus techniques.[2] In particular, finite changes may well result in changes in the pattern of production, i.e., changes in *which* commodities get produced. This is a situation more often found in the field of international trade than in other fields of economics that do not assume that some or all markets are global. The focus of this chapter examines the manner in which the comparison between trade models is severely affected by the *size* of the shocks that lead to new equilibria.

8.2   Standard Results for the Two Models with Small Changes

The Specific-Factors model is generally agreed to be the simpler of the two trade models. Although formal analysis of this model was not provided until thirty years after the 1941 appearance of the Stolper–Samuelson paper, it provides a set of results that correspond more closely to the well-recognized findings of partial equilibrium reasoning.[3] The basic scenario has each country producing a pair of commodities, each of which uses a factor of production, usually considered to be labor, freely mobile between sectors. In addition, each sector uses another factor of production, one that is *specific* in its use to that sector.[4] This leads to a form of a three-factor,

---

[1] The emphasis on multi-factor scenarios rules out the important Ricardian trade model with a single factor of production. However, the Ricardian emphasis on the opening of trade leading to a great *concentration* in production is maintained in my discussion, a feature often neglected in standard analysis of the Heckscher–Ohlin model with two factors and two commodities.

[2] Earlier treatments of finite changes are found in Jones and Marjit (1992) as well as Jones (2008).

[3] Formal analysis is found in Jones (1971, Chapter 1; 1975) and Samuelson (1971), who called the model the Ricardo–Viner model and emphasized the link to partial equilibrium results.

[4] Two key articles, those by Mayer (1974) and Neary (1978) interpret the Specific-Factor Model as a *short-run* version of the Heckscher–Ohlin model. They assume that in the long run "specificity" is removed, perhaps by depreciation and a change in new capital created. In Sanyal and Jones (1982), it is the possibility of international trade in "middle products"

two-commodity model in which the immobility of capital between sectors provides a simpler setting than that of the (2×2) Heckscher–Ohlin model.

In a competitive international trade setting, assume that a country actively produces both commodities 1 and 2 so that competition drives commodity prices in equilibrium to the level of production costs:

$$a_{L1}w + a_{K1}r_1 = p_1 \tag{8.1}$$

$$a_{L2}w + a_{K2}r_2 = p_2 \tag{8.2}$$

The notation for the input–output variables, a_{ij}, the factor prices (wage rate, w, and return to capital in sector j, r_i), and commodity prices, p_j, are all standard (with each a_{ij} depending upon the ratio of wages to capital rentals in sector j). For small (infinitesimal) shocks in prices let a "hat" over a variable represent a relative change, e.g., $\hat{x} = \frac{dx}{x}$. Note that the distributive share average of the relative changes in input-output techniques is a "second-order small," so that Eqs. (8.3) and (8.4), showing distributive share averages of input prices on the left-hand side, portray the competitive profit equations for changes of commodity prices, where θ_{ij} is factor i's share in production in industry j:

$$\theta_{L1}\hat{w} + \theta_{K1}\hat{r}_1 = \hat{p}_1, \tag{8.3}$$

$$\theta_{L2}\hat{w} + \theta_{K2}\hat{r}_2 = \hat{p}_2 \tag{8.4}$$

That is, the relative change in each commodity's price is flanked by the relative changes in appropriate factor returns. Assuming that the relative change in the first commodity's price exceeds that of the second, this leads directly to the following inequality ranking:

$$\hat{r}_1 > \hat{p}_1 > \hat{w} > \hat{p}_2 > \hat{r}_2 \tag{8.5}$$

Not surprisingly, with this change in relative commodity prices, the specific capital in the favored first sector must be the greatest winner, and that in the other sector the greatest relative loser. The wage rate change lies between that of the two commodity prices since labor is mobile between sectors.

---

such as capital goods that serves to convert a type of capital in one sector into the type useful in the other.

To get further results it is necessary to turn to market-clearing for mobile labor:

$$a_{L1}x + a_{L2}x_2 = L \qquad (8.6)$$

In addition, output in each sector is constrained by the quantity of capital in use there:

$$a_{Kj}x_j = K_j \qquad (8.7)$$

Expressed in terms of rates of change,

$$\hat{x}_j = -\hat{a}_{Kj} + \hat{K}_j \quad \text{(for } j \text{ equal to 1 or 2)} \qquad (8.8)$$

Now differentiate the full employment condition for labor, (8.6), and then substitute for the output changes shown in Eq. (8.8) to obtain:

$$\lambda_{L1}(\hat{a}_{L1} - \hat{a}_{K1}) + \lambda_{L2}(\hat{a}_{L2} - \hat{a}_{K2}) = \hat{L} - [\lambda_{L1}\hat{K}_1 + \lambda_{L2}\hat{K}_2] \qquad (8.9)$$

Each λ_{Lj} denotes the fraction of the labor force that is allocated to the jth sector. The changes in the ratios of labor to capital used in each sector depend upon the elasticity of demand for labor in that sector or, in more basic terms, the elasticity of the marginal product curve for labor in each sector. Denote such an elasticity by γ_{Lj}:

$$\gamma_{Lj} \equiv -\frac{(\hat{a}_{Lj} - \hat{a}_{Kj})}{(\hat{w} - \hat{p}_j)} \qquad (8.10)$$

Finally, substitute these elasticities into Eq. (8.9) and solve for the equilibrium change in the wage rate:

$$\hat{w} = [\beta_1\hat{p}_1 + \beta_2\hat{p}_2] - \left(\frac{1}{\gamma_L}\right)[\hat{L} - (\lambda_{L1}\hat{K}_1 + \lambda_{L2}\hat{K}_2)] \qquad (8.11)$$

The new terms appearing in this solution reflect the effect of price changes on the wage rate if endowments are kept constant, the β_j's. Consider the first sector's β_1. It equals $\lambda_{L1}\gamma_{L1}/\gamma_L$, where the denominator is an aggregate measure of the elasticity of demand for labor in the economy, $(\lambda_{L1}\gamma_{L1} + \lambda_{L2}\gamma_{L2})$. β_1 is a positive fraction, as is β_2. Now consider β_1 as the product of λ_{L1} and the term γ_{L1}/γ_L. The latter ratio exceeds unity if and only if (roughly speaking) the *flexibility* of technology or elasticity of demand for labor in the first sector exceeds that in the second (or the economy's aggregate, γ_L). Call this term (s_1), where the "s" stands for "substitutability", one of the features of the difference in technology between sectors.

Another feature of technology is well known — which sector is the more labor intensive. Although it is literally inappropriate to compare capital/labor ratios between industries, since the units do not match, the first industry is deemed to be labor intensive if and only if the fraction of the labor force used in the first industry (λ_{L1}) exceeds the output share of the first industry in the national income (θ_1). That is, the expression (λ_{L1}/θ_1) compared with unity reveals another aspect of the technological difference between the two industries. Call this ratio, (i_1), the "relative labor intensity", so that β_1 can be written as:

$$\beta_1 = \theta_1\{i_1, s_1\} \tag{8.12}$$

Thus the relative impact an increase in the price of the first commodity has on the relative change in the wage rate is a *fraction* that consists of the product of the two attributes of technology — (i) the relative *flexibility* of technology in the first industry (s_1) and (ii) the relative *labor intensity* of the first industry (i_1), all multiplied by a third characteristic, (iii) the relative *importance* of the first industry in the national income, shown by θ_1. As is well known, when attention is shifted to the (2×2) Heckscher–Ohlin model, only a single one of these three characteristics connects changes in commodity prices to changes in the wage rate — the relative labor *intensity* comparison between sectors.

Before turning to more details on the Heckscher–Ohlin (2×2) model, note from the expression for the change in the wage rate in Eq. (8.11) that even if commodity prices remain unchanged any change in factor endowments has an independent effect on factor prices. An increase in the labor force tends to lower the wage rate, while increases in either type of specific capital tend to raise the wage rate. This result seems to correspond strongly to common sense, although once again the (2×2) Heckscher–Ohlin model typically shows different results when calculus is used to ascertain the separate effects of changes in commodity prices and factor endowments on wages and rents.

The scenario for the (2×2) Heckscher–Ohlin model is well known — the economy has two factors, say labor and capital, both mobile between the two sectors. The formal lay-out of such an economy would be simplified if commodity prices are taken as parameters — given in world markets to an economy too small to influence commodity prices because of the relatively small size of its economy relative to global totals of supply and demand. Even with such a simplification, we are left with an equilibrium with 8 equations to determine 8 unknowns.[5] Not surprisingly such a system can be simplified so that subsets of equations can be solved in terms of other variables. For example, the common technique over 50 years ago was to cite as unknowns the set of 2 outputs, 2 factor prices, and the allocation of each factor to the two industries. As for equations, two of them equated total demand for one of the factors to the (assumed) given factor supply. Two more equations were found in stating the technology whereby a pair of *production functions* linked each output to the amounts of inputs of both factors.[6] The final set of four equations posited that each of the two factors earned a return that matched the value of its marginal product in each industry. A problem with this format is that the four unknowns measuring the allocation of the two factors to each of the two industries are composites of the variable input/output coefficients and the equilibrium level of outputs in the two industries. However, the two output levels are already variables. The amount of capital, say, used in the second industry is a composite of the amount used per unit output (the "how") and the amount of the good produced (the "how much"). The former depends more simply only upon factor prices, while the latter have already been counted as a pair of unknowns. As a consequence, the set of eight equilibrium equations can be solved without going any higher than solving a pair of equations at a time.

In any case, much can be learned by the pair of equations indicating that in equilibrium in competitive markets unit costs are brought into alignment with market output prices, just as they did for the Specific-Factors model. In the (2×2) Heckscher–Ohlin setting this implies that a pair

---

[5] If countries are not small, commodity prices in the world market can be determined by equating world demand and supply for each commodity. The set of 8 equations referred to here would need to be solved for the general producer *supply* relationships in a country with given prices, much as knowledge of taste patterns and ownership patterns for resources lead to consumer *demand* for each commodity as a function of all commodity prices.

[6] The way this was done underlies many key results in Heckscher–Ohlin trade theory because it *presumed* that there was no joint production. That is, each output was produced separately with an explicit pair of quantities of the two inputs. *Inter alia* this assumption implied that commodity price changes would have a *magnification* effect on factor returns. Such a result meant that, say, in the Stolper and Samuelson (1941) paper, a country imposing a tariff on imports of the labor-intensive product would unambiguously raise the *real* wage rate, without any reference to the taste patterns of workers.

of such equations involves only two input prices, and thus *factor prices get completely determined by commodity prices.* In the Specific-Factors model, the equations of change for the competitive profit conditions in Eqs. (8.3) and (8.4) involved 3 unknowns and 2 equations. The corresponding pair of equations for Heckscher–Ohlin is shown by (8.13) and (8.14):

$$\theta_{L1}\hat{w} + \theta_{K1}\hat{r} = \hat{p}_1 \tag{8.13}$$
$$\theta_{L2}\hat{w} + \theta_{K2}\hat{r} = \hat{p}_2 \tag{8.14}$$

Recall that the assumption about production that is commonly made is that there is no joint production. This implies that the two factor price changes flank each of the two commodity price changes. For example, if we once again assume that the price of the first commodity rises relative to that of the second, the relative factor price changes are *magnified* relative to commodity price changes, and the only question left is which factor price change tops the list. If we assume that the first industry is more labor-intensive, this must be labor, as expressed in the inequalities of (8.15):

$$\hat{w} > \hat{p}_1 > \hat{p}_2 > \hat{r} \tag{8.15}$$

Comparing this ranking with that of the Specific-Factors model, (8.5), it is clear that the two models have a distinctive difference as to the effect of a commodity price change on wage rates. The Heckscher–Ohlin ranking in (8.15) supports the 1941 Stolper–Samuelson conclusion that an increase in the relative price of the labor-intensive commodity must unambiguously increase the wage rate by a greater relative amount than either price change. By contrast, in the Specific-Factors model the wage rate increases in terms of one commodity but diminishes in terms of the other.

Just as striking a difference between the two models is revealed by the apparent lack of influence on the wage rate of the importance of the commodity whose relative price has been raised. Consider the pair of competitive profit equations of change in the Heckscher–Ohlin setting. The easiest exercise is to subtract Eqs. (8.14) from (8.13) to obtain (8.16):

$$|\theta|(\hat{w} - \hat{r}) = (\hat{p}_1 - \hat{p}_2), \tag{8.16}$$

where the determinant of coefficients in (8.13) and (8.14), $|\theta|$, equals the difference in labor shares in the two sectors, $(\theta_{L1} - \theta_{L2})$. This will be a positive fraction if the first industry is relatively labor intensive.[7] Absent in the solution is any information about the relative importance of the first industry, θ_1, or about the comparison between industries in the *flexibility* of technology when factor prices change. In order to appreciate what difference it makes to consider price or endowment changes that are *finite* in size, simple diagrams can reveal what the calculus leaves out.

8.3   Finite Changes and Diagrammatic Tools

The basic diagram that proves useful in analyzing the effect in the Heckscher–Ohlin model of changes in commodity prices and factor endowments on outputs and factor prices, say in a possible 3-commodity world, is displayed in Figs. 8.1 and 8.2.[8] The vertical axis displays the wage/rental ratio and the horizontal axis the endowment capital/labor ratio. Technology for three commodities is displayed by the positively-sloped curves labeled 1, 2, and 3. At any given wage/rental ratio the capital/labor ratio indicated by the technologies illustrates that the third commodity would be the most capital intensive and the first commodity the most labor intensive. In this two-factor setting, trade allows a country to be somewhat specialized in production; it never needs to produce all three goods (unless it was a very large country in the global community so that to satisfy its consumption it needs to produce at least some quantity of each commodity). Depending on technology, factor prices, and endowment proportions it may produce only a single commodity, or perhaps a pair of commodities. The three rising curves show technological possibilities, whereas the darker portions of each illustrate, for a *given set* of commodity prices, the country's possible production pattern, depending upon its endowment of factors. Thus if it is a very labor-abundant country it would only produce the first commodity, and a relatively low value of the wage/rental ratio would prevail in equilibrium. At slightly higher capital/labor endowment proportions

---

[7] The solution for the change in the wage rate by itself also displays a *magnification* effect, just as the ranking in (8.15) reveals. Details of the structure of the Heckscher–Ohlin model are found in Jones (1965), or Chapter 4 in this book.

[8] This diagram was presented in Jones (1974), reprinted as Chapter 2 in R. Jones, *International Trade: Essays in Theory,*" (North Holland, 1979), and discussed in Edition 2 (and subsequent editions) of the textbook, *World Trade and Payments,* Caves, Frankel and Jones, 2007.

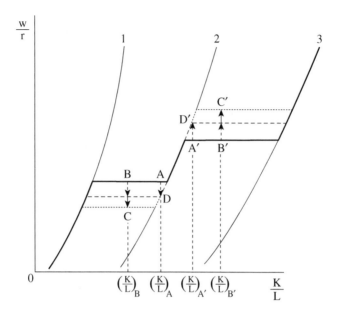

Figure 8.1.   An Increase in p_2

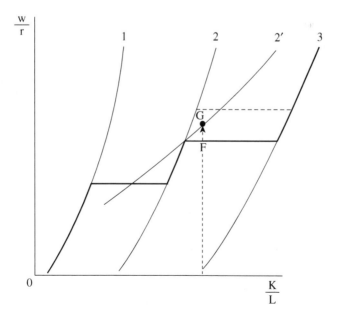

Figure 8.2.   More Flexibility in Production

it could start producing some quantity of the second commodity, which requires more capital-intensive techniques. The dark horizontal line connecting curves 1 and 2 illustrates that actual production of two goods at given commodity prices would determine completely the factor price ratio of the two factors-the common (2×2) Heckscher–Ohlin result. Furthermore, if growth of the overall capital/labor ratio reflects only an increase in capital with constant labor, simultaneous growth in both commodities 1 and 2 *cannot* occur, a variation of the Rybczynski (1955) result. Instead, as the country becomes more capital abundant it increases its production of relatively capital-intensive commodity 2 by releasing resources from production of the first commodity. Eventually it produces only the second commodity, and at this point as it becomes even more capital abundant the wage/rental ratio is driven upwards, until the country is able to compete in the market for the third commodity. Even higher endowments of capital relative to labor eventually result in the country becoming completely specialized in producing only the third commodity, the most capital-intensive of the presumed three commodities.

The country is in Heckscher–Ohlin mode along the two flats, where given commodity prices uniquely determine factor prices. What label should be attached to the darker part of the growth pattern in which the country is completely specialized? It is commonly accepted that a (3×2) model is the lowest dimension for the Specific-Factors model. I suggest that the dark rising curves could be labeled *degenerate* forms of the Specific-Factors model. With only a single commodity being produced, the distinction between being a mobile factor or a specific factor is not evident. This is a (2×1) version of the Specific-Factors model.

In Fig. 8.1, two further sets of "flats" have been introduced. The "dashed" set indicates Heckscher–Ohlin segments when the price of commodity 2 is increased by a finite, but relatively small, amount (For simplicity the prices of the first and third commodities are kept constant throughout). The "dotted" set indicates the Heckscher–Ohlin segments when the price of the second commodity has been increased by a somewhat greater amount than in the "dashed" set Note that an increase in p_2 increases the *range* of endowment proportions that would lead the economy to become specialized in producing the second commodity, precisely because it has gone up in price.

Consider, now, points A and B indicating, for the initial set of prices, two possible endowment levels that lead the country to produce the first and second commodities in a Heckscher–Ohlin (2 × 2) setting. The downward movements to the dashed line illustrate how, in either endowment situation, the increase in p_2 represents, for this country, an increase in the price of the more capital-intensive of commodities 1 and 2. The consequence for the wage rate is a relative decrease–of the same amount whether the country was initially at B or at A. However, when initially at A the economy is more highly engaged in producing the second commodity than it would be if it were at B. This is of no consequence for the effect on factor prices. However, suppose now that instead of the initial price rise for the second commodity leading to this same consequence for factor prices, the increase in the price of capital-intensive commodity 2 would have been larger, say as depicted by point C on the horizontal *dotted* line. The nature of the effect of this larger price rise if initially the endowment point were indicated by point B is once again a deterioration in the wage rate, but now more severely, as indicated by point C. However, if the endowment point initially were at A, the greater increase in p_2 would cause the economy to "shift" in its "model specification" because it is now in a (2 × 1) scenario. There is no further drop in the wage/rental ratio. Indeed, as in the Specific-Factors model the further price rise for the second commodity now *increases* the wage rate (and return to capital) by the *same* relative amount as the increase in p_2. For the economy starting at A in Heckscher–Ohlin fashion, the still higher price rise causes the economy to *change* its production pattern — no longer producing the labor-intensive first commodity. This implies that its further behavior is that of the degenerative form of the Specific-Factors model.

How does this argument about the importance of having the price change be for the commodity that is initially relatively more important in the production of national income perhaps become different if the economy originally produced commodities 2 and 3? A rise in p_2 now represents an *increase* in the price of the more labor-intensive commodity (since it produces the third commodity instead of the first). Repeat the earlier process by considering initial points A′ and B′ (on the dark horizontal section where the second and third commodities are produced). The relatively small increase in p_2 now leads to the dashed level shown by point D′. Whether the economy is originally at A′, with a relatively more concentrated production of the second commodity, or at point B′, the magnified increase in the wage rate (or wage/rental ratio) is the same. However, a larger increase in p_2 to the *dotted* horizontal segment would lead to an even larger magnified effect if originally the economy were at B', but not if the original point were at A'. In the latter case, the change in the factor price *ratio* stays at D', although the wage rate would increase by the same (instead of magnified) relative amount as the increase in p_2. In either of these cases (whether originally producing the first and second commodity or the second and third) a finite increase in the relative price of the commodity relatively more important in production may differ from that of an increase in the relative price of the other commodity in its effect on the wage rate if the price rise is sufficiently large. In that sense the Heckscher–Ohlin behavior for finite price changes becomes more like that found in the Specific-Factors model even for cases of infinitely small changes in which the calculus is applied.

Does the feature of technological differences between commodities that refer to the *flexibility* or degree of factor substitutability that is important in Specific-Factors model become important if originally the model is that of Heckscher–Ohlin? Not for infinitesimal changes in commodity prices. But it may become important if the shock to the economy is sufficiently finite in size. In order not to clutter Fig. 8.1, consider Fig. 8.2. Suppose, now, that instead of the technology for producing the second commodity being given by the original upward sloping curve 2, it is shown by the more flexible technology illustrated by curve $2'$, in which labor and capital have a higher degree of flexibility than shown by curve 2. Furthermore, suppose that initial production is at point F, with the economy producing the second and third commodity and suppose that an increase in p_2 serves to raise the horizontal section upwards to the dashed level. If the initial point of production is shown by F, the price increase would increase the wage/rental ratio to point G, at which point the country becomes specialized in production of the labor-intensive second commodity. After the country becomes specialized the wage and rental then rise in the same proportion as the price increase, not to the level indicated by the dashed flat. As a consequence, with the more flexible technology $2'$ the price rise does ensure an increase for the wage rate, but not as much as the magnified increase that would be the result if (as with the less flexible technology shown by curve 2) the economy were to continue to produce both commodities two and three.

In the Specific-Factors model the effect of a commodity price increase was shown by the product of the three features shown in Eq. (8.12): the

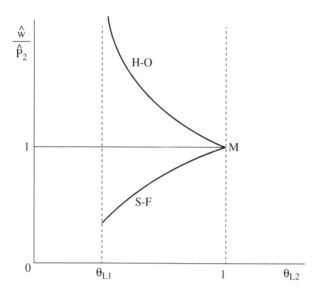

Figure 8.3.   Wage Rate Changes in the Two Models

relative importance in the national income of the commodity (now commodity 2 instead of the first commodity) that rises in price, and the two features of technology, the relative flexibility of technology for the good whose price has been raised and the ranking of the labor-intensity of the two commodities. In the Heckscher–Ohlin scenario only the last feature matters for infinitesimal changes in price. However, Figs. 8.1 and 8.2 illustrate that the two other features become important once the country becomes specialized in what I have called a *degenerate form* of the Specific-Factors model. But more can be said about the importance of the *factor-intensity ranking* which appears in both models even for infinitesimal changes. This comparison is illustrated in Fig. 8.3.

The vertical axis shows the relative change in the wage rate as a ratio of the relative change in p_2 as it is increased while p_1 is kept constant. The horizontal axis shows the labor share in the second industry, and I assume that the second industry is labor intensive, i.e., restricting the values of θ_{L2} to lie between the presumed constant value of θ_{L1} and unity. Consider, first, the Heckscher–Ohlin model, as shown by the curve H–O in which the price rise in the labor-intensive commodity, 2, has a *magnified effect* on the wage rate. The impact on the wage rate is almost infinitely large for values close to the fixed value of labor's share in the first sector, but diminishes and reaches a value of unity when θ_{L2} is unity. By contrast consider the curve for the Specific-Factors model, once again assuming a fixed value for labor's share in the first industry. Recall Eq. (8.12), but assume it is the fraction for the *second* industry. The term "i_2" would be unity at the point where the two labor shares are equal, but would increase as the second industry becomes more labor-intensive relative to the first. (I assume the other two terms in (8.12) remain constant and the product of the three terms of course is less than unity). When θ_{L2} reaches its maximum value of unity, only labor is used to produce the second commodity, and the price increase must therefore cause the wage rate to rise by the same relative amount. One important conclusion: Yes, the ranking of industries by factor-intensity is important both in the Heckscher–Ohlin model and in the Specific-Factors model. However, these two models differ in two respects: (i) a price increase for the labor-intensive sector raises the wage rate by a *magnified* amount in the Heckscher–Ohlin model but by a *smaller relative* amount in the Specific-Factors model, and (ii) in the Specific-Factors model the wage rate increase becomes *larger* the greater the labor-intensity advantage in the second sector while it becomes *smaller* in the Heckscher–Ohlin model as the gap between labor intensities gets larger. The reasoning in the Specific-Factors model is clear: A commodity price increase in either sector increases the wage rate, but by a relatively greater extent if the price increase is for the commodity that is more intensive in its use of labor. The reasoning in the Heckscher–Ohlin model is rather different. A price rise only in the more labor-intensive sector must be matched by an increase in the unit costs of producing the labor-intensive commodity relative to the capital-intensive commodity. If the degree to which these two intensity magnitudes differ is small, the increase in the wage rate that brings about an equality of price with unit costs must be large. On the other hand, if labor shares differ a lot, less of an increase in the wage rate is required to match the given commodity price change. In any case, although in both models the role of factor intensity is important, its influence on changes in the wage rate is *minimized* in the Heckscher–Ohlin model when factor intensity difference is maximized, although in the Specific-Factors model it is *maximized* at the same point, marked *M* in Fig. 8.3.

The reason I choose this letter is that at M there is one sector (sector 2) where in a two-sector model one sector uses capital and labor while the second sector uses only labor. In 1939, a chapter by Marion Crawford appeared in the *Quarterly Journal of Economics*, a chapter that discussed the Brigden Report on protection in Australia, with a model with the properties at point *M* of Fig. 8.3: One sector uses two factors while the other only uses labor. Suppose, instead, that the sector using only labor should then use another factor as well. Is that the same as the nonlabor factor used in the two-input sector? If so, the scenario becomes that of Heckscher–Ohlin, or more pointedly that of Stolper and Samuelson (1941). Alternatively, if instead the new factor introduced is different from the nonlabor factor used in the second sector (say land instead of capital) the scenario is that of the Specific-Factors model. As Samuelson points out, in his tribute to Stolper in the 1994 volume edited by Deardorff & Stern, *The Stolper-Samuelson Theorem: A Golden Jubilee*, Marion Crawford soon became Marion Samuelson and her paper can be viewed as a "fountain-head" for these two models.[9]

8.4 Technical Progress and Factor-Saving Bias

One of the often repeated remarks made about comparative static results in the Heckscher–Ohlin (2×2) model is concerned with the effect of *technical progress* on factor prices when commodity prices are given. Using calculus techniques, and assuming that progress is limited to the second commodity (assumed to be more capital-intensive than is the first commodity, with both the second and first commodities produced), the answer is that the wage rate will fall, both in nominal and real terms. Indeed the extent of the fall is the same as if, instead of technical progress, the price of the second commodity should rise. Thus the effect on factor prices is similar

---

[9]It is not so surprising that moving to higher dimensions for factors and commodities in general makes the analysis of the relationship between Specific Factors and Heckscher–Ohlin properties less precise. However, there is a connection between the two that is related to the Stolper–Samuelson Theorem. Consider the n-commodity, $(n + 1)$ Specific-Factor version, and suppose the single mobile factor, usually taken to be labor, is, instead, *produced* by all (or most of) the otherwise specific factors. Such a change alters the Specific-Factor model into an $(n \times n)$ version of the Heckscher–Ohlin model. As shown by Jones and Marjit (1985), such a difference leads to the *Strong-form* of the Stolper and Samuelson (1941) article. By this is meant that each commodity is associated with a unique productive factor such that an increase in the price of such a commodity (other prices constant) causes a *magnified* increase in the rate of return to the associated factor as well as a fall in rates of return to *all* other factors. That is a stronger version of the Stolper–Samuelson result than found in most Heckscher–Ohlin models.

to that illustrated in Fig. 8.1, where the increase in p_2 is illustrated by the extension of the range along which production of the second commodity is concentrated, at both ends, to the stretch DD'. However, if there is technical progress in the second commodity and it is produced, not only would the output of the second commodity be increased for any given set of inputs, but the *manner* in which production takes place might also be affected. That is, technical progress might have a *bias*, for example, one that uses labor more intensively, in the sense of lowering the capital/labor ratio used at any given wage/rental ratio. In such a case, progress would be associated with a *leftward shift* in the position of the positively sloped curve 2 in Fig. 8.1. The case in which no such shift, in either direction, takes place is known as one of *Hicksian neutrality*. If calculus techniques are appropriate, of course, no such changes (either showing any bias or indeed showing shifts in the flats along which both commodities 1 and 2 are produced) would be visible to the naked eye. But the horizontal shift of the 2-locus is referred to as a *second-order small* compared with the shifts in the flats since for any (differential) change in techniques at initial factor prices the distributive share average of any such changes is zero (or second order) because techniques used in the initial equilibrium *minimize* average costs.[10]

Maintaining the scenario of the Heckscher–Ohlin model in which calculus methods are invoked in order to ascertain the effect of technical progress on wage rates, the conclusion can be reached that the effect of technical progress on factor prices depends *only* upon the (Hicksian) *extent* of progress and not at all on the *bias*, whether of the labor-saving variety or of the capital-saving variety. Such a conclusion typically is not well received by labor economists who have not studied international trade theory. It is as if, with commodity prices taken as given, changes in the supply of labor to the economy would not affect the wage rate. That, however, *is* the conclusion of changes in the Heckscher–Ohlin setting where, if both commodities are produced and prices are given, changes in the supply of either factor get absorbed *only* at the *extensive* margin, i.e., by a change in the relative amounts produced of the labor-intensive commodity and the capital-intensive commodity. This leaves the labor economists with the view that *bias* in technological change cannot by itself affect the

---

[10]That is, the first derivative of the cost curve is zero.

outcome for wages and rents. However, suppose that technology changes by a *finite* amount. Could *bias* then have any role to play in the change in factor prices? Indeed, might it be the case that bias could be sufficiently capital-saving that the wage rate *increases* even if progress takes place only in the capital-intensive sector? Perhaps surprisingly, the answer to both of the queries is a positive *yes*. Labor economists are correct in thinking that bias has an important effect on the determination of wage rates if technical progress is finite. As well, earlier in this chapter, the suggestion was made that the relative importance in national production of the commodity that increases in price (or, here, has an improvement in technology) does indeed affect the resulting outcome of factor price changes if the change is finite.

Figure 8.4 illustrates the various possibilities.[11] The economy initially produces the first and second commodities, with several possible initial production points shown by A, A', A'', or A'''. There is technical progress only in the second commodity, and it is biased such that the technology curve for the second industry shifts to the left. That is, if after progress

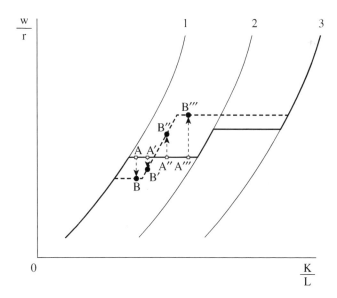

Figure 8.4.   Biased Technological Progress

---

[11] This diagram was used in Jones (2008).

the economy is specialized in producing the second commodity the new technology is capital-saving in the sense that at any factor price ratio the ratio of inputs of capital to labor will be diminished. The possibilities are:

(i) The economy is at **A**, producing very little of the second commodity. After technical progress favoring the capital-intensive sector, the wage rate is driven down (to **B**), as is typically the case found in the trade literature for small changes.

(ii) The economy is at **A′**: The wage rate once again falls (to **B′**), not by as much as shown by **B**. The economy leaves its Heckscher–Ohlin (2 × 2) situation and becomes completely specialized in the second commodity, the commodity that has experienced technological progress.

(iii) The economy is at **A″**: The effect of the bias becomes even more important as now the wage/rental ratio actually *increases*, (to **B″**).

(iv) The economy is at **A″**: Before technical progress the economy is in Heckscher–Ohlin mode, producing commodities 1 and 2, but especially the second commodity, in which there is technical progress. After technical progress the improvement in the wage rate becomes so great that the economy once again is in Heckscher–Ohlin mode but with the most capital-intensive commodity 3 replacing the most labor-intensive commodity 1 as the commodity produced along with the second commodity (at **B‴**).

This wide range of possibilities allows room both for the typical "trade" position that if progress takes place in (the initial) capital-intensive sector the wage rate must fall (despite the nature of the capital-saving bias in technical progress), and as well for the "labor" position that bias matters a lot, i.e., that if less capital is required per unit production, the economy reacts as if it had more capital, and ends up with a magnified increase in the wage rate and with new production of the even-more capital-intensive third commodity.

8.5   Concluding Remarks

Both the Heckscher–Ohlin simple (2 × 2) model and the (3 × 2) version of the Specific-Factors model have been extensively used in the competitive theory of international trade. They reveal distinctly different outcomes to the question of the effect of commodity price changes on factor prices when this issue is examined for the "small" changes that characterize the use of calculus. In the Specific-Factors model the two aspects of the technological discrepancy between commodities as well as the relative importance of the commodity (in production) whose relative price has been raised have important roles to play in the resulting change in wages and rents. By contrast, in the Heckscher–Ohlin model in which two factors, say capital and labor, produce two distinct commodities, an increase in the relative price of the more labor intensive commodity must increase the real wage rate *regardless* of differences in the flexibility of technology between sectors or of the importance in the output mix of the labor intensive commodity which has risen in price. This result follows because factor prices depend *only* upon commodity prices if the number of produced commodities equals the number of productive factors. However, if the changes in commodity prices are *finite* in size, the pattern of production might change. In particular, for finite changes in prices the economy may become completely specialized in producing a single commodity (the one whose relative price has increased). If so, all three characteristics that have a role to play in the Specific-Factors model emerge as important in the outcome of price changes for factor rewards. The (2×2) Heckscher–Ohlin model melds into the (2×1) model of complete specialization, a model which serves as a degenerate type of Specific-Factors model.

In my view, issues like the ones that are discussed in this chapter have an important role to play in the study of growth and development for economies that are *open* to world trade. Once trade is allowed, a growing or developing country need not produce all the commodities that it consumes. In a competitive setting for open economies, growth may be accompanied by the demise of certain industries and the new development of others. This suggests that growth theory for open economies needs to be allowed to portray a *blending* of models such as the Heckscher–Ohlin model and the Specific-Factors model, blends that may occur naturally and are easily understood when finite changes are considered.

References

Caves, R., Frankel, J., and Jones, R. (2007). *World Trade and Payments* (10th edn.). Boston, MA: Addison Wesley.

Crawford, M. (1939). The Australian Case for Protection Re-examined. *Quarterly Journal of Economics*, 54(1), 143–151.

Deardorff, A. and Stern, R. (Eds.). (1994). *The Stolper-Samuelson Theorem: A Golden Jubilee*. Ann Arbor, MI: University of Michigan Press.

Jones, R.W. (1965). The Structure of Simple General Equilibrium Models. *Journal of Political Economy*, 73, 557–572.

Jones, R.W. (1971). A Three-factor Model in Theory, Trade and History. In: Bhagwati, Jones, Mundell, & Vanek (eds.), *Trade, Balance of Payments and Growth*. Amsterdam: North-Holland.

Jones, R.W. (1974). The Small Country in a Many-commodity World. *Australian Economic Papers*, 13, 225–236.

Jones, R.W. (1975). Income Distribution and Effective Protection in a Multi-commodity Trade Model. *Journal of Economic Theory*, 11, 1–15.

Jones, R.W. (1979). *International Trade: Essays in Theory*. Amsterdam: North-Holland.

Jones, R.W. (2008). Key International Trade Theorems and Large Shocks. *International Review of Economics and Finance*, 17, 103–112.

Jones, R.W. and Marjit, S. (1985). A simple production model with Stolper-Samuelson properties. *International Economic Review*, 19, 565–567.

Jones, R.W. and Marjit, S. (1992). International Trade and Endogenous Production Structures. In: W. Neuefeind, and R. Riezman (Eds.), *Economic Theory and International Trade: Essays in Memoriam J. Trout Rader* (pp. 173–196) Berlin: Springer-Verlag.

Mayer, W. (1974). Short-run and Long-run Equilibrium for a Small Open Economy. *Journal of Political Economy*, 82, 955–967.

Neary, J.P. (1978). Short-run Capital Specificity and the Pure Theory of International Trade. *The Economic Journal*, 88, 488–510.

Rybczynski, T.M. (1955). Factor Endowments and Relative Commodity Prices. *Economica*, 22, 336–341.

Samuelson, P.A. (1971). Ohlin Was Right. *The Swedish Journal of Economics*, 73, 365–384.

Sanyal, K. and Jones, R.W. (1982). The Theory of Trade in Middle Products. *American Economic Review*, 72, 16–31.

Stolper, W. and Samuelson, P.A. (1941). Protection and Real Wages. *Review of Economic Studies*, 9, 58–73.

CHAPTER 9

Bubble Diagrams in Trade Theory*

Ronald W. Jones

Abstract

"Bubble" diagrams are quite useful in revealing some of the properties found in the competitive models of international trade. These diagrams use circles (bubbles) to indicate commodity outputs and connecting lines to indicate factor inputs. Models such as the 2×2 and $n \times n$ Heckscher–Ohlin models as well as the 3×2 (and extensions) Specific-Factors model are discussed. For example, a model with some factor mobility between countries (say capital into a foreign enclave) is discussed for both model types. As well, close analogies are made to issues in labor economics in which both skilled and unskilled labor are used as inputs.

9.1   Introduction

The word "diagrams" was inserted into the title because otherwise the reader might be expecting a trade theorist to expound wisdom on an economy's actions leading to (or from) macroeconomic "bubbles." Instead, my objective in this chapter is to discuss the range of uses possible in competitive international trade theory for diagrams depicting the myriad of relationships among commodity outputs and factor inputs. A glance at the diagrams should make it clear that the bubble symbol is used to represent commodity outputs and connecting lines represent factor inputs. Bubble diagrams were used fairly frequently in my Ohlin lectures in 1997 (published in 2000) focused on ways of modelling international capital movements in real trade theory. These diagrams are also useful in issues concerning economic development (e.g., Jones and Marjit, 2003). Although bubble diagrams were not used in the Jones and Dei (1983) paper, the

---

*Originally published in *Pacific Economic Review*, 18(5), (2013), pp. 561–573.

model developed there provided the inspiration to remodel that and other material (discussed below) into the bubble diagram format.

9.2   The Classical Building Blocks: Simple and General Forms

The pair of simple models that highlights the role of endowment differences in competitive models of international trade are the Heckscher–Ohlin 2×2 model (two factors, usually denoted by labor and capital, and two commodities) and the 3×2 Specific-Factors model (e.g., Jones, 1971; Samuelson, 1971; Chakraborty, 2009) with one factor mobile between sectors (usually taken to be labor) and the other pair of factors specifically used only in a single sector. Figure 9.1 illustrates how a bubble diagram displays the important linkages between produced commodities and required factor inputs. The striking difference between these two models is that despite the greater number of factors found in the Specific-Factors model (three instead of two), only a single factor (here labor, L) is mobile between sectors, whereas in the standard 2×2 Heckscher–Ohlin model there are two productive inputs that are mobile between sectors.

For an economy engaged in trade with other countries but not important enough to be able to influence world prices, the differences between these two models with respect to how changes in factor endowments are assimilated, on the one hand, or how the economy adjusts to a change in commodity prices in world markets, on the other hand, can

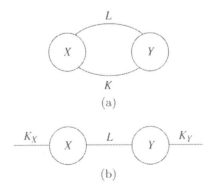

Figure 9.1.   The Basic Classical Building Blocks: (a) (2×2) Hecksher–Ohlin and (b) (3×2) Specific Factors

be summarized as follows. In the 3×2 Specific-Factors model an increase in the endowment of any factor (at given prices) is absorbed by adjustments made both in the intensity with which factors are used in any industry (the *intensive* margin) and in the composition of commodity outputs (the *extensive* margin). Thus, an increase in the endowment of X-type capital would lower its return and cause more capital intensive means of production to be used in the X-sector. This change in techniques would be prompted by a reduction in r_x (the return to X-type capital) and an increase in w (the wage rate). With labor mobile between sectors, the wage rate increase is equilibrated between sectors and, with commodity prices assumed given, the return to capital in the Y-sector (r_y) is driven down. As a consequence, more capital-intensive techniques are also used in the Y-sector in response to its loss of labor. In summary, the return to capital in both sectors falls and the wage rate (in both sectors) increases.[1] By contrast, an increase in the endowment of labor would, at constant prices, lower the wage rate and, thus, benefit capital in both sectors. Techniques in both sectors would become more labor-intensive. As for alterations at the *extensive* margin, an increase in the endowment of X-type capital, which also serves to attract labor away from its use in the Y-sector, unambiguously serves to increase output of commodity X and to reduce output in the Y-sector.

As for the other kind of shock considered here, say an increase in the world price of commodity X, the big winner is the return to X-type capital, while the big loser is the return to Y-type capital. Labor, used in both sectors, finds its return rising, but not by as much, relatively, as the price of commodity X.

The behavior in response to an increase in the endowment of capital in the Heckscher–Ohlin 2×2 case is strikingly different and reveals why early results in this model (especially the factor-price equalization theorem [Samuelson, 1948, 1949]), proved so surprising. Endowment changes (with given commodity prices and the economy actively producing both commodities) are absorbed *only* by changes in the *extensive* margin. Indeed,

---

[1] Indeed, r_Y may fall by more than the return to X-type capital even though the supply of Y-type capital has not increased. This perhaps surprising possibility ensues if the Y-sector is more labor-intensive (in the sense of a higher labor distributive share), forcing a greater fall in r_Y than r_x to compensate for the increase in the wage rate at constant commodity prices.

local factor prices are completely determined by world commodity prices, so that factor-intensity changes *cannot* be brought about. For two countries differing in factor endowments but facing the same world prices for the pair of commodities they produce, and sharing the same basic technologies, factor prices will be equalized even though there are no international markets (assumed) for factors of production. As for the reaction to an increase in the price of commodity X, both the wage rate change and that of the return to capital are relatively *magnified* compared with the commodity price changes (p_x increasing and p_Y remaining constant). This is because in each sector the change in unit costs must be matched in the competitive market place by the relative change in the commodity price. Hence, in the X-sector at least one factor return must increase. In the Y-sector at least one factor price must fall. The winner will be the wage rate and the loser the return to capital if (and only if) the X-sector is relatively labor-intensive.

A question that has long been analysed by trade theorists is whether these two basic models can be generalized to higher dimensions. The general Heckscher–Ohlin model has n commodities and n productive factors, all of which are mobile among all sectors. By contrast, the Specific-Factors model has each of n sectors using an input that is specific to that sector whereas all sectors use a single mobile factor (usually assumed to be labor). The answer to this query is drastically different in the two cases. The bubble diagrams for these two generalizations are illustrated in Fig. 9.2. Comparative static results for endowment changes or commodity price changes for the $n \times n$ Heckscher–Ohlin model without further detailed assumptions are impossible to obtain. As in the 2 × 2 version, factor intensity comparisons between sectors are the only technological characteristic that matter.[2] However, strong and explicit ordering of these intensities is necessary to obtain any specific results.[3]

---

[2] The other characteristic of technology is the degree of flexibility in intensities in response to any change in factor prices, as captured by elasticities of substitution or elasticities of demand curves for labor. Because factor prices are completely determined by commodity prices if n commodities are actually produced (in this $n \times n$ case), flexibility of technology issues are not relevant.

[3] The papers by John Chipman (1969) and Murray Kemp and Leon Wegge (1969) attest to the difficulties of obtaining strong results even in the 3 × 3 or 4 × 4 cases.

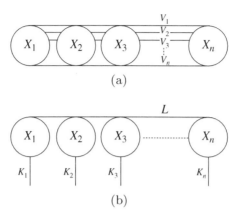

Figure 9.2. Generalized (a) ($n \times n$) Heckscher–Ohlin and (b) $\{(n+1) \times n\}$ Specific Factor Models

Figure 9.2b illustrates the specific factor generalization to the $(n+1) \times n$ case. Here the results are almost as easy to obtain as in the 3×2 case: The increase in the endowment of any specific factor will, if commodity prices are given, lower the return to that specific factor, serving to increase the wage rate for mobile labor which, in turn, squeezes the return to all other specific factors. One output increases, and all others fall. As for a change in the price of commodity X_i, the return to its specific factor will increase by relatively more than the commodity price and the wage rate increases by relatively less than the commodity price. As a consequence of this wage increase, capital used in any other sector suffers losses and outputs in these sectors all are reduced as labor is released to the ith sector.

One of the characteristics of this $(n + 1) \times n$ generalization of the Specific-Factors model is that the production process for any and all commodities requires the employment of exactly two inputs. In what follows I shall maintain this assumption for mixtures of Specific-Factor and Heckscher–Ohlin models. There may be more than two commodities producible (and there may be more than two factors of production), but throughout I shall assume that each commodity produced uses only two factors. An example of this is the form of the Heckscher–Ohlin model illustrated in Fig. 9.3. There are only two productive inputs, labor (L) and capital (K), but a total of n commodities are technologically producible. If the economy were in autarky, dependent upon its own production base for any commodity consumed at home, commodity prices would adjust so that all goods are produced. Of more interest, suppose the economy is in a competitive free-trade equilibrium with the rest of the world. Trade allows a great degree of concentration in production, and if world prices are given and independent of what the autarky prices would be in this country that would allow all goods to be produced, the economy needs, at most, to produce only two commodities (the same number as the factor count), and perhaps could be completely specialized to a single best commodity at world prices (such as in the Ricardian model of trade). Assume, in Fig. 9.3, that the numbering of commodities is in sequence of their capital–labor ratios, with X_1 being the most labor-intensive and X_n the most capital-intensive. As a consequence, if a very labor-abundant country is growing over time (in the sense of becoming more capital abundant), it goes from producing just the first commodity to producing both the first and the second until becoming specialized in the second commodity. As growth continues, such a pattern is repeated: Moving from being specialized in one commodity to adding some production of the next, followed by becoming completely specialized in that commodity before devoting some resources into starting production of the next in line as well. In ranges in which only a single commodity is produced, an increase in the endowment of capital (relative to labor) would be associated with an increase in the wage–rental ratio. In contrast, growth of capital–labor endowments when a pair of commodities is produced would have no effect on factor prices if commodity prices were given (the 2×2 Heckscher–Ohlin case). This general growth pattern is the version of the Heckscher–Ohlin model that over the years I have found to be of greater interest to students. After all, it raises the question of *which* commodities a country produces and trades and reveals the ever-churning patterns of production as a country's stock of capital per unit of labor grows.[4]

Before moving on to less general situations, there is a model associated with the names of Fred Gruen and Max Corden (1970) that is a special case

---

[4]If having only two factors seems too severe a limitation, a variation I introduced (Jones, 2007a) allows for sector-specific capital to encourage a greater pattern of production at any point in time. Let there be a sector that produces a capital good that becomes specific to the sector that, at that time, would yield the highest return to capital. That is, at any time there may be more than two commodities produced, where some of them have a lower rate of return to specific capital than that period's current best sector. If a sector's specific capital yields too low a return, over time the sector vanishes.

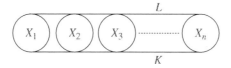

Figure 9.3. The (2 × *n*) Heckscher–Ohlin Model

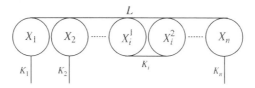

Figure 9.4. The Extended Gruen–Corden Model

of a three commodity and three factor model, but one that can easily be generalized to higher dimensions. With their country (Australia) in mind, suppose in the agricultural sector there are two commodities produced, grain and wool, and they require inputs of labor and land. As well, there is a manufacturing sector producing only a single commodity, textiles, which employs labor and capital. (They used such a model to illustrate how a tariff placed on textiles might worsen the country's terms of trade.) Figure 9.4 illustrates how their model can be expanded to higher dimensions (Jones and Marjit, 1992). As background, assume that initially (before trade) this economy is composed of *n* sectors, each employing a type of capital specific to that sector's collection of a number of different industries. The opening up of this economy to the world market results in a great deal of concentration of production. Indeed, in most sectors there will be only one industry that survives, the industry that would earn the highest rate of return to that sector's capital at world commodity prices. If this were the case in all sectors, the resulting economy would be of the generalized specific factors type, with (n + 1) factors (mobile labor plus *n* types of capital) and *n* commodities. However, as in the Gruen and Corden case, there may exist a single sector in which two industries survive despite the greater extent of competition found in the world market place. We call such a sector a *Nugget*, and in Fig. 9.4 this is sector *i*, in which two industries, X_i^1 and X_i^2 operate, leading to a Heckscher–Ohlin type of model with (n + 1) factors and the same number of industries. In Jones and Marjit (1992), we discuss how finite endowment or commodity price shocks can lead to changes in the composition of industries in each sector as well as result in endogenous changes in the type of model (specific factor *vs* Heckscher–Ohlin).

9.3 The 4 × 3 Model: Two Interpretations

In the Introduction I referred to the Jones and Dei paper (1983), in which we presented both a graphical and an algebraic analysis of real international capital flows from a country (call it Home) that is completely specialized to a single commodity (call it X), with a given endowment of sector-specific capital, K_X, and labor, L. All labor stays at Home, but some of Home's capital stock gets sent to an *enclave* of another country (Foreign) that supplies labor to work with capital. Foreign produces a different commodity, Y^*, and has a fixed amount of sector-specific capital, K_Y^*. This situation leads to a useful type of bubble diagram that is also relevant to a completely different setting in which there is no concern with international capital mobility. Figure 9.5 illustrates both of these scenarios.

Figure 9.5a allows focus on the following question: Suppose world demand for commodity X increases, leading to a rise in its price, with p_Y remaining constant. Does more X-type capital flow from Home towards the enclave abroad, or is the capital flow back towards Home instead? The answer is clear, and can be understood by asking what would happen to the rate of return to X-type capital in both locations if no further changes in the location of such capital were allowed? At Home the rise in p_X would cause both the Home wage rate and return to capital to rise by the same relative amount as the commodity price. The situation would be similar in the

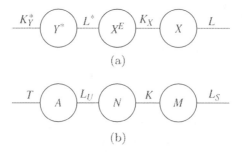

Figure 9.5.   The (4 × 3) (a) Model: International Capital Flow and (b) Heterogeneous Labor

enclave if there were also a freeze on labor mobility. However, the wage rate in the enclave is driven up by the rise in p_x, and this induces a greater inflow of Foreign labor into the enclave, inducing a predictable further increase in the rate of return to X-type capital there. Consequently, once capital becomes mobile again there is a flow from Home to the enclave until rates of return equalize between the two sources. The underlying rationale for this outward flow of capital from Home is that Foreign supplies a *hinterland* from which labor can flow to the enclave; Home has no such hinterland. (Such an asymmetry is corrected in the 5×4 model discussed in the next section.)

What can be said about the change in wage rates at Home and in Foreign (or in the enclave)? Clearly the Foreign wage rate, w^*, is driven up. Could it increase by more, relatively, than Home's wage rate, w? Perhaps surprisingly the answer is in the affirmative, and the criterion for such a possibility (i.e., for $\hat{w}^*$ to exceed $\hat{w}$) is easy to understand. In each locale, the common return to capital has risen by a greater relative amount than has the price of X, implying that the wage rate increase must be relatively smaller than $\hat{p}_x$. Both at Home and in Foreign the distributive share-weighted average of capital's relative rate increase and the relative change in return to labor must be equal to $\hat{p}_x$ (by the competitive profit equations of change). Therefore, if Home's production of X is more capital intensive than that in the enclave (with intensity measured by a comparison of distributive shares), Foreign's wage rate must increase relative to Home's. Indeed, although the algebraic criterion is more complicated, Home's wage rate could even fall, with the positive effect of the commodity price rise more than outweighed by the loss in the local supply of X-type capital.[5]

A different scenario is provided by Fig. 9.5b. Suppose that agriculture (A) uses two productive factors, land, T, and unskilled labor, L_U. Unskilled labor has an alternative employment possibility, in the sector producing a low-technology manufactured commodity, N, with the aid of capital, K. Capital is also used, along with skilled labor, L_S, to produce a more high-technology manufactured commodity, M. Note that the two scenarios in Fig. 9.5 have something in common: One productive activity (enclave production of X in Fig. 9.5a and low-technology manufacturing in Fig. 9.5b)

---

[5] Algebraic details can be found in Jones and Marjit (2003).

shares the Heckscher–Ohlin property wherein a commodity is produced with the use of two mobile factors. Each scenario also has a pair of activities that use one mobile factor and one specific factor: Y^* in Foreign and X in Home in Fig. 9.5a and, in Fig. 9.5b, agriculture and high-technology manufacturing. Thus, these 4×3 models share attributes of both of the basic models illustrated in Fig. 9.1.[6]

In the context of a developing country (such as India) suppose that agricultural production, which previously had been hampered by price controls, has these controls lifted with an ensuing increase in the price of A (closer to the world market value), with assumed unchanged price for either manufacturing commodity. Ask, first, what effect this would have on income distribution if the allocation of capital between the two manufacturing sectors is frozen. This would make the A and N sectors part of a specific factors 3×2 model, leading to a rise in the return to land relatively higher than the increase in p_A, a relatively smaller increase in the wage rate for unskilled labor, and an actual reduction in the return to capital. Once capital mobility is allowed between manufacturing sectors, some capital leaves low-technology manufacturing (N) for high-technology manufacturing (M), which mitigates (to some extent) but not erases the fall in capital's return. The wage rate for skilled labor is thus driven up, and a question analogous to that asked previously for Fig. 9.5a can be put forward: Could skilled labor, used only in a sector (M) that has enjoyed no price increase, experience a relatively higher wage increase than unskilled labor partly employed in a sector (A) that has seen its price increase? The answer is in the affirmative, and the emphasis on a comparison of distributive factor shares is similar in the two cases: The unskilled wage rate increases by relatively less than the skilled wage rate if (and only if) the high-technology manufacturing activity (M) is capital intensive relative to the low-technology (N) sector, with intensity rankings given by a comparison of distributive capital shares.[7]

---

[6]This same feature will be found in the next section's 5×4 model. Thus, neither the 4×3 model nor the 5×4 model is strictly a smaller-dimensional example of the general Specific-Factors model shown in Fig. 9.2b. In Jones and Marjit (2003) these scenarios are called "linear neighborhood models."

[7]The skilled wage rate must rise relatively more than the unskilled rate if skilled labor is the relatively unimportant input in producing M compared with unskilled labor in producing N: an example of "the importance of being unimportant" (Jones, 2007b).

9.4 The 5 × 4 Model: Two Interpretations

In the higher dimensional scenario in this section, I switch from a linear sequence of bubbles and lines to a more circular one. In Fig. 9.6, I return to the case examined in Fig. 9.5a in which Home invested some capital in an enclave also serviced by Foreign's labor force but now more symmetry is introduced by letting Home, as well as Foreign, have a hinterland from which resources could be drawn to accompany any inflow of internationally mobile capital. More specifically, in Fig. 9.6 Home labor can be used to produce Y as well as X, with the aid of sector-specific K_Y. I assume that Home and Foreign X-sectors, on the one hand, and Y-sectors, on the other, may not produce identical commodities (they may be *varieties* of the same commodity) so that neither country is driven out of production by world competition. However, both Home's X-sector and Foreign's X^*-sector use a homogeneous type of internationally mobile capital.

As in the smaller dimensional case, I focus on the scenario in which world demand shifts away from Y-type goods to X-type goods, raising (uniformly) the price of X-type goods with a constant price maintained for Y-type goods. Once again the question concerns the reallocation of internationally mobile X-capital between countries, and the analysis can be broken down into two steps. First, ask what would happen to the rate of return to X-type capital in each country if capital's location were initially frozen. Basically, that setting converts Fig. 9.6 into a pair of basic 3 × 2

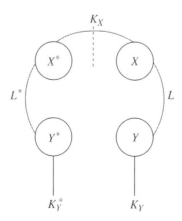

Figure 9.6. The (5 × 4) Model: International Capital Mobility

Specific Factor models, one for each country, in which the return to X-type capital increases by a greater relative amount than the price rise, the wage rate increases but by a smaller relative amount than the price rise, and the return to Y-type capital is driven down. Is there any *presumption* that the rate of return to capital will increase by a greater amount in Foreign, inducing, at the next step of the analysis, an increased flow of X-type capital from Home to Foreign? Now there emerges the typical economist's response: It all depends.

A formal algebraic analysis of this question is possible, but not pursued here. Instead, the present study focuses on a simpler question: What happens to the wage rate in each country? The standard specific factor's answer to this query (Caves, Frankel, and Jones, 2007) is that the relative wage rate increase, say $\hat{w}$ for Home, is a fraction of $\hat{p}_x$, where this fraction is the product of three terms: θ_X, the share of GNP represented by Home's production of X; and two features of Home's technology, i_x, the relative labor intensity in the X-sector, and s_X, a measure of the relative substitution possibilities in producing X.[8] To focus on the importance of the hinterland, assume that at Home the technology for producing X is quite similar, in labor intensity and flexibility of technology, to that for producing Y. If so, the relative wage gain will be greater the more important is production of X in the national income, as measured by θ_X. Making similar assumptions in Foreign about technology in the two sectors, Foreign's wage change (before international movements of capital) will be shown by θ_X^* times $\hat{p}_x$. In each country the extent of the wage increase helps to determine the extent of the increase in capital's rate of return. Thus, if Foreign has a larger hinterland than does Home (in the sense of θ_X^* being smaller than θ_X), there is a presumption that its labor market is less "heated up" by the increase in p_x than is Home's (i.e., $\hat{w}^* < \hat{w}$) and, thus, the increase in the return to X-type capital (which in relative terms must in any case increase by more than $\hat{p}_x$) is presumptively larger than in Home. That is, once capital is freed up, it will tend to move from Home to Foreign.[9]

---

[8]More explicitly, i_x is the ratio of labor's share in producing X to the economy's overall share of labor's income, while s_x is the ratio of the elasticity of the marginal product of labor schedule for X to the elasticity of the economy's overall demand for labor.

[9]The more detailed treatment in Jones (1989, 2000) suggests as well that with such a presumption of the direction of international capital flows as the price of X increases, it

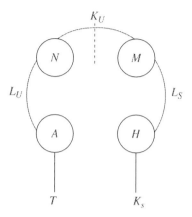

Figure 9.7. The (5 × 4) Model: Heterogeneous Labor and Capital

Figure 9.7 shifts attention to a 5 × 4 model for development. A new productive activity is introduced, call it high-technology R&D, (labelled H), which requires, as well, an input of more modern capital (called K_S to match the label for skilled labor, L_S). Jones and Marjit (2003) pursue several issues related to this and the associated smaller dimensional 4 × 3 model, such as the effect of education on changing unskilled labor into skilled labor, with the consequences for the level of wages and the wage premium for skills. Here let me just consider the possibility of a simple price increase in a single commodity, such as agriculture (A). This sends out a ripple effect on factor prices.[10] Freeze, at first, the allocation of K_U between the N and M manufacturing sectors. Then an increase in p_A causes a magnified increase in r_T, and a less than proportionate increase in w_U.

Given assumed fixed prices for commodities N, M, and H, the increase in w_U sets off a ripple effect on subsequent factor returns: r_U must fall, causing w_S to increase and, thus, forcing r_S to fall. The factor prices in each fixed price industry must alternate between rising and falling. Note that both wage rates increase; L_U works with K_U to produce N at fixed price and K_U works with skilled labor to produce M at a fixed price. Thus, the

---

will also be the case that the world X-industry becomes less concentrated, and that the volume of international trade will be reduced.

[10]The term "ripple effect" was used in Jones and Kierzkowski (1986) to describe a similar sequence of factor price changes.

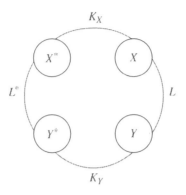

Figure 9.8.   The (4 × 4) Model: Neighborhood Production Structure

fall in r_U is what supports an increase in the wage rates of both types of labor because the prices of N and M are given. Could skilled labor have its wage rate increase by relatively more than unskilled labor (and, thus, have an increase in the wage premium)? Yes. All it would take is to have capital's distributive share in producing M be larger than its share in producing N.

Finally, Fig. 9.8 shows how the nature of the model changes if Y-type capital becomes internationally mobile as well. This is a type of Heckscher–Ohlin structure, with all factors mobile (but only between a pair of industries) and the same number of factors as produced commodities (a 4 × 4 example), what in Jones and Kierzkowski (1986) is called the *Neighbourhood Production Structure*. Each productive activity only makes use of a pair of factors: those in the nearby neighborhood. Each factor has only two outlets for employment: those in the nearby neighborhood. In the Fig. 9.8 interpretation there are two kinds of factor mobility: between sectors within a country for labor; and intra-industry but international for capital. What would be the income distribution fallout of a worldwide increase in the price of the X-type commodity with a fixed price for the Y-type commodity? Once again, it depends. Could the return to X-type capital increase by a magnified amount, wage rates in both countries increase, but by a dampened amount relative to the price rise, and the return to Y-type capital fall? Yes, and this would be the kind of response expected in specific factor kinds of models. However, much different results may be obtained. For example, an increase in the price of X-type goods might result in labor in both countries being the big gainers and lead to some increase in returns to

Y-type capital but depress the return to X-type capital! Of course, in this 4×4 setting all depends upon factor-intensity rankings, but such a result depends more on intra-sectoral intensity rankings than on the comparison between capital–labor ratios in the two different industries in each country. Details of how this might happen are left to the original Jones and Kierzkowski (1986) paper.

9.5   Concluding Remarks

Is a picture worth a thousand words? Perhaps in economics it might be a comparison of pictures with equations that is measured. Here I have used what I call "bubble diagrams" to illustrate scenarios involving commodities and the particular inputs required in production. This diagram is useful in illustrating general equilibrium relationships with dimensionality a bit higher than 2 (or 3), whether talking about international trade or purely domestic scenarios with land, heterogeneous labor and perhaps capital. Although some questions in these higher dimensional cases need to rely on rather extensive algebra, others can be answered fairly simply with the aid of these bubble diagrams. For example, in the Jones and Dei (1983) piece on investment activity in foreign enclaves, a diagram for the 4×3 case easily suggests the direction of international capital flows when commodity prices change, as well as suggesting the *possibility* of surprising results, such as in the case in which Home labor, used only to produce a commodity that has gone up in price, experiences less of a rise in its wage rate than does Foreign labor, used mainly to produce a commodity whose price is unchanged but also as an input in an enclave receiving international capital from Home. This is the sort of potential result that can be explained in general equilibrium models of competitive markets with somewhat higher dimensionality than in the basic Heckscher–Ohlin 2×2 scenario or in the 3×2 Specific-Factors model even before more formally obtaining comparative statics solutions.

References

Caves, R., Frankel, J., and Jones, R. (2007). *World Trade and Payments* (10th edn). Boston, MA: Addison Wesley.

Chakraborty, B.S. (2009). Protection and Real Rewards: Some Antinomies. *Pacific Economic Review*, 14(1), 56–70.

Chipman, J. (1969). Factor Price Equalization and the Stolper–Samuelson Theorem. *International Economic Review* 10, 399–406.

Gruen, F. and Corden, W.M. (1970). A Tariff That Worsens the Terms of Trade. In: I. McDougall and R. Snape (Eds.), *Studies in International Economics*. Amsterdam: North-Holland.

Jones, R.W. (1971). A Three Factor Model in Theory, Trade and History. In: J. Bhagwati, R. Jones, R. Mundell and J. Vanek (Eds.), *Trade, Balance of Payments and Growth*. Amsterdam: North-Holland.

Jones, R.W. (1989). Co-Movements in Relative Commodity Prices and International Capital Flows: A Simple Model. *Economic Inquiry*, 27, 131–141.

Jones, R.W. (2000). *Globalization and the Theory of Input Trade*. Cambridge, MA: MIT Press.

Jones, R.W. (2007a). Specific Factors and Heckscher–Ohlin: An Intertemporal Blend. *Singapore Economic Review*, 52, 1–5.

Jones, R.W. (2007b). Who Is Better Able to Get Protection? *Asia-Pacific Journal of Accounting and Economics*, 14, 1–5.

Jones, R.W. and Dei, F. (1983). International Trade and Foreign Investment: A Simple Model. *Economic Inquiry* 21, 449–464.

Jones, R.W. and Kierzkowski, H. (1986). Neighborhood Production Structures with An Application to the Theory of International Trade. *Oxford Economic Papers*, 38, 59–76.

Jones, R.W. and Marjit, S. (1992). International Trade and Endogenous Production Structures. In: W. Neuefeind and R. Riezman (Eds.), *Economic Theory and International Trade*. Heidelberg: Springer-Verlag.

Jones, R.W. and Marjit, S. (2003). Economic Development, Trade and Wages. *German Economic Review*, 4, 1–17.

Kemp, M. and Wegge, L. (1969). On the Relation between Commodity Prices and Factor Rewards. *International Economic Review*, 10, 407–413.

Samuelson, P.A. (1948). International Trade and the Equalization of Factor Prices. *Economic Journal*, 58, 163–184.

Samuelson, P.A. (1949). International Factor-Price Equalization Once Again. *Economic Journal*, 59, 181–197.

Samuelson, P.A. (1971). Ohlin Was Right. *Swedish Journal of Economics*, 73, 365–384.

CHAPTER 10

Trade, Technology, and Income Distribution*

Ronald W. Jones

Abstract

The functional distribution of income can be affected by price changes in international markets, by changes in technology which may be biased in factor saving, and by reductions in cost which allow vertically-integrated production processes to be fragmented and spread over several countries. Simple 2 × 2 Heckscher–Ohlin models yield predictions about income distribution which are at odds with frameworks allowing a wider variety of commodities to be produced and traded. In this framework a country losing out in labor-intensive segment of production to foreign competition may experience increases in real wages.

10.1   Introduction

Recent debates, primarily in the United States, about the effects of international trade on unskilled wage rates, have involved trade economists and labor economists in empirical and theoretical investigations as to the reasons why and how inequalities in the distribution of income have been brought about.[1] American experience does not support the view that unskilled labor must continuously lose to skilled labor in a wage comparison, since in the postwar period up to the 1970s, unskilled labor's relative wage was rising. My purpose here is not to examine the causes of changes

*Originally published in *Indian Economic Review*, 32(2), (1997), pp. 129–140.
Text of a lecture delivered at the Delhi School of Economics.
[1] See the contributions in Collins (1997), as well as Freeman (1995), Richardson (1995), Wood (1995), and Jones and Engerman (1996).

in income distribution in any one country or any particular time period. Instead, I wish to appraise several simple strands of reasoning in the international trade literature which serve to link income distribution to changes in relative prices of internationally traded products, to changes in technology which may be biased by sector or by factor-saving, and by recent tendencies to split vertically integrated production processes into separate components which may be produced in different regions of the world. I shall argue that excessive reliance on the standard two-commodity, two-factor Heckscher–Ohlin model yields predictions about income distribution which are significantly at odds with theoretical frameworks that allow a richer and wider variety of commodities to be produced and traded, or permit some factors to be limited in their mobility from sector to sector.

10.2   A Price Change in the World Market

Probably the easiest place to start is with the Stolper–Samuelson theorem, since this seems to provide most of the rationale behind popular and media coverage in the United States. This theorem, more than 50 years old in the professional literature (1941), is referred to by name in the *Economist* and other current sources.[2] It states that if a country produces a pair of commodities with two factors, say unskilled labor and capital (a composite of physical and human capital), and if the import-competing product is intensive in its use of unskilled labor, a fall in the world price of such a commodity would (unless protective measures are taken) eventuate in a decline in the real return to unskilled labor. That is the bottom line; no caveats are made about technological parity between this country and the rest of the world. This theorem, seemingly so applicable to describing the fate of unskilled workers in the United States or (in terms of high unemployment rather than decreased wages) in Western Europe, is often confused with the Factor-price Equalization Theorem, which points to the effect of free trade in equalizing wage rates among trading regions. Thus opponents of the NAFTA accord in North America, or to its extension to Chile and other countries of the Western Hemisphere, point to the drastic

---

[2]For an appraisal of this theorem after 50 years, see Deardorff and Stern (1994).

consequences for American wages should freer trade result in bringing wage levers down to the levels in their partner areas. Most international trade economists would hesitate to suggest that this latter proposition is relevant to today's trading world, since unlike the Stolper–Samuelson theorem the factor-price-equalization dictum presumes that countries not only share the same technology including the requirement of comparable labor skills) but that their capital/labor endowment proportions are sufficiently close together that the countries will produce the same pair of commodities.

One of the fundamental results in international trade theory is that countries which are linked together by trade rid themselves of the necessity to produce as many commodities as their populace demands. Specialization in production can be severe, and it takes a model with many commodities effectively to underscore the consequences for income distribution of the possibilities of widespread concentration of productive activity with trade. Consider, therefore, a country facing an initial set of world prices for commodities 1–5. Suppose, furthermore, that this country's factors are not well suited to producing commodity 5, either because technology is inferior to that found elsewhere, or the skills of its labor and capital are deficient, but that there are techniques available for producing the other four commodities which would allow this country to compete effectively with the rest of the world at prevailing prices in a competitive setting. Stated more formally, the home country's technology and the given set of world prices determine a set of *unit value isoquants* for these commodities, and the *convex hull* of these isoquants is illustrated by the heavy curve in Fig. 10.1. This is made up of curved sections, along which only a single commodity is produced with trade, and of linear segments along which two commodities are produced; for points along any such segment the standard 2 × 2 results of Heckscher–Ohlin theory are relevant for small changes. Suppose the world price of commodity 2 is reduced, say as a consequence of increased world market participation by countries whose output is primarily in industry 2's sector. This has the effect of shifting the unit value isoquant for commodity 2 radially away from the origin, since now a greater input bundle must be employed to produce enough of commodity 2 to earn $1 on world markets. The new Hicksian composite unit value isoquant is illustrated by curve 2′ in Fig. 10.2.

The same set of information is illustrated in Fig. 10.3. The lightly sketched upward sloping curves reveal the home country's technological

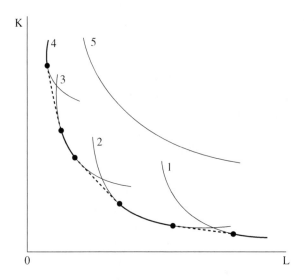

Figure 10.1.   Composite Unit Value Isoquant

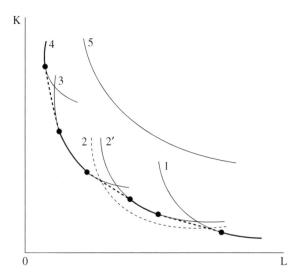

Figure 10.2.   Fall in 2′s Price

link between the factor price ratio, w/r, and the capital/labor ratios that
would be adopted. Prevailing world prices determine which techniques
could be used. As Figs. 10.1 or 10.2 reveal, at very low relative wage rates,
only commodity 1 is produced. At a slightly higher relative wage it becomes

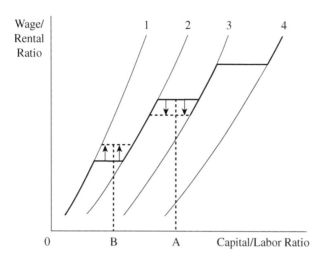

Figure 10.3.   Factor Prices and Endowments

possible to produce commodity 2 as well as 1, and such a factor price ratio is consistent with many combinations of outputs of these two commodities. For higher wage/rental ratios the composition of production changes yet again alternating between patterns of complete and incomplete specialization. The dashed lines in Fig. 10.3 correspond to the situation illustrated in Fig. 10.2, in which commodity 2's world price has fallen. Thus there is now a more narrow range in which commodity 2 would be produced.

Figure 10.3 is useful in illustrating how such a fall in commodity 2's price would affect real and relative wage rates for unskilled labor. This effect clearly depends upon the pattern of production in the home country, which in turn is based upon its endowment proportions. Consider, first, the position of a very labor-abundant country producing only the first commodity. Its relative wage rate is unaffected, and the *real wage* for unskilled workers would rise since the price of one of the consumption goods has fallen with no change in the nominal wage. A similar promising result holds for unskilled labor in very capital abundant countries producing no commodity 2. The fate of countries producing commodity 2 is different. Their terms of trade have deteriorated, so the welfare of the entire country is reduced. Such a welfare loss is shared by both types of income recipients if the country's endowment proportions have it producing only commodity 2 before and after the price rise. But if another commodity is produced as

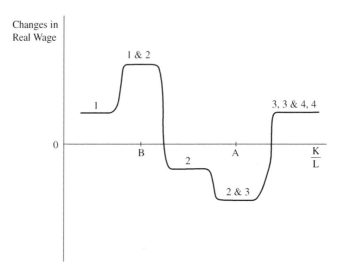

Figure 10.4.   Changes in Real Wage as P_2 Falls

well, the effect of the price change on unskilled labor is even more damaging for relatively capital abundant countries producing commodities 2 and 3·(such as a country with endowment proportions shown by point A), since commodity 2 is relatively labor-intensive. This is the *magnification effect* familiar in 2×2 models. For a more labor abundant country (such as shown by point B's endowment ratio) the price drop serves unambiguously to *raise* the real wage of unskilled labor, since commodity 2 is the more capital-intensive commodity produced there. These results on the *change* in the *real wage* are summarized in Fig. 10.4.

The fact that the same world price change can be unambiguously favorable to unskilled workers in some countries but damaging to the same kind of workers in another, even if it is assumed they have access to the same technology, is a property of simple trade models exhibiting *factor-intensity reversals*. In the literature stimulated by the Leontief Paradox in the 1950's and 1960's such a phenomenon could reflect a comparison of technologies of producing the *same* pair of commodities in two countries, wherein the commodity using capital-intensive techniques in one country uses labor-intensive techniques in another, so that a price change for that commodity results in factor prices moving in opposite directions in the two countries. Here something different is at work — there are not assumed to be any intensity reversals of this kind. Instead, it *must* be the case that for two countries having sufficiently close endowment proportions (and sharing the same technology) such that they produce some commodity in common but are each incompletely specialized to a different other commodity, a price change for the commonly-produced commodity will cause real wages of unskilled workers to rise in one country and fall in another. Thus compare the situation of countries with endowment proportions shown by *A* and *B* in Figs. 10.3 and 10.4. Note that it is the unskilled workers in the more capital-abundant country which are the losers. (Nonetheless, for such workers in even more capital-abundant countries no longer producing commodity 2, its price fall in world markets serves to raise real wages.)

10.3 Technical Progress

Many economists point to the nature of technical progress as a better explanation of why in some countries the wage rate of unskilled workers has fallen, especially relative to the return on human capital. If technical progress, e.g., developments in computer software, is biased in saving on the use of unskilled labor, what does standard 2×2 international trade theory tell us about the effect on the distribution of income? Nothing. We need to know more-in particular, in which sector has technical progress taken place? (And we assume here commodity prices remain unchanged). If, say, Hicksian labor-saving technical progress takes place only in the labor-intensive sector, real wages will unambiguously *rise*, whereas if such progress, with whatever factor bias one assumes, takes place in the other sector, the real wage rate will fall. This is standard fare in this kind of trade model *if* the degree of technical progress is very small. In such a case, the sector in which technical progress takes place causes the distribution of income to change precisely as would a (small) price rise-the Stolper–Samuelson result once again. But with finite changes in a world in which many commodities can be produced, technical progress may have the effect of shifting the pattern of production and thus resulting in a different response of wage rates and returns to human or physical capital. And, if the change is finite, the factor bias of technical progress may influence the production pattern.

This issue is illustrated in Fig. 10.5 for the two-commodity case. Commodity 2 is capital-intensive, and in the initial equilibrium it uses technique A along its unit-value isoquant, while labor-intensive commodity 1 adopts technique B. The initial wage/rental ratio is shown by the slope of the line

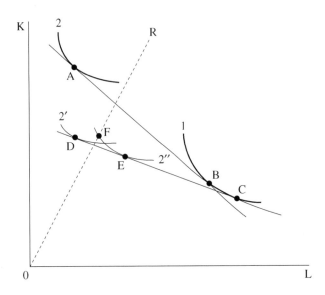

Figure 10.5.   Technical Progress in Capital-Intensive Sector (2)

tangent at A and B. Factor endowment proportions are shown by ray OR. Now suppose technical progress takes place only in capital-intensive sector 2. Two possibilities are shown, with different factor biases: 2′ and 2″, either of which would lead to the same new lower wage/rental ratio shown by the slope of DEC *if* both goods should be produced after the technical change. But this is a big "if," one not satisfied for this economy with indicated endowment ray OR if technical progress leads to the new isoquant 2″ instead of 2′. Such an economy would drop its production of commodity 1 and produce only the second commodity with a wage/rental ratio shown by the slope at F. That is, if the bias in technical progress leads this country to shift its production pattern (to specialize in the capital-intensive product), a rise in the real wage could result from technical progress in the capital-intensive sector.

There is no doubt that the frequent reliance trade theorists place on the 2 × 2 Heckscher–Ohlin model to trace out the effects of price changes or technical progress on income distribution leads to results at odds with the intuition which many labor economists place on partial equilibrium techniques. The Specific-Factors model helps to bridge the gap. It is a legitimate form of production structure for use in general equilibrium analysis, but leads to more common sense results for some questions. For example, in the 2×2 setting with given commodity prices, a nation would respond to an influx of immigration of unskilled labor by altering the production mix without any change in factor prices. By contrast, suppose in each of two sectors a type of capital (human and physical) is used that is specific to that sector and not used in the other. As well, suppose each sector dips into a common pool of unskilled labor. Increased supplies of such labor would unambiguously lead to wage declines. As for technical progress, in the Specific-Factors model the factor bias does matter, along with the rate at which each individual sector is affected. (See Jones, 1996 for details). If technical progress were Hicksian neutral (so that at an unchanged factor-price ratio the same capital/labor proportions would be utilized as in the initial state), the wages of unskilled labor would rise regardless of the sectoral distribution of technical progress. If progress were biased in the labor-saving direction, which most commentators fear has been the case for recent advances in technology, downward pressure on wages would indeed exist, much as in the case of increases in labor supply. However, a mobile factor such as labor would tend to gain from the very existence of technical progress, as would all income earners in the neutral case. What can be said of the balance in these opposing forces? As proved in Jones (1996), even in the case of pure Hicksian labor-saving progress at the same rate in each sector, labor's real wage will rise if technology is sufficiently "flexible." By this is meant if the elasticity of substitution between labor and capital in the two sectors is high enough. A value of unity is more than sufficient. (On average a value exceeding the ratio of capital to labor shares will be enough).

10.4   Fragmentation and Loss of a Labor-Intensive Activity

Developed countries in the United States and Western Europe are fearful that technological advances in service sectors such as telecommunications and transportation will encourage previously vertically-connected production processes to fragment, with more labor-intensive segments losing out to foreign competition. Need this be a concern? Figure 10.6 helps to clarify the issue.

For convenience, it is assumed in Fig. 10.6 that each productive activity displays absolutely rigid technology in the sense that no substitution possibilities between labor and capital are available. Thus originally suppose the

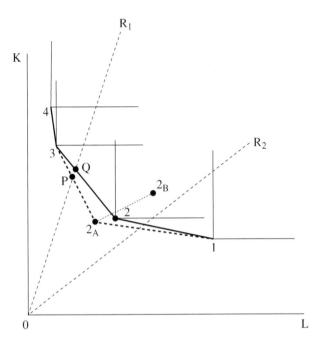

Figure 10.6.   Fragmentation in Sector 2

home country's Hicksian unit-value isoquant is made up of comer points
for producing activities 1 through 4, and the linear segments connecting
these points. This state of affairs is disturbed by developments in service
activities (not shown) which allow vertically-integrated activity 2 to be
fragmented into two fixed-coefficient activities, one more capital-intensive
than the other. In particular, suppose that this finer division of productive activities allows world gains in productivity in that a more intensive
application of the Ricardian doctrine of comparative advantage tends to
result in a lower world price for the aggregate of the two components of
commodity 2 than previously. This is revealed in Fig. 10.6 by the two fragments 2_A and 2_B, and the fact that the convex combination of these two
points lies above the corner of previously integrated activity 2. (Details of
this fragmentation procedure are found in Jones and Kierzkowski, 1997.)
Arbitrarily shown in Fig. 10.6 is the dominance of capital-intensive activity
2_A over the labor-intensive component 2_B, ensuring that with fragmentation the latter activity lies strictly within the convex hull denoted by the
dashed lines.

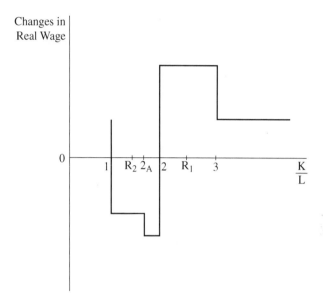

Figure 10.7. Fragentation and Changes in Real Wage

What are the consequences for factor prices and employment in the home country in this new, more fragmented world? This depends on the country's factor-endowment proportions. For example, if the capital/labor endowment ray is shown by OR_2, the wage/rental ratio falls. Indeed, the replacement of activity 2 by the fragment 2_A in the country's portfolio of production (it also produces commodity 1) is akin, in its effect on factor prices, to a labor-saving technical progress in the country's capital-intensive activity. Thus the real wage unambiguously is driven down. Figure 10.7 explicitly reveals this loss in the real wage. (For a capital/labor endowment ratio between rays 02_A and 02, the drop in the real wage is especially severe since wages were originally higher when the country originally produces commodities 2 and 3). By contrast, the situation at home if it originally had the higher capital/labor endowment proportions shown by ray OR_1 is different. In this case the country is originally producing commodities 2 and 3, so that the replacement of integrated activity 2 by the more capital-intensive segment, 2_A, has its analogy in a technical progress in producing the labor-intensive commodity. This results in standard 2×2 fashion in an increase in the wage/rental ratio and, as Fig. 10.7 illustrates, an increase in the real wage as well. For countries so capital abundant that commodity 2 is not initially produced, there results the standard improvement in the real wage as a consequence of the lowering of commodity 2's price to consumers.

Although this model is not designed to address the issue of aggregate employment (indeed it assumes factor prices represent market-clearing wages and returns to human and physical capital), it can show what happens to employment in sector 2, in which this country is shown to lose the labor-intensive fragment, 2_B, to world competition. The answer to this question depends on whether the country is relatively capital abundant, such as shown by ray OR_1, or labor-abundant, as shown by ray OR_2. In the latter case not only do wages fall, but sectoral employment shifts away from commodity 2 to more labor-intensive commodity 1. Consider the fate of a more capital-abundant country, the very type of country which is apt to be worried about the effect of losses of labor-abundant fragments on wage rates in a more competitive and fragmented world market. Its real wage rises, as previously noted, and employment of labor in the capital-intensive segment 2_A actually *exceeds* previous employment levels in the fully integrated activity 2. The reason: Point P in Fig. 10.6 is a weighted average of points 3 and 2_A, with a greater weight given to 2_A than is given to 2 in point Q's weighted average of points 3 and 2. Finally, compare the shapes of the loci in Figs. 10.4 and 10.7. If greater international competition forces down the price of commodity 2, it is the real wage in more capital abundant countries (producing 2) that is lowered. By contrast, increased fragmentation which causes a country to lose the labor-intensive fragment, 2_A, results in a lowered real wage not for more capital abundant producing countries, but for those which are more labor-abundant.

10.5   Concluding Remarks

The analysis of the effects of changing terms of trade or a change in technology or the degree of fragmentation in world markets on a country's distribution of income stressed in these remarks is based on a multi-commodity trading world. Abandoning the standard assumptions of 2×2 international trade theory leads to a wider variety of results without any substantial increase in the difficulty of analysis. To be sure, a drop in the world price of a commodity produced in a country by labor-intensive techniques still spells difficulty for the return to unskilled labor. But even this conclusion needs to be qualified. For suppose that the price drop is itself the consequence not of new supplies of the commodity as new developing countries enter the world market, but rather of technological progress which is shared by the country in question. In such a case the price drop is accompanied by an *increase* in the real wage. Indeed, this was the analogy pointed out in the preceding section, in which reductions in costs of fragmentation caused a country to lose the labor-intensive segment of a previously vertically integrated activity, an activity which utilized labor-intensive techniques relative to another actively produced commodity.

A Heckscher–Ohlin world in which factors are mobile between sectors is one in which production is concentrated to a few commodities if trade allows consumption to be obtained from abroad. This implies that as prices fall for some traded commodities, many countries may experience a rise in real incomes for all factors because none of that commodity is produced. This was the source of gain in real wages at very low and very high capital/labor endowment ratios in Figs. 10.4 and 10.7. Suppose instead there are many specific factors, indeed an $(n + 1) \times n$ version of the model in some country, then all commodities are produced. However, the lower the price for any commodity, the less labor will be devoted to its production, so that once again the gains to workers as consumers will eventually exceed any losses in real wages as the price to local producers falls.

The Specific-Factors model is both simple and useful if a distinction is desired between human capital and physical capital as well as unskilled labor. For example, suppose for the American case that import-competing goods are produced with unskilled labor and physical capital whereas in the export sector the specific factor is skilled labor (human capital) and physical capital is mobile between sectors. If a fall in the price of imports is the primary shock coming from world markets, such a scenario suggests a rise in real wages for skilled workers, a fall in real wages for the unskilled, and not much real change in the return to physical capital. Not a bad fit for the American scene.

There is no doubt that changing conditions of international trade can have important repercussions on the distribution of income in all trading nations. And so can changes in other conditions, such as technical progress or advances in services which allow an international dispersal of previously vertically integrated components. These changes are more sensibly analyzed in models with many commodities. The competitive forces of trade can then encourage greater degrees of concentration so that even countries with similar technologies and factor skills but somewhat different endowment proportions can produce a different range of commodities. The effects of any world shocks on real wages and returns to human and physical capital may then be different from one country to another.

References

Collins, S, (ed.) (1997). *Imports, Exports and the American Worker.* Washington, DC: Brookings Institution.

Deardorff, A. and Stern, R. (1994). *The Stolper-Samuelson Theorem: A Golden Jubilee.* Ann Arbor, MI: University of Michigan Press.

Freeman, R. (1995). Are Your Wages Set in Beijing? *The Journal of Economic Perspectives,* 9(3), 15–32.

Jones, R. (1996). International Trade, Real Wages, and Technical Progress: The Specific-Factors Model. *International Review of Economics and Finance,* 5(2), 113–124.

Jones, R. and Engerman, S. (1996). Trade, Technology, and Wages: A Tale of Two Countries. *American Economic Review,* 86(2), 35–40.

Jones, R. and Kierzkowski, H. (1997). "Globalization and the Consequences of International Fragmentation," reprinted in *Money, Capital Mobility, and Trade: Essays in honor of Robert A. Mundell,* Cambridge, MA: MIT Press, 2001, 365–383.

Richardson, J.D. (1995). Income Inequality and Trade: How to Think, What to Conclude. *The Journal of Economic Perspectives,* 9(3), 33–56.

Wood, A. (1995). How Trade Hurt Unskilled Workers. *The Journal of Economic Perspectives,* 9(3), 57–80.

CHAPTER 11

Factor Bias and Technical Progress*

Ronald Findlay and Ronald W. Jones

Abstract

The role of factor bias in technical progress has been a bone of contention between labor economists and international trade theorists. By considering progress that results in finite changes in techniques these two views can be reconciled. For example, labor-saving technical progress can result in lowered real wages, even if it is concentrated in the more labor-intensive of two commodities initially produced.

The fate of wage rates for unskilled workers in recent years has been the focus of analysis both of labor economists and international trade theorists.[1] Labor economists often favor partial equilibrium analysis and trade theorists frequently rely on the standard general equilibrium 2×2 model of Heckscher and Ohlin. These approaches sometimes lead to different conclusions, and such differences can prove to be contentious in the ongoing debate. Much of the disagreement concerns the role of factor bias in technical progress. Thus if Hicksian labor-saving progress (i.e., at initial factor prices the improvement in technology reduces the optimal labor–capital ratio utilized in production) takes place in some sector of the economy, labor economists would argue that there would be pressure on market wages to fall, and that such downward pressure would be greater than in the case of Hicksian neutral or capital-saving progress. By contrast, standard Heckscher–Ohlin trade theory suggests that factor bias would

---

*Originally published in *Economics Letters*, 68, (2000), pp. 303–308.
[1] See, for example, the recent work of Collins (1998).

be unimportant for the issue, whereas wages would rise or fall depending completely on whether the improved sector is labor-intensive or capital-intensive. The trade theory result would be illustrated using a model in which two traded commodities are produced, their world (and domestic) prices remain unchanged, and production requires the use of two inputs.[2]

This trade result shares company with much of trade theory in its assumption that the shocks to the equilibrium, such as technical progress, are *small* — with the general rationale being a desire to exclude second-order changes. In this note we examine what would happen to the trade argument about unskilled wages and biased technical progress if the change in technical progress is not small — rather is of finite size.[3] In such a case *bias* does indeed matter. The surprise is that bias *may* matter in a manner *opposite* to the supposed harm which a Hicksian saving in the use of unskilled labor would bring to the wage rate.

Our first two diagrams illustrate these possibilities. In both of these it is assumed that technical progress takes place in the capital-intensive sector (2) in a two-sector model. In Fig. 11.1, it is assumed for convenience that the possibilities for factor substitution are absent, so that unit-value isoquants are right-angled at initial points A and B. A parallel line, through points C and D, is drawn, and two alternative possibilities for technical progress in the capital-intensive sector are represented by points C and D. If commodity 2's isoquant shifts to point C, at the initial wage–rent ratio the ratio of labor to capital has been reduced — a Hicksian labor-saving technical change. The same *degree* of technical progress is captured in the alternative possibility, that the new unit-value isoquant touches at point D, although in this case progress is Hicksian capital-saving. In either of these two cases the effect of technical progress in the capital-intensive sector is to lower wage/rental rates. Unlike the case of infinitesimal changes,

---

[2] The issues related to the impact of technological progress on the terms of trade and factor prices first arose in the "trade and growth" literature of the 1950s and 1960s. Our own main contributions to this literature are in Findlay and Gruber (1959) and Jones (1965). The present article draws on the insight in both of these papers.

[3] The contemporary empirical literature on the causes of the decline in unskilled wages attaches considerable importance to the impact of a major technological or quality innovation, viz. the computer revolution. Clearly, the assumption of a finite technological improvement is the more appropriate for this case.

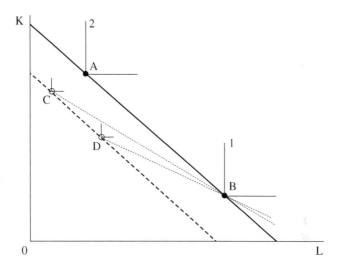

Figure 11.1.   Technical Progress in Capital-Intensive Sector

bias does matter. But wages are driven down *more* in situation D than in situation C. That is, workers lose more in cases in which technical progress is *labor-using.*

In Specific-Factors models, a neutral degree of progress in either sector of the economy would tend to help labor, assuming labor is the mobile factor. If the technical progress is labor-using, wages are driven up even more.[4] In Fig. 11.1 the results are the opposite — the more labor-using the bias, the more are wages driven down. The reason? Such a bias in technical progress in the capital-intensive sector of the economy serves to bring closer together the factor intensities in the two sectors. And a standard result in Heckscher–Ohlin theory is that the magnification effects of commodity price changes (or changes in technologies) on factor prices are stronger the closer are the factor intensities (Jones, 1965). That is, when intensities do not differ as much between sectors, factor prices must change by more in order to accommodate any given change in commodity prices or technical progress. In Fig. 11.1 the same kind of result would emerge if technical progress took place in the labor-intensive sector instead. As can easily be verified, the more labor-saving the bias in technology among

---

[4] An analysis of technical progress in the Specific-Factors model is found in Jones (1996).

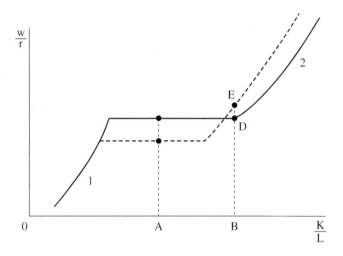

Figure 11.2. Capital-Saving Technical Progress

alternatives of the same degree, the greater will be the increase in relative wages.

Finite changes in technology do not always lead to this ranking of biases on factor prices. Consider Fig. 11.2. The relationship shown there between relative factor prices and factor endowments reflects both technology and world commodity prices (as did Fig. 11.1). The original three-part heavy curve shows that, at low capital–labor endowment ratios, the country is specialized in producing the first commodity and, since factor substitution is now allowed, relative wages rise with increases in endowment capital–labor ratios. Such a monotonic relationship also holds for high capital–labor endowment ratios when the economy is specialized in the second commodity. For endowments in between, the country produces both commodities and, since world prices for these commodities are given, factor prices are determined — the middle section of the locus is flat.

Consider, now, technical progress in the capital-intensive good, progress that is capital-saving. That is, if the second commodity is the only commodity produced, at any given factor–price ratio the techniques of producing commodity 2 would be adjusted to show higher labor–capital ratios; at initial factor prices more labor would be demanded per unit of capital. The existence of technical progress in the second commodity (of any bias) causes the new middle "flat" portion in Fig. 11.2 to shift downwards; the wage–rental ratio would be reduced by this progress in the capital-intensive commodity (of the two being produced). Therefore, if the endowment ratio is given by point A, wages suffer. But if the endowment point is at B, finite technical progress that has a capital-saving bias causes the wage rate to *rise* (from level D to E), in conformity with the expectations put forth in the labor economics literature. A finite degree of technological progress has encouraged the economy to devote all its resources to producing the favored commodity, thus altering the specialization pattern and, with it, the consequences of progress for the distribution of income.

These two possible results on the effect of biased progress on relative (and real) wage rates are brought together in Fig. 11.3. The solid broken line illustrates the factor price–factor endowment relationship initially. Also illustrated is the dashed locus and the dotted locus. The dashed locus reflects the effect of *labor-using* (or capital-saving) technical progress in the second sector (all at constant commodity prices); the dotted locus reflects *labor-saving* technological progress of the same Hicksian extent. If both commodities are produced before and after the technological change, the drop in wages is more severe in the case of labor-using progress — the

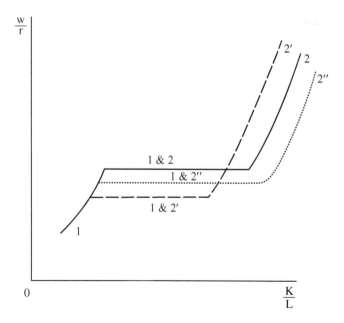

Figure 11.3.   Comparison of Factor Biases

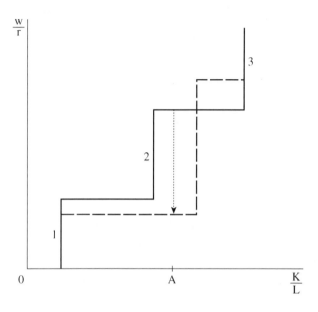

Figure 11.4.   Progress in the Labor-Intensive Sector Leading to Fall in Wage Rate

same result as shown in Fig. 11.1. At the other extreme, if only the second commodity is produced before and after the change, the wage rate falls if and only if technical progress is biased in a labor-saving direction — a result consistent with partial equilibrium analysis. And, as Fig. 11.2 reveals, if technical progress is capital-saving instead and if, initially, both commodities are produced, the wage rate could nonetheless rise if the country is driven to specialize completely in the second commodity.

In the final diagram, Fig. 11.4, we illustrate a case that perhaps serves to crystallize the different points of view held by trade economists and labor economists. We return to the fixed-coefficient technology illustrated in Fig. 11.1, but now consider a three-commodity case using the kind of diagram illustrated in Figs. 11.2 and 11.3. Along the three solid vertical sections the country has an endowment ratio that allows it to achieve full employment by producing a single commodity. For other endowment proportions it must split its resources to produce two goods — commodities 1 and 2 in the lower horizontal section and commodities 2 and 3 for a more capital-rich endowment proportion. Now suppose that a *labor-saving* technical progress takes place in commodity 2, and that the country's endowment proportions are shown by point A, so that the country is initially producing commodities 2 and 3, with commodity 2 representing the more labor-intensive activity. Has technical progress in this labor-intensive good raised the wage rate? No. Instead, the labor-saving bias of the progress has caused the wage rate to fall. The fact that progress has not been assumed to be small has allowed a change in production patterns such that all production of commodity 3 ceases and in the new situation commodities 1 and 2 are produced. Presumably a labor economist would be pleased at this outcome, whereas the trade theory result that factor bias is unimportant (with only sectorial bias counting) would be confounded. Care must obviously be taken in making sweeping generalizations about the unimportance of factor bias in discussing the effects of technical change on income distribution.

References

Collins, S.M. (Ed.) (1998). *Imports, Exports and the American Worker*. Brookings, Washington, DC: Brookings Institution.

Findlay, R. and Grubert, H. (1959). Factor Intensities, Technological Progress, and the Terms of Trade. *Oxford Economic Papers*, 11, 111–121.

Jones, R.W. (1965). The Structure of Simple General Equilibrium Models. *Journal of Political Economy*, 73, 557–572.

Jones, R.W. (1996). International Trade, Real Wages and Technical Progress: The Specific Factors Model. *International Review of Economics and Finance*, 5(2), 113–124.

CHAPTER 12

Sense and Surprise in Competitive Trade Theory (2010 WEAI Presidential Address)*

Ronald W. Jones

Abstract

Economic models are often judged by the reality of their assumptions or their success at predicting realistic outcomes. In this chapter, I suggest a different criterion for judging models in international trade theory in competitive settings: (i) Does the model conform to common sense in leading to results that even suggest the model is not necessary, and yet (ii) can the same model be used as a tool to reveal in simple terms why certain outcomes that may appear surprising (often labeled a paradox in trade theory) nonetheless are correct. Many trade theory paradoxes appear as the result of income effects in simple general equilibrium models. Here attention centers instead on two of the familiar production models: The Specific-Factors model and the Heckscher–Ohlin model, either separately or when combined. It is shown that very basic properties of production underlie many of the surprising results in competitive trade theory.

12.1   Introduction

The competitive theory of international trade is well known for its abundance of "paradoxes." Perhaps the most widely known is the Leontief Paradox, associated with the rather startling results presented by Leontief (1953) that the trade pattern of the United States suggested that its export sectors were more labor-intensive than factor proportions found in its import-competing sectors. This result stimulated decades of research, but is not the focus of the present paper. Other so-called paradoxes include the Metzler (1949) result, wherein a country levying a tariff on an imported item may

---

*Originally published in *Economic Inquiry*, 49(1), (2011), pp. 1–12.

end up with a *lowering* of its domestic price. That is, a tariff may not be protective.[1] Lerner (1936), who earlier hinted at the Metzler outcome, emphasized the possibility that a tariff might instead worsen a country's terms of trade, which is at the opposite extreme to the Metzler result. Both of these paradoxes are attributed to possible *income effects* in demand.

More recently, income effects stemming from asymmetry in demand patterns (among countries) were shown to open the door to paradoxical results if one country makes a transfer to another in a world in which other countries are also engaged in trade in the same commodities. The surprising results: The Giver in the transfer might end up better off (i.e., it may pay to give rather than to receive), and/or the Recipient of the transfer may end up worse off.[2] Finally, a classic result that does not depend on asymmetries in taste patterns, but rather upon the degree of elasticity in demand and the nature of growth is the question of whether a country that unequivocally grows (transformation schedule shifts out) can be made worse off as a consequence of growth (the so-called *immiserizing growth* paradox).[3] This is an issue familiar to particular sectors of the economy, for example, agriculture — can a good harvest yield lower returns because of the subsequent price fall?

Instead of revisiting these familiar paradoxes here, I wish to concentrate on the production side of competitive models used in international trade and to focus on the question involving ways of judging economic models. Clearly the question of realism often comes up, whether it is in terms of assumptions made or of outcomes expected. Here I suggest a different criterion: Does the model conform in many ways to common sense? (That is, would one be tempted to suggest that the model is not necessary because

[1] This result also served to query the argument put forward by Stolper and Samuelson (1941) that a tariff imposed by a country importing a labor-intensive product (a country presumably like the United States) would unambiguously raise the real wage. As a consequence, the Stolper–Samuelson wording was frequently changed to asking about the effect of a change in the *domestic relative price* of a commodity upon the real wage.

[2] The literature on what came to be called the Three-Agent Transfer Problem is quite extensive (and, at times, a bit contentious), and includes Johnson (1960), Komiya and Shizuki (1967), Gale (1974), Chichilnisky (1980), Brecher and Bhagwati (1981), Yano (1983), Bhagwati, Brecher, and Hatta (1983), and Jones (1984, 1985).

[3] The literature goes back to Edgeworth (1894) and, in the 1950s, to Johnson (1953, 1955), and Bhagwati (1958).

common sense would lead to the same results?) And, if it does, do the outcomes in certain scenarios seem to be paradoxical or surprising? If so, can the model reveal in simple terms why these somewhat surprising results make sense?[4] I shall restrict myself to a pair of basic models of production used in competitive trade theory — the Specific-Factors model on the one hand, and the Heckscher–Ohlin model on the other. I shall argue that in many ways both conform to common sense, but, in addition, provide the very *tools* that expose the underlying rationale for surprise.

12.2 A Preliminary Question

Consider *any* economy that is characterized by competitive markets and constant returns to scale technology. Suppose, for such an economy, there is an increase in the factor endowment bundle. To fix on an example, suppose there is an increase in the economy's labor force. The very general question I wish to ask is: How does such an economy absorb this increased endowment to maintain full employment of all factors? Note that if this economy is not engaged in international trade there will likely result a change in commodity prices as they adjust in order to equilibrate local supply and demand. Given the points I wish to make later, let me assume that the country is engaged in free trade with the rest of the world. If this economy were particularly small, world prices could be taken as given. Even if world prices are disturbed, it is legitimate to ask how the economy absorbs the extra supplies before any change in commodity prices takes place. (I shall mention an alternative use later that concerns a comparison of two trading communities that face the *same* world prices in equilibrium.) The general answer to the question is that there are two ways in which a greater labor supply can be absorbed in competitive models: (a) by changing the way in which commodities are produced, that is, increasing the quantity of labor used per unit of capital in all sectors in response to a lowered wage rate and (b) by changing the composition of its output, that is, reallocating resources toward the labor-intensive good(s). To use a more classical language, method (a) refers to changes at *the intensive margin*, and method (b) refers to adjustments at

---

[4]When I was an undergraduate student at Swarthmore College, I recall mentioning to a History Professor (Prof. George Cuttino) that I was thinking of majoring in Economics. In an effort to dissuade me, Prof. Cuttino remarked, "Economics is just horse sense couched in verbiage." That sounded great to me, so I did decide on Economics.

the extensive margin. The production and trade models examined in the next two sections react quite differently to this question.

12.3   The Specific-Factors Model

The Specific-Factors model is often referred to as the general equilibrium model that best tends to capture processes assumed in most partial equilibrium models. Used verbally by Haberler (1936) and others, it received more formal algebraic treatment in the works of Jones (1971, 1975) and Samuelson (1971), who labeled this the Ricardo–Viner model. The most frequently used and simplest form of the model is for an economy with only two sectors. Both sectors employ an input that is mobile between sectors, usually thought of as homogeneous labor, a factor that works in each sector with a kind of capital that is specific to that sector. A variant, often used in textbooks, considers two industries using mobile labor, with one industry using land as a second input, and the other sector using capital.[5] The multisector version has the advantage that it is almost as easy to analyze, with mobile labor used in all sectors and with each sector employing a factor (say a form of capital) that is only used in that sector.[6]

Consider one such industry, say industry i, and examine the consequences of an increase in the price of the ith commodity, all other commodity prices constant. Such a price rise leads to very common sense output changes: The ith industry attracts labor from *all other* sectors of the economy, thus causing output in all other sectors to fall. The effect on income distribution also satisfies common sense: The wage rate, w, is driven up by the price increase, but, given that no other commodity prices change, not by as much as the return to the specific-factor in the ith sector, r_i. The wage increase causes a reduction in the rate of return to specific capitals in all *other* sectors. In more detail, the unit cost change in the ith sector is, in a competitive equilibrium, brought into equality with that sector's change in commodity price. Furthermore, the relative change in unit costs must

---

[5]See, for example, Chapter 5 of Caves, Frankel, and Jones (2007).

[6]The recent focus (in so-called "new, new" trade theory) is on the heterogeneity of firms *within* an industry. The Specific-Factors model can usefully be used in such an analysis by letting the returns to a factor specifically tied to a firm differ among the industry's various firms. This allows for a competitive model to be used in firms having different *productivities*, as captured by Ricardian "differential rents" to specific-factors within an industry.

equal the weighted average of the changes in the two input prices, with the weights reflecting each factor's importance in total costs, the factor's distributive share, θ_{Li} for labor and θ_{Ki} for specific capital:

$$\theta_{Li}\hat{w} + \theta_{Ki}\hat{r}_i = \hat{p}_i \tag{12.1}$$

In sector i, the relative change in the return to capital, $\hat{r}_i$, must exceed the change in the commodity price, $\hat{p}_i$, because the relative change in the economy's wage rate, $\hat{w}$, although positive, is prevented from increasing as much as the commodity price because labor is used as well in all other sectors.[7] Now consider the cost situation in one of the sectors in which price has not increased. The increase in the wage rate common to all sectors must, for each such sector without a price increase, put *downward* pressure on the return to specific capital, because the distributive share weighted average of the relative changes in input prices is zero. The effect of a single price change on the distribution of income well satisfies the criterion of common sense. The equations of change for the competitive profit conditions (i.e., that changes in equilibrium costs are equal to that of price for any commodity produced, as set out in Eq. [12.1]), are of fundamental use in exploring subsequent surprises in trade theory, both for the Specific-Factors model and for the Heckscher–Ohlin model.

The principal characteristic of competitive general equilibrium models is their ability to examine the effect of an economic shock in one sector of the economy on outputs and income distribution in other sectors of the economy as well. Consider, now, the effect of an increase in the economy's endowment of the specific capital used only in sector i on all outputs and the distribution of income assuming that *all* commodity prices are held constant. Not surprisingly, the return to such capital must fall, attracting labor from all other sectors. With the commodity price in sector i kept constant, such a fall in capital's return puts upward pressure on the wage rate, and this increase in labor costs serves to reduce the returns to all types of specific capital used in other sectors. Although these results make

---

[7] The "hat" notation for the relative change in the wage rate, say, equals dw/w. Note that for the left-hand side of Eq. (12.1) to represent the relative change in unit costs for small changes, it is not necessary to assume that technology is rigid (i.e., fixed input/output coefficients), because for small changes the alterations in techniques of production called for by factor price changes lead to second-order changes in unit costs.

good sense, consider the *extent* to which the return to sector i's specific-factor (whose endowment expands) falls compared to the fall in some other sector's specific-factor, say that used in commodity j. In both sectors, the wage rate increases, forcing the returns to specific-factors, r_i and r_j, both to fall. Equation (12.1) would reflect factor-price changes if the change in commodity price for each sector were zero. The possibility that the return to sector j's specific-factor, which has not increased in supply, could fall by *more* than that of the specific-factor that has experienced a supply increase depends upon a simple comparison of distributive labor shares in the two sectors. Such a comparison reveals which of the two sectors is more *labor-intensive.*[8] If θ_{Lj} were to exceed θ_{Li}, that is, if labor costs loom larger in sector j than in sector i, the increase in the wage rate, common to both sectors, would drive down the return to the specific-factor used in the jth sector by *more*. To many this outcome would seem rather surprising.

Suppose a country wants to raise revenue by imposing an import duty only on *one* of a pair of import-competing industries. Which industry should it choose? Alternatively stated, what arguments for trade protection could an industry mount? This pair of industries is part of a much larger set of industries not involved in the question of protection, but that would be affected by any subsequent increase in the wage rate (assuming that commodity prices they face are constant throughout). The more labor-intensive of the pair of import-competing industries might argue that *it* should be the sector to enjoy protection, because labor would likely be more favorably affected. I return to that issue below. But first suppose that the more labor-intensive industry is industry 1, and ask how the specific-factors would be affected if protection of a given relative amount is granted the first industry as opposed to the same degree of protection granted the second industry (i.e., the more capital-intensive industry). Make use of relationship (1) in the comparison, with the same relative increase in price offered in each case. Whether it is the first or the second industry that gains

---

[8] It may seem surprising to speak about factor-intensity rankings in Specific-Factors models where commodities employ different kinds of capital. However, commodities do use labor as a common factor, and thus a labor distributive share comparison can be made. It turns out that in the 2 × 2 Heckscher–Ohlin model in which both commodities use a *common* type of capital (as well as labor), so that physical factor proportions used in the two industries can be compared, such an intensity ranking corresponds exactly to a comparison of labor distributive shares.

protection, the wage rate will increase, but by a small relative amount given all the other industries in which labor is employed, and the specific-factor in the favored sector would gain even relative to the degree of protection. But such a gain is bound to be larger for the labor-intensive industry. That industry (industry 1) might try to attract favor because θ_{L1} exceeds θ_{L2}; and this is precisely the argument that the gain to r_1 would be greater than that to r_2 if the second sector had obtained protection instead. This is what I have referred to (with apologies to Oscar Wilde) as *the importance of being unimportant.*[9]

Although the wage increase would in either event be quite small in this multisector economy, could the wage rate (as well as the return to capital) really increase more if the labor-intensive sector were the one receiving protection? Details are easy to obtain, but are not provided here.[10] In the specific-factors setting, if commodity i is the only sector in which the price increases, the wage increase depends upon two features of technology, as well as upon the importance of commodity i's output relative to the national income, θ_i. Let s_i denote the elasticity of demand for labor in sector i compared with the aggregate elasticity of demand for labor in the overall economy, and i_i denote the relative labor intensity in the ith sector (this equals the ratio of labor's distributive share in the ith sector to the overall share of labor in the national income, θ^L). Equation (12.2) shows that the relative wage change is the product of these three elements times the price change, where the product is a positive fraction:

$$\hat{w} = \theta_i[i_i s_i]\hat{p}_i. \tag{12.2}$$

Suppose industries 1 and 2 are of the same size (i.e., $\theta_1 = \theta_2$) and relative degree of flexibility in technology (i.e., suppose $s_1 = s_2$), the wage rate *must* increase by *more* if sector 1 were the sector provided protection. That is, in this case *both* factors of production in the labor-intensive sector would benefit more from protection than would labor and specific capital if the second commodity were the one provided protection.[11] Specific capital

---

[9] See Jones (2007b).

[10] See Caves, Frankel, and Jones (2007), Supplement to Chapter 5.

[11] This result, wherein both wage rate and return to capital in one sector might increase more than in another even for the same degree of industry protection may seem less surprising by considering Eq. (12.1). With $\hat{p}_i > \hat{p} > \hat{w}$ for either industry (if each get protection), both

in the labor-intensive sector could argue that industry 1 should receive protection because of its greater importance to labor, while labor, in turn, would indeed favor protection in the first sector as well, and be willing to lobby the government for this choice.

Other surprising results can appear in a specific-factor setting in which one country (call it Home) is completely specialized in producing commodity X, which uses labor and a specific type of capital, K_X. Suppose not all of X-type capital is used at Home. Although owned by Home, some of this capital has been placed in a Foreign *Enclave*, where X^E is also produced with the help of some Foreign labor, L^*, most of which is used in the Foreign country to produce a different commodity, Y^*, with the help of their sector-specific capital, Ky^*.[12] Now suppose that the world price of commodity X (relative to that of commodity Y) increases. If X-type capital is freely mobile between Home and the Foreign Enclave, what can be said about the effect of the world-wide price increase in X on the location of capital between Home and Enclave? The answer is simple, which may sound surprising: More of Home's X-type capital moves to the Foreign Enclave. To see why, suppose that at first no X-type capital is allowed to move between its two locales. In such a case, in Home, the wage rate increases by the same relative amount as the return to capital, each equal to the relative increase in p_X. If the location of Foreign labor is also frozen, in the Enclave both w^E and the return to capital also rise by the same relative amount as p_X. However, rescinding the ban on factor mobility implies that more Foreign labor would then be attracted to the Enclave, which would serve to raise the return to capital there, thus attracting as well more X-type capital from Home. The new equilibrium will exhibit greater production of X^E, with more use of capital from Home as a consequence of more Foreign labor coming into the Enclave.

The key to the direction of capital flow induced by the commodity price change is the assumption that Home is completely specialized to commodity X, whereas Foreign has an Enclave into which Foreign labor can flow, released from its production of commodity Y^*. That is, the Foreign Enclave has a *hinterland* (Y^* production) from which resources (labor)

$\hat{w}$ and $\hat{p}_i$ could be larger in the first sector than comparable values for the second sector as long as labor's share is larger in the first sector than in the second, which I am assuming.

[12]See Jones and Dei (1983) as well as Jones (2000), Chapter 3.

can be released to help production of X^E in the Enclave, whereas Home has no hinterland. Now suppose that such a strong asymmetry is removed by letting Home produce Y as well as X (with a fixed amount of Y-type capital specific to Y-production), but letting X-type capital be the only kind that is internationally mobile.[13] Such a change raises the dimension of the model from a specific-factors setting with four inputs and three productive activities to a 5×4 model (five productive factors and four activities). Although such a change alters the possible direction of the international flow of X-type capital, somewhat surprisingly it does *not* change a simple criterion that reveals how the effect on wage rates at Home compares with that in the Foreign enclave. This comparison of wage change in the two locales depends *only* upon the question of whether X is produced at Home with more or less capital-intensive techniques than those adopted abroad. The result follows directly from the competitive profit equations of change shown in Eq. (12.1): both Home and Enclave face the same relative price rise for X as well as the same equilibrium change in the return to X-type capital. If the production of X at Home is more capital-intensive than in the Enclave (i.e., if θ_{KX} exceeds θ_{KX}^*), and given that the wage increase in either country must be smaller than the increase in price, the relative increase in w (if it is an increase) must be less than the relative increase in w^*.[14]

12.4   The Heckscher–Ohlin Model

The most commonly used general equilibrium competitive model of production owes its origins to the pair of Swedish economists, Heckscher (1919) and Ohlin (1933). They both frequently described the model as using three factors (labor, land, and capital), and the more well-known version, the two factor, two commodity model, owes much of its formal development to the work of Samuelson, especially in his joint work with Stolper (Stolper and Samuelson, 1941) and his two articles on factor-price

---

[13] For details, see Jones (1989).

[14] This is an example of how, even in a fairly large dimensional general equilibrium framework (17 equations in this 5×4 setting with given commodity price for commodity Y [and Y^*] and a given price increase for commodity X), some results do not need the full set of equations of change — here only the use of Eq. (12.1) for Home and the comparable equation for X-production in the Enclave is required. Of course more information would be necessary to determine in which direction X-capital moves.

equalization (Samuelson, 1948, 1949). If used as a model of a country not engaged in international trade, its properties are sensible with few surprises. The bowed-out transformation curve was used even in first-year textbook discussions, and, after the Stolper and Samuelson (1941) paper introduced the concept of a *production box*, patterned after earlier use of the *consumption box*, movements along the transformation curve could be seen to be the outcome of shifts of resources from one industry to another along a contract curve in the production box, a collection of points for which ratios of marginal input products are equated between sectors.

The Stolper–Samuelson paper did at the time seem somewhat surprising.[15] It showed how the imposition of a tariff on imports of a labor-intensive commodity would unambiguously result in a higher *real* wage rate because the nominal wage rate would increase more than either commodity price. Although this result was set in a context of international trade, the theorem is basically a reflection of the consequence for factor returns of any change in commodity prices whether or not international trade takes place. Such behavior is a direct consequence of an assumption about technology typically made in most models: Production in each sector uses two factors to produce a single commodity. That is, *joint production* is ruled out.[16] To some economists there was indeed a somewhat surprising result posited in the Stolper–Samuelson paper: An economy with fixed overall bundles of capital and labor *could*, by expanding production of the labor-intensive commodity, raise the capital/labor ratios utilized in *both* sectors of the economy. Indeed, the "could" should be replaced by "must." The reason: both sectors adopt techniques appropriate to factor prices, and as the wage/rental ratio is driven up by expansion of the labor-intensive commodity, *both* sectors respond by switching to more capital-intensive techniques.[17]

---

[15] It was rejected by the *American Economic Review*, and published later by the *Review of Economic Studies* in the United Kingdom.

[16] For a discussion (and disagreement) about the importance of ruling out joint production see Samuelson (1992) and Jones (1992). In this two factor setting, the lack of joint production means that each of the two production activities uses both factors to produce a *single* commodity.

[17] In the Stolper–Samuelson paper, techniques are assumed to be sensitive to factor prices, so that a tariff on labor-intensive importables causes both labor and capital to move along

The great element of surprise in the profession with the 2 × 2 model in a trade context emerged with Samuelson's article in 1948 in the *Economic Journal* arguing that under appropriate conditions factor prices would be brought into *equality* between two freely trading economies despite the *absence* of any world market in capital or labor as reflected in international factor mobility. Of course a major assumption is made, *viz.* that the two countries have exactly the same technology. (This assumption is often made in Heckscher–Ohlin models in order to isolate conditions at work separate from the technology differences featured in Ricardian-type modeling.) As well, competitive conditions prevail and, very importantly, it is assumed that both countries are actively producing the *same* pair of commodities. The fact that there was general surprise at this result is evident from what might be termed "revealed journalism": One year later (1949) in the same journal Samuelson was encouraged to write another article, "*International Factor-price Equalization Once Again.*"[18]

The analysis supporting the factor-price equalization theorem rests very much on a setting of free international trade between the two countries (a) that share the same technology; and (b) in which in equilibrium commodity prices are brought together internationally (assuming away all transfer costs or tariffs). The argument: In each country, wage rates and rental rates are related to commodity prices by the equilibrium condition that unit costs of production are equal to commodity prices. Unit costs depend on factor prices. If it is assumed that each country produces both commodities, and if both countries face the same commodity prices they *must* have the same

---

the contract curve in the production box towards production of importables, raising capital/labor ratios in both sectors. This kind of argument is correct, but a question can be raised about this result if technology is rigid in both sectors, in which case there is no change in either output and capital/labor ratios used in each sector remain constant. The result still holds. Indeed, a more simple argument suffices (whether or not technology is flexible): Use Eq. (12.1) with a positive price change for the labor-intensive industry and a similar equation with a zero price change for the capital-intensive sector, and solve the pair for the factor-price response This leads to a wage rate response to a change in a commodity price as shown below in Eq. (12.3). See Jones (1965).

[18] Some years later Hicks (1960), in referring to the simple Heckscher–Ohlin 2 × 2 model with fixed input/output coefficients, thought it strange that with given commodity prices the returns to labor and capital would be independent of factor supplies and that full-employment levels of outputs seemed to be determined independent of demand for given factor supplies.

factor prices because the zero profit condition of competitive equilibrium in a 2 × 2 model provides a pair of equations in two unknowns.[19] The reasoning is fortified by the discussion in Section II on how an economy adjusts to a change in factor endowments if commodity prices are constant. With the same number of factors as commodities in the Heckscher–Ohlin 2 × 2 context, commodity prices uniquely determine factor prices, so that adjustment to any factor endowment changes must be made only at the *extensive margin*. Thus despite having different factor endowments, with free trade both countries face the same commodity prices and therefore their factor prices (and production techniques used) are also the same.

What happens to the factor-price equalization theorem if countries do *not* share the same technology? Obviously there is no longer any tendency for free trade to bring about equalization. However, even in this case a strong result obtains, and this might be described as the "Factor-Price Determination" theorem: If a country produces as many commodities that are freely traded on world markets as it has factors of production (two apiece in the simple model), all (both) its factor prices are completely determined by the set of commodity prices ruling in world markets. That is, even though there are presumed to be no direct world markets in factors of production, the country has no power to affect its distribution of income among factors unless it purposely interferes with free trade (e.g., by levying tariffs on imports or taxes or subsidies on exports). It is sometimes argued that free trade is the optimal policy for a *small* country, that is, one unable to affect world commodity prices. However, the country may put some value on being able to affect its local distribution of income, in which case free trade might be considered too heavy a price to pay. Furthermore, even without equivalence in productivities, consider the possibility that immigration takes place in the more advanced country. As long as traded commodity prices stay constant there will be no pressure for the wage rate to fall. (Try this out on your labor economist colleague.)

---

[19]This of course assumes that relative factor intensities differ between commodities. As well, as Samuelson emphasized in his 1949 article, it assumes that the relatively labor-intensive commodity in one country is the same as that in the other. The opposite case leads to *the factor-intensity reversal* problem, much discussed after the appearance of the Leontief (1953) Paradox. As discussed later, in the multicommodity case equalization of factor prices with trade requires that both countries produce the *same* pair of commodities.

12.5   Mix and Match

There are numbers of possibilities wherein the setting involves a mixture of the Specific-Factors model and the Heckscher–Ohlin model. The former has been interpreted by Neary (1978) and others in a temporal setting as a short-run version of a model in which capital is specific between sectors, but with the passage of time capital can move and the model becomes a Heckscher–Ohlin model with both factors of production mobile between sectors.[20] In many ways this seems quite realistic, but for some purposes the consequences may appear to be surprising.

Regulations and forms of licensing sometimes have the effect of granting specificity to a form of capital (physical or human) in a setting in which other forms of capital may be exactly similar, but are not allowed to relocate to an industry that makes use of the "licensed" form of capital. Figure 12.1 makes use of a box diagram showing an initial situation at point *A*, a point on the contract curve arbitrarily chosen so that the return to capital is the same between industries 1 and 2. Now suppose that there is an increase in the price of the first sector, in which the "licensed" owners of capital work. If these regulations prevent capital from moving from the second industry to the first, labor is the only mobile factor and there is a movement to

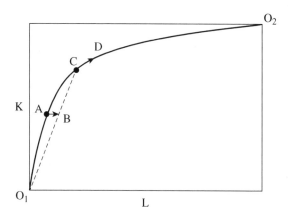

Figure 12.1.   Competition May Help

---

[20] An alternative method in which specific capital can be convened to mobile capital was suggested by Sanyal and Jones (1982) in which capital of one specificity can be converted to capital of another through international trade.

point B. Capital owners in the first sector are delighted, and their return, r_1, increases by a greater relative amount than the price increase, with the wage rate rising, but by less than does r_1. What would be the fate of the return to capital in the first sector if the "licensing" provision were no longer allowed? If capital in the second sector joined labor in flowing to the first sector in the same proportions used by the first sector until point C on the contract curve is reached, there would be no change in the return to capital in the first sector. However, free mobility of capital as well as labor would prompt an even greater flow of factors until a point such as D is reached.[21] The new equilibrium wage rate, once capital as well as labor becomes mobile, actually falls because I have assumed the second sector is more labor-intensive. Capitalists in the first sector are originally concerned when capital from the second sector invades their turf — but such capital brings with it a higher labor/capital ratio than used in the first sector at B (the equilibrium if only labor were mobile). Higher labor/capital ratios serve to increase capital's return and, although r_1 has increased more than price if the "licensing" restrictions were in effect (moving the equilibrium to B), r_1 is increased *even more* as the labor/capital ratio is raised by the even greater flow of factors from the first industry. (This possibility might prove a hard sell to capitalists in the first industry, and depends, of course, on sector 1 being capital-intensive.)

Such an example serves to contrast the way in which price changes alter wages and capital returns in the Specific-Factors model and the Heckscher–Ohlin model. Equation (12.2) for the Specific-Factors model shows that the effect of a price change (say in the first sector only) on the wage rate is dampened, the expression $\{\theta_1 i_1 s_1\}$ being a fraction that multiplies two relative features of technology (the relative labor-intensity ranking, i_1, and the relative flexibility in sector 1, s_1), together with the relative importance of the first sector in the national income, θ_1. What would the comparable expression for the wage change in the Heckscher–Ohlin model reveal? Refer back to Eq. (12.1), and consider the *pair* of competitive profit equations of change that would consist of an expression for sector I as in Eq. (12.1), and

---

[21] The movement from B to C first, and then to D is quite arbitrary; the important movement is from B to D, revealing that when capital also becomes mobile both factors move towards the capital-intensive first sector in a way that increases the labor/capital ratio used in both sectors (in response to a lower wage rate).

a second for sector 2 that would have a zero value for the price increase. Solve this pair for the relative change in the wage rate to obtain the value shown in Eq. (12.3):

$$\hat{w} = \{\theta_{K2}/[\theta_{K2} - \theta_{K1}]\}\hat{p}_1 \tag{12.3}$$

In the setting of the preceding paragraph, this shows a drop in the wage rate accompanying an increase in p_1. What is noteworthy (in comparing this with the specific-factors result shown in Eq. [12.2]) is what is missing: The only feature of technology that is relevant in Eq. (12.3) is the factor-intensity ranking, *not* the relative degree of factor substitutability and, what may be even more surprising is the *absence* of any parameter suggesting the importance of the industry that has received an increase in price. In the Heckscher–Ohlin model, it seems to make no difference whether the first sector comprises 50% of the national income or only 2%.[22]

This difference between the two models in the manner in which commodity price changes affect income distribution is also found if technical progress takes place (and, to simplify, commodity prices are kept constant). The two features of any technical progress that takes place in a single industry are the *extent* of the technical progress and the *bias* in technical progress. By the *extent* of technical progress here is meant the Hicksian measure of technical progress, the relative reduction in unit costs of production that would take place if there were *no* change in factor prices. For infinitesimal changes in technical progress at constant prices in industry i, the effect on income distribution would follow by replacing $\hat{p}_i$ in Eq. (12.1) by π_i, the Hicksian measure of the extent of technical progress. The *bias* in technical progress indicates the relative extent to which the ratio of labor to capital that would be utilized after technical progress at initial factor prices would be reduced.[23] For small changes the *bias* in technical progress does not

---

[22] Recall that expressions such as (12.2) and (12.3) refer to infinitesimal changes. For finite price changes these solutions are roughly correct, but if the first sector is very small, not much of a price *reduction* in the first sector would be necessary for the economy to become *completely specialized* in the second sector, thus making further price reductions for the first having no effect on the economy's nominal wage rate, although it does on *real* wages.

[23] Let $\hat{b}_{Li}$ and $\hat{b}_{ki}$ denote the relative *decreases* in unit labor and capital requirements per unit output in the ith sector that would take place with technical progress if factor prices were kept constant. The labor-saving *bias* in technical progress in sector i would be measured by $\{\hat{b}_{Li} - \hat{b}_{Ki}\}$.

affect factor prices in the Heckscher–Ohlin setting for the same reason that changes in endowments would not affect factor prices unless commodity prices changed. In the 2×2 basic version of the model, the real wage rate increases (and the return to capital falls) if technical progress only takes place in the first industry and this industry is relatively labor-intensive, regardless of whether technical progress is of the Hicksian labor-saving or capital-saving kind.[24]

Things are different if technical progress takes place in a specific-factors setting: the bias in technical progress indeed affects factor prices for a given extent of the progress even in the infinitesimal case where calculus is used in comparative static exercises (and this, of course, is standard procedure in most trade theory analyses). With more factors than commodities in Specific-Factors models, changes in factor endowments affect factor prices even if commodity prices are constant, so that factor bias in technical progress does have an influence on factor prices independent of the extent of progress. Surprises are to be found nonetheless. The analysis in Jones (1996) for a specific-factors setting investigates a case in which *all* sectors of the economy (for any number of commodities) experience technical progress of the same extent in each, progress that is *purely Hicksian labor saving* — at initial factor prices a unit of each good would be produced with the same amount of capital but less labor input. Although a natural response in such a case would be that the wage rate (*real wage*, in the case in which prices are held constant) must fall, note that *some* factor(s) of production must benefit from technical progress. The surprise that may be in store: labor might be a factor that gains from such progress. What would

---

[24] Bias does matter if technical progress is of *finite* size. However, there is still a surprise left: In the previous chapter of this book, an illustration is provided that contrasts two possibilities of technical progress in the capital-intensive sector (in the 2×2 setting), with each possibility yielding the same (Hicksian) extent of technical progress. One possibility illustrates a slight capital-saving bias in technical progress that also saves on labor. The other exhibits labor-using technical progress in the capital-intensive sector. In both cases, wages fall (since progress is only in the capital-intensive sector). However, the fall in the wage rate is *more severe* in the case in which progress has a labor-using bias. The rationale for this surprising result is found in the fact that if there is a labor-using bias in the capital-intensive commodity the gap separating factor intensities between sectors is *narrowed*. (For example, note the denominator in the solution for the wage change in Eq. [12.3], which, if it is narrowed in absolute terms, causes the wage rate to fall even more if the first sector is capital intensive.)

be required is that elasticities of substitution in production throughout the economy are, on average, sufficiently high. Would Cobb–Douglas suffice? That would be more than sufficient; the condition for labor's real wage to increase in this case of pure labor-saving technical progress is that the average value (over all sectors) for elasticities of substitution in production exceed the ratio of the average relative share of capital to the relative share of labor, a ratio usually taken to be less than 1/2.

So far the remarks about the Heckscher–Ohlin model have been focused on the case of two produced commodities. If a country is engaged in free international trade the case of many commodities is simple to handle because trade allows a great concentration in the number of commodities produced without restricting the number of commodities a country might consume. (The Ricardian model, of course, shows this in the extreme case in which the movement to free trade allows a country to concentrate on producing the single commodity in which it has the greatest comparative advantage.) The reason: No more commodities need be produced than the number of factors of production — one in the Ricardian case, and two in the 2 × 2 Heckscher–Ohlin model. Suppose in a trading world with many commodities only a pair of factors, capital and labor, is required to produce each. Figure 12.2 illustrates how a country that is growing and developing, such that its overall capital to labor endowment ratio increases, changes the pattern of its production with growth. The input requirements for each of four different commodities are shown in Fig. 12.2, with required capital/labor input ratios rising monotonically as wage/rental rates increase.[25] Furthermore, assume that as the country (call it Home) develops, world commodity prices remain unchanged. Such given prices lead to the heavily lined locus whereby production patterns systematically change with growth: If Home's endowment capital/labor ratio is quite small, Home concentrates on producing the most labor-intensive commodity 1. When Home becomes more capital abundant, its wage/rental ratio improves until it is able to start producing the second commodity as well as the first.[26] At this stage, further small increases in the endowment capital/labor ratio leave factor prices unchanged because Home is producing both commodities at

---

[25]These curves are drawn (arbitrarily) so that no factor-intensity reversals take place.

[26]Figure 12.2 is based upon what is called the "Hicksian Composite Unit Value Isoquant," as found in the work of Jones (1974) and Caves, Frankel, and Jones (2007, pp. 106–108).

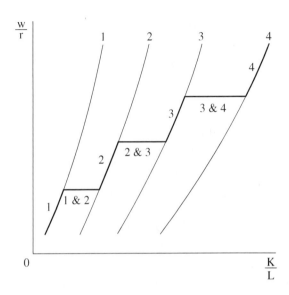

Figure 12.2.   Factor Endowments and Factor Prices

given prices. Asymmetrical changes are taking place along this first "flat" in Fig. 12.2: As K/L increases, Home shifts resources out of the first commodity into the second, until it is completely specialized to the second commodity. Further increases in K/L from that point do result in increases in the wage/rental ratio, until Home can begin producing commodity 3, even more capital/intensive than commodities 1 and 2. Such a process with endowment growth continues for any number of commodities traded on world markets (only four commodities in Fig. 12.2).

My own experience teaching this material to undergraduates is that the kind of situation shown in Fig. 12.2 is more interesting to them than is the basic 2 × 2 Heckscher–Ohlin model. Here the basic question becomes, "*Which* commodities does a country produce?" Because a country can specialize to a great extent when it enters into international trade, as its circumstances change (becoming more developed — increasing its capital/labor endowment proportions) the answer to this question systematically changes. As well there is the question: "As capital is accumulated, or as immigration occurs, are wages and returns to capital changing?" The answer is *maybe*, sometimes *yes* and sometimes *no*. And if more than a single commodity is produced, note that at the microlevel growth is *not* apt to be balanced. That is, in a context of trade, there typically will be some (one in this simple case) sector expanding while another contracts. *Uneven growth* patterns at the microlevel are to be expected even if at the macro level (i.e., in the aggregate) the country were to grow at a fairly regular rate.[27]

Although Fig. 12.2 does exhibit Home concentrating its production when engaged in trade either to a single or a pair of commodities, suppose that there are many more commodities consumed and produced on world markets. Without increasing the number of productive factors used in an industry beyond two (and thus maintaining the simplicity of not having to deal with the possibility of factor complementarity or different degrees of substitutability) it is possible to alter this setting by creating a *hybrid* model making use of both of the two production models being discussed in this chapter, the Specific-Factors model and the Heckscher–Ohlin model.[28] Let some labor (or capital as well as labor) be used each period to *produce* new capital equipment (i.e., to engage in *investment*). To simplify (leaving some of the alternative important features to macro-economists), assume that it is a constant flow of inputs each period that is used for investment purposes. The crucial feature is that newly created capital is of the form that is *specific* to the particular sector, or pair of sectors, that in that period yield the highest rate of return to capital. This selection (to the best single or pair of commodities) may not be the same as was made in the previous period or the period previous to that. In other words, there may be several or more sectors actively producing this period because in the past these sectors have been the winners attracting new investment even though they are no longer winners in the current period. Eventually the return to specific capital in some sectors may no longer remain positive, leading Home to stop producing that commodity. (As well, technical progress may result in better types of specific capital so that older types no longer stay in use.) Thus labor not used for current investment is absorbed in two other kinds of activity: (a) it is used with the new capital to produce (or increase production of) this period's sector(s) yielding the highest return to capital,

---

[27]Further details are found in the work of Jones (2004). This explanation assumes that oil commodities are traded on world markets, a situation that does not take account of nontraded commodities.

[28]This hybrid model is described briefly by Jones (2007a).

and (b) it is used in cooperation with the specific capital found in other sectors that have been favored in the past and are still actively producing. The consequence: History matters, and although any producing sector uses only a pair of inputs, the panoply of current production of commodities and array of specific-factors is much less compressed than in the $2 \times n$ version of the Heckscher–Ohlin model. Furthermore, it might even be the case that new investment is not made in any export sector, but instead is received by a sector that competes with imports.[29]

12.6   Concluding Remarks

As mentioned in Section I, competitive trade theory has on display a number of surprising results (or paradoxes) whose source resides primarily in the nature of income effects in demand.[30] These are results which can be developed in the so-called Exchange Model which, I would argue, can be thought of as one of a set of four prominent competitive models of production that are used in trade theory. The Exchange Model is one in which outputs of each commodity available in supply are considered fixed (or, as in the case of immiserizing growth, change by an arbitrary amount, independent of any change in commodity prices). To introduce production in such a setting let the economy have a pair of different kinds of labor, each suited only to a particular occupation so that if the factor endowment bundle is fixed, so is the commodity endowment vector. The opposite extreme is the Ricardian model, in which the transformation schedule exhibits a constant rate at which production of one commodity can be reduced to produce more of the other. The final two sets are those discussed in this chapter, the Specific-Factors model and the Heckscher–Ohlin model.

There is a recent example in competitive trade theory that serves to illustrate the theme that a good criterion for a model is that it corresponds to common sense as well as being capable of yielding (and explaining) surprising results. The multicommodity version of the Ricardian model was used by Samuelson (2004) to admonish those economists who seemed to be excessive in their praise for the benefits flowing from the world's movement

---

[29]That is, this period's highest rate of return to capital might be found in a sector in which output is quite a bit less than current consumption.

[30]Once again I ignore the Leontief Paradox in this catalogue.

toward greater degrees of globalization. It was not that Samuelson disagreed with the general favorable outcome of such globalization, but he was anxious to emphasize that not every country would gain all the time, because more trade might result (and generally would) with terms of trade turning against some countries. At the time of his article, pointing to oil-importing countries would provide a good example. In terms of results found with this Ricardian model, I mention in passing the possibility analyzed in Chapter 3 of this book concerning gains or losses to a country (call it Home) which has an absolute advantage in many goods (say all) compared with another (call it Foreign). Suppose Foreign acquires through stealth or gift the superior technology whereby Home's best export commodity is produced. Could Home gain by such a loss? The answer we found seemed to us surprising: Consider the relative size of the two trading countries, L^*/L. There is a sequence of such relative sizes such that, with some restriction on demand (say Cobb–Douglas with equal spending shares among commodities for both countries), Home would actually *gain* even though it has lost its best export commodity. Involved is a balancing of the gain to Home consumers from being able to take advantage of a lower price for its former best export commodity and the potential loss from an increase in price of other goods produced in Foreign and imported by Home when Foreign's wage rate increases from the technological acquisition. The word "when" should be changed to an "if " because for some pairs of country size the foreign wage rate either does not increase, or at least not by very much. This result would indeed seem surprising.[31]

A common characteristic is found in all these cases discussed here and mentioned earlier: They all reflect possibilities that are found in competitive

---

[31] Another example in which trade theory suggests a surprising possibility for wage rates has emerged from the literature on fragmentation of production activities whereby various parts or "fragments" may separately be produced in different locales, sometimes in different countries. In this literature, there emerges the possibility that a quite labor-intensive fragment of production might be outsourced from a highly developed country to a country with much lower wage rates. The commonly accepted view that such outsourcing must result either in greater unemployment or lower wage rates in the developing country does not necessarily follow — Home wages might increase. The Heckscher–Ohlin framework is exploited by Jones and Kierzkowski (2001) to describe how this can happen. More recently this kind of phenomenon has been discussed by Grossman and Rossi-Hansberg (2008) and Baldwin and Robert-Nicoud (2010).

general equilibrium models of production, in which there is always more than one market — some are commodity markets and some are factor markets. Surprising results can be found when these markets interact, even though the structural form for production may seem to be very simple and to reflect common sense. This is what gives these models value in trying to understand, say, the possibilities involved when countries trade with each other.

References

Baldwin, R. and Robert-Nicoud, F. (2014). Trade-in-goods and Trade-in-tasks: An Integrating Framework. *Journal of International Economics*, 92(1), 51–62.

Bhagwati, J. (1958). Immiserizing Growth: A Geometrical Note. *Review of Economic Studies*, 25, 201–205.

Bhagwati. J., Brecher, R., and Hatta, T. (1983). The Generalized Theory of Transfer and Welfare: Bilateral Transfers in a Multilateral World. *American Economic Review*, 73, 606–618.

Brecher, R. and Bhagwati, J. (1981). Foreign Ownership and the Theory of Trade and Welfare. *Journal of Political Economy*, 89, 497–511.

Caves, R.E., Frankel, J.A., and Jones, R.W. (2007). *World Trade and Payments: An Introduction* (10th ed.). Boston, MA: Addison Wesley.

Chichilnisky, G. (1980). Basic Goods, the Effects of Commodity Transfers and International Economic Order. *Journal of Development Economics* 7, 505–519.

Edgeworth. F.Y. (1894). The Theory of International Values: 1. *Economic Journal*, 4, 35–50.

Findlay, R. and Jones, R.W. (2000). Factor Bias and Technical Progress. *Economics Letters*, 68, 303–308.

Gale, D. (1974). Exchange Equilibrium and Coalitions: An Example. *Journal of Mathematical Economics*, 1, 63–66.

Grossman, G. and Rossi-Hansberg. E. (2008). Trading Tasks: A Simple Theory of Offshoring. *American Economic Review*, 98, 1978–1997.

Haberler, G. (1936). *The Theory of International Trade*. London: W Hodge.

Heckscher, E. (1919). The Effect of Foreign Trade on the Distribution of Income. *Ekonomisk Tidskrift*, 21, 497–512.

Hicks, J. (1960). Linear Theory. *The Economic Journal*, 70, 671–709.

Johnson, H.G. (1953). Equilibrium Growth in an International Economy. *The Canadian Journal of Economics and Political Science*, 19, 478–500.

Johnson, H.G. (1955). Economic Expansion and International Trade. *The Manchester School of Economic and Social Studies*, 23, 95–112.

Johnson, H.G. (1960). Income Distribution, the Offer Curve, and the Effects of Tariffs. *The Manchester School of Economic and Social Studies*, 28, 215–242.

Jones, R.W. (1965). The Structure of Simple General Equilibrium Models. *Journal of Political Economy*, 73, 557–572.

Jones, R.W. (1971). A Three Factor Model in Theory, Trade and History. In: J. Bhagwati, R. Jones, R. Mundell, and J. Vanek (Eds.), *Trade, Balance of Payments and Growth* (pp. 3–21). Amsterdam: North-Holland.

Jones, R.W. (1974). The Small Country in a Many Commodity World. *Australian Economic Papers*, 13, 225–236.

Jones, R.W. (1975). Income Distribution and Effective Protection in a Multi-Commodity Trade Model. *Journal of Economic Theory*, 11, 1–15.

Jones, R.W. (1984). The Transfer Problem in a Three-Agent Setting. *Canadian Journal of Economics*, 17, 1–14.

Jones, R.W. (1985). Income Effects and Paradoxes in the Theory of International Trade. *The Economic Journal*, 95, 330–344.

Jones, R.W. (1989). Co-movements in Relative Commodity Prices and International Capital Flows: A Simple Model. *Economic Inquiry*, 27, 131–141.

Jones, R.W. (1992). Jointness in Production and Factor-Price Equalization. *Review of International Economics*, 1, 10–18.

Jones, R.W. (1996). International Trade. Real Wages and Technical Progress. The Specific Factors Model. *International Review of Economics and Finance*, 5, 113–124.

Jones, R.W. (2000). *Globalization and the Theory of Input Trade*. Cambridge, MA: MIT Press.

Jones, R.W. (2004). Micro-Churning with Smooth Macro Growth: Two Examples. In S. Dowrick, R. Pitchford, and S. Tumovsky (Eds.), *Economic Growth and Macroeconomic Dynamics: Recent Developments in Economic Theory* (Ch. 8). Cambridge University Press.

Jones, R.W. (2007a). Specific Factors and Heckscher-Ohlin; An Intertemporal Blend. *Singapore Economic Review*, 52, 1–6.

Jones, R.W. (2007b). Who Is Better Able to Get Protection? *Asia & Pacific Journal of Accounting Economics*, 14, 1–5.

Jones, R.W. and Dei, F. (1983). International Trade and Foreign Investment. A Simple Model. *Economic Inquiry*, 21, 449–464.

Jones, R.W. and Kierzkowski, H. (2001). Globalization and the Consequences of International Fragmentation. In: G. A. Calvo, R. Dornbusch, and M. Obstfeld (Eds.), *Money, Capital Mobility and Trade: Essays in Honor of Robert A. Mundell* (pp. 365–383). Cambridge, MA: MIT Press.

Jones, R.W. and Ruffin, R. J.(2008). The Technology Transfer Paradox. *Journal of International Economics*, 75, 321–328.

Komiya, R. and Schizuki, T. (1967). Transfer Payments and Income Distribution. *The Manchester School of Economic and Social Studies*, 35, 245–255.

Leontief, W. (1953). Domestic Production and Foreign Trade: The American Capital Position Re-examined. *Proceedings of the American Philosophical Society*, 97, 332–349.

Lerner, A.P. (1936). The Symmetry between Import and Export Taxes. *Economica*, 3, 306–313.

Metzler, L. (1949). Tariffs, the Terms of Trade, and the Distribution of National Income. *Journal of Political Economy*, 57, 1–29.

Neary, J.P. (1978). Short-run Capital Specificity and the Pure Theory of International Trade. *Economic Journal*, 88, 488–510.

Ohlin, B. (1933). *Interregional and International Trade*. Cambridge, MA: Harvard University Press.

Samuelson, P.A. (1948). International Trade and the Equalisation of Factor Prices. *Economic Journal*, 58, 163–184.

Samuelson, P.A. (1949). International Factor-Price Equalization Once Again. *Economic Journal*, 59, 181–197.

Samuelson, P.A. (1971). *Ohlin Was Right. Swedish Journal of Economics*, 73, 365–384.

Samuelson, P.A. (1992). Factor-Price Equalization by Trade in Joint and Non-Joint Production. *Review of International Economics*, 1, 1–9.

Samuelson, P.A. (2004). Where Ricardo and Mill Rebut and Confirm Arguments of Mainstream Economists Supporting Globalization. *Journal of Economic Perspectives*, 18, 135–146.

Sanyal, K. and Jones, R.W. (1982) The Theory of Trade in Middle Products. *American Economic Review*, 72, 16–31.

Stolper. W.F. and Samuelson, P.A. (1941). Protection and Real Wages. *Review of Economic Studies*, 9, 58–73.

Yano, M. (1983). Welfare Aspects of the Transfer Problem. *Journal of International Economics*, 15, 277–289.

Part III

Fragmentation of the Production Process and International Trade

Chapter 13 begins with the statement: "The bulk of international trade consists of the exchange of intermediate products, raw materials, and goods which require further local processing before reaching the final consumer." The first *diagram* (not Fig. 13.1) suggests why, in the production process, the international trade that takes place between (or among) countries is referred to here as "trade in middle products." In the early stages of the production process (that we called the *Input Tier*), local labor and local resources produce goods that enter into the trading process (although some are kept back for use at home) to exchange for other middle products. The array of middle products in the *Output Tier* of the economy is then joined by local labor further to process the production of final consumption goods to satisfy local *consumption* demands. The chapter then continues with formal explanations of various elasticities and demand changes. The Appendix adds more formal touches.

The remarks in Chapter 13 set the stage for most of the remaining chapters in Part III, and, in a sense, Chapter 14 probes more thoroughly into the role of "middle products" discussed in the previous chapter. The focus now is on the role of *services* in the production of commodities. We wanted to focus on what services do. There was much interest in the 1970s and 1980s in the nature of services, and how and why they are different from commodities. The production process depicted in Chapter 14, Fig. 14.1 emphasizes the importance of *production blocks* and *service links* (and admits as well the role of other kinds of services that connect final production outcomes to consumers). Service links help in the process of *fragmentation* (not a nasty word) of the production process especially by allowing the connection of various production blocks that might be located in different firms or different countries. However, our interest or concern was not on finding which countries had a comparative advantage in producing the service links, but on finding countries that might have a comparative advantage in producing different production blocks that then are allowed by the existence of service links to be joined together through international trade.

In the decade or two before the 1990 paper (Chapter 14), and increasingly in the years since, the fastest growing types of items have been *parts and components* that are produced in a variety of countries and then brought together through international trade in order that one country can assemble them to produce a final (tradeable) commodity. The concept of *intra-industry trade* covers not only final commodities that are *varieties* of each other but also of the parts and components used in their production. The costs involved in linking together parts and components that are produced in several different countries have been drastically reduced in the past few decades, and this helps to account for the high rates of their growth in international trade. Why would producers of the final product wish to demand this fragmentation of the production process? The answer lies in the 200-year old Ricardian concept of *comparative advantage*. A country's labor force involved in producing parts and components may not directly enter world markets but the items produced by such labor can be traded across country borders if the required service link costs to final producers are outweighed by the gains allowed by having various components being produced in countries that have the greatest comparative advantage in the component assigned to them.

Chapter 15 is a different kind of paper, not at all filled with formal demonstrations of how mathematical training can be put to work in discussing "general equilibrium" models used in the theory of international trade. However, it does focus on a broader set of questions involving the fragmentation in production processes that concern the role of international trade in the less developed countries of the world.

The particular feature of this chapter is the focus on the connection between the younger generation in less developed countries and the older generation in developed countries. For example, early educational opportunities that students in developing countries now have when doors of universities in America and Europe are more open to them can, in subsequent years, lead to business connections between foreign graduates and American or European firms, such as access to loans from American and European sources that the foreign younger generation may find difficult to obtain in their own countries. It is generally the case that *physical capital* is held mostly by the older generation and *human capital* is often held relatively more by the younger generation. Indeed, Chapter 15 ends with an interesting and perhaps surprising remark found in *The Economist* (in 2000) about the views the Japanese older generation has for their younger generation. It is interesting to us how these attitudes have a role to play in the recent changes in the nature of International Trade.

Chapter 16 returns to my remarks about the importance and relevance of previous statements about fragmentation. The second section of this chapter focuses on two alternative scenarios that might capture the basic changes and consequences of the type of international trade in the later years of the 20th century. In both scenarios, the concept of *increasing returns to scale* is important. Some economists make use of the arguments found in the *Chamberlinian monopolistic competition* model, in which firms face cost curves that are still in their negatively sloped section because the demand curve they face is negatively sloped (instead of horizontal as in perfect competition models) which, therefore, emphasizes there are still increasing returns. That is, an increase in output lowers the average costs of production. The alternative source for increasing returns in the model we use in this chapter (and throughout Part III) relies on the great fall in the prices of many service link activities that help to allow a greater degree to which the production process can be fragmented to allow a variety of firms in other countries to supply parts and components to another firm that makes use of them in producing the final product. This is what allows "increasing returns" *not* on the factory floor, but in the provision of lower cost service links leading to a greater degree of gains from comparative advantages from many production blocks. Figs. 16.1 and 16.2 illustrate the difference between "Agglomeration" within a country and "Disagglomeration" as greater use is made of production blocks produced in a variety of different countries. Thus the arguments we use in this chapter differ from those found in Fujita, Krugman, and Venables: *The Spatial Economy: Cities, Regions and International Trade* (1999), MIT Press, Cambridge, Mass.

Chapter 17 is the last paper in this section and, in effect, serves as a summary of the more basic remarks made in the other chapters of Part III. A repetition on my part now seems superfluous.

CHAPTER 13

The Theory of Trade in Middle Products*

Kalyan K. Sanyal and Ronald W. Jones

The bulk of international trade consists of the exchange of intermediate products, raw materials, and goods which require further local processing before reaching the final consumer. Furthermore, few items in international commerce are pure raw materials or primary factors which have not received any value-added from other local inputs. If production is viewed as a spectrum of activities whereby local primary resources help produce and transform commodities into the final state required by consumers, these observations suggest that international trade takes place in "middle products."

One immediate consequence of this view of the nature of trade is that small countries which are price takers in world markets nonetheless exert some influence over local costs and prices of consumer goods. For raw materials or goods in process, this influence on consumer goods' prices clearly reflects local additional value created by the process of manufacturing and assembly. However, even for commodities which physically appear in final form in the world market, consumers typically pay prices which include local transportation and retailing services. The purpose of this

*Seminar Paper/Institute for International Economic Studies, Stockholm University, ISSN 0347-8749; 128.

This research was supported in part by National Science Foundation grant no, SOC 78-16159. The chapter is a completely revised version of a paper of the same title. No. 128 in the Seminar Paper Series of the Institute for International Economic Studies. University of Stockholm.

chapter is to analyze the consequences for a small trading community of changes in world conditions or local policies when the basic role of trade is to allow the composition of outputs of productive activity at early stages of the productive spectrum to differ from the composition of intermediate products and raw materials required as inputs in the final stages in which consumption goods are produced.

The model developed in this chapter has several antecedents. The theory of effective protection has given central attention to the role of trade in intermediates. However, this theory has not allowed prices of consumer goods to be determined by local cost conditions and local taste patterns since all prices reflect given world prices raised by the relevant rate of duty.[1] As well, standard trade theory has developed models in which some final consumer goods are traded while others, because of high transport costs (natural or man-made), are nontraded.[2] In the present chapter, this evenhanded treatment of commodities which give rise to consumer satisfaction (both tradeables and nontradeables enter the utility function) is replaced by the view that *all* consumption goods are nontradeables, differing from one another in the proportions in which they require inputs of traded middle products as opposed to local resources.

The view that all international trade takes place in what we call middle products suggests that local economic activity can be segregated into two "tiers." The *Input Tier* combines local resources to produce outputs (middle products) *for* the world market. The *Output Tier* makes use of traded middle products (of a different composition than represented by production in the Input Tier) as inputs combined with local resources to produce final consumption goods.[3] Thus one tier of the economy is connected to world markets at the output level whereas the other tier has its contact at the input stage. One factor of production, labor, is capable of moving between these two tiers in response to changing economic incentives. Indeed, the

---

[1] See, for example, the discussion of effective protection in W. Max Corden (1971a).

[2] For example, see W. G. Salter, or, Jones (1974).

[3] This view of the productive spectrum neglects the use of traded middle products as inputs in the production of other traded middle products. For an earlier use of a two-tier breakdown, involving a distinction between exportables and importables, on the one hand, and consumption goods and investment goods on the other (in a Heckscher–Ohlin context), see Corden (1971b).

allocation of labor between tiers turns out to be a crucial determinant of the internal distribution of income.

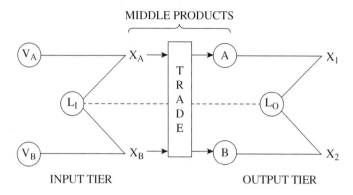

These interrelations are illustrated schematically in the accompanying chart, showing the two tiers of the production spectrum connected by the possibility that trade in middle products frees the Output Tier from item-by-item dependence upon the products of the Input Tier. The V_i are the economy's ultimate specific-factors (say raw materials not yet processed). The quantities of x_A and x_B produced in the Input Tier can be supplemented and exchanged in trade for inputs A, B used to produce final outputs, x_1 and x_2, in the Output Tier. The structure of the model allows for a multiplicity of goods to be produced in both tiers of the economy. However, we proceed by first considering a stripped-down model in which the economy produces only *one* commodity that is traded on world markets (x_B). It engages in trade in order to obtain quantities of some other middle product (A) which, in the Output Tier, is combined with local labor to produce a single consumption good (x_1). Two broad types of questions are raised, namely, how are local income distribution and production patterns affected by (i) changes in aggregate spending — for example, triggered by transfers (or exchange rate changes), and (ii) changes in relative prices of middle products, reflective either of alterations in the terms of trade in world markets or of changes in commercial policy.

Although this simple prototype serves starkly to reveal many of the features that characterize the more general model, the assumption that only one final commodity from the Output Tier is consumed severely restricts the role of local taste patterns in affecting the distribution of income. Therefore, Sec. 2 of the chapter broadens the model in allowing each tier of the economy to produce two commodities, as is shown in the chart. At this point, algebraic details are relegated to the Appendix. Sec. 3 is devoted to showing how the model of middle products may be generalized and extended in a number of directions. Throughout the chapter, monetary issues are swept aside by the assumption that sufficient changes in local supplies of money are provided to support whatever changes in the general price *level* are called forth by the model. The reason the price level emerges as a variable in what purports to be a real general equilibrium model of trade is that prices of all (nontraded) consumption goods are determined relative to given world prices of traded middle products.[4]

This model of trade in middle products makes use of two more simple models found in trade theory: the Heckscher–Ohlin model with two occupationally mobile productive factors; and the Specific-Factors model. Although our model is considerably richer in allowing for structural detail than either of these precursors, it at times leads to less ambiguous or different results. For example, an export surplus, perhaps representing the short-run impact of an exchange rate devaluation, not only signals an overall reduction in the economy's consumption, it also redistributes earned income away from labor. The real wage must fall. To take another example, a tariff that protects an industry producing a traded middle product may lower the real wage even if that industry is more labor intensive than every other industry in the economy.

13.1   The Two-tier Approach

The key feature of the model is that international trade serves to demarcate all productive activity into two tiers. (1) In the Input Tier, primary productive factors and labor produce commodities (middle products) which can be traded on world markets but are never consumed directly as final products. 2) On the contrary, the Output Tier combines middle products obtainable on the world market with labor to produce final (nontraded) consumption goods. In this section, we focus on the significance of this two-tier approach by assuming that, in the Input Tier, labor, L_1, is combined with a fixed factor (used only in the Input Tier), V_B, to produce a

---

[4]The interaction of monetary and real factors in a model of trade in middle products is analyzed in Jones and Purvis (1983).

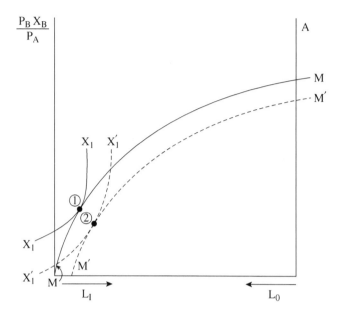

Figure 13.1.

single, traded middle product, x_B. In addition, the Output Tier consists of a single sector producing a final consumption good, x_1, by means of labor and a traded middle product, A. To highlight the role of international trade, we assume that the entire output of the middle product produced in the Input Tier (x_B) is exported in exchange for a different, unique middle product (A) to be used in the Output Tier as an ingredient in producing final consumption, x_1.[5]

The relationships determining an initial balanced-trade equilibrium are illustrated in Fig. 13.1.[6] The MM curve shows the value of middle product output, x_B, in units of commodity A (at given world prices p_A and p_B). The curve rises at a diminishing rate as more labor (L_1) is allocated to the Input Tier to be used with a factor (say natural resource V_B) specifically used only to produce x_B and given in fixed supply. The slope of the MM curve shows labor's marginal product in producing middle product B,

---

[5]A more general stance, allowing some local production of the middle product which is imported, is adopted in Section 2.

[6]A similar type of diagram, with the horizontal axis representing the intercountry allocation of the world's capital supply, has been used by Ronald Findlay.

evaluated in A units. The community's total supply of labor (L) is assumed constant. Labor not used in the Input Tier is allocated to the Output Tier and is measured leftwards from the right-hand origin. Quantity of middle product A, which is combined with labor to produce final output, is measured on the right-hand vertical axis so that isoquants for producing final consumption rise homogeneously from the right-hand origin. The slope of these isoquants would reflect, in equilibrium, the wage rate measured in units of A. Equilibrium is shown by point 1 where isoquant $X_1 X_1$ is tangent to MM and the market- clearing wage rate (in A units) is reflected in the common slope at point 1. Furthermore, the vertical distance from point 1 to the labor axis measures both the equilibrium value (in A units) of the output of middle product B and the community's total imports of middle product A. Trade is balanced.

We first ask how the allocation of labor and the internal distribution of income are altered if this trading community is forced to run an export surplus of a predetermined amount. Such an outward transfer payment is illustrated in Fig. 13.1 by drawing a curve $M'M'$ parallel to but lower than MM. For any given allocation of labor between tiers the vertical distance to the MM curve still shows the value (in A units) of the economy's production of traded middle products (x_B). By contrast, the $M'M'$ curve shows quantities of A available as inputs to the Output Tier. The shorter distance to $M'M'$ reflects the assumption that an export surplus is created (the vertical gap between MM and $M'M'$). As a consequence, less final consumption is possible. The equilibrium point shifts from 1 to 2 on the lower isoquant $X_1' X_1'$. (Note both points 1 and 2 are shown in circles.)

This reduction in real consumption levels is not neutral in its impact on internal income distribution. Relative to the given world prices of middle products A and B, the wage rate has been reduced; isoquant $X_1' X_1'$ at 2 is flatter than at $X_1 X_1$ at 1. Labor has been reallocated from the Output Tier to the Input Tier, and this move drives down the return to labor and increases the return to the factor used specifically in the Input Tier.

This direction of change in factor rewards holds also in *real* terms. To see this, consider the competitive profit conditions in the two tiers of the economy. In the Output Tier any change in the wage rate and /or the price of middle product A is passed on to affect the cost and price of producing a unit of final consumption, p_1. More explicitly,

$$\theta_{L1}\hat{w} + \theta_{A1}\hat{p}_A = \hat{p}_1, \tag{13.1}$$

where θ_{L1} and θ_{A1} reflect the distributive shares of labor and middle product A, respectively, and "hats" represent relative changes, for example, $\hat{p}_i = d \ln p_i$. In the present circumstances, the price of middle product A is kept constant. The wage rate falls, dragging down the price of final consumption goods, but not by as much. That is, the *real wage* must fall as a consequence of the outward transfer. Similarly, in the Input Tier the competitive profit conditions of change in general are shown by (2),

$$\theta_{LB}\hat{w} + \theta_{VB}\hat{r}_B = \hat{p}_B, \qquad (13.2)$$

where θ_{VB} is the specific-factor's distributive share and r_B is its rental return. With the price of traded middle product B held constant, the decline in the wage rate must cause the return to the specific-factor to rise — more so in real terms than in nominal terms.

Whereas Fig. 13.1 was designed to illustrate how labor loses when the trade account goes into surplus at given world prices, Fig. 13.2 shows how labor gains when the country's terms of trade improve. In particular, suppose that the world price of middle product B, the only middle product produced domestically, rises and the price of imports, p_A, remains constant.

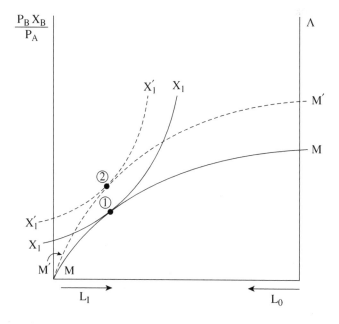

Figure 13.2.

The proportional upward shift of the MM curve to $M'M'$ shows that any given labor allocation now allows greater imports of A. Output of final consumption goods rises from 1 to 2 on the new isoquant $X_1'X_1'$. The comparison between 1 and 2 shows a slight reallocation of labor towards the Output Tier. This need not be the case. In particular, if labor and middle product A are highly substitutable in producing final consumption, labor could flow towards the Input Tier. Nonetheless, labor's real wage rises to some extent. We turn now to a brief algebraic account in order to make these and other points explicit.

Labor is fully employed. If the aggregate labor force is fixed, as we assume, any increase in labor used to produce traded middle product B must reduce the use of labor in the Output Tier. In relative terms,

$$\lambda_{L1}\hat{L}_1 + \lambda_{L0}\hat{L}_0 = 0, \tag{13.3}$$

where λ_{L1} and λ_{L0} denote the fractions of the aggregate labor force allocated to each tier. L_1 depends upon the technology whereby B is produced, as well as the world price of B. Given the amount of the fixed factor available to produce $B(V_B)$, the demand for labor in the Input Tier is linked to the wage rate (relative to p_B) by a downward-sloping marginal product schedule whose elasticity, γ_1, is defined by (13.4):

$$\hat{L}_1 = -\gamma_1(\hat{w} - \hat{p}_B). \tag{13.4}$$

Alternatively, (13.4′) shows the dependence of the wage rate on the price of output, p_B, and the labor allocated to the Input Tier, L_1:

$$\hat{w} = \hat{p}_B - (1/\gamma_1)\hat{L}_1. \tag{13.4′}$$

In the Output Tier, the demand for labor depends both upon total output of the consumption good, x_1, and the intensity with which labor is used per unit output, a_{L1}, and is the product of the two. Therefore, if there is any change in the intensive or extensive margin,

$$\hat{L}_0 = \hat{a}_{L1} + \hat{x}_1. \tag{13.5}$$

We assume here that there is some degree of substitutability between labor and the middle product (A) used in production of the consumption good. Indeed, let σ_1, denote the elasticity of substitution between the two inputs in the Output Tier. Then[7]

$$\hat{a}_{L1} = -\theta_{A1}\sigma_1(\hat{w} - \hat{p}_A). \tag{13.6}$$

Therefore, $\hat{L}_0$ can be written as in (7):

$$\hat{L}_0 = -\theta_{A1}\sigma_1(\hat{w} - \hat{p}_A) + \hat{x}_1. \tag{13.7}$$

Finally, these expressions for the change in each tier's demand for labor can be combined in (3) to yield the required change in the wage rate that preserves full employment:

$$\hat{w} = \zeta_A\hat{p}_A + \zeta_B\hat{p}_B + (\lambda_{L0}/\omega)\hat{x}_1,$$

$$\text{where } \zeta_A \equiv \lambda_{L0}\delta_L/\omega : \zeta_B \equiv \lambda_{L1}\gamma_1/\omega; \tag{13.8}$$

$$\text{and } \omega \equiv \lambda_{L1}\gamma_1 + \lambda_{L0}\delta_L, \text{ where } \delta_L = \theta_{A1}\sigma_1.$$

The term ω brings together (and literally averages) the two means by which an increase in the wage rate causes labor to be released from both tiers of the economy for any given level of final output. In the Input Tier a 1 percent rise in the wage rate would, at constant prices of middle products, yield a γ_1 percent reduction in labor demand, while in the Output Tier a 1 percent rise in the wage rate encourages a release of labor at the intensive margin of δ_L percent. Therefore, if substitution possibilities in general are quite high, increases in final consumption (say by running trade deficits at constant world prices) necessitate a release of labor to the Output Tier, but such labor could be released without exerting much upward pressure on the wage rate.

The explicit solution for the wage rate change provided by Eq. (13.8) confirms that should a small country facing fixed world prices for middle products run a trade surplus, its required reduction in final consumption, x_1 must lower the wage rate. And Eq. (13.1) showed how the price of the consumption good is thus driven down, but by less than the nominal wage. The Figure 13.2 illustration of an improvement in the terms of trade and its impact on wages is captured only in part by the fraction ζ_B in Eq. (13.8). An increase in p_B, the price of the nation's export commodity, must improve

---

[7] This is easily derived from two relationships. On the one hand, cost minimization requires the distributive share weighted average of $\hat{a}_{L1}$ and $\hat{a}_{A1}$ to equal zero. On the other $(\hat{a}_{A1} - \hat{a}_{L1})$ divided by $(\hat{w} - \hat{p}_A)$ is equal to σ_1, by definition. Further details are found in Jones (1965).

aggregate real income and expenditure by an amount proportional to the price rise and the fraction which trade represents of the national income. Since trade is assumed balanced, θ_{A1} reflects both the share of imported middle product A in the production of final consumption and the share of exports (of middle product B) in the national income. Thus when the terms of trade improve,

$$\hat{x}_1 = \theta_{A1}\hat{p}_B. \tag{13.9}$$

Substitute this into (13.8) to obtain

$$\hat{w} = \{[\lambda_{L1}\gamma_1 + \lambda_{L0}\theta_{A1}]/[\lambda_{L1}\gamma_1 + \lambda_{L0}\theta_{A1}\sigma_1]\}\hat{p}_B. \tag{13.10}$$

This expression confirms our earlier remark that an improvement in the terms of trade may reallocate labor between tiers, but in either direction. If σ_1 is large, the wage rate is not driven up by much. In Fig. 13.2, very elastic X isoquants would show point 2 above and to the right of point 1; labor would be attracted to the Input Tier. Low values of σ_1, benefit labor more. With substitution possibilities low, the increase in final consumption necessitates dragging labor away from the Input Tier and thus raising the wage rate even more than the price of exports. Equation (13.10) reveals that unity is the critical value of σ_1 in terms of labor allocation.

The *real* wage must rise when the terms of trade improve. Nominal wages may rise by more or less than the price of exports, depending upon the value of σ_1. But by Eq. (13.1), any increase in the wage rate (at constant price of imports of middle product A) pushes up the price of the consumption good by less. If wages rise by less than the price of exports, the return to the specific-factor in the Input Tier rises by more (by Eq. [13.2]). But if substitution possibilities are low, the wage rate rises by more than the export price and rentals are squeezed. Indeed, it might be the case that rentals actually fall, in nominal as well as real terms. In such a case, the fixed factor in the export sector is hurt more by the departure of labor to the Output Tier than it gains by the rise in export price which allowed consumption and production in the Output Tier to expand.

This example of an improvement in export prices is equivalent to an alternative change, namely, an upward shift in productivity in the Input Tier (at a uniform Hicksian rate). With the simplifications made in this section, the entire production of middle products is exported. In a more general setting in which exports account for only a fraction of production, technical progress would have a more widespread impact than would a change in the terms of trade.

A deterioration in the terms of trade could of course be analyzed in parallel fashion by considering a rise in A's price. Instead, suppose that p_A rises because the country levies a tariff. Since the country is assumed to be small, world prices of A and B are unaffected. Additionally, suppose that the tariff is small, and initially markets are undistorted. In such a case *aggregate* welfare change is second-order small and the impact on wages in Eq. (13.8) is approximated by setting $\hat{x}_1$ equal to zero. The positive coefficient for $\hat{p}_A$ suggests that labor benefits in nominal terms. The wage rate rises, but by a fraction of the increase in p_A. Therefore, by Eq. (13.1) the wage rate rises by less than the price of the consumption good and the real wage is seen to fall.

Although the tariff unambiguously lowers labor's real wage, it would be erroneous to conclude that labor is made worse off by the tariff. By the profit conditions in the export sector (Eq. [13.2]), any nominal rise in wages (as of fixed price of middle product B) sends rentals downward, especially in real terms (since p_1 has risen). Although earnings of both productive factors have fallen, tariff revenue is collected. When this revenue is redistributed, aggregate welfare is (by the small country, initial free trade assumption) approximately kept constant. Therefore, for roughly evenhanded revenue distribution arrangements, labor benefits and the specific-factor loses by the tariff. The key to this result is that the tariff makes the use of middle products in producing final output artificially expensive. Substitution possibilities force labor out of the Input Tier in order to keep aggregate production constant (roughly) in the Output Tier. By thus changing factor proportions in the export sector, labor gains relative to the factor used specifically in the Input Tier.

13.2 Relative Prices and the Role of Demand

The consequences of multiple productive activities in each tier of the economy can most readily be analyzed by allowing two separate middle products to be produced in the Input Tier and two final consumption goods to be produced in the Output Tier, as in the chart. In the Input Tier this can allow some local production of a middle product that is also imported, so that the degree to which the economy relies upon international trade to provide essential middle product inputs becomes an important characteristic of the economy. In the Output Tier, the existence of more than one final commodity whose price is locally determined allows a more important role for the community's taste pattern.

The two tiers of the economy are assumed to possess symmetrical productive structures in that each sector of each tier labor, which is drawn from a common pool, is combined with some factor or input used only in that sector to produce output. That is, production relationships in both tiers are basically those of the Specific-Factor model.[8] However, international trade ruptures this symmetry since contact with the world market takes place at the output level in one tier (the Input Tier), and at the input level for the other tier. As we demonstrate, this tends to convert the Output Tier into a 2 × 2 model with two mobile factors, the model associated with Heckscher–Ohlin theory. Furthermore, prices of goods produced in the Input Tier are exogenous to the economy (except for changes in commercial policy), whereas final commodity prices in the Output Tier are endogenous.

For any given allocation of labor between tiers, and with specific-factors (V_A to produce x_A and V_B to produce x_B) assumed throughout to be fixed in supply, a bowed-out transformation schedule can be drawn for the Input Tier. World prices of middle products determine the competitive production point. Should more labor be allocated to the Input Tier, this transformation schedule would shift outwards such that outputs of both middle products would expand if prices are kept constant. On the pricing front the competitive profit conditions for the two sectors producing middle products x_A and x_B are shown in Eqs. (13.11). These replace Eq. (13.2) for the one-commodity case.

$$\theta_{LA}\hat{w} + \theta_{VA}\hat{r}_A = \hat{p}_A \qquad (13.11)$$

$$\theta_{LB}\hat{w} + \theta_{VB}\hat{r}_B = \hat{p}_B$$

The elasticity of demand for labor in the Input Tier, γ_1, is now a weighted average of the separate demand elasticities in each sector;

$$\gamma_1 \equiv \lambda_{LA}\gamma_A + \lambda_{LB}\gamma_B.$$

---

[8] For example, see the descriptions in Jones (1971), Paul Samuelson (1971), Wolfgang Mayer, and Michael Mussa.

Should changes in middle product prices take place, wages are affected since labor is involved in their production. Equation (13.4′) for the one-sector model is replaced by (13.12):[9]

$$\hat{w} = \beta_A \hat{p}_A + \beta_B \hat{p}_B - (1/\gamma_1)\hat{L}_1$$

$$\text{where } \beta_A \equiv \lambda_{LA}\gamma_A/\gamma_1, \beta_A + \beta_B = 1. \tag{13.12}$$

That is, for given labor allocation to the Input Tier, a 10 percent rise in p_B no longer gets transmitted to a comparable rise in the wage rate; competition from the sector producing middle product A keeps the wage rise below 10 percent.

Two final commodities, x_1 and x_2, are produced in the Output Tier. Middle product A and labor produce the first commodity while B and labor produce the second. The competitive profit conditions in the Output Tier (previously shown by (13.1)) are given by Eqs. (13.13):

$$\theta_{L1}\hat{w} + \theta_{A1}\hat{p}_A = \hat{p}_1; \tag{13.13}$$

$$\theta_{L2}\hat{w} + \theta_{B2}\hat{p}_B = \hat{p}_2.$$

Figure 13.3 illustrates a final equilibrium for consumption goods at point 1 with local tastes balancing local production of the two commodities of the Output Tier. The endogenously determined equilibrium relative price of the first commodity is shown by the slope of the common tangent at 1. Hidden from explicit view are the reallocations and price changes involved in movements along the transformation schedule. The set of "endowments" of middle products and labor supporting the transformation schedule all change in a systematic fashion along the curve. This serves to make the transformation schedule more elastic than if these endowments were fixed.

The full-employment condition for a given allocation of labor to the Output Tier is shown by

$$a_{L1}x_1 + a_{L2}x_2 = L_0. \tag{13.14}$$

The economy's derived demand for middle product A equals $a_{A1}x_1$, and for middle product B equals $a_{B2}x_2$, since each middle product is associated with just one output.[10] Let T_0 denote the aggregate value of middle products

---

[9]Derivations can be found in Richard Caves and Jones, supplement to Chapter 6.
[10]As discussed below, the model easily accommodates the use of each middle product in a number of output sectors.

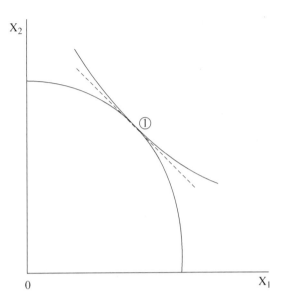

Figure 13.3.

available for use in the Output Tier, a_{T1} denote $p_A a_{A1}$, and a_{T2} denote $p_B a_{B2}$. Then a further linear constraint on final outputs is shown by

$$a_{T1}x_1 + a_{T2}x_2 = T_0. \tag{13.15}$$

Although each sector is assumed to use a unique middle product, the existence of trade at given world prices allows these middle products to be aggregated into a Hicksian composite input (T_0). Such an aggregation serves to transform the specific-factor structure of the Output Tier into the standard 2×2 mobile factor Heckscher–Ohlin structure. Free trade in world markets for middle products A and B substitutes completely for their sectoral specificity in producing x_1 and x_2.[11]

In drawing the linear constraints on outputs represented by Eqs. (13.14) and (13.15) in Fig. 13.4, we have arbitrarily assumed x_1, to be labor intensive. Suppose the economy is initially at point 1 in Fig. 13.4 and wishes to

---

[11] Mayer pointed out how a Specific-Factor model could, over time, be transformed into a Heckscher–Ohlin model as one kind of specific capital is gradually changed into another, perhaps via depreciation and replacement. Here the transformation takes place through international trade in middle products. As Doug Purvis remarked in a conversation. "Heckscher–Ohlin does not explain trade, trade explains Heckscher–Ohlin."

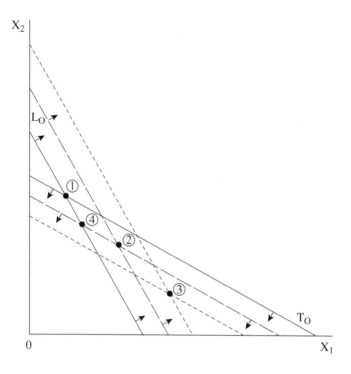

Figure 13.4.

produce a greater quantity of the first commodity. Labor is clearly more of a binding constraint than is the available supply of middle products. If more x_1 is desired, it pays to release labor from the Input Tier and reallocate it to the Output Tier. If techniques of production are fixed, this reallocation would directly serve to shift the L_0 constraint in Fig. 13.4 outwards and the T_0 constraint inwards, allowing a new intersection at 2. But at given world prices this labor reallocation must (by Eq. [13.12]) drive up the wage rate. When labor becomes more expensive relative to traded middle product inputs, labor is used less intensively in both sectors of the Output Tier and middle products more intensively. These substitutions serve further to relax the labor constraint on outputs and tighten the constraints emanating from the value of output of middle products in the Input Tier. In Fig. 13.4, these further shifts lead to a new intersection at 3. The economy's transformation schedule passes through points 1 and 3.

Although the algebraic details describing these adjustments are left to the Appendix, it is easy to show why the transformation schedule based on these endogenously changing "endowments" of L_0, A and B is strictly bowed out. Changing the composition of final outputs in favor of the labor-intensive first commodity must increase the wage rate. By the competitive profit conditions in the Output Tier, such a wage increase pushes up costs in both sectors. But it pushes up costs relatively more sharply in labor-intensive sector 1. More formally, subtracting the bottom from the top Eq. in (13.13), with middle product prices held constant, shows

$$|\theta|\hat{w} = (\hat{p}_1 - \hat{p}_2), \tag{13.16}$$

where $|\theta|$ indicates the difference $(\theta_{L1} - \theta_{L2})$ and is a positive fraction since x_1 is labor intensive. Thus increasing production of x_1 drives up its relative cost of production.

If trade is balanced, the aggregate value of middle products available for use in the Output Tier, T_0, equals the value of middle product production, T_1, although international trade allows the composition of production to differ from that of derived demand. But now suppose the country runs an export surplus so that T_0 is reduced below the production value, T_1. In the one-sector case described in the preceding section, such an export surplus not only reduces aggregate final consumption, it redistributes earned income away from labor towards the specific-factor employed in the Input Tier. In the present two-sector analysis, the extent of this redistribution of income depends in part on the nature of consumer demand.

Curves showing relative demands and relative supplies varying with price are shown in Fig. 13.5, which is based on Fig. 13.3. Define the elasticity of substitution in demand, σ_D,

$$(\hat{x}_1 - \hat{x}_2) = -\sigma_D(\hat{p}_1 - \hat{p}_2). \tag{13.17}$$

The relative demand curve in Fig. 13.5 would cut more steeply through the initial equilibrium point C the lower is σ_D. The details of the comparable elasticity on the supply side, σ_s, are provided in the Appendix. σ_S shows for the transformation schedule in the Output Tier how a rise in the relative price of labor-intensive good 1 expands relative output of good 1 by attracting more labor to the Output Tier and, through the consequent rise in the wage rate, releasing labor at the internal margin (lowering the a_{Lj}'s) at the expense of a more intensive use of both middle products.

The move from balanced trade to an export surplus has a strongly biased effect on commodity markets. In Fig. 13.5, the relative supply curve for the

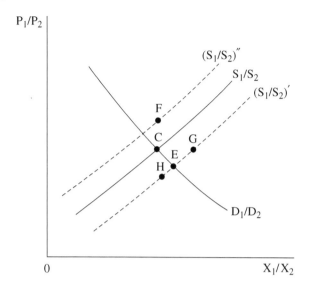

Figure 13.5.

first commodity is shifted to the right, to $(S_1/S_2)'$. Consider the extent of this rightward shift — from C to G at initial relative prices. By (16), it is clear that if relative prices of final consumption goods are kept constant, so is the wage rate. At unchanged wage rate and constant prices for middle products, the allocation of labor between tiers is unaltered (by Eq. [13.12]), and, as well, techniques of producing final consumer goods stay the same. With reference to Fig. 13.4, this implies that the L_0 labor constraint line does not shift as a consequence of an export surplus at initial final commodity prices. But the T_0 constraint shifts inwards. Aggregate production of middle products, T_1, is unchanged, but the value available for further use in the Output Tier is reduced by the amount of the export surplus. Since factor intensities are assumed to differ, a reduction in T_0 has a biased impact on outputs; production of middle-product-intensive x_2 is reduced while labor-intensive x_1 actually expands. This is the well-known Rybczynski effect found in Heckscher–Ohlin models and is represented in Fig. 13.4 by the move from 1 to 2. In Fig. 13.5, relative outputs move from C to G.

If the relative demand curve in Fig. 13.5 were flat, representing downward-sloping straight line indifference curves (an infinite value for σ_D), the export surplus would not alter the distribution of income or output levels in the Input Tier. Aggregate consumption would be reduced, and the composition of consumption radically altered. However, any resistance on the part of consumers to such a change in the composition of consumption, represented by a less than infinite value for σ_D, must serve to reduce the relative price of labor-intensive commodity 1 (for example, the move from C to E in Fig. 13.5) and, via the Heckscher–Ohlin type of relationship between output prices and the wage rate captured by Eq. (13.16), to reduce the wage rate as well. This is the kind of result characteristic of the one-sector model. The wage rate is reduced, and this encourages a reallocation of labor to the Input Tier. With reference to Fig. 13.4, the original transformation curve for the Output Tier (not drawn) passed through point 1. The export surplus caused this transformation curve to shift inwards so that it passes through 4 with, at that point, the same slope the original schedule had at 1. If demand is less than infinitely elastic, the relative price of the first commodity falls and outputs move along the new transformation curve through 4 in a northwesterly direction.

Whereas high degrees of substitutability in demand allow the country to run an export surplus without much reduction in the wage rate, low values for σ_D force severe drops in the relative price of the labor-intensive commodity and thus in the wage rate. (The returns to both specific-factors in the Input Tier must rise.) As the Appendix formally proves, low values for the elasticity of relative output supply, σ_s, would also conspire to cause a severe drop in the relative price of labor intensive x_1 and the wage rate. The reduction in the wage rate that accompanies the export surplus is in real terms. By Eq. (13.13), the nominal wage reduction pulls down the prices of both final consumption goods, but each by a fraction of the wage drop. Therefore, real wages must fall. By contrast, the competitive profit equations of change in the Input Tier show that returns to both types of specific resources rise in nominal and real terms. The export surplus harms the mobile factor (labor), which is pushed into the Input Tier and suffers a consequent toss in its marginal productivity.

In the preceding section, we analyzed two types of changes in prices of middle products. In one case, the terms of trade changed, while in the other, the relative price change took the form of a self-inflicted small change in tariffs. Aggregate income effects are important when the terms of trade change, but of second-order magnitude if a small country imposes a small tariff from a position of initial free trade. In the case of tariffs, nominal wages were shown to rise, real wages to fall, although labor will be in a somewhat improved situation when the redistribution of tariff proceeds are included. This scenario can be significantly altered when the Output Tier turns out more than one consumption good if demand elasticities are high.

Although full details are left to the Appendix, the extreme case of infinitely elastic relative demands can be easily handled on the basis of competitive profit conditions in the Output Tier, Eqs. (13.13). If indifference curves are downward-sloping straight lines, relative prices of final commodities do not change.[12] Thus $\hat{p}_1 = \hat{p}_2$. Assume that commodity A is imported, and that a tariff drives up the domestic price of A although world prices of both A and B remain constant. Subtraction of the second equation from the first in (13) shows that

$$\hat{w} = -\{\theta_{A1}/|\theta|\}\hat{p}_A, \tag{13.18}$$

where $|\theta|$ is the positive fraction, $\theta_{L1} - \theta_{L2}$. That is, the tariff on A must lower the wage rate if, as assumed, A is the middle product used in the labor-intensive first industry. Note that commodity A is assumed to be locally produced in the Input Tier and it may be the case that this industry is more highly labor intensive than the other three (in the sense that θ_{LA} may exceed other θ_{Li}'s). Even so, if demand is highly elastic, protection of the A industry must harm labor. This result is reminiscent of the theory of effective protection, in which the factor used intensively in the sector of the economy whose effective price has fallen must suffer. Here it is the labor-intensive first industry that has been squeezed.

In terms of Fig. 13.5, the tariff shifts the relative supply curve upwards to $(S_1/S_2)''$. If demands are less than infinitely elastic the relative price of the industry that has been squeezed rises. At the extreme in which individuals resist any change in the proportions in which they consume final commodities ($\sigma_D = 0$), the nominal wage rises by a fraction, E_A, of the rise in the tariff, much as it did in the one-sector model. As the Appendix proves, this polar case and the other, in which σ_D is infinite, between them trap the wage change that would result if both demand and supply elasticities were finite. For explicit reference, the solution for the impact of a tariff on the

---

[12]We are assuming that consumption remains incompletely specialized. If only one commodity is consumed (since σ_D is so high), we are thrown back to the analysis in the preceding section.

wage rate is shown by

$$\hat{w}/\hat{p}_A = \{\sigma_S/(\sigma_S + \sigma_D)\}\{\varepsilon_A\} + \{\sigma_D/(\sigma_S + \sigma_D)\}\{-\theta_{A1}/|\theta|\}. \qquad (13.19)$$

Equation (13.19) reveals that the effect of the tariff on the wage rate is a weighted average of the two extremes of demand response to price, $\sigma_D = 0$ and $\sigma_D = \infty$. The weights, in turn, are familiar from simple analyses of tax shifting and incidence, where a tax levied on supply serves partly to raise price to consumers and partly to lower price to producers; the relative sizes of demand and supply elasticities are crucial. In Fig. 13.5, the relative supply curve for commodity 1 is shifted upwards to $(S_1/S_2)''$, from C to F if relative outputs are unchanged. The lower is σ_D relative to σ_S, the more will the relative price of labor intensive x_1 rise to its maximum value at F, and the wage rate rise to the fraction ε_A of the tariff rise. By contrast, large values of σ_D relative to σ_S imply little rise in p_1/p_2 and hence a fall in wages close to their Heckscher–Ohlin value, $\{-\theta_{A1}/|\theta|\}$. Thus labor's fate when a tariff is imposed depends in part on the flexibility of consumer response to relative price changes.

In this analysis, the domestic price of A has risen because a tariff has been levied. Instead, suppose the *world* price of A rises. Aggregate home real income will fall if A is imported, but rise if A is exported. Let θ_x denote the fraction of the country's national income represented by *exports* of commodity A : θ_x will be negative if A is imported. As developed in the Appendix, the impact of the world rise in A's price on the wage rate is shown by

$$\hat{w}/\hat{p}_A = \{\sigma_S/(\sigma_S + \sigma_D)\}\{\varepsilon_A + \lambda_{L0}\theta_x/\omega\} + \{\sigma_D/(\sigma_S + \sigma_D)\}\{-\theta_{A1}/|\theta|\}$$
$$(13.20)$$

where

$$\omega \equiv \lambda_{L1}\gamma_1 + \lambda_{L0}\delta_L$$

and

$$\delta \equiv \lambda_{L1}\theta_{A1}\sigma_1 + \lambda_{L2}\theta_{B2}\sigma_2.$$

The comparison of (13.20) and (13.19) reveals how closely labor's gains or losses are associated with gains or losses for the entire community. Compare two economies quite similar in their productive structures, but with economy I possessing a strong taste bias for the first commodity and thus importing A, and with economy II possessing a taste bias for the second commodity (which uses B) and, therefore, exporting A. If the price of A rises on world markets, economy I is hurt and economy II gains. The wage rate increases more in economy II. And, the higher the wage rise the lower, other things equal, will be the return to specific-factors in the Input Tier. In this sense, labor's interests are identified with those of the community as a whole whereas specific-factors are not.

A change in world prices of middle products serves to shift the transformation schedule in the Output Tier and, therefore, the menu of consumption choices available to the economy. For example, a rise in the price of middle product A causes the transformation curve in Fig. 13.6 to rotate clockwise around point 1, which represents the autarky point. For output combinations southeast of 1 the economy's derived demand for middle product A used to produce x_1, exceeds its local production of A in the Input Tier. Similarly, northwest of 1 commodity A is exported.[13] Since a rise in the

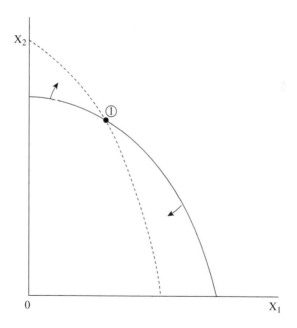

Figure 13.6.

---

[13] As x_1 production expands along the transformation curve, outputs of both middle products fall since labor leaves the Input Tier. By contrast, the rise in the wage rate causes σ_{A1} to

world price of A harms consumption possibilities for importers of A, the transformation curve must rotate as shown in Fig. 13.6. The identification of labor's interests with that of the community follows since the greater is aggregate welfare, the more must the mobile factor (labor) be attracted to the Output Tier. All commodities yielding direct utility are nontradeables (x_1 and x_2) which must be produced at home in the Output Tier.

13.3   Generalizations

The move from the one-sector model in Sec. 1 to the two-sectors-in-each-tier approach in Section 2 introduced some genuinely new elements. Local taste patterns helped determine relative commodity prices and the degree of dependence upon trade became an endogenous variable. Further dis-aggregation carries few surprises, and this is an advantage of this form of model. In the Input Tier, the specific-factor structure assures this ease of generalization as long as labor remains the only mobile factor.[14] If middle product prices remain unchanged, the Hicksian composite commodity the-orem allows the entire Input Tier to be treated as a single sector. Similarly, in the Output Tier a fixed set of prices for traded middle products suggests that only two basic inputs are required in production: labor and a Hicksian composite traded middle product. Indeed, it is easy to lift the assump-tion that each final commodity makes use of only a single middle product. Instead, middle products like oil, used in a number of industries, may be considered. Of course changes in middle product prices can be analyzed, much as in Sec. 2. But for a small country, such changes can be treated as exogenous and examined singly, so as to retain the use of the Hicksian composite theorem for the remaining sectors.

Not only can the model be extended to allow multiple activities in each tier, the balance in *number* of activities between tiers can be removed. Considering the opportunities afforded by international trade to concen-trate production for the world market, it may be desirable to envisage the Input Tier as being more concentrated than the Output Tier. Of course the existence of multiple outputs in the Output Tier raises the usual question of

---

increase so that total derived demand for A, $a_{A1}x_1$, rises as more x_1 is produced. At point 1, local production matches derived demand.

[14]The multisector version of the Specific-Factors model is analyzed in Jones (1975).

the shape of the transformation surface when there are more commodities than factors (labor and a composite traded middle product). It is ruled. If outputs were traded at given world prices this would create the typical situation in which the country becomes highly specialized. But with all outputs being nontraded in the Output Tier, specialization is avoided. Local prices adjust so that many commodities gel produced along multidimensional flats. Any indeterminacy as to production levels is resolved by local demand conditions.

Changes in conditions of trade affect final output prices according to factor intensities. For example, if the country develops an import deficit, labor is attracted from the Input Tier, the wage rate rises, and the relative prices of the more labor-intensive consumption goods rise compared with commodities intensive in their use of middle products. The "Heckscher–Ohlin" Tier of the economy (the Output Tier) feeds input price changes in orderly fashion into changes in unit costs.[15] Gone is the necessity of inverting this process to have commodity prices determine factor prices (in the Output Tier). Changes in traded middle product prices exert their influence on wages and returns to specific-factors in the more orderly fashion associated with the Specific-Factor model (in the Input Tier).[16]

This model of trade in middle products could also be extended to consider a wider variety of productive inputs, especially produced means of production. Two routes are possible. On the one hand, we could envisage the country having available locally a fixed quantity of physical capital. It might be mobile, as in the typical Heckscher–Ohlin setting. Or it may be heterogeneous and occupationally specific (such as our V_A and V_B). Clearly in this conception if capital goods are used in both tiers the strong

---

[15]This distinction among factor intensities for commodities in the Output Tier represents one way in which factor-intensity rankings are important in the model. Another follows from the observation that all final nontradeables are produced with middle products *plus* labor. In this natural sense, nontradeables art labor intensive compared with tradeables. (The analogy with Wicksell's wine is apparent: In Wicksell's model, the consumer good — final vintage wine — is capital intensive because it is produced with good-in-process, "capital," plus more time.)

[16]Equation (13.12) shows how wages are determined by changes in middle-product prices. Of course the allocation of labor between tiers needs also to be determined, but this does not require any matrix inversion such as is characteristic of Heckscher–Ohlin models.

conclusions as to the effects of tariffs or export surpluses on the wage rate (and returns to specific-factors) gets moderated.

We would prefer an alternate route. Instead of the form (and overall quantity) of capital goods locally used being determined, capital is more "footloose,"[17] much as are traded middle products. A country's heritage wills it a certain level of wealth in the form of heterogeneous capital. The international location and form of this capital depends upon the world market. Like middle products, one type of capital can be transformed into another via world trade, at prices determined in world markets and given to the small country. And the value of capital employed within a country need not match the value of the nation's ownership of capital goods. A country engaged in positive net foreign investment may run import deficits — allowing a greater availability of traded middle products to be used in the Output Tier than is locally produced in the Input Tier. Thus three major features characterize an economy: (i) Its distribution of natural resources, waiting to be developed in the Input Tier; (ii) its labor force, occupationally mobile but trapped within the national borders, and (iii) its level of accumulated wealth which, by trade, need not be restricted in form or national location.

The central feature of our model has been the location of international trade in the middle of a nation's productive spectrum instead of at the end. Trade affects the menu of commodities available to consumers, not because final commodities can be directly exchanged, but because middle product trade enriches the availabilities of inputs. Part of the nation's resources are used to produce middle products for the world market and the remainder are involved in making use of middle products from the world market to help produce final nontraded consumption goods.

Appendix

A. The elasticity of supply along the transformation schedule

The transformation schedule for final consumer goods for the model in which two sectors in the Output Tier combine labor and middle products is illustrated in Fig. 13.3. Although middle product A is specifically used

---

[17]For a discussion of trade theory with such a footloose factor, see Jones (1980).

only to produce x_1 and middle product B to produce x_2, trade at given world prices allows A and B to be combined into a Hicksian composite input, T_0. Eqs. (13.14) and (13.15), showing the two constraints provided by labor and the aggregate value of middle products, can be differentiated to yield

$$\lambda_{L1}\hat{x}_1 + \lambda_{L2}\hat{x}_2$$
$$= \hat{L}_0 - \{\lambda_{L1}\hat{a}_{L1} + \lambda_{L2}\hat{a}_{L2}\} \tag{A.13.1}$$

$$\lambda_{T1}\hat{x}_1 + \lambda_{T2}\hat{x}_2$$
$$= \hat{T}_0 - \{\lambda_{T1}\hat{a}_{T1} + \lambda_{T2}\hat{a}_{T2}\}. \tag{A.13.2}$$

On the right-hand side, all terms are linked to changes in the wage rate. $\hat{L}_0$ and $\hat{L}_1$ are related by Eq. (13.3), which reflects overall full employment, and $\hat{L}_0$, in turn, is linked to the wage change for given world prices of traded middle products by Eq. (13.12). Therefore,

$$\hat{L}_0 = (\lambda_{L1}\gamma_1/\lambda_{L0})\hat{w}. \tag{A.13.3}$$

Similarly, with balanced trade $\hat{T}_0$ equals the change in the aggregate value or output of middle products from the Input Tier, $\hat{T}_1$. At constant prices the wage rate w must equal the value of labor's marginal product in the Input Tier, $\partial T_1/\partial L_1$, so that T_0 equals the share of labor in the Input Tier, θ_{L1}, times $\hat{L}_1$. Again using Eq. (13.12) to link $\hat{L}_1$, to the wage change we get

$$\hat{T}_0 = \theta_{L1}\gamma_1\hat{w}. \tag{A.13.4}$$

Finally, the bracketed expressions for changes in input-output coefficients in (A.13.1) and (A.13.2) depend on the degree of substitution between labor and traded middle products in the two sectors of the Output Tier and the change in the wage rate. Explicitly, with p_A and p_B constant, $a_{tj} = -\theta_{Tj}\sigma_j\hat{w} : \hat{a}_{Tj} = \theta_{Lj}\sigma_j\hat{w}$,

so that (A.13.1) and (A.13.2) can be rewritten as

$$\lambda_{L1}\hat{x}_1 + \lambda_{L2}\hat{x}_2 = \{(\lambda_{L1}\gamma_1/\lambda_{L0}) + \delta_L\}\hat{w} \tag{A.13.5}$$

$$\lambda_{T1}\hat{x}_1 + \lambda_{T2}\hat{x}_2 = -\{\theta_{L1}\gamma_1 + \delta_T\}\hat{w} \tag{A.13.6}$$

$$\text{where} \qquad \delta_L \equiv \lambda_{L1}\theta_{A1}\sigma_1 + \lambda_{L2}\theta_{B2}\sigma_2$$

$$\delta_T \equiv \lambda_{T1}\theta_{L1}\sigma_1 + \lambda_{T2}\theta_{L2}\sigma_2.$$

To derive the expression for σ_S, the elasticity of relative output response to a change in relative prices, subtract (A.13.6) from (A.13.5) and substitute Eq. (13.16) in the text for $\hat{w}$ in terms of the change in the output price ratio. This yields

$$(\hat{x}_1 - \hat{x}_2) = \{[\delta_L + \delta_T + \theta_{L1}\gamma_I/\theta_{L0}]/|\lambda||\theta|\}(\hat{p}_1 - \hat{p}_2). \qquad \text{(A.13.7)}$$

σ_s is the positive coefficient of $(\hat{p}_1 - \hat{p}_2)$ where $|\lambda|$ refers to the determinant of coefficients in (A.13.1) and (A.13.2) and equals $(\lambda_{L1} - \lambda_{T1})$, and $|\theta|$ refers to the fraction $(\theta_{L1} - \theta_{L2})$. Its value incorporates the kinds of substitutions between inputs familiar in Heckscher–Ohlin models,[18] plus the reallocation of labor between the Input Tier and the Output Tier. For example, should p_1/p_2 rise, not only can the relative output of the labor-intensive first commodity expand as a consequence of substitutions away from labor, but also more labor is provided to the Output Tier as production levels in the Input Tier are cut back.

B. Outward transfer: An export surplus

As in the text, consider the consequences of the country's arbitrarily running an export surplus. Let $\hat{t}_0$ represent this surplus relative to the initial value of total production in the Input Tier. Whereas Eq. (A.13.4) points to the change in the aggregate value of production in the Input Tier that will follow any change in the wage rate (at constant prices of middle products), an export surplus implies that in addition T_0 is cut back for any value of T_1. Thus in the case of transfer, (A.13.4) is replaced by

$$\hat{T}_0 = -\theta_{L1}\gamma\hat{w} - \hat{t}_0. \qquad \text{(13.A4')}$$

Once this substitution is made into Eq. (A.13.2), the change in relative outputs can be obtained as before to yield

$$(\hat{x}_1 - \hat{x}_2) = \sigma_s(\hat{p}_1 - \hat{p}_2) + (1/|\lambda|)\hat{t}_0.$$

The change in relative demands is shown by Eq. (13.17). Thus the change in the value of market-clearing relative prices is

$$(\hat{p}_1 - \hat{p}_2) = -\{1/|\lambda|(\sigma_s + \sigma_D)\}\hat{t}_0.$$

---

[18] In the standard two-sector model, δ_S is given by $(\delta_L + \delta_T)/|\lambda||\theta|$. See, for example, Caves and Jones, supplement to Chapter 7.

and the resulting change in the wage rate is

$$\hat{w} = -\{1/|\lambda||\theta|(\sigma_S + \sigma_D)\}\hat{t}_0. \tag{A.13.8}$$

C. Changes in middle product prices

The convenience of the concept of a Hicksian composite input for middle products must to some extent be sacrificed if the relative price of one middle product changes vis-à-vis the other. Suppose p_A rises and p_B remains constant. Instead of following the procedure of linking output changes to changes in labor and middle product availabilities, as in Eqs. (A.13.1) and (A.13.2), we keep the labor constraint and add to it a statement that the aggregate change in real consumption (and real income if trade is balanced) depends upon the change in the terms of trade. Let θ_i, denote the share of income spent on good i. Then the weighted average, $\theta_1\hat{x}_1 + \theta_2\hat{x}_2$, shows the change in real expenditure. With θ_x denoting the share of the national income represented by exports of middle product A,

$$\theta_1\hat{x}_1 + \theta_2\hat{x}_2 = \theta_x\hat{p}_A. \tag{A.13.9}$$

With the price of middle product A rising, the expressions for changes in the labor constraint line will be more complicated than previously shown. At the extensive margin. $\hat{L}_1$ and $\hat{L}_0$ are still connected as in Eq. (13.3), but Eq. (13.12) now shows that the reallocation of labor depends upon the extent of the wage change compared to $\beta_A\hat{p}_A$. With the appropriate substitutions, (A.13.3) converts into

$$\hat{L}_0 = (\lambda_{L1}\gamma_1/\lambda_{L0})(\hat{w} - \beta_A\hat{p}_A). \tag{(A3')}$$

At the intensive margin, $\hat{a}_{L1}$ is now shown as

$$\hat{a}_{L1} = -\theta_{A1}\sigma_1(\hat{w} - \hat{p}_A)$$

whereas $\hat{a}_{L2}$ is, as before, linked only to $\hat{w}$:

$$\hat{a}_{L2} = -\theta_{B2}\sigma_2\hat{w}.$$

If the wage rate were constant, no substitution could take place in the second industry, but labor would be used more intensively in the first. By contrast, should the wage rate rise by the same relative amount as the price of middle product A, techniques in the first industry would be unaltered but substitution against labor would occur in the second. Therefore, there is some fractional value for the wage rise relative to $\hat{p}_A$ that would keep the *average* intensity in the two sectors unchanged (i.e., would set $\{\lambda_{L1}\hat{a}_{L1} + \lambda_{L2}\hat{a}_{L2}\}$ equal to zero). Call this fraction ρ_A. Then

$$-\{\lambda_{L1}\hat{a}_{L1} + \lambda_{L2}\hat{a}_{L2}\} = \delta_L\{\hat{w} - \rho_A\hat{p}_A\} \qquad (A.13.10)$$

$$\text{where} \quad \rho_A \equiv \lambda_{L1}\theta_{A1}\sigma_1/\delta_L.$$

The value of ρ_A depends upon technology in the Output Tier. The value of β_A in (A.13.3$'$) depends upon technology in the Input Tier. Their relationship to each other helps determine the required direction of labor reallocation. Combining (A.13.3$'$) for the extensive margin with (A.13.10) for the intensive margin yields (A.13.11) as the rewritten form of (A.13.1):

$$\lambda_{L1}\hat{x}_1 + \lambda_{L2}\hat{x}_2 = (\omega/\lambda_{L0})\{\hat{w} - \varepsilon_A\hat{p}_A\} \qquad (A.13.11)$$

$$\text{where} \quad \omega \equiv \lambda_{L1}\gamma_1 + \lambda_{L0}\delta_L$$

$$\text{and} \quad \varepsilon_A \equiv (\lambda_{L1}\gamma_1/\omega)\beta_A + (\lambda_{L0}\delta_L/\omega)\rho_A.$$

The expression for ε_A is a weighted average of the two fractions, β_A and ρ_A. If the wage rate change equals this fraction times $\hat{p}_A$, there would be no shift in the labor constraint line.

Changes in relative outputs can be obtained by subtracting (A.13.9) from (A.13.11). Note that $(\lambda_{L1} - \theta_1)$ is positive if x_1 is labor intensive and, indeed, this fraction can be rewritten as $\theta_{T0}|\lambda|$. Making use of the expression for σ_s on the output side[19]

$$(\hat{x}_1 - \hat{x}_2) = |\theta|\sigma_s\{\hat{w} - [\varepsilon_A + \lambda_{L0}\theta_X/\omega]\hat{p}_A\}.$$

On the demand side, make use of Eq. (13.17), noting that from Eq. (13.13) with $p_B = 0$,

$$(\hat{p}_1 - \hat{p}_2) = |\theta|\hat{w} + \theta_{A1}\hat{p}_A.$$

Thus when commodity prices adjust to clear the market,

$$\hat{w}/\hat{p}_A = \{\sigma_S/(\sigma_S + \sigma_D)\}\{\varepsilon_A + \lambda_{L0}\theta_X/\omega\} + \{\sigma_D/(\sigma_S + \sigma_D)\}\{-\theta_{A1}/|\theta|\}.$$

---

[19]In more detail, it can be shown that $|\theta|\sigma_S$, which by (A.13.7) equals $\{\delta_L + \delta_T + \theta_{L1}\gamma_1/\theta_{L0}\}/|\lambda|$, equals $\omega/\lambda_{L0}\theta_{T0}|\lambda|$ or $(1/|\lambda|)\{(\delta_L/\theta_{T0}) + \lambda_{L1}\gamma_1/\lambda_{L0}\theta_{T0}\}$.

This is Eq. (13.20) in the text, showing how a change in the world price of middle product A has an effect on wages that blends the Heckscher–Ohlin term, $-\theta_{A1}/|\theta|$, with the fraction ε_A, augmented by an expression that is positive if and only if the community exports A. The case in which the price of A rises because of a self-imposed tariff leads to Eq. (13.19), which would follow if in (A.13.9) the right-hand side is put to zero to capture the negligible impact of a small tariff on aggregate welfare.

References

Caves, R.E. and Jones, R.W. (1981). *World Trade and Payments* (3rd edition). Boston, MA: Little, Brown and Company.

Corden, W.M. (1971a). *The Theory of Protection*. Oxford: Oxford University Press.

Corden, W.M. (1971b). The Effects of Trade on the Rate of Growth. In: J. Bhagwati *et al.*, (Eds.), *Trade, Balance of Payments, and Growth* (Ch. 6). Amsterdam: North-Holland.

Findlay, R. (1979). Economic Development and the Theory of International Trade. *American Economic Review Proceedings*, 69, 186–190.

Jones, R.W. (1979). The Structure of Simple General Equilibrium Models. *Journal of Political Economy*, 73, 557–572.

Jones, R.W. (1971). A Three-Factor Model in Theory. Trade, and History. In: J. Bhagwati *et al.*, (Eds.), *Trade, Balance of Payments and Growth: Papers in International Economics in Honor of Charles P. Kindleherger* (pp. 3–21). Amsterdam: North-Holland.

Jones, R.W. (1974). Trade with Non-Traded Goods: The Anatomy of Interconnected Markets. *Economica*, 41, 121–138.

Jones, R.W. (1975). Income Distribution and Effective Protection in a Multi-Commodity Trade Model. *Journal of Economic Theory*, 11, 1–15.

Jones, R.W. (1980). Comparative and Absolute Advantage. *Schweiz Zoitschrift für Volkswirtschaft und Statistik*, 3, 235–260.

Jones, R.W. and Purvis, D. D. (1983). International Differences in Response to Common External Shocks: The Role of Purchasing Power Parity. In: Claassen, Salin (Eds.), *Recent Issues in the Theory of Flexible Exchange Rates*, (pp. 33–55) Amsterdam: North-Holland.

Mayer, W. (1974). Short-Run Equilibrium for a Small Open Economy. *Journal of Political Economy*, 82, 955–968.

Mussa, M. (1974). Tariffs and the Distribution of Income: The Importance of Factor Specificity, Substitutability, and Intensity in the Short and Long Run. *Journal of Political Economy*, 82, 1191–1204.

Salter, W.G. (1959). Internal and External Balance: The Role of Price and Expenditure Effects. *Economic Record*, 35, 226–238.

Samuelson, P.A. (1971). Ohlin Was Right. *Swedish Journal of Economics*, 73, 365–384.

CHAPTER 14

The Role of Services in Production and International Trade: A Theoretical Framework*

Ronald W. Jones and Henryk Kierzkowski

14.1 Introduction

International trade in services is currently the subject of intense scrutiny among academics. Whereas most contemporary discussions of services attempt to uncover an all-encompassing definition of tertiary activities, in the present chapter, we deliberately avoid this issue, asking instead what services do. We share in common with other observers the conviction that it is important to liberalize regulations covering services and international trade, but depart from the dominant focus on establishing the determinants of comparative advantage in services. Instead of trying to ascertain which countries will end up exporting or providing services, we concentrate on the manner in which developments in the service sector have encouraged and promoted the general level of international trade in goods.

In asking what services do, we acknowledge the importance of retail activities in facilitating the absorption of the nation's output by its consumers. Other activities, such as those provided by the medical and legal professions, link in a more direct fashion producers and consumers of services. In the present chapter, we shift attention from these consumption

*Originally published in R. Jones and A. Kruger (Eds.), *The Political Economy of International Trade* (pp. 31–48). Oxford, UK: Blackwell.

activities to the way in which services are involved in the production process. Two key concepts are introduced: *production blocks* and *service links*. The chapter discusses how, with growth of a firm's output level, increasing returns and the advantages of specialization of factors within the firm encourage a switch to a production process with *fragmented* production blocks connected by service links. These links, bundles of activities consisting of coordination, administration, transportation, and financial services, are increasingly demanded when the fragmentation of the production process allows joint use of production blocks located in different regions.

Such fragmentation spills over to international markets. The greater disparity in productivities and factor prices found between countries (as compared to within a country) may encourage, via the Ricardian doctrine of comparative advantage, the use of several international locations for production blocks comprising a given production process. This dispersion is aided and abetted by the possible existence of increasing returns within production blocks.

It seems to us that one of the stylized facts characterizing recent developments in world trade is the fall in relative prices of many services, especially those found in the transportation and communication section.[1] This relative price change further encourages the process of fragmentation, whereby increasing use is made of disparate locations in which parts of the production process take place, with more intensive use required of connecting service links. Furthermore, it can be argued that technological advances in the provision of services lower especially the relative costs of international coordination and communication. As services become cheaper, service links at the international level become more frequently and intensively utilized as integral ingredients in the production process.

Section 2 introduces our framework in the context of an economy trading only final commodities. The use which can be made of international markets earlier in the production process and the importance of recent developments in major service industries is spelled out in more detail in

---

[1] Transport costs have been steadily declining for decades. North (1958) cites ocean freight costs in 1910 as one-thirtieth of their level in 1800.

Secs. 3 and 4. In Sec. 5, we relate our framework to Vernon's concept of the product cycle (1966), the importance of national and international returns to scale analyzed in two basic papers by Ethier (1979, 1982), as well as to a contribution by Markusen (1986) applying Ethier's model to the issue of trade in services. In our concluding section, we discuss a number of policy issues: Liberalization under the Uruguay Round, fragmentation and North–South trade, and the role of government policies in influencing absolute advantage and attracting internationally mobile service inputs.

14.2   Services in the Process of Expansion and Fragmentation

Our framework is best revealed by considering an initial early stage in a production process, in which an integrated activity exists in a single location. Figure 14.1(a) depicts this early mode as a single *production block*. Service inputs are not absent at this early stage; they are required to coordinate activities within the production block as well as to connect production and consumption via distribution and marketing operations.

We assume that technology within the production block, contains elements of increasing returns to scale. Although such scale economies may take many forms, we shall assume in our diagrammatic exposition that productive activities require fixed, or set-up, costs, and that marginal costs of operation are constant. Thus in Fig. 14.2, line 1 depicts the manner in which total costs expand with scale of output. Vertical intercept Oa represents set-up and other fixed costs associated with the production block while the slope of line 1 shows marginal costs of the production run.

As production expands, alternative techniques embodying a greater division of labor may emerge as superior. Increased specialization of productive tasks and division of labor of the kind envisaged as early as Adam Smith could result in a *fragmentation* of the production block as illustrated in Figure 14.1b. In his classic presidential address, Allyn Young in 1928 emphasized the importance of Smith's views on the division of labor and remarked that

> ... over a large part of the field of industry an increasingly intricate nexus of specialized undertakings has inserted itself between the producer of raw materials and the consumer of the final product. (p. 538)

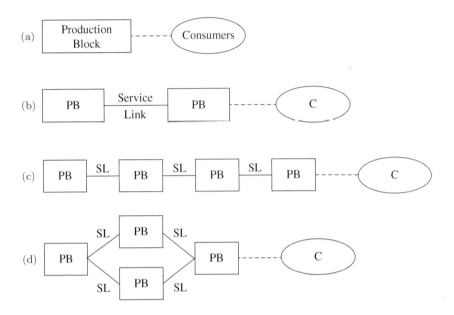

Figure 14.1. The Production Process

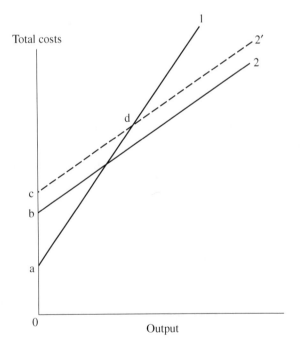

Figure 14.2. Total Costs and Output

We assume that such fragmentation alters the trade-off between fixed and variable costs; lower marginal costs of output are obtained at the expense of a greater total sum of fixed costs in the pair of production blocks. An illustration of the relationship between total costs and output for this fragmented technology is depicted by line 2 in Fig. 14.2.

At this stage, a new role emerges for service activities. The two production blocks pictured in Fig. 14.1(b) need to be coordinated and linked by use of service resources. The activities of the two production blocks cannot be combined without cost. *Service links* are required to join *production blocks*. These may include transportation costs if the separate physical locations of production blocks warrant. At the minimum, there is a need to plan and synchronize the two streams of production with respect to timing, size and quality. These service links represent inputs additional to any service resources required within each production block. The total costs of production with fragmented technology, represented by line 2 in Fig. 14.2, need to be augmented by the costs of the service link joining the two production blocks (to yield total cost line 2′). In Fig. 14.2, we have illustrated these service costs as being somewhat independent of the scale of output (the vertical intercept is shifted from Ob to Oc and line 2′ is parallel to line 2). However, if the costs of the service link are driven up with the level of production, line 2′ could be drawn steeper than line 2. Marginal costs inclusive of services are still assumed to be lower than with the more concentrated techniques (1).

The process represented in Fig. 14.2 can be repeated to higher orders (see Fig. 14.3(a)), creating an increasing number of production blocks and connecting service links. Indeed, the process of industrial development has been historically documented to be one of increasing specialization and division of labor, resulting in a growing degree of fragmentation and an increasing role for producer services. Numerous patterns of interdependence among production blocks and service links can be envisaged. Figure 14.1(c) represents a production process whereby each production block utilizes as inputs the outputs of the preceding block. Figure 14.1(d) illustrates an alternative grouping: the simultaneous operation of a pair of production blocks, the outputs of each requiring an assembly process at the final stage of fabrication.

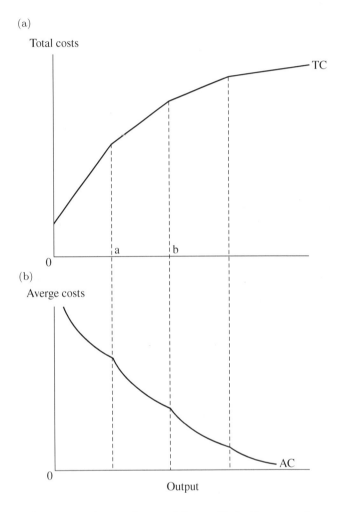

Figure 14.3.   Average Costs and Output Under Fragmentation

This process of development, as illustrated in Fig. 14.3 over several stages of fragmentation, embodies two sources contributing to continuously decreasing average costs. For any degree of fragmentation the combination of fixed costs and (fairly) constant marginal costs within production blocks (coupled with a relatively heavy fixed cost component in each service link) ensures that average costs decline with output. This rate of decline is accelerated at every point at which a switch is made to technologies incorporating a higher degree of fragmentation.

Figure 14.4 illustrates the dependence of marginal cost upon output as production growth encourages a switch to more fragmented technologies. Assuming production remains within the confines of a single firm and that market demand is less than infinitely elastic, the firm would maximize profits by selecting an output level at which marginal revenue equals marginal costs. However, there may be multiple intersections for any given marginal revenue curve. Consider that demand has grown sufficiently to support the MR_1 curve in Fig. 14.4. Point b shows marginal revenue equal to marginal cost, but is a point of local profit minimization — a small contraction or expansion of output would increase profits. The contenders are points a and c. Profits at a are clearly superior to those at c — a movement from a to c involves primarily marginal losses as marginal costs exceed marginal revenue with the lower order of fragmented technology, and fall short of marginal revenue only for the small stretch (from b to c) where the firm adopts the more fragmented technology.

If we envisage a smooth growth of demand, and with it an associated growth in marginal revenue schedules, at the critical MR_2 curve (when

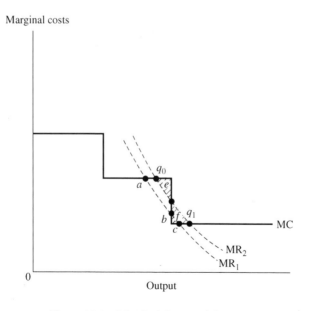

Figure 14.4.   Marginal Costs and Output

shaded area e equals area f) the firm could produce either q_0 or q_1. For a slightly higher level of demand, output level slightly exceeds q_1. The range $q_0 q_1$ is never observed. That is, a smooth growth or demand leads to gradual transitions to more fragmented technologies, but the price drops corresponding *to* such transitions lead to jumps in output volumes. Such jumps are more noticeable if marginal revenue (and associated demand) are more elastic.

Little has been said so far about the role of firms and the relationship between the number of production blocks and service links and the number of firms. The idea that firms may wish to incorporate functions which might otherwise be provided less efficiently or at higher costs by market transactions has been stressed by Ronald Coase (1937) and his followers. However, the evolution of the production process, with its increasing a complexity, opens up the possibility of vertical specialization and the appearance of new firms. In the limit every production block and service link might represent a separate firm. The producer of the final good located at the end of a production chain might rely completely on the market to supply necessary intermediate product and services.

The process of spinning off new firms could be reinforced if various production blocks and service links can be utilized by more than one sector, or by more than one firm producing a differentiated product in the same sector. Telecommunication services, with high fixed costs, provide a good example of an activity which would be too costly to develop by a single firm in a different industry. The firm would rely on the market. It is, on the other hand, possible that the emerging new production blocks and service links will be retained within the firm.

In our view, the process of increasing fragmentation and use of service links is consistent either with patterns of development involving a greater scope of activity by a single firm or with heavier reliance upon the market to coordinate activities of newly emerging independent firm. For example, Stigler (1951) cites the case of the small-arms industry in Birmingham in 1860. The master gun-maker engaged in market transactions with independent manufacturers, each performing separate, differentiated tasks. An alternative is exemplified by a typical large US corporation, with its own legal department, a fleet of corporate jets, publishing facilities and an internal transportation network. Even such a large corporation, however, is likely to rely on the market for some major inputs such as telecommunication and financial services.

Fragmentation involves extra costs. Recently firms have become more aware of how expensive it is to hold inventories. "Just-in-time" technology has been shown to be effective in holding down production costs.[2] Improvements in computer technology and telecommunication have allowed a greater degree of reliability of deliveries and synchronization of output streams required by "just-in-time" inventories strategy.

14.3   International Markets and the Production Process

International markets have not been excluded from the account of the development process described in the preceding section. Heretofore, we assumed that goods appearing at the completion of the production process were traded on world markets, but that intermediate products and service inputs were not. The array of goods selected for production at home already reflected positions of comparative advantage and the further bias towards concentration encouraged by increasing returns to scale. As compared with complete autarky, the extent of specialization brought about by allowing free trade in final goods itself promotes welfare gains; the cut-back in the number of different production processes undertaken allows a higher degree of fragmentation in each.

The new possibility for international trade which we now wish to consider involves the role of services in linking production blocks across national boundaries. If the assumed overall position of comparative advantage in a particular good does not imply lower national costs for each production block and service link used, efficient production process may involve a mixture of domestic and foreign activities. Recent developments in the world automobile industry have encouraged widespread trade in components. For example, in 1986 Japan ran a surplus in car-components trade with the United States to the tune of $5.6 billion. Bosch of West Germany has captured 75 percent of the world market for anti-lock braking systems.[3] In 1983, around 60 percent of imports and exports for the United

---

[2] For an alternative view of the significance or "just-in-time" technology see Kumpe and Bolwijn (1988).

[3] These figures come from the *Economist*, December 17, 1987, p. 57.

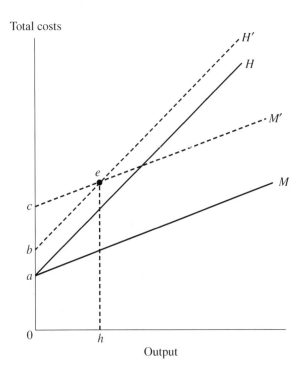

Figure 14.5.   Total Costs and Output: Effect of Foreign Service Links

States and the Economic Community consisted of intermediate goods; consumer goods and capital goods counted for roughly 20 percent and 10 percent, respectively.[4]

Figure 14.5 displays cost comparisons for the same degree of fragmentation — two production blocks connected by a service link. Line H shows fixed and variable costs when both production blocks are located at home, and H' adds in the costs of the required service link. Suppose that in comparing each production block separately, the foreign country would have a lower marginal cost for the second block and the home country for the first. The combination of home first production block and foreign second block is represented by line M, and we assume the same fixed costs are involved as for line H. However, we also assume that the service costs of linking a

---

[4] These figures are cited by Kol (1987).

domestic and a foreign production block are greater than those required if both blocks are nationally based. (In Fig. 14.5, distance *ca* exceeds distance *ba*.) The possibility of service inputs linking internationally dispersed production units lowers the best cost-output line from be H' (i.e., line H') to broken line be M'.

In our framework, production blocks are each located entirely at a single location, but service links may involve inputs from more than one country, or, indeed, inputs from a third country. (Lloyd's of London could provide insurance for shipments of automobile parts from Canada to the United States.) In our illustration (Fig. 14.5), we have assumed that the fixed costs associated with domestic production blocks are equivalent to those found abroad. This assumption was purely arbitrary. If the foreign country possesses a cost advantage in the second production block, it might have been embodied in elements of fixed costs as much as in variable costs. What is less arbitrary is the assumption that the service costs of linking production blocks in more than one country exceed those involved in purely domestic links. However, even in this respect there could be exceptions. In the case of Canada, for example, connecting production blocks in British Columbia and Ontario may involve higher-priced service links, e.g., transportation, than required for British Columbia and the State of Washington.

Further insights into the manner in which international trade involving fragmented production blocks yields extra gains *to* producers can be obtained by looking at two basic models of trade, viz. Ricardo and Heckscher–Ohlin.

(i) A Ricardian framework:

In the Ricardian context suppose that initially the home country uses two production blocks with the marginal labor input coefficients in each block denoted by a_{L1}. (Comparable input coefficients abroad are denoted by a_{L1}^*). Assume that units of output in the two blocks must be matched one-for-one to obtain a unit of final output. Further assume that fixed costs within production blocks and between countries are identical. If no trade in producer components were allowed, let us assume that the home country possesses an overall comparative advantage in producing this commodity. Letting w and w^* represent wage rates in the two countries, such a ranking according to comparative advantage implies that:

$$\frac{a_{L1}^* + a_{L2}^*}{a_{L1} + a_{L2}} > \frac{w}{w^*}.$$

Our assumption of the foreign country's superiority in the second block, and the home country's in the first block, is captured by the Ricardian inequality,

$$\frac{a_{L1}^*}{a_{L1}} > \frac{w}{w^*} > \frac{a_{L2}^*}{a_{L2}}.$$

Allowing the foreign country to take over production of the second block would lower marginal costs and thus allow gains. For such rationalization of production to be undertaken, the scale of output would have to be large enough for lower variable costs to outweigh the extra costs of international service links.

(ii) A Heckscher–Ohlin model:

Whereas a Ricardian framework allows us to focus on the possibility that the relative efficiency of labor varies among countries and commodities and, further, from one production block to another, a Heckscher–Ohlin framework recognizes the use of many factors in the production process. The factor intensities required in one production block may differ from those in another. (We ignore, here, the further possibility that service links as well require factor proportions which might differ from country to country. Indeed, one possibility is that service links are provided by the lowest-cost source in world markets.)

To take an example, suppose that the first of a two-part fragmented technology for producing a certain commodity is more capital intensive than the second. Factor endowments differ between countries, and suppose the foreign country is relatively so well endowed with labor that even with free trade allowed in parts of the production process factor prices are not equalized. If international service links can be forged, relatively cheap labor abroad and cheap capital at home could establish the basis for an internationally mixed production process. The international market place, with its variety of factor productivities (Ricardo) and factor prices and factor intensities (Heckscher–Ohlin) provides the richer possibilities associated with trade in production blocks according to comparative advantage to add gains to those associated with increasing returns and fragmentation as the scale of output expands.

The hypothetical comparison which we have been making is between trade patterns in a world in which trade takes place only in final commodities, with each country responsible for the entire integrated production process involved in its final exports, and those in which the production process can be fragmented so that production blocks for a given final output can be located in a number of countries. If each production block is identified with only one final output and if each final output is produced in only one country, allowing trade in components of the production process could be expected to yield gains from world resource reallocation more closely corresponding to lines of comparative advantage. However, the potential for gain is even greater if final goods trade reflects a sizeable degree of intra-industry trade and/or if production blocks can in principle be used to support output of completely different industries. In such cases, the existence of service activities providing international links for production blocks opens up the possibility of an even greater degree of international specialization, with concurrent gains from increasing returns to scale and greater degrees of fragmentation. The automobile example cited previously illustrates how the output of one component (antilock braking systems) can be used in a number of differentiated products. Furthermore, some service links, e.g., those exemplified by telecommunication, may be required by production blocks used in a wide variety of different industries.

Whatever the sources of comparative advantage, the possibility that separate production blocks can be dispersed in their geographical location increases the chances for less developed countries to participate to some extent in the industrialization process. In a world in which all production blocks must be located in a single country in an integrated process, less developed regions always have a comparative advantage in some commodities. But these may represent agricultural or raw-material extraction activities in which, we suppose, labor does not possess the opportunity to acquire sets of skills which are associated with certain types of learning-by-doing. The role of services in fostering the fragmentation of the production process over a number of different countries becomes important. Through such fragmentation countries may partake in some part of industrial activity even when a comparative advantage in the integrated process is still out of reach.

14.4   Price Changes and the Role of Services in Trade

Recent decades have witnessed a technological revolution in service sectors. This would certainly have surprised Adam Smith. The very man who brought us the concept of gains from the division of labor viewed services as being "unproductive of any value." A more muted modern view would still claim that services tend to get left behind in society's steady march on the technological front. The source for such a view stems in large part from identifying service activities as extremely labor intensive. Furthermore, services tend to be associated with sheltered non-traded sectors.[5]

The type of inputs required for service links in the production process shares few of these characteristics. Foremost among these inputs must be ranked telecommunications and financial services. Rapid technological change has increased the case and reduced the cost of linking different production blocks. Furthermore, domestic deregulation pursued by governments in countries such as the United States, Canada, and the United Kingdom has accelerated the pace of these cost reductions.

Economies in the cost of providing service links promote the process of fragmentation. Total production costs fall for any given level of output, and a switch to a more diversified production process can be attained at lower levels of output. This is illustrated in Fig. 14.2. Lower service costs shift line 2' downwards, moving switch-point d south-westwards along line l.

We would argue that the type of technological breakthrough and innovation that has characterized section such as telecommunications, transportation and financial services has had especially pronounced effects in reducing the relative costs of *international* service links. A bank manager in New York can communicate with an associate in Hong Kong as rapidly and almost as cheaply as he can with a colleague in Chicago. National boundaries scarcely impede transmission of large bodies of data. By utilizing innovations such as fax, a fashion designer in Paris can transmit graphic details and instructions to cutting-room floors in Taipei instantly and at a fraction of the costs of international courier service.

The clothing industry provides an interesting example of how relative costs, reliability and speed of providing service links influence the

---

[5]See Balassa (1964) and Bhagwati (1984), as well as the literature on the so-called Scandinavian model of inflation.

internationalization of the production process. Spurred by the US offshore assembly (807) scheme, the American textile industry profited from a finer international division of labor by reallocating some production stages to developing countries. As pointed out by Morawetz (1981), Colombia and several Far East Asian countries were in direct competition for the task of assembling fabrics which had been cut in the United States. Colombia was a winner in this competition in the early 1970s, with the outcome largely determined by its favorable geographical location which resulted in relatively low costs of airfreight and telecommunications service links. Morawetz points out that ill-advised national macro and exchange rate policies soon reversed the Colombian cost advantage. In any case, technological advances in transportation and telecommunications since that time have done much to remove the advantage which proximity to market brings.

Service links have benefited from learning-by-doing at the international level. Decades or rapid growth of international trade and expansion of foreign investment resulted in an accumulation of a wealth of knowledge about foreign countries, their markets, and their political systems. Business firms are especially concerned with property rights and procedures for contract enforcement available to nonnationals. The legal climate in which international transactions are undertaken now seems less hostile and more predictable. As a consequence of these developments, the scope for international participation and interpenetration of markets at the production level has been greatly expanded. The reduction in the cost of services generally has fostered increased fragmentation and division of labor in production; the greater relative cost reductions for services linking international operations have had a profound effect in stimulating the use of international markets at every stage of the production process. This, we would claim, is the primary connection between services and international trade. One of the stylized facts of international commerce is the increasingly large share of trade represented by exchanges of producer goods and middle products.

We would further argue that the reduction of uncertainty regarding foreign production activities and the greater reliability provided by international service links are especially important in encouraging trade within the production process. The precision of delivery dates, for example, is of much more concern to producers weighing the possibility of repeated reliance on foreign components than it is to individuals who are engaged in one-shot purchases of the final consumer good.

Just as in the domestic sphere, we emphasize that the process of increasing fragmentation and use of international markets does not preclude a variety of organizational structures for farms. Although it may be in the firm's interest to avoid arms-length international transactions in favor of establishing a multinational presence, our framework encompasses as well interconnected production processes involving many firms. Certainly many of the service links could be provided by outside suppliers, perhaps some of them multinationals in their own right.

14.5   Comparisons with Existing Models

Currently it is fashionable in discussions of international trade theory to elevate the phenomenon of increasing returns to scale to a level of importance at least equal to that of comparative advantage in explaining sources of gains from trade. We have described a framework which highlights the role of services in encouraging international trade. In this framework, the traditional grounds for international trade based on the doctrine of comparative advantage have been supplemented by two ways in which production processes exhibit decreasing costs. Our treatment of increasing returns to scale owes much to Ethier's (1979, 1982) fundamental papers. However, we have pursued a Jess formal modeling strategy and differ in the manner in which we interpret the relationship between international trade and increasing returns.

National increasing returns to scale in Ethier's (1982) paper are embodied in cost functions which relate bundles of factors linearly to levels of national output. These functions can be interpreted as combining elements of fixed and variable costs, a procedure we adopted in modelling increasing returns within a production block.[6] Each such process yields as output a "component" which differs from any other "component," albeit produced in an entirely symmetrical fashion. These components, some of which (in a trading context) will be produced abroad, are combined in a production function for "finished manufactures" which allows for increasing returns

---

[6] Earlier use of this simple method of capturing increasing returns to scale can be found in Krugman (1979).

from the use of a larger array of components. The form of this latter function is similar to that presented by Dixit and Stiglitz (1977) in a different context — one showing how an individual can benefit from having access to a wider variety of consumer goods.[7] Ethier's production function for finished manufactures expresses what he labels international returns to scale.

There is no analog in Ethier's formulation to the role of services in linking production blocks, with or without international trade. Instead, his components are costlessly assembled. International increasing returns are introduced by allowing trade in components, thereby increasing the variety of components available to any given producer at any output level. By stark contrast, in our framework it is an expansion in the scale of output encouraged by growth in demand (whether domestic or international) which leads to an increased degree of fragmentation in the production process. The consequences of opening a trade in producer components in our model and in Ethier's are thus fundamentally different. In the Ethier formulation, producers seize upon the possibility of utilizing a greater variety of components in order to expand output because his international increasing returns depend on the extent of variety and not, as in our treatment, on the scale of output and the attendant degree of fragmentation. In our framework the potential for international dispersion of production blocks, made possible by connecting service links, yields gains to the extent that a finer degree of disaggregation and specialization according to comparative advantage results in traditional fashion in greater efficiency in resource allocation. This is a feature absent in Ethier's model.

Markusen (1986) builds directly upon the Ethier framework in his discussion of services and trade. If trade in producer goods is allowed, it *must* be trade in services, for the "components" in the Ethier model are re-defined as producer services. This interpretation of the role of services differ sharply from ours. In our treatment services may or may not be traded; their main function in trade is in allowing fragmentation over production blocks located both at home and abroad.

Some of the concepts underlying the "product cycle" introduced by Ray Vernon (1966) are present in our formulation. Early stages in the

---

[7]Romer (1987) gives a continuum version or the Dixit-Stiglitz function and applies it to growth in a closed-economy context.

cycle of development of a product are located in a country having available a host of potentially usable factors and skills, because the techniques required in product development arc still uncertain. As this uncertainty is resolved, and production techniques simplified, the location of production may shift abroad if a foreign source has a comparative advantage with the new, simplified, techniques.[8] As in our treatment, Vernon allows for the international relocation of a production process. Missing, however, is the same use of comparative advantage to argue that *part* of the production process be located at home and part abroad. Our framework, focusing on the development of separate production blocks connected by service links, opens up a scenario in which the production process can be finely divided into stages. The international location of each block (or stage) is heavily influenced by international comparisons of factor prices and productivities, with the scale of output indicating the extent to which the entire process can be fragmented.

14.6   Concluding Remarks

Our framework can shed some light on issues under discussion in the Uruguay Round and in particular on consequences of international trade liberalization in services for North–South trade. Countries such as India and Brazil have expressed fears that comparative advantage in service activities resides in more highly developed countries. Even if one is willing to assume that the most efficient providers of service links are all located in the developed countries, it has to be realized that liberalization of services and a subsequent fragmentation of production could result in a finer international division of labor in which developing countries could actively share. Certain production blocks, especially the ones requiring labor-intensive techniques, could be more cheaply produced in LDCs. The gains from liberalization of trade in services would then manifest themselves in a greater participation of developing countries in goods trade. It is therefore important that the participants in the Uruguay Round see gains and losses in the overall context rather than in the context of service sectors alone.

---

[8] It is perhaps tempting to use the Dixit-Stiglitz formulation to model the advantages which having a wide array of productive factor available conveys when uncertainty exists as to technology.

Consider the position of a country which does not have a comparative advantage in supplying services on the world market. What should its stance be towards negotiations aimed at liberalizing service trade? We have already emphasized that such a country's export activities can gain by virtue of less expensive service links which allow some production blocks within the country to be made part of an international production process. Furthermore, the literature on the Dutch Disease alerts us to the consequences for trade in traditional export sectors of technological progress in one sector — in this case service sector. If services become freely tradeable, they are available not only in the source country but in others as well. However, the extra activity in the source country could, by raising wage rates or other input prices, hurt the relative international position of other industries in the source country compared with similar industries abroad. That is, less developed countries may think they will not succeed in the competition for internationally liberated service activities, but as consumers they may have relatively more to gain in service-using sectors than do the developed countries.[9]

Even if trade in services is opened up, a less developed country may deal with outside service activities more harshly relative to other countries via-à-vis domestic regulations (e.g., concerning banking or the financial sector) or levels of taxation or of uncertainty in terms of governmental attitudes towards private business activity within its borders. Here it is important to emphasize that differences between nations in governmental policies, domestic regulations and levels of taxation all bear upon patterns of international trade in a manner which is absent if international exchange is limited to final consumer goods. Trade in the latter instance is governed by comparative advantage; high business taxes, for example, may hit all local activities fairly evenly and thus not affect the comparatively best assignment of resources and factors which are trapped behind a nation's boundaries. But once trade seeps down into factors and inputs utilized in the production process, *absolute* levels of government interference bear upon the ability of one country's production blocks to come in at a lower cost than those of another country. The traditional question, what should a nation's own immobile resources do (answered by criteria of comparative advantage),

---

[9]This argument is described in further detail in Jones, Neary, and Ruane (1987).

needs to be supplemented by asking where internationally mobile service inputs are employed (answered in part by criteria of relative attractiveness of one country versus another as a stable locale to host internationally connected productive activities).[10]

We conclude by emphasizing what we stated at the outset. We are concentrating on one of the things which services *do* in the production process: Service links have the function of connecting production blocks in separate locations, perhaps among several countries. But other roles are available for services. Aside from those mentioned earlier, whereby services are utilized within production blocks and aid in marketing the product for consumption, we should note the role of services in research and development. More broadly interpreted, services may be used to explore future possibilities for fragmentation and re-alignments within the production process, in a manner going beyond their operational role in bilaterally linking pairs of production blocks. In all these uses, services are important for the manner in which international commerce is encouraged, whatever their direct status in trade.

References

Balassa, B. (1964). The Purchasing Power Parity Doctrine: A Reappraisal. *Journal of Political Economy*, 72(6), 584–596.

Bhagwati, J. (1984). Why Are Services Cheaper in the Poor Countries? *Economic Journal*, 94, 279–288.

Coase, R. (1937). The Nature of the Firm. *Economica*, 4, 386–405.

Dixit, A. and Stiglitz, J. (1977). Monopolistic Competition and Optimal Product Diversity. *American Economic Review*, 67, 297–308.

Ethier, W.J. (1979). Internationally Decreasing Costs and World Trade. *Journal of International Economics*, 9, 1–24.

Ethier, W.J. (1982). National and International Returns to Scale in the Modern Theory of International Trade. *American Economic Review*, 72, 389–405.

Jones, R.W. (1980). Comparative and Absolute Advantage. *Swiss Journal of Economics*, 3, 235–260.

Jones, R., Neary, J.P., and Ruane, F. (1987). International Capital Mobility and the Dutch Disease. In H. Kierzkowski (Ed.), *Protection and Competition in International Trade*, Oxford: Basil Blackwell.

Kol, J. (1987). Allyn Young Specialization and Intermediate Goods in International Trade. Mimeo.

---

[10]This issue is discussed in more detail in Jones (1980).

Krugman, P. (1979). Increasing Returns, Monopolistic Competition, and International Trade. *Journal of International Economics*, 9(4), 469–479.

Kumpe, T. and Bolwijn, P. (1988). Manufacturing: The New Case for Vertical Integration. *Harvard Business Review*, 66(2) 75–81.

Markusen, J.R. (1986). Trade in Producer Services: Issues Involving Returns to Scale and the International Division of Labor. Discussion Paper, Series on Trade in Services, The Institute for Research on Public Policy.

Morawetz, D. (1981). *Why the Emperor's New Clothes are Not Made in Colombia*. Oxford: Oxford University Press.

North, D. (1958). Ocean Freight Rates and Economic Development 1750–1913. *Journal of Economic History*, 18(4), 537–555.

Romer, P. (1987). Growth Based on Increasing Returns Due to Specialization. *American Economic Review*, 77, 56–62.

Stigler, G. (1951). The Division of Labor is Limited by the Extent of the Market. *Journal of Political Economy*, 59(3), 185–193.

Vernon, R. (1966). International Investment and International Trade in the Product Cycle. *Quarterly Journal of Economics*, 80, 190–207.

Young, A. (1928). Increasing Returns and Economic Progress. *Economic Journal*, 38, 527–542.

CHAPTER 15

The Role of International Fragmentation in the Development Process*

Ronald W. Jones and Sugata Marjit

Much of what has been written about the process of economic development has concentrated on macroeconomic factors that affect the growth process, such as the community's savings rate, its ability to attract foreign investment, and the composition and quality of its factor-endowment base. Less formally dealt with, but nonetheless often cited as important in the development process, is the nature of government regulations and the type of institutions that are reflective of the community's own cultural inheritance.

The tide of globalization in its many forms is making it more difficult for countries to insulate their citizens from those foreign influences and information that often pose a challenge to existing national regulations and cultural norms. World news and country-specific information about opportunities are the kinds of information now readily available from the media and on the World Wide Web. One feature of the current move worldwide toward increased trading contacts is the every-larger extent of international outsourcing. Production processes that traditionally have been vertically integrated within countries become *fragmented* into separate parts which can be located in countries in which factor prices are well matched to the factor intensities of the particular fragments. In this chapter, we sketch

---

*Originally published in *American Economic Review*, 91(2), (2001), pp. 363–366. We are indebted to Frances Ruane for helpful discussions.

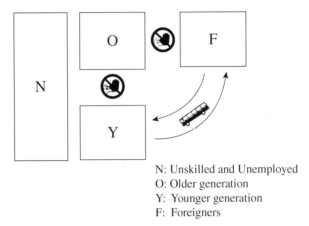

N: Unskilled and Unemployed
O: Older generation
Y: Younger generation
F: Foreigners

Figure 15.1.   Interest Groups

out a scenario that captures some of the principal features of many less-developed areas. This sketch serves to illustrate how the process of increased international fragmentation of production can encourage changes in those regulations and national habits that have typically held back the process of economic development.

Let the populace of a less-developed region be broken down into the four groups illustrated in Fig. 15.1. One of these groups, N, refers to unskilled labor as well as unemployed workers, either of the younger or older generation, and has little role to play in the scenario. The remaining two domestic groups are defined by age: an *older generation*, O, and a *younger generation*, Y. The older generation owns the physical capital and the existing businesses that operate within the economy. The younger generation consists of recent graduates of educational institutions as well as even younger members who are still somewhere in the educational system. A fourth group is identified in Fig. 15.1, *foreigners*, indicated by F. This group has commercial contacts with the national groups, either through international trade or through foreign investment.

The basic hypothesis of the scenario that we sketch out is that the panoply of government laws and regulations, as well as the mores and culture of the society as it has developed over time, are motivated by a desire to protect the position of the older generation, O, from the potential or actual competition from two sources: foreigners and the younger generation. The defense against foreign pressures takes the traditional form of commercial policy restrictions (e.g., tariffs and quotas against foreign imports), foreign-exchange regulations, and strict controls over the types of foreign investment allowed. As well, there may be tight control over foreign immigration, although the desire of people from other countries to emigrate to this country may be limited. As for the younger generation, it will admittedly be allowed entry to the older group, in time, but the options available to the younger generation are proscribed. There may be apprenticeship schemes that channel younger recruits into the businesses already established. The primary constraint may take the form of restraints on credit available to individuals in the younger group if not sanctioned by members of the older generation. Thus, it would be difficult, if not impossible, for a member of the younger generation to obtain funding to form an enterprise operating independently of existing traditional firms.

Just as restrictions on international trade and investment typically militate against the development process, so also do the restrictions imposed on the economic activity of the younger generation. However, the nature of the globalization phenomenon is working somewhat systematically to loosen the constraints imposed by national culture and regulations on the activities of the younger generation. For example, there is now much more traffic in young members from less-developed regions into educational establishments in the United States and Western Europe. This younger group is now well represented in many MBA or Ph.D. programs (*The Economist* of [16 November 1991] reported that a full 25 percent of doctorates in engineering granted by American universities were awarded to students who came from Taiwan). Those students who return to their native lands not only receive an education that could be useful in their professional careers and in starting their own businesses, but also they forge contacts with foreigners in the F group. These contacts may open up opportunities in foreign credit markets that serve to circumvent the restrictions they would face at home. Even those students who remain abroad serve a useful function for other members of the younger generation, for they establish themselves as role models and form networks that ease entry into foreign educational establishments. As for even younger members of the Y generation who are still engaged in studies in the home country, they now have much greater access, via radio, television, and the Internet, to information and points of view that may challenge the nationally accepted traditional norms concerning regulation and culture. Not only can the use of the new information technology aid in the process of education, the younger members are also learning the skills involved in using this technology, skills that will serve to enhance their productivity in the market place.

Putting aside the restraints on credit that make starting a business difficult for members of the younger generation, consider the contrast between such a business and one owned by established members of the older generation. The latter have been at it longer and may well have benefited from "learning-by-doing" that has given them an absolute advantage in current production methods. Suppose, however, in this age of fairly rapid technological change, that some new techniques originally associated with other sectors of the economy (or other parts of the world) are developed, and the possibility of their application to the business at hand is considered by the two groups. For each, developing the new technology means forgoing (at least to some extent) the old. As analyzed in Michihiro Ohyama and Jones (1995), a business launched by members of the younger generation is more likely to switch to the new technology than is a business of the established older group. The reason resides in the theory of comparative advantage. Having a presumed absolute advantage in the older technology, the older generation has a tendency to have a comparative disadvantage in the new. This comparison could hold even if the older generation was a bit better at the new: it is *comparative* advantage that matters, and the older generation has a higher opportunity cost of switching to the new. In other words, in a period in which new technologies and ideas are being developed in a number of industries globally, the payoff to switching to the new techniques may be greater for the latecomers — the members of the younger generation.

To this scenario, we now add the phenomenon of fragmentation of production processes. The movement toward deregulation, especially of services, and the technological changes that have drastically reduced the costs of communication as well as making transportation less expensive have all encouraged a fragmentation of previously vertically integrated production processes (as spelled out in Jones and Kierzkowski (1990, 2001) and Jones (2000)). The spillover into international markets has been striking in a number of industries: electronics, textiles and clothing, automobiles, and radio and television are only a few examples. If it becomes less costly to coordinate activities in more than one location or country, the attraction provided by lower relative wages in some countries for labor-intensive fragments becomes obvious.

Suppose, then, that a member of the F group finds this low-wage country an attractive locale in which to locate a labor-intensive fragment. It has to make contact with some of the local population in order that a separate firm is located to provide this fragment or so that personnel can be recruited for a joint venture or a branch of a multinational organization. Should the foreigner seek out members of the older generation or members of the younger generation? Members of the O group may have an advantage in that they already have established businesses in the same kind of activity. Although they may possess an absolute advantage in production over that possessed by members of the Y group, as argued above this may serve to put them at a comparative disadvantage if the foreigner wants to make use of newly developed techniques unfamiliar either to the local O group or to the Y group. The older generation would face a higher opportunity cost. Furthermore, productive activity in the older generation may have survived in large part because of protective tariffs or quotas. More importantly, such activity may be exemplified by vertically integrated production processes, with some fragments of local production unsustainable once fragmentation in the rest of the world allows international competition from foreign sources possessing an absolute advantage either of the Ricardian type or because factor intensities are a better match for factor prices abroad. The firm owned by the older generation would be loath to jettison those parts of the integrated process that would not be competitive in the new trading environment.

The advantages of an alliance of foreign entrepreneurs with local members of the younger generation are several. The younger generation has an endowment that is heavily skewed toward human capital as opposed to physical capital, and in a world of rapidly changing technology the relative value of human capital is rising compared with that of physical capital. Contacts with foreigners have the added value to local members of the Y group because they allow them to circumvent onerous restrictions imposed by local regulations and cultural norms. This would certainly be the case if the younger members could establish credit facilities abroad, aided by previous personal contacts with foreigners. Admittedly it is generally more difficult to obtain credit based upon human capital as collateral. Foreign sources with more direct information, however, may prove more open to supplying credit. But the fragmentation process goes further than this. It provides business opportunities to the younger generation, opportunities arising from the potential demand in world markets for less-expensive local production of labor-intensive fragments.

Of course it is not only the less-developed countries of this world that have cultural attitudes and regulations that tend to hobble the ability of the young to proceed in business. A quote from *The Economist* (29 April 2000, pp. 58–59) provides a good illustration of how members of the established older generation in Japan view the younger generation. Early in the year a new high-tech firm, Hikari Tsushin, found its shares in deep trouble, mirroring the difficulties of high-tech firms in the United States in the spring. The firm's president, Yasumitsu Shigeta, was in severe financial trouble. What was the reaction of the older generation in Japan? To quote:

> Japan's banks and big businesses have watched the recent rise of entrepreneurs such as Mr. Shigeta with real revulsion. To them, Hikari Tsushin and its sort are an aberration. Brash, young, aggressive, loud and on the make, these companies ooze with the type of values that Japan's old business elite finds distasteful and dangerous.

A world in which the costs of service links are falling drastically and competition is spreading globally is one in which production processes worldwide are becoming fragmented, encouraging outsourcing of labor-intensive segments of the production process to countries in which labor costs are relatively low. This offers new opportunities to less-developed areas, countries which previously could not engage in the vertically integrated processes unless tariff or quota protection were allowed and foreign investment opportunities were proscribed. An alliance between foreigners and members of the younger generation seems a more likely outcome in promoting local production of these fragments. Resistance is to be expected from established members of the older generation, whose firms would not only compete with such an alliance in the home market, but could not survive without local protection that cuts them off from exporting to world markets. Inherited cultural norms and a deliberate web of regulations often limit opportunities for members of the younger generation to obtain credit and establish their own firms. With globalization, greater exposure to foreign cultures, opportunities afforded by world capital markets, and international fragmentation of production, the younger generation now has possibilities of circumventing local restrictions on their activities. The expected outcome should be a more active and rapid process of economic development.

References

Jones, R.W. (2000). *Globalization and the Theory of Input Trade.* Cambridge, MA: MIT Press.

Jones, R.W. and Kierzkowski, H. (1990). The Role of Services in Production and International Trade: A Theoretical Framework. In: R. Jones and A. Krueger, (Eds.), *The Political Economy of International Trade* (pp. 31–48). Oxford, UK: Blackwell.

Jones, R.W. and Kierzkowski, H. (2001). A Framework for Fragmentation. In: S. Arndt and H. Kierzkowski, (Eds.), *Fragmentation: New Production Patterns in the World Economy* (pp. 17–34). Oxford, UK: Oxford University Press.

Ohyama, M. and Jones, R.W. (1995). Technology Choice, Overtaking and Comparative Advantage. *Review of International Economics*, 3(2), 224–34; longer version In: Jim Levinsohn, Alan V. Deardorff, and Robert, M. Stern, (Eds.), *New Directions in Trade Theory* (pp. 199–236). Ann Arbor, MI: University of Michigan Press.

CHAPTER 16

International Trade and Agglomeration: An Alternative Framework*

Ronald W. Jones and Henryk Kierzkowski

Abstract

The New Economic Geography, as expounded by Krugman and others, high-lights the importance of greater extent of agglomeration as incomes grow in the world economy. In this chapter, we suggest an alternative framework in which, as incomes grow, greater degrees of economic fragmentation, and disagglomeration are encouraged. In both approaches increasing returns to scale are crucial, but in ours these are found in service sectors that allow separate production blocks to be coordinated instead of being found within separate production blocks.

16.1 Introduction

In the vast array of fields in economics, international trade and economic geography should be neighbors sharing similar interests and preoccupied with a strongly overlapping range of issues. Alas, one could say that the scientific telescopes of each specialization had been trained for a long time in different directions. This state of isolation could not last and either an international trade economist would discover that commerce, within or across countries, involves geography; or a geographer would have observed that trade is one of the best examples of spatial displacement.

In the event, Paul Krugman was the first to seize the connection in a 1991 *Journal of Political Economy* paper and has been running with the main

---

*Originally published in *Journal of Economics*, Supplement 10, (2005), pp. 1–16.

idea ever since.[1] Other trade economists soon saw a new opening and a way of enriching their discipline. Having "discovered" geography, international trade economists had no hesitation telling economic geographers how their field really *should* be structured and developed.

As in the case of the "new" trade theory, the breakthrough in the "new" economic geography has come from the application of increasing returns to scale, especially in the context of monopolistic competition utilizing the functional form made famous by Avinash Dixit and Joseph Stiglitz (1977).

Increasing returns to scale could not alone do the trick of re-orienting the field of economic geography; in addition to increased realism, transportation costs have been called in to give the new models an increased complexity in order to generate interesting results. There is no doubt that the tools and the analytical machinery developed in the course of the new trade revolution have proved very popular. However, it seems pertinent to ask what purpose is served by applying them to geography. A convincing answer would be that the traditional economic geography framework and the tools it employed were not capable of explaining the existence of some important stylized facts.

Recall that the existence of intra-industry trade and the alleged inability of the traditional international economics models to explain this trade, ushered in the "new" trade revolution almost two decades ago. Was there, more recently, a corresponding stylized fact related to economic geography

---

[1] In the economics literature concern over spatial aspects was expressed earlier by Stephen Enke (1951) and Paul Samuelson (1952). Samuelson remarked,

> "Spatial problems have been so neglected in economic theory that the field is of interest for its own sake." (p. 284).

In 1976, a symposium was held in Stockholm, and the Foreword to the publication of the Proceedings (see Bertil Ohlin, Per-Ove Hesselborn and Per Magnus Wijkman, Eds, 1977) commented,

> "A special aim of the symposium was to bring about an exchange of ideas between economists and economic geographers interested in trade and movements of the factors of production."

The "new" economic geography has expanded in leaps and bounds. Even reviews of the existing work have become numerous. Among most comprehensive surveys are: Neary (2001), Martin and Sunley (1996), Sunley (2001), Sheppard (2001) and Urban (2001).

that escaped explanation until the increasing-returns-to-scale artillery was brought in? The question of the agglomeration of economic activities or its opposite could be thought of as requiring proper modeling and explanation. It is not obvious, however, that there is some overwhelming empirical evidence demonstrating clear trends regarding agglomeration (or disagglomeration) on a country, regional or global basis. The desire to understand the mechanisms driving these processes may provide sufficient justification for an interest in this subject.[2]

There exists evidence showing that the global economy does *not* consist of a single core or even a limited number of centers and peripheries. Instead, the world economy becomes an increasingly, even though not evenly distributed, complex industrial structure spanning not only individual continents but the entire globe. International production networks have emerged in a manifold of industries and products: sports footwear, mobile phones, cars, clothing, computers, and furniture to name only a few. While there obviously are agglomeration forces operating in some areas, dispersion of economic activities is also a fact of life. One of the consequences of disagglomeration manifests itself in a rapid expansion of international trade in parts and components.

The empirical study by Francis Ng and Alexander Yeats (2001) shows this new phenomenon for East Asia. Between 1984 and 1996 East Asian imports and exports of manufactured components grew annually between 2 and 3 times as fast as imports and exports of traditional production. It is highly probable that the trade in parts and components also trumped intra-industry trade. The *maquiladora* phenomenon also shows that disagglomeration of production takes place in the US–Mexico context.[3] Further north, Canada and the United States had undertaken sharing of production

---

[2]One of the critics of the new economic geography models based on the Dixit Stiglitz approach takes Masahisa Fujita, Paul Krugman, and Anthony Venables, the authors of The Spatial Economy (1999), to task:

"While such formal modeling may increase the credibility and popularity of the ideas with the economists, it provides no evidence as to their actual empirical significance and their initial assumptions appear mainly to be made on the basis of modeling convenience rather than with any regard to empirical relevance." [Sunley (2001), p. 136.]

[3]Interesting work on the phenomenon of outsourcing in the Mexican context is found in Robert Feenstra and Gordon Hanson (1996).

many years ago, especially in the automobile industry. More recently, India has emerged as a powerful attractor for a range of intermediate activities in manufacturing and services. Europe is certainly moving in the same direction.[4]

All in all, it has been estimated by Yeats (2001) that about 30 percent of global manufactured goods trade takes the form of trade in parts and components. Corresponding numbers for the 1950s and 1960s do not exist, but they surely must have been very small indeed. It follows that growth of intra-industry trade must have been outpaced by a new type of trade associated with disagglomeration.

The phenomenon of international production networks and trade in parts and components reinforces the importance of transportation costs stressed in the new economic geography. But what kind of transportation costs — producers-to-consumers or producers-to-producers? Surely it must be the latter in a world where production of a pair of jeans can be broken down into 24 stages and allocated among Pakistan, Mainland China, Hong Kong, and Malaysia with more than a dozen border crossings being executed before the final product is shipped off to consumers.[5] Are producers-to-consumers transportation costs so important as to neglect

---

[4]Interestingly enough, the grand project of a supersonic passenger plane, Concord, conceived primarily by the French and British back in the 1960s could have been one of early examples of dispersion of production across Europe.

[5]The Economist of December 27th 2002 reports on a rapid growth of logistic companies operating on a global scale.

> "So what exactly can smart logistics do for companies? One example is TPG's contract with Ford to service its Toronto factory. This plant produces 1,500 Windstar minivans a day. To keep it running virtually round the clock, TPG has to organize 800 deliveries a day from 300 different part makers. Its software must be tied into Ford's computerized production system. Loads have to arrive at 12 different points along the assembly lines without ever being more than 10 minutes late."

But TPG is a traditional freight company. The new type of logistics company, such as Exel, does much more. It is like the chef of an orchestra. The Economist continues:

> "One of Exel's biggest contracts is with Ford, for which it organizes supplies for seven factories around Europe. Exel also works for Volkswagen in its operations in Spain and Mexico. The factory in Puebla, Mexico, turns out 1,400 new Beetles a day. And Exel helps with Nokia's logistics as well, especially in China and South-East Asia."

producers-to-producers transportation costs? It would seem likely that the industrial landscape generated by our theoretical models looks different depending upon which transport links are brought to the fore of the analysis.

As Peter Neary (2001) commented in discussing the appearance of *The Spatial Economy* (1999) by Masahisa Fujita, Paul Krugman, and Anthony Venables, "*New economic geography has come of age.*" While recognizing its important and numerous contributions, we should advance other explanations of phenomena arising in the common grounds shared by two neighbors — economic geography and international trade.

16.2   Two Alternative Scenarios

In suggesting an alternative framework for examining whether economic growth is accompanied by a greater degree of agglomeration or, instead, by a spread of productive activity or disagglomeration, we alter somewhat the focus provided in the work of Krugman and others in order to provide a benchmark comparison. We leave out of account the question of costs involved in having produced final goods reach the consumer and, instead, enquire about the possibility of breaking an integrated production process into separate *fragments* that could be located in other areas or other countries. In asking about links among producers instead of between final producers and consumers we also dispense with the need for utilizing the Dixit–Stiglitz utility function to express taste patterns for consumers facing an array of differentiated final goods. This function has provided yeoman service in "new trade theory", growth, and political economy in supplying a foundation at the micro level for Chamberlinian monopolistic competition with firms operating in the range in which increasing returns to scale are still found. Increasing returns are essential in our alternative scenario, but they are assumed to take place in what we call *service link* activities such as communication and coordination services that are required to establish a functioning network among fragments of *production blocks* that are located in different geographical locations (Ronald Jones and Henryk Kierzkowski, 1990, 2001a). These service activities include (but are not limited to) transportation services, the ones that play such a crucial role in the "new economic geography," albeit assumed there to be of the constant-cost variety. Herein lies a crucial distinction with our alternative: Increasing returns are assumed to reside in service link activities (including transportation) instead of on the factory floor (within production blocks). In section 4 we suggest what empirical work has to say about the nature of service links.

In each of the two alternative scenarios, we now present we compare the costs of producing a final commodity when an integrated production location (or firm, **IF**) is used as opposed to having the production process split into two fragments located in different regions or countries, perhaps produced by two different firms. If such a split occurs, costs of production (neglecting transport costs or other coordinating service link activities) are lowered since it is possible to select locations such that factor prices and/or factor productivities are for each fragment more suited to factor proportions in that fragment. Regions in which labor is relatively inexpensive are used for the more labor-intensive fragment. For example, Nike, in making sports apparel, does the design work in the United States but outsources almost all the actual production activity to firms in Asia. Likewise, the Swedish furniture firm, Ikea, early on sent its actual production activity to Poland and used its Swedish labor force to design the individual pieces. In both Figs. 16.1 and 16.2 final output, **Y**, is shown on the horizontal axis and a pair of total production cost loci are drawn, labeled **IF** when all

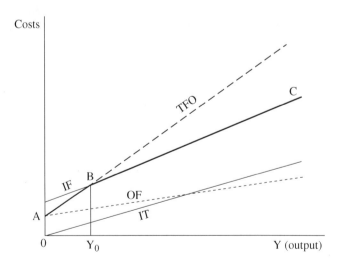

Figure 16.1.   Agglomeration. IF: Integrated Firm. OF: Outsourced Fragments (Production). IT: "Iceberg" Transportation. TFO: Total Fragmented Operation. ABC: Minimum Cost Schedule

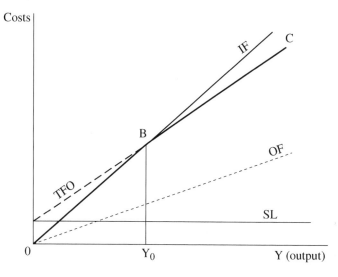

Figure 16.2. Disagglomeration. IF: Integrated Firm. OF: Outsourced Fragments (Production). SL: Service Link Costs. TFO: Total Fragmented Operation. OBC: Minimum Cost Schedule.

activity takes place in a single location with one firm, and **OF** (outsourced fragments) when the costs in the two separate fragments arc added up (production costs only). These two fragments provide the appropriate balance of necessary output for any value of **Y**.

If production is split between two fragments located in different areas, these fragments must be brought together and coordinated, thus incurring extra costs of transportation, communication, and obtaining knowledge of where best to locate the fragments. These service link costs tend to be higher if fragments are located in different countries than if they are merely placed in different regions of a single country. Where Figs. 16.1 and 16.2 differ is in the kind of activity in which increasing returns are found. Figure 16.1 characterizes our version of the assumptions made in the Fujita, Krugman, and Venables model, in which increasing returns are found *within* production blocks. The simple way of modeling such increasing returns is to combine fixed costs (along the vertical axis) with constant marginal costs (shown by the slope of the total cost curve), leading to the rising **IF** and **OF** loci in Fig. 16.1. (Note that with two regions from which to choose, the costs of production along **OF** are everywhere lower than along the **IF**-locus if production is positive.) Following their treatment, we assume that the entire costs of linking the two fragments together is in the form of transport costs between fragments where the so-called *iceberg* model of such costs is used. (The iceberg analogy was introduced by Paul Samuelson in his 1954 *Economic Journal* discussion of the international transfer problem when transport costs exist.[6]) In that scenario, a unit of output exported from one locale will arrive at a different locale diminished in size, much as part of an iceberg would melt if transported from one region to another. The crucial aspect to notice is that this makes transportation a constant-returns-to-scale activity — doubling the output transferred between locations will double the loss eaten up in transport. There is no doubt that such an assumption is useful in avoiding separate activities whereby factors of production are combined to produce the services of transportation. However, it introduces a form of service link in Fig. 16.1 not matched in Fig. 16.2's alternative. The **TFO** (total fragmented operation) costs are found by adding the **OF** locus to the ray from the origin representing transportation costs.

In the alternative portrayed in Fig. 16.2, constant returns to scale are assumed both for the integrated production block (**IF**) and for the costs (production only) of the combined activities for the separate production blocks (**OF**), which are lower because each fragment is located in an area in which there is a better match among factor prices, technology, and factor proportions. Service link costs are required in order to coordinate the outputs of the separate fragments, and we make the extreme assumption that all such costs are constant regardless of the scale of activity. Thus the **TFO** cost schedule is a shifted-up version of the **OF** locus.

In each diagram the cost of the best mode of production is shown by a broken heavy line, with the break appearing at output level Y_0. Do larger scales of output encourage or discourage agglomeration? The contrast between the two scenarios is striking. In Fig. 16.1, the characterized version of the Fujita, Krugman, and Venables model with iceberg transportation costs, disaggregated output in two locales is appropriate for small levels of output, up to Y_0. Up to this point the costs of connecting the two fragments by incurring transport costs are outweighed by the benefits of

---

[6]As a matter of fact, Michael Rauscher has pointed out to us that the grand master of economic geography, Johann Heinrich von Thunen, 130 years previously, described how a horse that transports wheat from the country side to a city market eats a fraction of it en route.

lower marginal costs in each fragment, but for higher levels of output it pays to combine all output in an integrated production block subject to increasing returns to scale and thus to obviate the need to pay for transportation. By contrast, in Fig. 16.2, it is a large scale of output (greater than Y_0) that encourages disagglomeration. With increasing returns found in the service link activities (including the costs of transportation), it pays to outsource the originally vertically-integrated production process into two fragments in different locales especially well-suited to their factor proportions.

In Sec. 4, we shall dwell more extensively on the nature of the costs of service links, including transportation. There is general agreement that there have been significant technological improvements that have brought about a lowering in the costs of service links. This is especially true of the costs of communication, which now have almost reached the vanishing point. It also holds, to a lesser extent, with the general costs of obtaining information and, as well, costs of transportation between producing regions. The consequences of such downward shifts in these costs in the two alternative settings are profound. In Fig. 16.1, a lowering of the iceberg transportation costs causes the (**TFO**) schedule of costs of total fragmented operation to rotate in a clockwise direction from the initial point on the vertical axis. As a result, the change-over point of output, Y_0, moves to the *right*. In Fig. 16.2, a technologically-inspired reduction in the costs of service links shifts the TFO schedule downwards, causing the change-over level of output, Y_0, to move to the *left*. The result: In *both* cases, the range of outputs in which disagglomeration is the preferred mode of production increases. In Fig. 16.1, as output expands the consolidation of production in one location is delayed, whereas in Fig. 16.2, the desirability of fragmented production occurs at an earlier stage of growth.

One of the widely-recognized asymmetries on the international scene is the greater ease of moving commodities and middle products (including physical capital) among countries than it is to move labor. The large international migrations of labor witnessed at the end of the 19th century and beginning of the 20th century seem now a thing of the past, although some migration, both legal and illegal, still takes place. This asymmetry provides the basis for the doctrine of comparative advantage and suggests limits on the degree of international agglomeration that can be expected. Whereas within a country relatively mobile labor can aid and abet a process of agglomeration into a few urban nodes, on a global scale we have witnessed a greater degree of outsourcing of fragments of the production process in a manner reflecting both the Ricardian and Heckscher–Ohlin rationale for the nature of trade. Such disagglomeration among countries is encouraged by the increasing returns to scale found in many service link activities as world incomes rise, by the significant improvements in technology in the service area, as well as by a general lowering of regulatory barriers to international trade. With labor relatively immobile between countries, the doctrine of comparative advantage guarantees that no country will empty out as a consequence of the forces of agglomeration.

16.3 Fragmentation may Encourage Agglomeration and Growth

In the preceding section, we have suggested that greater levels of output in an industry tend to encourage a fragmentation of a vertically integrated production process, with outsourcing reaching even beyond a nation's borders. Suppose such a process is taking place not only in a single sector but also in many industries world-wide. Then it is possible to argue that fragmentation may provide a stimulus to subsequent _agglomeration_ at a global level!

The argument for such a possibility rests in part on what we have termed the "_horizontal aspects of vertical fragmentation_" (see Jones and Kierzkowski, 2001b). Suppose that in a number of industrial sectors economic growth, technical progress, increasing returns in connecting service-link activities, and deregulation efforts have all conspired to promote a fragmentation, both locally and internationally, of production processes. We assume that some of these fragments more closely resemble each other in an interindustry comparison than do the original integrated activities. This encourages further technical progress serving to make such fragments even more uniform and useful in a number of different sectors of the economy. (Consider the spread in the use of computer chips from computers to a wide range of uses ranging from toasters to automobiles.) Furthermore, the overall techniques of production (or factor proportions) of such fragments may be rather similar. All this serves to encourage an agglomeration of a new industry producing such fragments for a wide array of sectors both locally and internationally.

The time-honored arguments about labor with certain skills being attracted to a center where a variety of productive activities require such skills seem appropriate in this setting. Alfred Marshall (1890) was an early exponent of the kind of externalities that may emerge when fragments of different industries share somewhat similar factor proportions and types of labor skills are located in the same region. In his words,

> "The mysteries of trade become no mystery; but are as it were in the air. Good work is rightly appreciated, invention and improvements in machinery, in processes and general organization of businesses have their merits promptly discussed: if one man starts a new idea, it is taken up by others and combined with suggestions of their own; and thus it becomes the source of further new ideas."

This Marshallian view has been picked up by other geographers. Thus,

> "Economists since Alfred Marshall have argued that cities facilitate the flow of ideas. However, most urban research focuses on the role that the density plays in reducing transportation costs between suppliers and customers (Krugman, 1991). However, Dumais et al. (1997) show that manufacturing firms in the USA since 1970 have not based their location decisions on the presence of suppliers and customers. Instead, firms locate near other firms that use the same type of workers."[7]

These ideas are consistent with a Heckscher–Ohlin basis for trade between countries based on differences in factor endowments and factor requirements in production, even without strong elements of imperfect competition. It would not be difficult formally to model externalities whereby factor productivities in one sector are positively affected by increases in activity of similar factors in other sectors closely related in their input and skill requirements.

The process of agglomeration outlined above presents an alternative to the agglomeration story told by the new economic geography. Perhaps it follows more closely what traditional economic geographers tell us is important. It presents a more complex world in which fragmentation of production results initially in a dispersion of economic activities. However,

---

[7] Edward Glaeser (2000, p. 84). Others expressed similar views. Martin and Sunley (1996) state on pages 285–286,

> "one of the most important limitations of Krugman's geographical economics is his stubborn concentration only on those externalities that can be mathematically modelled, and thus his reluctance to discuss the geographical impacts of technological and knowledge spillovers. The recent geographical literature has begun to assign key importance to technical change and technological externalities in shaping and transforming the space economy".

as a realignment of production patterns takes place within and across countries, the forces of agglomeration once again are in evidence. The addition of these externalities allows the forces of fragmentation and subsequent agglomeration to become engines of growth.[8]

As fragmentation and technical progress take place, the locales in which such pressures for agglomeration occur may change over time. An example of this was provided years ago in Ray Vernon's discussion of the product cycle (1966). At early stages of production a search is under way for the best techniques of producing a new product. In the face of uncertainty, the location of production is guided largely by the existence of labor (and perhaps capital) of a number of different skills. This leads (so Vernon argued) to a locale in an advanced country such as the United States. Eventually things settle down, and a technology requiring relatively heavy use of less skilled labor is formulated. As a consequence, the industry moves to a less developed country in which such labor is relatively inexpensive.

There is another route whereby fragmentation may eventually lead to a greater degree of agglomeration. The international fragmentation of production blocks is only made possible by the use of connecting service links, and it is in these service activities that we have argued that strong increasing returns are found. Just as in the arguments put forth by Krugman and others that increasing returns foster agglomeration, such agglomeration might be expected within the service sector. Indeed, this seems to be the case in activities such as financial services and insurance. Deregulation should certainly be given much of the credit for allowing more open trade in services, and one of the by-products of international fragmentation and its role in disagglomeration is the tendency for activities that provide service links themselves to agglomerate. This is consistent with the observed concentration of many service activities in advanced countries and international outsourcing of production blocks to less developed areas.

16.4   Increasing Returns and Technology in Service Link Activity

Where are increasing returns to be found? The crude assumptions that we have made is that they are found exclusively in the service link activities

---

[8] For somewhat similar views, see the discussion of "clusters" as providing externalities and influences on productivity growth in Michael Porter (2000).

that facilitate a coordination of fragmented production blocks as opposed to constant returns to scale within such blocks. We need not rely on such a stringent dichotomy. Instead, we would argue that the kind of economic activities that are most often associated with increasing returns are ones in which economic information is gathered, where financial aids to trade are obtained, where shipments are insured, where communication between locations far apart are required, and even where transportation activities are involved.[9]

Although some service activities are found within production blocks, it seems difficult to find strong evidence of increasing returns in actual production. In a relatively estimate of production functions in the United States, Susanto Basu and John Fernald (1997) have come to the following conclusion:

> "A typical (roughly) two-digit industry in the United States appears to have constant or slightly decreasing returns to scale" (p. 249)

and furthermore

> "most plants and engineering studies find essentially constant returns to scale." (p. 263).

The evidence from Canadian manufacturing industries provides some support for the opposite view that there are increasing returns to be found in production.[10] Technological progress in service link activities, including transportation, has been an impressive feature of the past few decades. For example, one can hardly discuss global production without making reference to telecommunications. It is generally accepted that launching telecommunications services involves high fixed costs. By contrast, the marginal cost is miniscule. In a bygone era telephone operators struggled to

---

[9] Alfred Marshall (1890) has this to say about transportation:

> "A ship's carrying power varies as the cube of her dimensions, while the resistance offered by the water increases only a little faster than the square of her dimensions; so that a large ship requires less coal in proportion to its tonnage than a small one. It also requires less labour, especially that of navigation. In short, the small ship has no chance of competing with the large ship between ports which large ships can easily enter, and between which the traffic is sufficient to enable them to fill up quickly."

[10] Michael Benarroch (1997, p. 1084).

make speedy connections. Today a user dials a number practically anywhere in the world and is put through immediately. Long-distance transmission of text or images has also become much less costly. Sending production plans from England to Singapore became significantly easier with the introduction of fax technology and DHL. Today it is possible to transmit text and images in living color instantaneously and almost costlessly.

16.5   Concluding Remarks

Both "old" and "new" geographers have cited many reasons why economic activity is not spread uniformly within a country or, indeed, among countries. Despite the standard economic doctrine of diminishing returns, many reasons can be cited for a "bunching up" of productive activities and residences. Individuals desire to consume services and products difficult to obtain in thinly settled communities (theatre, variety in shopping malls, proximity to friends and relatives, etc.) and externalities are provided by the co-existence in one locale of productive activities requiring inputs of labor of similar skills.

In the "new" economic geography, exemplified by the book by Fujita, Krugman, and Venables, increasing returns in production and transportation costs of the Samuelsonian "iceberg" variety between consumers and producers are important ingredients in the analysis of agglomeration. In their models, consumer behavior is explicitly modeled with the aid of the Dixit–Stiglitz utility function allowing a love of variety among commodities of the same general type, leading to a Chamberlinian form of monopolistic competition. At the outset of our chapter, we have taken liberties with this setting, concentrating instead on the costs of connecting fragments of a production process that can be outsourced, perhaps to other countries, and leaving final consumers aside. The crucial issue is where are the increasing returns found — on the factory floor (i.e., within the production unit) or among the services required to link disparate fragments of the process.

If increasing returns are found within each production block, which is our transformation of the Fujita, Krugman, and Venables model to consider the outsourcing phenomenon, we argued that if transportation services are required to link two blocks, and if these services exhibit constant returns to scale (as in the iceberg model), larger scales of output will indeed tend to cause production fragments that are initially separated spatially, to agglomerate. However, we also provided an alternative scenario that leads to opposite conclusions, one based on the model we presented initially in 1990. A production process consists of a number of production blocks that can be fragmented and located in different geographic regions of the same country, or can be outsourced to a variety of countries. The incentive to do so is provided by the different skills or factor combinations required in various fragments and the variety of factor prices and/or factor skills available in different regions or countries. Fragmentation allows a better "fit" for each production block. But extra costs are involved - those of trans-portation, but also of finance, coordination, communication, etc., and we argue that it is in these service link activities that strong degrees of increas-ing returns and decreasing costs are to be found. To take extreme examples we assumed that production blocks exhibit constant returns to scale, while service link activities are purely of the fixed cost variety, independent of scales of output. This difference in the location of the increasing returns activity is sufficient to lead to the result that eventually as output expands productive activity exhibits disagglomeration — a dispersal of productive activity to locations in which Ricardian and/or Heckscher–Ohlin differ-ences among countries provide a better fit for the separate fragments as the scale of production expands.

Recent decades have witnessed profound productivity improvements in service links, whether of the transportation variety or in other service activ-ities. The changes in communication costs have probably been the most significant in lowering the service costs required to coordinate spatially separated production fragments. We have argued that such changes have encouraged disagglomeration *both* in the modified Fujita, Krugman, and Venables scenario as well as in our model of international fragmentation.

A melding of the two strands of argument concerning agglomeration was suggested in that international fragmentation of economic activity, promoted by larger scales of output and technological progress reducing the costs of service links, may lead to a subsequent agglomeration of frag-ments from different industries, fragments that nonetheless require similar relative quantities and qualities of productive inputs. This can eventu-ate in a realignment of the location of production, with encouragement for further technological progress and externalities that serve, as well, to promote economic growth.

Finally, we should note that in this, and our previous chapters, we have remained relatively silent on such questions as: Will fragmentation take place within the firm or at arms-length in market transactions? Will large firms, possibly multinationals, dominate the process of international fragmentation while small firms are pushed away? *These* are legitimate and difficult issues, and our silence reflects a lack of comparative advantage.[11]

Acknowledgments

The authors wish to thank seminar participants in Helsinki and Osaka for valuable comments, as well as two anonymous referees. Bjarne Jensen has been very helpful in the revision of the manuscript.

References

Arndt, S. and Kierzkowski, H. (Eds.) (2001). *Fragmentation: New Production and Trade Patterns in the World Economy.* Oxford: Oxford University Press.

Basu, S. and Fernald, J. (1997). Returns to Scale in U.S. Production: Estimates and Implications. *Journal of Political Economy,* 105, 249–283.

Benarroch, M. (1997). Returns to Scale in Canadian Manufacturing: An Interprovincial Comparison. *Canadian Journal of Economics,* 30, 1083–1103.

Cheng, L. and Kierzkowski, H. (2002). *Globalization of Trade and Production in South-East Asia.* New York: Kluwer Academic Press.

Dixit, A. and Stiglitz, J. (1977). Monopolistic Competition and Optimum Product Diversity. *American Economic Review,* 67, 297–308.

Dumais, G., Ellison, G., and Glaeser, E. (1997). Geographic Concentration as a Dynamic Process. *NBER Working Paper 6270.*

Enke, S. (1951). Equilibrium among Spatially Separated Markets: Solution by Electric Analogue. *Econometrica,* 19, 40–47.

Feenstra, R. and Hanson, G. (1997). Foreign Direct Investment and Relative Wages: Evidence from Mexico's Maquiladoras. *Journal of International Economics,* 42, 371–394.

Fujita, M., Krugman, P., and Venables, A. (1999). *The Spatial Economy: Cities, Regions and International Trade.* Cambridge, MA: MIT Press.

Glaeser, E.L. (2000). The New Economics of Urban and Regional Growth. In: G. L. Clark *et. al.,* (Eds.), *The Oxford Handbook of Economic Geography.* Oxford: Oxford University Press.

---

[11] For an informed view, consider Henry Wan, Jr. (2001). He uses the concepts of closed and open networks in discussing relations between subcontractors and assemblers. He argues persuasively, with many examples from Japan, Hong Kong, Korea, and Taiwan, that no unique arrangement should be expected to emerge. Which particular organizational structure is appropriate and most efficient to carry out fragmentation depends on the nature of an industry, the existence of information externalities, the speed of response to global transformation by individual firms and the economy as a whole.

Jones, R.W. and Kierzkowski, H. (1990). The Role of Services in Production and International Trade: A Theoretical Framework. In: R. W. Jones and Anne Krueger (Eds.), *The Political Economy of International Trade* (Ch. 3). Oxford: Blackwell.

Jones, R.W. and Kierzkowski, H. (2001a). A Framework for Fragmentation. In: S. Arndt and H. Kierzkowski (Eds.), *Fragmentation: New Production and Trade Patterns in the World Economy*. Oxford: Oxford University Press.

Jones, R.W. and Kierzkowski, H. (2001b). Horizontal Aspects of Vertical Fragmentation. In: L. Cheng and H. Kierzkowski (Eds.), *Globalization of Trade and Production in South-East Asia*. New York: Kluwer Academic Press.

Krugman, P. (1991). Increasing Returns and Economic Geography. *Journal of Political Economy*, 99, 483–499.

Marshall, A. (1890). *Principles of Economics.* Book Four: The Agents of Production: Land, Labour, and Capital and Organization, Chapter 11, "Industrial Organization Continued. Production on a Large Scale" available on the Internet at: http://www.marxists.org/reference/subject/economics/marshall/ bk4ch11.htm.

Martin, R. and Sunley, P. (1996). Paul Krugman's Geographical Economics and its Implications for Regional Development Theory: A Critical Assessment. *Economic Geography*, 72, 259–292.

Neary, J.P. (2001). Of Hype and Hyperbolas: Introducing the New Economic Geography. *Journal of Economic Literature*, 39, 536–561.

Ng, F. and Yeats, A. (2001). Production Sharing in East Asia: Who Does What for Whom and Why? In: L. Cheng and H. Kierzkowski (Eds.), *Globalization of Trade and Production in South-East Asia*. New York: Kluwer Academic Press.

Ohlin, B., Hesselborn, P.O., and Wijkman, P.M. (Eds.) (1977). *The International Allocation of Economic Activity*. The Nobel Foundation.

Porter, M.E. (2000). Locations, Clusters, and Company Strategy. In: G. L. Clark *et. al.*, (Eds.), *The Oxford Handbook of Economic Geography*. Oxford: Oxford University Press.

Samuelson, P.A. (1952). Spatial Price Equilibrium and Linear Programming. *American Economic Review*, 42, 283–303.

Samuelson, P.A. (1954). The Transfer Problem and Transport Costs: The Terms of Trade when Impediments are Absent. *Economic Journal*, 64, 278–304.

Sheppard, E. (2001). How Economists Think: About Geography, for Example. *Journal of Economic Geography*, 1, 131–136.

Sunley, P. (2001). What's behind the Models? in Critical Forum. *Journal of Economic Geography*, 1, 136–139.

Urban, D. (2001). The Special Economy: One New Economic Geographer's View. *Journal of Economic Geography*, 1, 146–152.

Vernon, R. (1966). International Investment and International Trade in the Product Cycle. *Quarterly Journal of Economics*, 80, 190–207.

Wan, H., Jr. (2001). Function vs. Form in the Fragmented Industrial Structure: Three Examples from Asia Pacific Experience. In: L. Cheng and H. Kierzkowski (Eds.), *Globalization of Trade and Production in South-East Asia*. New York: Kluwer Academic Press.

Yeats, A. (2001). Just How Big is Global Production Sharing? In: S. Arndt and H. Kierzkowski (Eds.), *Fragmentation: New Production and Trade Patterns in the World Economy*. Oxford: Oxford University Press.

CHAPTER 17

International Fragmentation
and the New Economic Geography*

Ronald W. Jones and Henryk Kierzkowski

Abstract

Fragmentation of vertically integrated production processes implies that segments (production blocks) are located in different geographical areas, perhaps in
different countries, and that they may be undertaken by different firms. Service
links are required to coordinate such fragmentation, and it is in these links (such
as communication and transportation) that significant economies of scale are to
be found. This often leads to dis-agglomeration of economic activity, especially at
the international level, which runs counter to suggestions found in the "new economic geography" literature. This paper explores the implications of increasing
returns in service links for fragmentation and the dispersion of production.

17.1 Introduction

In a recent magisterial survey, Neary (2001) remarked that, "Economic
Geography has come of age." Several years later we are witnessing an
extended birthday bash — a newly published volume by Baldwin, Forslid,
Martin, Ottaviano, and Robert-Nicoud (2003), and a forthcoming volume 4
of the *Handbook of Regional and Urban Economics* (Henderson & Thisse,
2004). Most of this literature pays special tribute to the pioneering article
and book by Krugman, (1991a, 1991b), as well as Venables (1996), and
the detailed book, *The Spatial Economy*, by Fujita, Krugman, and Venables

*Originally published in *North American Journal of Economics and Finance*, 16, (2005),
pp. 1–10.

(1999). This book pays special attention to the so-called Core-Periphery model laid out in the earlier Krugman contributions, and to the central issue in this body of theory, i.e., the phenomenon of agglomeration of economic activity. Much of the effort in newer articles and chapters, including the Neary survey, is devoted to coming to grips with problems presented by the core-periphery account. As Baldwin *et al.*, attest, "This model... has the unfortunate feature of being astoundingly difficult to work with analytically" (2003, chap. 1, p. 2).

In this paper, we have no intention of adding to these efforts to make the new economic geography analyses more tractable, although we do empathize with the need to simplify the analytics of the issue. Instead, we discuss our alternative framework within which issues such as the agglomeration of economic activity can be understood. This work, starting with our original article in 1990, is supported by the emphasis placed in the theory of international trade on the increasing importance of trade in intermediate goods and goods in process. Such emphasis is reflected, of course, in the long-standing interest in foreign investment activity. Around four decades ago, the importance of international trade in intermediates was recognized by the many contributions to the theory of effective rates of protection. This theory contributed the valuable insight that the production of final commodities often relied on intermediates originating abroad, and that account of such trade should be taken in calculating the *effective* rate of protection to local productive activity provided by a country's tariff structure (e.g., Corden, 1966). In an era of intensive international tariff reductions, the theory of effective protection addressed a real-life issue: what is the essential meaning of reductions in tariff walls when industries are interdependent and interconnected in a global economy.

In the early 1980s, the concept of *middle products* was introduced (Jones & Purvis, 1983; Sanyal & Jones, 1982) to incorporate the notion that almost all final commodities make use of a pair of inputs — those available in national markets and those obtained in world markets. Here again, a real-life phenomenon suggested a research agenda: When inflation became a truly international event, could countries insulate their economies from global influences under a fixed exchange rate system? Traditional trade theory applied to open macro-economics seemed to be saying no, at least in the context of small countries that produced only tradable goods. And yet, inflation rates differed across countries, small and large, and even PPP did not hold particularly well.

The theory of trade in middle products suggested an explanation of the puzzle by postulating that productive activity within an economy could be separated into two *tiers — an input tier,* wherein labor and natural resources locally found can be combined to produce goods *for* the world market, and an *output tier* that combines goods *from* the world market with local inputs to produce final consumer goods. That is, almost all of international trade takes place in the middle of the production spectrum. While prices of middle products may equalize across the world rather quickly and completely (and be exogenous for small countries), the prices of goods actually consumed need not be the same.

No short review of economic phenomena and trends encouraging research and leading to new trade theories or models would be complete without the intra-industry trade described and documented by Grubel and Peter Lloyd in the 1970s. Considered initially by some economists as a statistical artifact, intra-industry trade triggered a revolution in international trade theory. For our purposes it is important to note that intra-industry trade not only refers to trade in final goods, such as different colors or makes of automobiles, but also to parts and intermediate goods (middle products) as well.

The focus of our modeling on *fragmentation* of production processes is on the possibility of using services to break up a vertically integrated production nexus into separate fragments, which may be located nearby, in the same firm, or at some distance, perhaps in a different country and under the control of different firms. That is, a lowering of the service-link costs of connecting parts of a production process may encourage the various parts to be located in geographically separate locales. Increases in the scale of production might also encourage such fragmentation, for reasons we discuss in the following section. Technically, fragmentation could be referred to as *outsourcing,* although that word is often used to signify removal to a different firm or, in current usage, a removal to a different country. Although in this paper we emphasize *international* fragmentation, the concept of fragmentation refers more broadly to the possibility that production blocks are separated by distance, which may be within a country. A vertically integrated production process at home might be moved to a foreign locale. This could be termed *outsourcing*, but it would not come under the rubric of *fragmentation*.

Even though international trade economists have turned their attention to fragmentation/outsourcing only recently, the phenomenon, and terms to describe it, are not new. David Landes in his magnificent book, *The Wealth and Poverty of Nations* (1998, Norton) traces the origin of outsourcing to 13th century Europe. It stemmed from attempts to reduce guild controls in the cities, and use abundant and cheap female and child labor available in the countryside. The term used to describe this process was *putting-out*:

> "Early on (thirteenth century), then, merchants began to hire cottage workers to perform some more tedious, less skilled tasks. In the most important branch, the textile manufacture, peasant women did the spinning on a putting-out basis: the merchant gave out (put out) the raw material — the raw wool and flax, and, later, cotton — and collected the finished yarn." (p. 43)

Interestingly enough, cities were up in arms complaining about "unfair competition"; in Italy and the Low Countries strict limits were imposed on the extent of the putting-out. Seven centuries later, the key political economy issues are not much different, but addressed on a global scale.

As opposed to the literature on the new economic geography, in our modeling efforts we have deliberatively by-passed the requirement that final produced goods must reach consumers. Instead, in keeping with the traditional paradigm of international trade theory, we have assumed that each country's labor force and consumers have their mobility limited by the national boundary and increasingly can easily be serviced by retail outlets and direct providers of services. This allows us to focus on the role of services in linking various fragments of the production process. In more modern terminology, we are stressing the importance of "B to B" activities rather than "B to C" ones. A recent article in *The Wall Street Journal* (Anguin, 2003, p. B1), in discussing the users of online services, remarks that in the year 2002 consumers in the U.S. spent $71 billion on goods and services online. This contrasts with U.S. businesses spending $482 billion in online transactions with other businesses. Furthermore, by ignoring the costs involved in reaching the final consumer, a central concern in the new economic geography literature, we avoid the analytical complexities introduced by focusing on consumer demand for variety. This love of variety is captured in the core-periphery models by the use of Dixit and Stiglitz (1977) utility functions, which leads at times to what Peter Neary refers to as "a near-impenetrable soup of CES algebra" (2001, p. 537). Emphasizing that consumers have a taste for variety served extremely well the analysis of intra-industry trade in "new trade theory," but perhaps does not as easily pass a cost/benefit test in the "new economic geography."

A crucial difference between the scenario found in the new economic geography literature and that in our paradigm of the fragmentation of production processes concerns not the existence of increasing returns, but their location. In the core-periphery models and variants found in the new economic geography, the love of variety embedded in consumer tastes is matched by a symmetric array of producers, each providing a different variety, with markets characterized by Chamberlinian monopolistic competition. In such equilibria, the firm is still at a decreasing-cost range of its average cost curve, and this is guaranteed by the assumption that for each firm costs are made up of a fixed-cost element and constant marginal costs. (Thus, the average cost curve never turns upwards.) That is, increasing returns are internal to the plant and firm. Our fragmentation scenario rests on a distinction between *production blocks* and *service links* (Jones & Kierzkowski, 1990). In the simplified version of the scenario, production blocks may exhibit constant returns to scale. A production process consists of a sequence of such production blocks, which need to be linked by the services of transportation, communication, and financial inputs. To these services must be added the general costs of co-ordination and the acquisition of relevant information. In the simplified version of our model, these service link activities are assumed to exhibit the kind of strong increasing returns associated with fixed costs that are invariant to scales of output. This makes most sense with communication and co-ordination activities, but even transportation costs are usually declining with quantities transported. In any case, it is in the service link sectors that we assume increasing returns are to be found rather than on the plant floor. And this difference leads to a significant reversal of the view, often expressed in the new economic geography literature, that increases in the level of economic activity are associated with increased spatial agglomeration of such activity.

The fragmentation paradigm is essentially a dynamic one. We do not attempt to explain why a particular country has the degree of agglomeration of productive activity it has inherited from the past. Instead, we ask what changes can be expected in the pattern of agglomeration by the steadily increasing trend in (i) levels of aggregate income and spending on particular goods, (ii) technological progress in the nature and costs of connecting service links as well as deregulation of service activities both nationally and between countries, and (iii) developments of new technologies for production blocks and the introduction of new products. We take as given that skill levels and productivity of factors of production and other inputs may differ widely from country to country as well as within regions of the same country. Differences in factor endowments and in country regulations and tax patterns often account for the variation in returns to factors found across countries.

Consider a particular final commodity. It could be produced in a vertically integrated process, with all activity taking place in one locale. However, the total costs of producing output might be lowered by outsourcing some *fragment* of the integrated activity, say one that makes relatively intensive use of unskilled labor, to another locale in which labor productivity is higher relative to its wage rate. This calls to mind the possibility of increasing returns suggested by Adam Smith, who pointed to the advantages of a division of labor (that was limited by the extent of the market). Such a geographical separation of production fragments introduces the necessity of establishing service links in the form of transportation, communication and other coordinating activities. It is the costs of these service links that we assume do not rise in proportion to levels of output, and in the simple version of our model we assume these costs are fixed. For example, the communication costs of establishing a shipment of one thousand units may be the same as those for ten thousand units. Transport costs, of course, are another matter. These play center stage in models of the new economic geography, and the assumption typically adopted there is that of the "iceberg" variety (suggested by Samuelson, 1952), wherein the "melting" of the product being shipped reflected a constant fraction of the amount being transported. (Much earlier, von Thunen suggested that horse-drawn hay was in part consumed by the means of transport.) However, it is widely recognized that costs per unit of the item being transported usually decrease with volume. If the extra costs of service link activities are more than balanced by the lower marginal costs obtained by a closer match of factor intensities with net factor productivities for each fragment, such

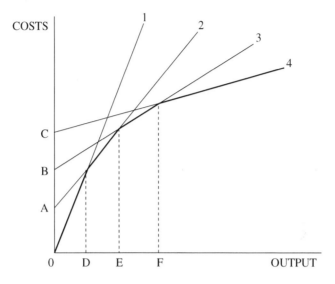

Figure 17.1.   Fragmentation and the Cost of Production

outsourcing will take place in order to minimize costs of production. For a given degree of fragmentation the nature of service link activities leads to a lowering of total average costs of production with output. However, further increases in output may suggest a finer degree of fragmentation of the production process, with the extra costs of connecting service links now more than matched by the lower assembled marginal costs of the production blocks. In the aggregate, average costs of production decrease with output for a given pattern of fragmentation, and *marginal* costs of total production are lowered discontinuously at the point at which the degree of fragmentation is increased (Jones & Kierzkowski, 1990).

Figure 17.1 is the kind of diagram we have frequently used to illustrate the growth of fragmentation when incomes and demand for output of a product increase. Ray 1 from the origin reveals what the costs of production would be if undertaken in a single production block exhibiting constant returns to scale, while line segment 2 with vertical intercept OA suggests an alternative process in which two different domestic locations are selected to take advantage of geographic differences in various factor costs and productivities. The use of these two locations lowers aggregate marginal costs (shown by the slope of A2), but their co-ordination requires service links that are shown by fixed costs, OA. Such fragmentation only becomes

cost-effective if output levels exceed OD. Line segments 3 and 4 illustrate
the increasing possibilities of decreasing marginal costs if a greater degree
of fragmentation is introduced, with foreign sources enlisted in order to
take advantage of differences in international factor prices that lower costs
because of differences in factor requirements among the separate fragments. Of course, such international fragmentation raises the costs of connective service links. The integrated minimum cost schedule is shown by
the heavy locus, with increases in the degree of fragmentation occurring at
output levels D–F. This schedule exhibits increasing returns to scale.

The role of international trade is crucial in this description. Although
fragmentation can, and often does, take place within a region or country, it
is not limited by national boundaries. The costs of connective service links
may be larger in supporting a production network that encompasses more
than one country, but the pay-off in lowering aggregate production costs
by taking advantage of a wider spread of effective factor costs between, as
opposed to within, a country encourages this broader spread. In this regard,
the modeling strategy typically found in the new economic geography literature, wherein varieties of goods produced may have different appeals
to consumers but are "horizontal" in their similar use of factors in production, makes little use of the commonly found wide disparity in factor
returns among nations. By contrast, such a wide disparity plays a central
role in international fragmentation. Furthermore, it is the fragmentation
possibility inherent in each variety that would be of interest in our model.

In recent decades, we have witnessed great productivity improvements
in the costs of providing connective service links. Perhaps foremost is the
reduction in costs of communication. Telephone costs have, of course, been
reduced dramatically, with reductions in relative costs in international communication even greater than that within countries. The introduction of
Fax technology, and then the widespread adoption of e-mail transmission
and the ability to send moving images (in color) from one part of the globe
to another instantaneously, have done much to facilitate broader international fragmentation and production networks. Figure 17.1 shows how
reductions in the costs of service links promote greater degrees of fragmentation for any given output level. At an international level, this reflects
the close positive association between lower service link costs and disagglomeration or dispersion of productive activity. In a recent manuscript
(Jones & Kierzkowski, 2005), we illustrated in a pair of simple diagrams

how greater levels of output encouraged such dispersion in the fragmentation scenario (as illustrated in Fig. 17.1), although if increasing returns are centralized on the factory floor, and service link costs consist only of "iceberg" type of transportation costs, greater output levels might well support greater levels of agglomeration. These paradigms lead to significantly different results.

The reduction in service link costs has also been aided by moves to de-regulate such activities, both within countries and, as in the efforts of the Uruguay Round of GATT talks, internationally. One of the misplaced concerns of less developed countries during these negotiations is, in our view, that these regions do not have a comparative advantage in providing services and thus would lose out by a freeing-up of services. Such a stance overlooks the fact that a lowering of costs for service link activities allows the transfer of comparative advantage in certain fragments to such developing countries. For example, a recent study (Ng & Yeats, 2003) points out that in East Asia from 1990 to 2001 the exports of parts and components to countries outside the region increased from nearly $56 billion to almost $118 billion, with an even greater rise for exports within the East Asia region from almost $34 billion to $110 billion, an almost three-fold increase. Furthermore, technical progress has also encouraged fragmentation *within* the service sector. The use made by businesses in Silicon Valley of software services provided many time zones away by personnel in Bangalore has been widely documented. Even local consumers in the United States may use the telephone to make travel arrangements for locales within the country and end up talking with service personnel in Jamaica or India.

Technical progress also takes place within production blocks. Frequently this is a concomitant of changes in the quality of the commodities being produced or, indeed, of introducing new commodities in which the optimal choice of technique has yet to be developed. This is the context in which Vernon's (1966) theory of the *product cycle* was set. He considered the geographical pattern in which a new commodity is at first produced in a developed country such as the United States and, after a sequence of trials with different technologies, simple methods of production are discovered that cause a shift in the pattern of comparative advantage: Less developed countries take over production that has become quite labor-intensive. Key to the early part of the cycle is the existence of a wide variety of human and physical capital and skills in the developed country at a time when there is uncertainty about the techniques that will evolve. This bears some resemblance to the assumption about production adopted by Ethier (1982) in his reinterpretation of the Dixit–Stiglitz utility function as a production function, wherein productivity is an increasing function of the variety of skilled inputs available. Such a reinterpretation for production has been used in the new economic geography literature. In Vernon's hands, it explains a sequence in which there is a continual outsourcing of production towards less developed areas as techniques simplify, accompanied by ever-emerging new products and technologies being developed in advanced areas. Such a view holds as well for fragments of a technology that become quite labor-intensive.

One of the most basic features of a country being able to engage in international trade is that it cuts the dependence of local consumption upon a corresponding range of local production. Trade allows a great degree of concentration of productive activity, so that any changes that reduce the cost of trading, whether natural or man-made, can be expected to lead to yet greater degrees of concentration of productive activity, often in urban areas with good port or rail facilities. Therefore, it is natural to associate an agglomeration of economic activity *nationally* with increases in levels of international trade. However, at an *international* level increased trade, especially when accompanied by greater levels of international fragmentation of production, is reflected in a global dis-agglomeration or dispersal of productive activity. Less developed countries that have little basis in comparative advantage in producing manufactured goods, when production processes must be vertically linked in one place and one time, can increasingly join in producing fragments of these processes, when increasing returns associated with service link activities allow a lowering of costs by outsourcing labor-intensive fragments. In other words, trade and fragmentation may lead both to an increased dispersion of production activity world-wide, while simultaneously encouraging national agglomeration.

We have argued that international fragmentation is best seen in a dynamic context. Apropos of the agglomeration issue, it is possible to argue that increases in the outsourcing of economic activity, whether nationally or globally, may lead to new forms of agglomeration. Production processes, when compared across industries, often have separate fragments that are more similar from one industry to another than is the integrated whole. That is, fragmentation sometimes leads to a horizontal spread in which the similarity between fragments across industries promotes technological progress to make fragments even more similar and thus to encourage new forms of agglomeration (Jones & Kierzkowski, 2001). Consider the outsourcing of accounting activities to new firms that may service many sectors. Or, perhaps the most cited case, the use of computer chips not only in computers but also in toasters, laser devices, and in countless productive activities in many industrial sectors.

Most new economic geography models have the perceived advantage (compared with the literature on fragmentation) of explicit modeling of imperfect competition. Typically, firms are in markets characterized by monopolistic competition. The emphasis in consumption on the existence of variety in the utility function is matched by the variety of goods produced, each one by a different firm in a monopolistically competitive equilibrium. As already noted, the imposition of identical technology for each variety serves to make international differences in productivities and factor prices of less importance in the determination of the geographical pattern of production. By contrast, such a wide global variation in the components of production costs is central to the discussion of international fragmentation. Global dispersion is precisely what is encouraged by the increasing returns from service sector activities. Although it foregoes the assumption of horizontal variety among commodities, the fragmentation literature does exhibit a different kind of variety — among a number of possible forms of market competition. For example, fragmented production blocks could be produced by purely competitive firms, on the one hand, or by large multinational firms, on the other. These firms may keep control over many of the production blocks for a commodity, and even for some of the service links. However, greater outsourcing to independent firms may be encouraged by the greater knowledge they possess of foreign market conditions, a higher density of foreign suppliers which makes "hold-up" less a danger, and less uncertainty about getting on-time delivery of fragments necessary for final assembly. Some service link activities, such as telephone or transportation, may be undertaken by oligopolistic producers, but in world markets in which technology is constantly changing, competition can easily render downward pressure on prices. Whatever the nature of the organization of firms, in the global market place firms are constantly aware of potential or actual suppliers of similar services or products in a competitive fashion. Furthermore, the extreme assumptions embodied in

Fig. 17.1, that constant returns prevail within production blocks, but service links costs are strictly invariant with respect to increases in outputs, can be moderated to allow some increasing returns on the factory floor and some degree of positive marginal costs in providing connective service links.

New economic geography models are becoming popular and indeed can provide much insight about issues concerning the agglomeration and spatial location of economic activity. However, like the proverbial elephant that is being viewed from different perspectives by different observers, the fragmentation paradigm also has much to offer. In a world in which advanced countries are witnessing a reduction in manufacturing activity and a great increase in services, and in which international trade in parts and components is increasing at a significantly faster rate than trade generally, it is important to understand the role of service links as a source of increasing returns in production processes by allowing fragments of these processes to be spread over several nations.

References

Angwin. J. (2003, November 20). Renaissance in Cyberspace. *The Wall Street Journal*, p. BI.

Baldwin, R., Forslid, R., Martin, P., Ottaviano, G., and Robert-Nicoud, F. (Eds.). (2003). *Economic Geography and Public Policy*. Princeton, NJ: Princeton University Press.

Corden, W.M. (1966). The Structure of a Tariff System and the Effective Protective Rate. *Journal of Political Economy*, 74, 221–237.

Dixit, A. and Stiglitz, J. (1977). Monopolistic Competition and Optimum Product Diversity. *American Economic Review*, 67, 297–308.

Ethier, W. (1982). National and International Returns to Scale in the Modem Theory of International Trade. *American Economic Review*, 72, 389–405.

Fujita, M., Krugman, P., and Venables, A. (1999). *The Spatial Economy: Cities Regions and International Trade*. Cambridge, MA: MIT Press.

Grubel, H. and Lloyd, P. (1975). *Intra-Industry Trade: The Theory and Measurement of International Trade in Differentiated Products*. London: Macmillan.

Henderson, V. and Thisse, J.-F. (2004). *Handbook of Regional and Urban Economics* (Vol. 4). Amsterdam, North-Holland.

Jones, R. and Kierzkowski, H. (1990). The Role of Services in Production and International Trade: A Theoretical Framework. In R. Jones & A. Krueger (Eds.), *The Political Economy of International Trade*. Oxford: Blackwell Publishing.

Jones, R. and Kierzkowski, H. (2001). Horizontal Aspects of Vertical Fragmentation. In L. Cheng & H. Kierzkowski (Eds.), *Global Production and Trade in East Asia*. Dordrecht: Kluwer.

Jones, R. and Kierzkowski, H. (2005). International Trade and Agglomeration: An Alternative Framework. In T. Palokanges *et al.* (Eds.), *Growth, Trade and Economic Institutions, Journal of Economics* (Suppl. 10), forthcoming.

Jones, R. and Purvis, D. (1983). International Differences in Response to Common External Shocks: The Role of Purchasing Power Parity. In E. M. Claassen & P. Salin (Eds.), *Recent Issues in the Theory of Flexible Exchange Rates* (pp. 33–55). Amsterdam: North-Holland.

Krugman, P. (1991a). Increasing Returns and Economic Geography. *Journal of Political Economy*, 99(3), 483–499.

Krugman, P. (1991b). *Geography and Trade.* Cambridge, MA: MIT Press.

Landes, D. (1998). *The Wealth and Poverty of Nations.* New York: Norton.

Neary, P. (2001, June). Of Hype and Hyperbolas: Introducing the New Economic Geography. *Journal of Economic Literature*, 39(2), 536–561.

Ng, F. and Yeats, A. (2003). *Major Trade Trends in East Asia* (World Bank Policy Research Working Paper 3084). Washington, DC.

Sanyal, K. and Jones, R. (1982). The Theory of Trade in Middle Products. *American Economic Review*, 72, 16–31.

Venables, A. (1996). Equilibrium Locations of Vertically Linked Industries. *International Economic Review*, 37, 341–359.

Vernon, R. (1966). International Investment and International Trade in the Product Cycle. *Quarterly Journal of Economics*, 80, 190–207.

Part IV

Final Thoughts on Competitive Trade Models

Part IV consists of Chapters 18 and 19. Each of them appeared in publications in 2015. Chapter 18 focuses on a number of features of *small-scale* general equilibrium models that are used in international trade theory. Not surprisingly, the first such model is the Ricardian model, discussed in Part 1 of this book. As well there are subjects not treated earlier in the book, such as the stability issues in models, the transfer problem and the Reciprocity Theorem. As the title of the chapter suggests, models that specifically are limited to dealing with small numbers of commodities, factors, and countries often reveal properties that can be found in models that are not so limited but are, therefore, more difficult to analyze.

Chapter 19, the longest chapter in the book, is itself a kind of pulling together of the discussions in earlier chapters. An emphasis concerns model building. Frequently economists are heard to ask, "Which model is better — which one wins?" The question itself is undoubtedly more reasonable if the economist is considering the features describing competitive *static* equilibria in a general equilibrium model. After establishing the appropriate equilibrium conditions, usually a question is asked: "If one of the properties of an economy that we assume are *givens* is changed, how is the set of *equilibrium unknowns* altered as the economy reaches a new equilibrium?"

Perhaps the best, and shortest, way of suggesting what topics are discussed in Chapter 19 is to list the title of each section in this last, but hopefully easy and useful chapter:

1. Introduction
2. The (3×2) Specific-Factors Model
3. The (2×2) Version of the Heckscher–Ohlin Model
4. Simple Diagrams for the Basic Models
5. The Multi-commodity International Trade Scenario
6. Specific-Factors: An Extended Version Blending with Heckscher–Ohlin
7. The Produced Mobile Factor Structure
8. More on the Multi-commodity Model: The Ruffin–Ricardo Model
9. How Concentrated Does Trade Make Production? A Hybrid Model
10. Middle Products
11. Non-traded Goods
12. Fragmentation and Outsourcing
13. Concluding Remarks

CHAPTER 18

On the Value of Small-scale GE Models*

Ronald W. Jones

Abstract

The field of international economics has made frequent use of general equilibrium models in order to investigate the nature of those possible comparative static equilibrium solutions that seem somewhat paradoxical. Frequently the analysis is done for settings in which the number of commodities, countries, and/or factors of production is assumed to be rather small. For example, the Classic Ricardian model making use of the concept of comparative advantage based on comparisons of efficient ratios of country productivities has solutions that hold for any number of countries or commodities. A number of different issues, such as stability conditions and the transfer problem, are discussed in which surprising equilibrium outcomes possible in a general situation can be understood more easily in a small-scale setting.

18.1   Introduction

Most trade theorists doing general equilibrium (at least those of my vintage) do not question the value of small-scale models in their research. Here I select a small sample of the work of trade theorists to show that small-scale models can often reveal in an *economic manner* properties of competitive equilibria that go beyond what partial equilibrium models provide. Indeed, it is not that difficult to reveal the ways that changes in one market serve to bring about alterations as well in prices and quantities of other markets, often with effects that significantly entail modifications or reversals of what could be expected when relying on *partial equilibrium* reasoning.

---

*Originally published in *International Journal of Economic Theory*, 11, (2005), pp. 155–168.

Also, I wish to illustrate how some work that has gone beyond the realm of "small-scale GE models" has, in its focus on mathematical technique, strayed away from the basic economic setting of the original small-scale results.

18.2   The Ricardian Model

It is perhaps appropriate to begin with the older Ricardian model that revealed the importance of *comparative* advantage in suggesting how not only there are gains to be had by international trade, but also that these gains do not exclude participation of countries that have rather low levels of technology compared with competing countries. As long as *comparative* advantage is the key to mutual gains, no country is excluded. This observation must clearly stand among the most profound results in our profession. Ricardo hypothesized a simple setting where two countries, say Portugal and England, could each produce two commodities, say wine and cloth, using only labor, with labor unable to move from one country to another if wage rates differ from country to country. He showed how Portugal could gain from trade by exporting wine and letting England provide its cloth even though Portugal could produce cloth more efficiently (i.e., with fewer man-hours per unit) than could England. England could compete with cloth exports despite its lack of productive superiority in an *absolute* sense, since it is only *comparative* advantage that counts if productive factors are trapped within country borders. English labor would, of course, receive lower wage rate than would Portuguese labor, but if labor is assumed not to be mobile between countries, two-way international trade could benefit both countries.

The formal logic requires a comparison of such relative costs. In England, let the amount of labor required per unit of wine be designated by a_W^E and that of cloth to be a_C^E. The *ratio* of these two figures could be compared with the comparable ratio for Portugal, a_W^P / a_C^P, which, in this example, is assumed to be smaller than the English ratio. Consequent mutually profitable trade flows could then be shown for this (2×2) simple model. It is extremely easy to extend this result to the case in which countries other than Portugal and England are also capable of producing wine and cloth, and whose relative costs can be ranked along with those of Portugal and England. Alternatively, in a two-country setting with many commodities it is easy to rank Portugal and England producing these other commodities as well. In either case demand patterns and country size conspire to separate a country's exports from its imports.

These remarks illustrate how concepts created for small-dimensional models can easily be obtained for *some* dimensional changes. But what can be said about situations in which the number of potential trading countries exceeds two and, as well, the number of commodities also exceeds two? In the early 1940s, Prof. Frank Graham, in his graduate trade class at Princeton, used to provide exercises for his graduate students for them to pick assignments of countries to commodities that satisfied comparative advantage for given sets of numbers of labor efficiencies for workers in various countries. When I started teaching at Rochester, Lionel McKenzie, a former Graham student, urged me to look at this problem to see if any easy process could be established to satisfy comparative advantages in this multi-commodity and multi-country case. Such a procedure eventually was established, and the logic of the process was, in hindsight, exceedingly simple. For the two-country or two-commodity case the procedure involved a comparison of a set of labor-cost *ratios*. Suppose, instead of comparing *ratios*, one cross-multiplied and compared *products*. That turned out to be the way to generalize comparative advantage.

An important concept is that of a *class* of *complete specializations* — one defined as requiring for each commodity how many countries are to be assigned to be *completely specialized* in producing that commodity. If there are two countries and two commodities, there will be three such classes: two of them have both countries producing the same commodity (and there obviously is only one possible assignment in each of these classes). For the class that has one country completely specialized to the first commodity and the other country completely specialized to the other commodity, there are two possible entries (with the "winner" being the one that satisfies comparative advantage). In the Ricardian 2 × 2 scenario, it would be Portugal producing wine and England producing cloth.

The competitive Ricardian model that assumes three commodities and three countries is discussed briefly in the Appendix, and has dimensionality that allows a view of the model with many countries and many commodities (not necessarily the same number). How many classes are there that have each country completely specialized in producing a single commodity? The answer is 10. The easiest class to consider is when all three countries produce the same commodity, and there are three of these classes, with only a single way of doing so for each commodity. How about classes in which only two commodities are produced? As in the Appendix, suppose the three commodities are corn, linen and cloth. There are six classes that have only two commodities produced: (i) two classes have corn produced in one country and linen produced in the other two countries, or corn produced in one country and cloth produced in the other two; (ii) another two classes have linen produced in only one country and corn produced in the other two, or linen produced in only one country and cloth in the other two; (iii) a further pair of classes has cloth produced in only one country and corn produced in the other two, or cloth produced in only one country and linen produced in the other two. Finally, there is the single class in which all three commodities are produced, and each country is specialized to a different commodity. There are six assignments possible in this class. Thus in three of the classes (where only a single commodity is produced) there is only one assignment (of countries to commodities), in a further six of the classes (in which two out of three of the commodities are produced) there are three possible assignments in each class. In the final class of assignments of complete specialization (the one in which a different country is assigned to each commodity), there are six possible candidates for such an assignment.

Market forces would determine, for each class, which of the possible assignments for that class are efficient, just as in the Ricardian 2 × 2 case the efficient assignment where both wine and cloth are produced has Portugal producing wine and England cloth. (There is no set of non-negative world commodity prices that would support a competitive equilibrium in which Portugal produces cloth and England produces wine.) In the 2 × 2 case, the world transformation schedule will be a convex combination of the linear transformation schedules for each country. A given set of commodity prices determines whether each country is completely specialized or whether one of the countries is incompletely specialized. Similarly, in the 3 × 3 case, there is a world transformation schedule in three dimensions made up of one-dimensional points (with all countries completely specialized), or straight lines (along which one of the three countries produces a pair of commodities), or planes (along which two of the three countries are each producing a pair (not the same pair) of commodities). The entire mapping along the world transformation three-dimensional surface is determined (once the size of each country's labor force and its labor requirements per unit output are given) by the set of optimal assignments in each of the classes. The optimal assignment in each class is the one satisfying the comparative advantage conditions in the 2 × 2 case or, more generally put, the assignment in each class that *minimizes* the product of the labor-input coefficients found in each assignment in that class.

In a competitive equilibrium, for every commodity selected for a country to produce, commodity price equals cost of production *and*, for each such country, there is *no* other commodity that is not produced even though price would exceed unit cost if it were. As just mentioned, the *efficient assignment* of countries to commodities for each class is the assignment that *minimizes* the *product* of labor-input coefficients. In the 2 × 2 case this could also be shown by the *ratios* of the two countries to satisfy comparative advantage. The generalization, once conceived, seems almost obvious, and is perfectly general, regardless of the number of countries and the number of commodities (Jones, 1961). Once all the classes *of complete assignments* are figured out, a global world transformation surface makes use of the fact that *any* designation of world outputs will be a linear combination of outputs found in the ones that have complete specializations. This shows how even the smallest-scale model (e.g., the Ricardian setting with Portugal and England producing a pair of commodities) leads recognizably to a generalization for any scale. Furthermore, the concept of comparative advantage in the simple 2 × 2 case, in which the *ratios* (instead of the product) of labor costs are compared, can be used as well in the many-commodity and many-country case. The Appendix to this chapter makes use of the numbers selected in Jones (1961) to illustrate that comparative advantage can in general compare the *ratio* of labor costs for a pair of commodities in one country with those in the rest of the world. Thus, the kinds of comparison so useful to Ricardo in the case of only a pair of countries and a pair of commodities can also be used in the general case of many countries and commodities. *Comparative advantage* is a key concept for a world in which labor is internationally immobile.

18.3   Leaders and Followers

If the doctrine of comparative advantage is such a powerful concept, can it be used in scenarios in which international trade is not the focus?

One example was provided in Ohyama and Jones (1995), and this might illustrate how very low-dimensional international trade models (as in the Portugal and England Ricardian case) have lessons that help to elucidate possibilities in other scenarios. The setting is one in which there are two firms in an industry, in which technology is improved in a learning-by-doing fashion and one of the firms, the *leader*, has been in the industry longer than the other firm, the *follower*. They both are using the same general kind of technology, call it the θ-technology, and the leader is the firm that has been in the business longer. This industry is just one of many, and new technologies (not of the θ-type), are being developed by a wide variety of other industries. The question that then arises concerns how these two firms react to the possibility of exploring and learning a different technology, say the β-type, which might or might not be superior after a period of somewhat costly learning. Here are the possibilities: Both firms might reject the β-type technology, or they both may be willing to make the switch, or a third possibility is that one of the firms does make the switch while the other firm stays with the θ-technology. We argue that in the third case there is a strong presumption that the follower makes the switch while the leader does not. Why? Because the leader has a *comparative advantage* over the follower in the θ-technology. The leader might rationally stick with the old even if it knows that in a couple of periods the present follower will have an advantage in the β-technology that gives it superior results. If elements of the standard "principal-agent" problem are present, this may strengthen the case. The "agent" in the research group in the leading firm may wish to preserve what it perceives as *its* higher rents from the θ-technology. This suggests that although comparative advantage helps to establish the better firm, in an intertemporal setting it may stand in the way of advances that could be made with different technologies. That is, today's winning technology may not remain so. The leader's decisions may be made by agents in the research lab who expect to retire before the new technology could be sufficiently adapted so as to be superior in the current season to the older technology.

18.4   Technology Transfer Surprise

There is another rather general lesson that the Ricardian model provides in thinking either about small-scale or large-scale models. It has to do with the *selection* of model that seems best suited to the question being asked. Consider a change that takes place to an international competitive equilibrium that suggests a particular question: Does a *country* win or lose as a consequence of the change? Note that this does not enquire about particular groups in the country. For example, it does not ask about the fate of landlords versus capitalists, or versus laborers. It only asks about the effect on *aggregate* real income in a country. The Ricardian model is ideal in the sense that each country only has a single type of input (homogeneous labor), so that the aggregate real income increases only if the real wage does. Consider the following example. Some large country, say the United States in a Ricardian scenario, can produce a number of commodities. Suppose its labor efficiency *in every commodity is* greater than that of another large economy, say China, and assume these two countries are the only ones in a global economy. Let the ranking by comparative advantage be such that the first commodity is the American best, and the nth is, comparatively speaking, its worst, although America is still more efficient than China for that commodity. Furthermore, suppose that American absolute advantage in all commodities is a reflection of better technology (rather than climate, or innate factor skills), and that China succeeds in stealing or otherwise obtaining the technology (or blueprints) the USA possesses for producing the *first* commodity, its best export good. No compensation is paid to America for this transfer. Query: If these are the only two countries trading on world markets, could America actually *gain* by this transfer? This is the type of question that is found fairly often in a GE setting. The answer is *yes*, it is possible (but not necessary) that America gains, even though, if China is large enough (after the stealth), American production of the first commodity is completely wiped out.[1] China, of course, would gain. A follow-up query: could America gain if China were to obtain American technology for all n commodities? No, because in such a case there would be no gains from trade for America to be had by removing barriers to trade China because relative prices would be the same in the two countries.

No fancy algebraic manipulation is required to understand how a result that seems to be paradoxical may be a result that could emerge. Simplify on the demand side by assuming taste patterns are the same between countries as well as leading to consumption shares that are the same for all

---

[1] Indeed, if American production of the first commodity is *not* wiped out, America must lose. Details of this model are provided in Jones and Ruffin (2008).

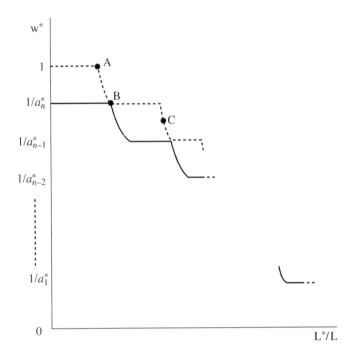

Figure 18.1.   Stealing Technology

commodities (e.g., common Cobb–Douglas tastes with the share of income spent on each good consumed the same for all commodities). A diagram (Figure 18.1) is useful, one that shows the Chinese wage rate (w^*) on the vertical axis when the *units* of each commodity have been (conveniently) chosen as the amount capable of being produced in an hour by an American worker. (This implies that whatever the outcome of trade, the American hourly wage rate is unity, and the price of any commodity produced in equilibrium in America is also unity. The vertical axis is therefore equivalently measuring the *ratio*, w^*/w.) Along the horizontal axis show the relative size of the Chinese labor force, L^*, to that in the USA, L. Let the vertical axis be "notched" at various levels, say $1/a_n^*$, $1/a_{n-1}^*$,..., down to the lowest possible foreign wage rate, $1/a_1^*$. *Before* the stealth takes place, consider what the Chinese curve (the solid locus) looks like. If China were to be very small relative to the USA, it would only need to produce *some* of its best commodity (n) in order to obtain sufficient funds to buy from America its desired consumption of every other commodity. Furthermore, as long as China's relative size is tiny enough, its wage rate (relative to the American value of unity) remains at a constant value of $1/a_n^*$ (less than unity). Once it is large enough, China can satisfy the entire world demand for the nth commodity. Suppose it gets a bit larger. In that case, China would produce a bit more of commodity n, which would serve to lower its price (and China's wage rate) until w^* becomes low enough that it can start competing in its next best commodity, $n - 1$. Once that level is reached, small further increases in L^* (with American L kept constant throughout) can be absorbed without a further drop in the Chinese wage rate until world demand for commodity $n - 1$ is satisfied at that price. Once again, should L^* increase a bit further, w^* would be driven down some more until China can compete in producing commodity $n - 2$. Thus this "staircase" figure for China's wage rate continues. If China's size were to grow sufficiently compared with America, it would have to produce *all* commodities, with America supplying only some of the world demand for the first commodity (in which America has its greatest comparative advantage).

The question that now emerges is how this locus for the relation of the Chinese wage rate to its relative country size differs (i.e., shifts) if it can obtain the technology that America possesses for producing the first commodity? China's new locus is now shown by the dashed curve. Clearly commodity 1 now becomes *China's* best commodity, and in the diagram the wage rate China would have if it were small enough that in the world market it cannot satisfy total (American plus Chinese) demand for the first commodity becomes *unity*, equaling the American wage rate. Indeed, the entire Chinese locus shifts upwards. However, and this is Crucial, the locus shifts upwards *and* to the left. Why? Because after the transfer, its productivity improvement in producing the first commodity allows it to satisfy world demand for this new "best" commodity at a *lower* country size (than was necessary when the nth commodity was its best). Call this point A. After that, more growth in the size of L^* causes w^* to fall (because p_1 falls) until it can start producing its next best commodity, the previous top one, commodity n. Given the assumptions made about demand, this can be shown to take place at corner point B.[2] If the relative size of L^*

---

[2]As explained in Jones and Ruffin (2008), the before-and-after meeting at point B reflects the Cobb–Douglas assumption. Without this, meeting-point B could be a bit to the left or right, but the argument concerning gains or losses is roughly the same.

happens to lead to point B, note that after the technology transfer the price of the first commodity faced by American consumers has dropped from unity to $1/a_n^*$, leading to *gains* for American workers. What is the situation at a point such as C? China is the only producer of the first commodity as well as that of commodity n. The price faced by importers in America of the first commodity has fallen (a gain for consumers), but with a higher Chinese wage rate than before stealth the price of commodity n has gone up for American consumers, and this, by itself, is a loss. The general result is that as China gets larger relative to America there are two changes that technology stealth would have on American consumers: the reduction in the cost of consuming the first commodity is a gain, but the increase in price for all commodities imported from China (from any increase in the Chinese wage rate) hurts American real income. The greater is China's relative size, the greater is the number of commodities imported by America. However, the greater also will be the drop in the price of the commodity whose technology has been transferred from America to China, which is a boon to American consumers. The outcome: American real incomes *may* rise, or may not, which is quite a different result from concluding American real incomes *must fall*.

18.5   Tariffs and Income Distribution

Let me turn now to a completely different scenario: A pair of cases in which a country engaged in trade produces at least two commodities and imposes a tariff on a commodity that it imports. First consider the situation similar to that used by Stolper and Samuelson (1941), an important paper I shall discuss in more detail a bit later. Suppose the country imports its labor-intensive commodity in Heckscher–Ohlin (2×2) setting in which two mobile factors, labor and capital, are inputs in production of each commodity. Stolper and Samuelson argued that a tariff on the labor-intensive imports will cause the domestic price of such imports to increase, leading to an increase in the wage rate that exceeds, in relative amount, the domestic price rise. The consequence is striking: the *real wage* of workers increases *regardless* of their taste patterns. However, Lloyd Metzler, in a 1949 article, showed how this was not necessarily the case. Why not? Because the tariff might have the (unintended) consequence of lowering the *foreign* price of imports by an amount even larger than the tariff. That is, the tariff may fail to benefit the factor of production used more intensively in local production of the imported commodity. This result was surprising, and may indeed hold regardless of how many commodities the country produces. It had the consequence of altering the scenario considered by trade theorists in subsequent work into one in which they assume *something* happens (it need not be a tariff) such that the *domestic* price of a commodity produced does increase.

The other case is based on a model that is a bit more complex. This is due to a surprising result found by Gruen and Corden (1970). The scenario is one in which there is a country like Australia producing two agricultural goods, say wheat and wool, where exports of the latter good are sufficiently large that changes in local production influence the world price. The inputs are labor and land, whereas the sole commodity produced in the manufacturing sector, textiles, uses labor and capital. Suppose the country levies a tariff on imports of textiles, and the country is too small to influence the world price, so that the domestic price of textiles increases by the amount of the tariff, and, assuming imports are labor-intensive, the wage rate increases. As a consequence, labor is drawn from the agricultural sector. This is where the international trade theory *dual* to the Stolper–Samuelson result comes in — that is, the effect on outputs of a change in the factor "endowments" used in the two-commodity agricultural sector. Assuming that wheat is the labor-intensive sector in agriculture, by the celebrated Rybczynski theorem (1955), the loss of labor will reduce the output of wheat, which not only sends more labor to manufacturing (and to wool) but also releases some land to the other activity in agriculture, the production of wool. Since Australia is a large wool producer, its larger output will serve to worsen the terms of trade for Australia. The consequence: *raising* the tariff has caused the terms of trade to *deteriorate*, a result that seemed paradoxical since it was proved (in more simple settings) that a tariff, if it could affect the terms of trade, would cause the terms of trade to *improve*. This is a simple example in which the 3 × 3 setting of Gruen and Corden allows an often held view as to the effects of a tariff in a 2 × 2 setting to be overturned. Sometimes an increase in dimensionality can matter, even if the setting can still be described *as* a "small-scale" model.

18.6   Stability of Equilibrium

Two of the four principle objectives of GE theory were to provide conditions that would ensure that there would exist a market equilibrium and that the equilibrium would be *stable*. In the older (small-scale) literature, a famous condition for stability was identified with the names of Alfred Marshall and Abba Lerner — the so-called Marshall–Lerner condition: in a two-country case the *sum* of the two countries' elasticities of demand for imports must exceed *unity*. I recall the instance of my oral exam at MIT, (not for the dissertation — in those days we also had oral field exams) in which two of my examiners were Paul Samuelson and Robert Bishop. Samuelson, of course, requires no introduction, and Bishop was a professor in the department who knew (and taught) economic theory, but as I recall had no background in international trade theory. During the course of the examination Samuelson raised the issue of stability of a trading equilibrium and we discussed the Marshal–Lerner condition. Upon leaving the exam Bishop turned to Samuelson and asked: "Paul, what is that number *one* doing in the stability criterion?" I thought this was a marvelous query that illustrated well the kind of difference training in international trade could provide, even for basic questions. GE theorists not versed in trade have in mind aggregate excess demand curves that must be negatively sloped to assure stability. So how does the number one enter? Answer: Trade theorists often focus on the response in each country of the country's demand for *imports* to changes in the terms of trade. But the pair of imports are for two *different* commodities. In expressions for income effects, the marginal propensity to consume one commodity is just "one" minus the marginal propensity to consume the other. Once attention is paid just to a single good in the market where one good gets traded for another, the number one disappears.

   I have noticed over the years that there is an additional difference in the way that trade theorists approach the stability issue and that adopted by same very famous theorists of the non-trade group. If all participants in a market are aggregated together the concepts of "inferior good" or indeed "Giffen good" may be used to suggest how income effects can be destabilizing. In contrast, many trade theorists would focus more attention on the behavior of net exporters (or sellers) of a commodity versus that of net importers. Neither group may exhibit any signs of inferiority in demand, and yet instability may arise. Why? Because the net exporters of a commodity are also consumers, and may have a higher propensity to consume the commodity in question than do net importers. In such a case, income effects are destabilizing because (ignoring substitution effects) a price rise for a commodity increases the demand for that commodity by exporters more than the negative income effects faced by importers causes them to lower demand.

18.7 The Transfer Problem

The transfer problem, so called when one country is required to make a gift or payment to another (say, after a war, as in the case of France after the war with Germany in 1870–1871, or the reverse requirement after World War I) raises the question: Do the terms of trade move against the transferor (this is a so-called "orthodox view") to make the real burden of making a transfer even more severe than suggested by the payment itself? Alternatively, do the terms of trade move in favor of the transferor? (Indeed, could a transfer so improve the terms of trade of the giver that the giver is better off? This is a question that some ask every Christmas season.) The answer to this query in the inter-war years pit Bertil Ohlin against John Maynard Keynes. Both men have articles on the "transfer problem" in the *Economic Journal* for 1929 (Keynes, 1929; Ohlin, 1929). Keynes was also famous for his (1920) book on the Treaty of Versailles that put forth the presumption that the reparations payments imposed on Germany would have a *secondary burden* in the form of a worsening of the terms of trade for Germany because of the necessity of its running an export surplus (to match the reparations). As the editor of the *Economic Journal*, Keynes deserves some credit for printing Ohlin's anti-Keynesian view. Keynes argued for the "orthodox" view and Ohlin argued that there is *no presumption*.[3] As for the *presumption* issue, I am on record (Jones, 1970) for arguing against both Ohlin and Keynes on this issue. That is, I have argued that there may be a presumption that is *anti-orthodox* in asking

---

[3] After the Treaty of Versailles, following World War I, Keynes argued strongly that the loss to Germany of having to make reparations payments to the Allies would bring about a *secondary burden* to Germany if, as he presumed, the payments would worsen the German terms of trade — an "orthodox" presumption.

about transfers. My argument is very simple (at least to me): if one knows that a country is an exporter of the first commodity and has no information as to whether it has a greater relative *supply* of the first commodity than the other country, I would bet that chances are better than even that this country has a *lower* marginal propensity to consume the good than does the other country. Alternatively phrased, if a country has a *taste bias* for a certain commodity I would argue that there is a *presumption* that it imports this good if nothing is known about supply differences in the two countries. (This assumes that tastes in each country are roughly homothetic, so that *marginal* propensities to consume a good (crucial for the *change* in direction of the terms of trade) are close to the *average* propensity to consume the good (of importance to the question of whether the good is exported or imported).

Suppose demand conditions are homothetic (but not the same) in the two countries and the amounts of each country's endowment or production of the two commodities are fixed. This allows use of a box diagram to reflect by its size the sum of the amounts produced in the two countries. Suppose taste patterns are different (but homothetic) in the two countries. In that case the contract curve (reflecting demand) is biased away from the diagonal of the box, creating two sections, one larger than the other. Which commodity Home exports depends upon where in the box its production endowment lies. If tastes are independent of production, there is a *presumption* that the endowment point lies in the larger of the two regions, and, as a consequence, Home will be an importer of the commodity in which it has a taste bias. If so, and if Home makes a transfer of purchasing power to the other country, net world demand for the commodity Home imports is reduced by the transfer and the terms of trade of Home (the giver) are improved by the transfer. This illustrates the *anti*-orthodox presumption. If production and consumption features are independent of each other, the trade pattern is not. In his articles on the transfer problem, Samuelson (1952, 1954) tended to assume that each country produced only a single commodity, so that the trade *pattern* was completely independent of tastes.

The "presumption" pattern described above also affects the stability issue. Assuming homotheticity in tastes once again, if the transfer from Home would improve its terms of trade, income effects work to establish the stability of equilibrium.

18.8   G.E. Extensions

Return, now, to the Stolper and Samuelson (1941) conclusion that a rise in the price (alone) of the labor-intensive commodity raises the real wage of labor. The simple model is that of (2 × 2) Heckscher and Ohlin, where a pair of inputs are perfectly mobile between two sectors. For some decades a set of trade economists have tried to move the setting to higher dimensions to attempt to *generalize* the results obtained in the small-scale (2 × 2) setting. The "spear-carriers" in this attempt were Kemp and Wegge (l969) on the one hand and Chipman (1969) on the other. Here, I focus on the Kemp and Wegge (1969) arguments which were concerned with what was known as the "strong form" of the theorem. Each factor is assumed to have an associated sector (industry) in which it is particularly intensive (defined below for the 3 × 3 case). A set of conditions was suggested in the hopes that it would follow that an increase in the price just for a single commodity would increase by a greater relative amount the real return to the factor associated moat intensively with that sector and, in addition, lower the return to all other factors. The criteria that Kemp and Wegge put forth for the 3 × 3 case stated that for each commodity there is a unique factor (with the same number as that of the commodity) such that the distributive factor share for that factor i in the associated industry, ϑ_{ii}, relative to that of any other factor, k, in the same industry, ϑ_{ki}, exceeds the ratio of these same two factor shares for any other industry, s, $\vartheta_{is}/\vartheta_{ks}$. Such a criterion, of course, need not be satisfied in all cases — it is an assumption imposed on the model. As well, the conclusion that the winning factor has its return increased by a greater relative amount than the price rise depends on an often unmentioned condition that there is no joint production. That is, each commodity is produced alone by a combination of both factors.[4]

Kemp and Wegge then tried to see if their criterion for the strong Stolper–Samuelson result in the 3 × 3 case would hold as well in the 4 × 4 case. Alas, it proved to be insufficient, as illustrated by a counter-example.[5] What was lacking was a condition that guarantees that distributive shares

---

[4]Query: Does the factor price equalization theorem also depend upon the "no joint production" assumption? For different points of view see Samuelson (1992) and Jones (1992).

[5]A 3 × 3 matrix of distributive shares has the property that the conditions comparing the ratio of distributive shares put forth by Kemp and Wegge make use of every element in the matrix. The same remark cannot be made for the 4 × 4 case, in which some ratio

for off-diagonal elements do not differ that much from each other so that the strong form of the Stolper–Samuelson theorem can be obtained. After all, a price rise is supposed to affect the unintensive factors in a *similar way* — they all lose. Such a condition was provided in Jones, Marjit, and Mitra (1993) for the general $(n \times n)$ case.[6]

This mathematical pursuit of the properties of the inverse of the distributive share matrix does raise some questions that should be of concern to trade economists. In asking about ways of using changes in commodity prices to raise the real return of any productive factor, why should all the "heavy lifting" be done by only raising the price of a single commodity? And, of course, why worry about having all other factors lose, when it might be more convenient for the factor that the price change is aimed at protecting to allow such a factor to point to the benefits going to *other* factors?

Is there a more general form of the Stolper–Samuelson theorem that taka account of these Concerns? Yes. Assume a competitive model with any number of factors and commodities (not necessarily the same number of each), and that allows joint production. For *any* productive factor there *does* exist a set of commodity price changes that will raise the *real* return to that factor. The proof of this existence theorem is extremely simple. The change in the particular factor's real income requires the relative change in its nominal wage rate to exceed the value of the relative change in that factor's cost of living. In any GE model, the relative change in the nominal wage is a weighted average of all commodity price changes, although many of the weights may be negative (as in the 2×2 case. In addition, the change in the factor's cost of living index is a non-negative weighted average of all commodity price changes. As long as these two vectors of price changes are *not identical,* there exists a set of commodity price changes that will increase the input's real income. This result should be of interest to those political scientists who are concerned with the scope of governmental power to reward certain groups, not by direct transfers, but instead in a *non-transparent* manner.

---

comparisons would involve only off-diagonal elements (e.g., the lower left and upper right elements of the matrix).
[6]See also Jones (2006) for a more general discussion of attempts to generalize the original (1941) Stolper–Samuelson argument.

18.9 Complementarity and Substitutability

Perhaps the most important service that GE models can provide is to show how a shock to one sector of the economy can have a ripple effect on other sectors. Of particular importance is the possibility of *complementarity* whereby a favorable shock that raises output in a single sector may also cause output in a different sector to increase despite the assumption that its price remains unaltered. One important feature of the Specific-Factors model is that a price increase in one sector has a *negative* effect on outputs in all other sectors. An effect much like this has been labeled the "Dutch disease," with reference to the discovery of natural gas deposits in the Netherlands some decades ago. The "disease" refers to the expected deleterious effect this would have on many other sectors of the economy, especially those sectors whose price remains constant.[7] The small-scale model by Gruen and Corden in describing how a country like Australia could worsen its terms of trade by levying a tariff, is capable of expressing a situation in which a price increase favoring a particular industry may create a severe Dutch disease in all other industries, or, instead, may bring about a complementary positive effect on almost all other sectors.

The setting is one explored in Jones and Marjit (1992), in a model that extended the Gruen–Corden (3 × 3) setting to a Heckscher–Ohlin ($n \times n$) model. Recall that in the Gruen–Corden setting there were only two sectors, agriculture and manufacturing, with the agriculture sector having two industries, each using labor and land, while in manufacturing there was only one industry, and it uses labor and capital. Extend this to an $(n+1) \times (n+1)$ setting by assuming that in $(n-1)$ sectors of the economy free trade leads each industry to use a unique (i.e., specific) form of capital not used by any other industry, while in the nth sector a different unique kind of capital is used by a *pair* of industries. We referred to this nth sector as a Heckscher–Ohlin *nugget*. A severe form of Dutch disease would follow if there is a price increase for the labor-intensive industry in the nugget, and since the nugget is itself a (2 × 2) Heckscher–Ohlin grouping, the wage rate

---

[7] I recall a remark the Canadian economist, Doug Purvis, made after he attended a conference in Oslo in which fears were expressed as to the possible harmful effect that the discovery of North Sea oil would have on many sectors of the Norwegian economy. Displaying his well-known tendency to capture odd events by careful use of language, Doug remarked, "It's strange about oil: whether a country has it, or does not have it, oil creates friction."

is a magnified reflection of the price increase. What is the effect on all the other $(n-1)$ sectors of the economy? They all suffer a Dutch disease type of fall in output. There is only a single gainer: the labor-intensive sector in the nugget.

In this large-dimensional setting suppose the price of the capital-intensive commodity in the nugget increases instead. This spreads to all other sectors because the fall in the wage rate leads to an increase in the rate of return to *all* the specific capitals in other sectors — an extreme form of *complementarity*. Some industry must, of course, contract — the labor-intensive industry in the nugget. It supplies labor to the capital-intensive sector in the nugget as well as to all of the specific-factor sector. That is not all — it also supplies some capital to the capital-intensive sector in the nugget. Note that since the wage–rental ratio everywhere has fallen, every industry outside the nugget must increase its labor–capital ratio in production. Perhaps surprisingly, therefore, the labor-intensive industry in the nugget loses relatively more of its capital than it does of its labor that it sends off to all other industries. Where does that capital go? To the capital-intensive industry in the nugget, the only other industry that uses that kind of capital.

This example illustrates two main possibilities that can be found in some (but not all) GE models. First, the range of possible outcomes for outputs in a large group of industries that do not experience any price change may vary from extreme Dutch disease to almost extreme complementarity. Second, the small-scale model (3×3) and the general large-scale model ($[n+1] \times [n+1]$) may exhibit the same detailed outcomes. In that sense, *scale* for the general-size model adds nothing to the possibilities found in the small-scale model. The rationale is simple: all sectors except one (the nugget) are of the specific-factor type, which has extreme simplicity in that the properties of the model are independent of the number of sectors.[8]

---

[8]There is an alternative and much less volatile reaction of outputs if in this model there is a price increase for a commodity not in the nugget. Because the prices of the pair of goods in the nugget do not change, there is no change in factor prices except to the rate of return to capital in the favored sector. In all other non-nugget sectors both the wage rate and return to capital do not change and neither do any associated outputs. The favored sector does, of course, expand, with the labor supplied by the labor-intensive commodity in the nugget.

18.10 Reciprocity Theorem

Let me conclude by mentioning another property of GE models that is dimension-free and widely used, certainly in international trade theory. I refer to the reciprocity theorem that was emphasized by Paul Samuelson (1953). Suppose that in a general equilibrium setting the commodity-price vector is represented by **p** for outputs $1, \ldots, n$, the factor-price vector by **w** for factors $1, \ldots, r$, the output vector by **x**, and the factor endowment vector by **v**. The theorem states that $\partial x_j / \partial v_i$, with all prices and other v's constant is equal to $\partial w_i / \partial p_j$ with V's and other p's constant.

This conclusion reflects the fact that the national income can be expressed either by the value of outputs, $\sum_j p_j x_j$, or *by* the value of inputs, $\sum_i w_i V_i$. The result follows because the second derivatives of Y (national income) with respect to a commodity price change and an endowment change are in every case independent of the *order* in which the two partial derivatives are obtained. Young's theorem in the calculus tells us not only that the effect of a price increase on the return to a specified factor of production has the same *sign* as an increase in that factor's endowment would have on the selected commodity output, but also that the *values* of the two derivatives are the same. In trade theory this result shows that the Rybczynsky theorem (1955) is *dual* to the Stolper–Samuelson theorem (1941). Such a result would, for example, cut the work in half of asking about the effect of international capital mobility on factor prices.

18.11 Appendix and Conclusion

In discussing, how the simple Ricardian argument about comparative advantage for the case of a pair of countries and a pair of commodities can be extended to higher dimensions, much can be gleaned from the particular case of the three-commodity, three country setting that I used in Jones (1961):

	A	B	C
Corn	10	10	10
Linen	5	7	3
Cloth	4	3	2

All three countries would require 10 units of labor to produce a unit of corn, whereas less labor is required per unit output of linen in country A, a bit more than this for a unit of linen in country B, and only 3 units of labor are required to produce a unit of linen in country C. Finally, the labor requirements per unit output of cloth are even lower for each country, especially only 2 units of labor in country C. In a world in which only corn and linen are produced and two countries, A and B, are engaged in trade, note that country A would have a bilateral comparative advantage in producing linen compared with country B and corn. If country C enters world trade and cloth can also be produced by all three countries, note that country C would have an *absolute* advantage in producing cloth compared with the other two countries. If each of the three countries were to be completely specialized in the pattern A in linen, B in corn, and C in cloth, each country compared with either of the others would have a comparative advantage in the commodity it produces relative to that assigned to the other country. It is probably surprising, therefore, to find that there is **no** set of non-negative commodity prices that would support (in pure competition) such an allocation of production in free trade![9] That is, *bilateral* comparisons of efficiency are *not sufficient* to establish efficient patterns of comparative advantage. Instead, there is an alternative allocation in which each country is completely specialized in producing a commodity and all commodities are produced. This allocation has country A producing corn, B producing cloth, and C linen. As suggested in the text, the product of the three labor costs per unit in the latter case is 90, which is less than the product in which A is in linen, B in corn, and C in cloth (yielding a product of 100):

$$a_{co}^A a_{cl}^B a_{lin}^C < a_{lin}^A a_{co}^B a_{cl}^C.$$

Now rewrite this inequality in the following form:

$$\frac{a_{co}^A}{a_{lin}^A} < \frac{a_{co}^B}{a_{cl}^B} \times \frac{a_{cl}^C}{a_{lin}^C}.$$

On the left-hand side the ratio shows for country A what the cost of corn would be if measured in units of linen instead of units of labor, — that is, the amount of linen that would have to be given up in order to free up enough labor to produce an extra unit of corn. This would represent

---

[9] Try it: let the price of corn be $1.

the *comparative cost* of producing corn in country *A*, expressed in units of linen. The right-hand side shows a comparable figure of the *comparative cost* of producing corn in the "rest of the world" (i.e., countries *B* and *C*). This would require country *B* to produce an extra unit of corn (by releasing labor from producing cloth), and, in order to keep the rest of the world's production of cloth unchanged, have country *C* take just enough labor out of producing corn to match B's cut in cloth production, and then measuring the required amount of reduction in *C*'s output of linen. That is, in the rest of the world another unit of corn is produced, there is no change in the production of cloth, but the production of linen would be reduced, by an amount that reflects the rest of the world's *comparative cost* of corn in units of the necessary sacrifice in linen production. In terms of the displayed labor costs for the three countries, the comparative cost of corn (in terms of linen) in country *A* (the left-hand side) would be 2/1 or 20/10, while the right-hand side for the rest of the world's comparative cost of corn production would be a *higher* value, 20/9, or 10/3 times 2/3.

References

Chipman, J. (1969). Factor Price Equalization and the Stolper/Samuelson Theorem. *International Economic Review*, 10, 399–406.

Gruen, F. and Corden, M. (1910). A Tariff that Worsens the Terms of Trade. In: I. McDougall and R. Snape, (Eds.), *Studies in International Economic Monash Conference Papers* (pp. 55–58). Amsterdam: North-Holland.

Jones, R.W. (1961). Comparative Advantage and the Theory of Tariffs: A Multi-country, Multi-commodity Model. *Review of Economic Studies*, 28, 161–175.

Jones, R.W. (1970). The Transfer Problem Revisited. *Economica*, 37, 178–184.

Jones, R.W. (1992). Jointness in Production and Factor-price Equalization. *Review of International Economics*, 1, 10–18.

Jones, R.W. (2006). 'Protection and Real Wages': The History of An Idea. *Japanese Economic Review*, 57, 457–466.

Jones, R.W. and Marjit, S. (1992). International Trade and Endogenous Production Structures. In: W. Neuefeind and R. Riezman (Eds.), *Economics Theory and International Trade: Essays in Memoriam J. Trout Rader* (pp. 173–196). Berlin: Springer-Verlag.

Jones, R.W., Marjit, S., and Mitra, T. (1993). The Stolper-Samuelson Theorem: Links to Dominant Diagonals. In: R. Becker, M. Boldrin, R. Jones, and W. Thomson (Eds.), *General Equilibrium, Growth and Trade II: The Legacy of Lionel McKenzie* (pp. 429–441). San Diago, CA: Academic Press.

Jones, R.W. and Ruffin (2008). The Technology Transfer Paradox. *Journal of Political Economics*, 75, 321–328.

Kemp, M.C. and Wegge, L. (1969). On the Relationship between Commodity Prices and Factor Rewards. *International Economic Review*, 10, 407–413.

Keynes, J.M. (1920). *The Economic Consequences of the Peace.* New York: Harcourt Brace and Howe.

Keynes, J.M. (1929). The German Transfer Problem. *Economics Journal,* 39, 1–7.

Metzler, L. (1949). Tariffs, the Terms of Trade, and the Distribution of National Income. *Journal of Political Economy,* 57, 1–29.

Ohlin, B. (1929). The Reparation Problem: A Discussion. *Economic Journal,* 39, 172–178.

Ohyama, M. and Jones, R.W. (1995). Technology Choice, Overtaking and Comparative Advantage. In: J. Levinsohn, A.Dearorff, and B. Stern (Eds.), *New Directions in Trade Theory* (pp. 76–93). Michigan: University of Michigan Press.

Rybczynski, T.M. (1955). Factor Endowments and Relative Commodity Price. *Economica,* 22, 336–341.

Samuelson, P.A. (1952). The Transfer Problem and Transport Costs: The Terms of Trade When Impediments Are Absent. *Economic Journal,* 62, 278–304.

Samuelson, P.A. (1953). Prices of Factors and Goods in General Equilibrium. *Review of Economic Studies,* 21, 1–20.

Samuelson, P.A. (1954). The Transfer Problem and Transport Costs: II. Analysis of Effects of Trade Impediments. *Economic Journal,* 64, 264–289.

Samuelson, P.A. (1992). Factor-price Equalization by Trade in Joint and Non-joint Production. *Review of International Economics,* 1, 1–9.

Stolper, W. and Samuelson, P.A. (1941). Protection and Real Wages. *Review of Economic Studies,* 9, 58–73.

CHAPTER 19

On Blending Competitive
Trade Models*

Ronald W. Jones

Abstract

Three standard models typically discussed in the theory of international trade are the Ricardian model, the Heckscher–Ohlin model and the Specific-Factors model. Models are often compared with each other, in an attempt to analyze which model is best or fits reality better. Instead, I suggest that these international trade models can often be *blended* to take account of finite changes when, as a country develops, the appropriate model to be used changes as the pattern of production changes. Trade allows countries to produce fewer commodities than it consumes, and which commodities are selected to be produced may change as the economy grows in the size of its endowment bundle and/or technology changes. At issue is not only the question of which commodities are produced, but also how many commodities are produced, especially with reference to the number of productive factors.

19.1   Introduction

The three most frequently used models found in the theory of international trade when pure competition is assumed are the Ricardian model, the Heckscher–Ohlin model and the Specific-Factors model.[1] Whereas the Ricardian model typically deals with a single factor of production (usually assumed to be labor) that can differ in its productivity from country to country, the latter two models are focused on industrial and country comparisons in the ratio(s) in which various factors of production are

---

*Originally published in *Pacific Economic Review*, 20(5), (2015) pp. 651–686.
[1]Later in the chapter, I also discuss the Ricardian model with a changed assumption of a variety of labor types found in each country, as developed in Ruffin (1988).

required for different commodities and the ratio(s) in which factors of production are found in the endowment bundles of different countries. The Ricardian model, the small-scale version of the Heckscher–Ohlin model (the (2 × 2) version with two factors and two commodities), as well as the small-scale version of the Specific-Factors model (the (3 × 2) version in which in each sector labor is combined with a factor used only in that sector while labor is mobile between sectors), have been subject to detailed algebraic analysis of a comparative statics variety. Differential calculus is often used in this type of analysis to examine how small shocks (e.g., commodity price changes, factor endowment changes, or changes in taste patterns or technology) affect commodity outputs and the internal distribution of income among factors of production as well as income distribution between countries.

The basic characteristic of the existence of international trade is that countries are not required to produce the entire array of commodities that are locally consumed. Instead, international exchange allows a great degree of specialization among countries in the pattern of production in each, with the basic result that production patterns tend to focus on commodities in which a country has a comparative advantage. As a consequence, although active production in any country may be limited to a small number (such as pair of commodities or, in the basic Ricardian model just a single best commodity), larger changes may induce a *change* in the *pattern of production,* and such a change is not covered by the techniques of calculus. Just as a diagrammatic representation is so useful (compared with the calculus) in depicting the gains from trade compared with autarky, such techniques can easily be deployed to illustrate required changes when patterns of production in each country must be altered following a large shock to equilibrium. Such shocks require alterations both in small scale as well as in larger-scale versions of Heckscher–Ohlin and Specific-Factors models, alterations that lead to *blends* of the two models as well as a use of the Ricardian analysis.[2]

19.2   The (3 × 2) Specific-Factors Model

The (3 × 2) version of the Specific-Factors model is the simplest example in which a country produces at least two commodities but makes use of at

---

[2] Earlier attempts at discussing these issues can be found in Jones and Marjit (1992) and Jones (2008).

least three inputs. The key to its simplicity is that each commodity makes use only of two of the inputs, which dictates that both sectors make use of a single input in common as well as an input not used in the other sector. Put differently, there is a single factor (usually taken to be labor) that is completely mobile between sectors as well as a pair of factors, each of which has absolutely no mobility between sectors. In reality, any particular factor of production may have some mobility among sectors. The specific-factors setting takes the degree of mobility to extremes: factors are either completely specific to a sector or completely mobile between (or among) sectors.

A condition of equilibrium in competitive models is that if production of a commodity is positive, unit cost must be equal to the commodity price. Let the commodities be denoted by numbers, and factors by L and K so that, letting the a_{ij}s denote input/output coefficients:

$$a_{L1}w + a_{K1}r_1 = p_1 \qquad (19.1)$$
$$a_{L2}w + a_{K2}r_2 = p_2. \qquad (19.2)$$

Letting a "hat" (^) represent a relative change (e.g., $\hat{x} = \frac{dx}{x}$) and recognizing that cost minimization requires (for small changes) that the distributive share average of the relative changes in input/output coefficients is a second-order small, Eqs. (19.3) and (19.4) represent the *competitive profit conditions of change*, where θ_{ij} is factor i's share in industry j:

$$\theta_{L1}\hat{w} + \theta_{K1}\hat{r}_1 = \hat{p}_1 \qquad (19.3)$$
$$\theta_{L2}\hat{w} + \theta_{K2}\hat{r}_2 = \hat{p}_2. \qquad (19.4)$$

In words, the relative change in unit cost equals the relative change in commodity price. As a consequence, each commodity price change is flanked by the relative changes in appropriate factor returns. This leads directly to the following inequality rankings if the price of the first commodity increases relatively to that of the second:

$$\hat{r}_1 > \hat{p}_1 > \hat{w} > \hat{p}_2 > \hat{r}_2. \qquad (19.5)$$

Thus, if commodity 1's relative price rises, the nominal wage change is trapped between the two rates of change of commodity prices, whereas the return to the fixed factor used in the first sector must increase in real terms, while that of the other fixed factor must decline in real terms. These returns to the fixed factors are, of course, better thought of as *rents*.

With labor the only mobile factor, a crucial concern is the re-allocation of labor between the two sectors as a result of the commodity price alterations. Attention thus focuses on the condition that the overall labor supply is fully employed:

$$a_{L1}x_1 + a_{L2}x_2 = L. \tag{19.6}$$

Note that each output is restricted by the quantity of the specific factor used in that sector:

$$a_{Kj}x_j = K_j \quad (\text{for } j = 1, 2). \tag{19.7}$$

Expressed in terms of rates of change,

$$\hat{x}_j = -\hat{a}_{Kj} + \hat{K}_j. \tag{19.8}$$

Now differentiate the full employment condition for labor, Eq. (19.6), and then substitute the output changes shown in Eq. (19.8) to obtain:

$$\lambda_{L1}(\hat{a}_{L1} - \hat{a}_{K1}) + \lambda_{L2}(\hat{a}_{L2} - \hat{a}_{K2}) = \hat{L} - [\lambda_{L1}\hat{K}_1 + \lambda_{L2}\hat{K}_2]. \tag{19.9}$$

Each λ_{Lj} denotes the fraction of the labor force allocated to the jth sector. The relative changes in the labor/capital ratios used in each sector depend upon changes in the wage rate relative to the change in the commodity price in each sector. In words, such a relation reveals the elasticity of demand for labor in each sector, or, in more basic terms, the elasticity of the marginal product curve for labor in that sector. Denote such an elasticity by γ_{Lj}:

$$\gamma_{Lj} \equiv -\frac{(\hat{a}_{Lj} - \hat{a}_{Kj})}{\hat{w} - \hat{p}_j}. \tag{19.10}$$

Substitute these expressions into Eq. (19.9) in order to solve for the equilibrium change in the wage rate:

$$\hat{w} = [\beta_1\hat{p}_1 + \beta_2\hat{p}_2] - \left(\frac{1}{\gamma_L}\right)[\hat{L} - (\lambda_{L1}\hat{K}_1 + \lambda_{L2}\hat{K}_2)], \tag{19.11}$$

where β_j equals $\lambda_{Lj}\gamma_{Lj}/\gamma_L$, the sum of the βs is unity, and γ_L is the economy's overall elasticity of demand for labor; that is, the weighted average of sector elasticities ($\lambda_{L1}\gamma_{L1} + \lambda_{L2}\gamma_{L2}$).

Equation (19.11) displays not only the effect of commodity price changes on the wage rate, but also the effect at constant commodity prices of any change in factor endowments. In particular, any increase in the endowment of labor lowers the wage rate, while any increase in either capital supply serves to increase the wage rate. If factor endowments stay constant, the effect of any change in commodity prices on the wage rate reveals that, as in Eq. (19.5), the wage rate increases by a smaller relative amount if a single commodity price increases. Furthermore, the expression for β_1, for example, can be altered: divide and multiply by θ_1, the share of the first commodity in the national product, to reveal that the expression for β_1 can be rewritten to highlight the role of the pair of technology features in the country as well as the importance of the relative size of the first commodity, θ_1. This leads to Eq. (19.12):

$$\beta_1 = \theta_1\{i_1 s_1\}, \qquad (19.12)$$

where the term i_1 refers to the expression λ_{L1}/θ_1, a comparison of the fraction of the labor force used in the first sector to the *overall* importance of the first sector in the national income, and, thus, is greater than unity only if the first sector is relatively labor-intensive. The term s_1 is greater than unity only if the technology in the first sector is *relatively flexible*, and is defined as the comparison between the elasticity of demand for labor in the first sector and the economy's overall elasticity of demand for labor, (γ_{L1}/γ_L). In addition to these two characteristics of technology, it is also the case that an increase in p_1 has a more powerful effect in raising the wage rate the more important in the economy is the value of output in the first sector.

This simple form of the Specific-Factors model was developed formally in Jones (1971) (see also Samuelson, 1971), and, in a less formal setting, by Haberler in the 1936s. As Samuelson often described the model, it is the one most closely associated with partial equilibrium analysis. Later I describe the ease with which it generalizes to higher dimensions.

19.3   The (2 × 2) Version of the Heckscher–Ohlin Model

Although both Heckscher and Ohlin discussed the relationship between trade and factor endowments in general terms, it was primarily Paul Samuelson who developed the more simple (2 × 2) Heckscher–Ohlin model.[3] This model was considered the standard general equilibrium model to be used in the trade area for decades. Before pursuing the fate of this model in higher dimensions, it may be useful to consider its basic features in the (2 × 2) version, especially as they differ in many respects from the specific-factors (3 × 2) model. Indeed, I would argue that focusing on the differences between these two basic models in low dimensional settings is a useful exercise for appreciating the similarity and shared properties in higher dimensions, leading to particular *blends* of the two basic models.

The key difference between these basic models is that whereas the specific-factors model has more factors of production (three) than commodities produced (two), the Heckscher–Ohlin small version has the same number (two) of factors as commodities. A major consequence of this is that there are as many factor prices to be determined as there are competitive profit conditions of equilibrium. Whereas the pair of price equal cost equations for the Specific-Factors model, Eqs. (19.1) and (19.2), and the corresponding profit equations of change, Eqs. (19.3) and (19.4), could not be solved uniquely for factor rewards if commodity prices (or changes in prices) are known, at least not without depending as well on factor endowments or their changes, the (2 × 2) Heckscher–Ohlin model exhibits zero profit Eqs. (19.13) and (19.14) that *do* link wage changes and the return to (the single type of) capital uniquely to the pair of commodity price changes[4]:

$$\theta_{L1}\hat{w} + \theta_{K1}\hat{r} = \hat{p}_1 \qquad (19.13)$$

$$\theta_{L2}\hat{w} + \theta_{K2}\hat{r} = \hat{p}_2. \qquad (19.14)$$

Although it is possible to solve separately for the wage change and the change in the return to capital, it may be more convenient merely to subtract Eq. (19.14) from Eq. (19.13) (recognizing that the distributive

---

[3]Of course other economists were also involved: for example, Wolfgang Stolper in his collaboration with Samuelson in their basic paper in 1941 and Abba Lerner in his unpublished student paper at the London School of Economics in the 1930s (published in 1952), which suggested factor-price equalization between countries.

[4]I am assuming that the first commodity is relatively labor-intensive compared with the second commodity, regardless of factor prices. This is tantamount to assuming the determinant of distributive factor shares in this equation set, $|\theta|$, or $(\theta_{L1} - \theta_{L2})$, is positive.

shares in each industry sum to unity) to obtain Eq. (19.15):

$$|\theta|(\hat{w} - \hat{r}) = (\hat{p}_1 - \hat{p}_2). \tag{19.15}$$

Because each commodity price change in Eqs. (19.13) and (19.14) is trapped between changes in the wage rate and return to capital, and because the first sector is assumed to be labor-intensive, any increase in the price of the first commodity compared to that of the second commodity leads to the following set of inequalities in factor returns:

$$\hat{w} > \hat{p}_1 > \hat{p}_2 > \hat{r}. \tag{19.16}$$

This ranking should be compared with that for the (3×2) Specific-Factors setting when the relative price of the first commodity increases: in the Specific-Factors model, once again the big winner and big loser in the rankings are both specific factors, but the wage change itself is trapped between the two commodity price changes, the ranking in Eq. (19.5). In the (3×2) setting, there is no *magnification effect* for mobile labor, while there is such an effect for the wage rate in the Heckscher–Ohlin ranking, shown by Eq. (19.16). There is an additional, more subtle, difference to be found between these two basic low-dimensional models. Although in both the increase in the relative price of the labor-intensive commodity has the effect of raising the nominal wage rate, in the Specific-Factors model the greater is the labor-intensity of the commodity whose price has increased, the greater will be the increase in the wage rate. The result is just the reverse in the Heckscher–Ohlin case. Admittedly, such a price change raises the wage rate by a magnified amount in the (2×2) Heckscher–Ohlin setting, but by a dampened amount in the Specific-Factors model. However, consider the comparison of Eqs. (19.11) and (19.12) for the Specific-Factors model with that of Eq. (19.15) for the Heckscher–Ohlin model.[5] In the Specific-Factors model, the wage rate increase is larger the greater is labor-intensity of the labor-intensive sector, while in the Heckscher–Ohlin model a greater gap in the comparison of labor intensities results in a smaller wage rate increase.

---

[5] Equation (19.15) refers to the change in the wage rate compared with the change in the rental rate. For a formal solution for the wage rate change by itself solve Eqs. (19.13) and (19.14) to obtain the solution for $\hat{w}$, holding p_2 constant: $\hat{w} = \{\theta_{K2}/|\theta|\}\,\hat{p}_1$. If for given intensities in the second commodity the labor intensity in the first sector would be larger, the denominator becomes larger, and the increase in the wage rate smaller. More details are found in Jones (1965).

19.4   Simple Diagrams for the Basic Models

As a prelude to the use of diagrams in higher dimensional cases, I review here the diagrams that best portray the scenario of pre-trade and post-trade for both the (3 × 2) and (2 × 2) models. I start with the Specific-Factors model with two commodities. Not reproduced here is the fairly standard four-quadrant diagram now found in many textbooks.[6] Such a diagram is used to illustrate how the production-possibilities curve in the first quadrant is derived using the total product curves for each commodity (quadrants II and IV) and the constraint that the labor force is fully employed (quadrant III) and, not shown explicitly, that the quantity of the specific factor in each sector is given and constant. Shown here in Fig. 19.1 is the oft-used diagram that illustrates how the equilibrium wage rate is determined by the intersection of two "front-to-front" curves showing the value of the marginal physical product of labor schedule for each sector. The equilibrium nominal wage rate is shown by point A, and the allocation of labor at point B. Special notice should be focused on what is measured on the vertical axis. It is the nominal wage rate, with the prices of both

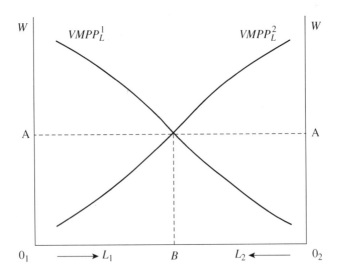

Figure 19.1.   Labor Market: Specific-Factors Model

---

[6]For example, see the diagram on page 94 of the 10th edition of *World Trade and Payments* (Caves, Frankel, and Jones, 2007).

commodities assumed given.[7] If the price of the first commodity should increase, say by 10%, the $\text{VMPP}_L{}^1$ schedule would be shifted upwards by 10%. As a consequence, the equilibrium wage rate can be seen to increase by a smaller percentage, as reflected in the positive fractional values for the βs in Eqs. (19.11) and (19.12). If, instead, the endowment of the specific factor in the first industry were to be increased by 10%, the $\text{VMPP}_L{}^1$ schedule would be shifted to the right by 10%, and the equilibrium wage rate increases (perhaps by more than 10% if the two curves were sufficiently inelastic).

Whereas the specific-factor model displays technology for each sector by using the marginal product schedule (physical or value), motivated by the immobility of the specific factors between sectors, the Heckscher–Ohlin model makes use of bowed-in isoquants for each sector. Here also there is both a physical version (the unit isoquant) and a unit value version. The latter depends upon knowledge of commodity prices. To save space, and in anticipation of the higher-dimensional cases, Fig. 19.2 illustrates the concept of the Hicksian composite unit-value isoquant in a four-commodity case. This is a concept used frequently in international trade theory, and it assumes that the technologies that are displayed are those in use in a particular country (and not necessarily found in common in other countries), whereas the commodity prices used are typically those ruling in world markets.[8] The composite unit-value isoquant in Fig. 19.2 is the inner locus, *DCBGA* (extended at both ends), composed of individual unit-value isoquants and connecting tangency cords. What these cords reveal is that for given endowment proportions (say with endowment rays passing through *DC* or *BA*), full employment of both factors would necessitate production of two commodities. For example, point *E* shows a bundle of capital and labor that would produce a dollar's worth of commodity 1. There is no way of producing a dollar's worth of any other single commodity using less labor and capital than shown by point *E*. However, a point such as *G*

---

[7]A curve showing the marginal product of labor schedule would have, on the vertical axis, the wage rate divided by the given commodity price, which would not be appropriate in Fig. 19.1 because commodity price units differ between commodities.

[8]If unit-value isoquants for these four different commodities' assumed domestic prices are given in an autarky situation in which all four commodities are produced, they would all be tangent to a common budget line with slope reflective of the autarky local wage/rent ratio.

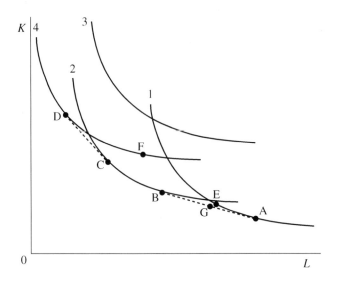

Figure 19.2.   The Hicksian Composite Unit-Value Isoquant

illustrates how a blend of around 50 cents worth of the second commodity using techniques shown by point B and around 50 cents worth of the first commodity using techniques shown by point A would require less capital and labor than would point E that produces only the first commodity. Note also that this diagram reveals that the technology that the country possesses for producing the third commodity is inferior to that possessed by some other country (or countries). For this country to produce a dollar's worth of commodity 3 more labor and capital would be used than is required by producing an alternative point on the Hicksian composite unit-value isoquant.

Unit-value isoquants combine knowledge of two important variables (technology and world commodity prices), whereas the two-quadrant diagram in Fig. 19.3 illustrates these separately, focusing here on the two-commodity case. The two positively sloped schedules in the top diagram show how the capital/labor ratio that would be utilized to produce each commodity is dependent upon prevailing wage/rent ratios. The arbitrary assumption that the first commodity is produced with relatively labor-intensive techniques for any factor price ratio is embodied by the locus for the first commodity lying everywhere below that for the second commodity

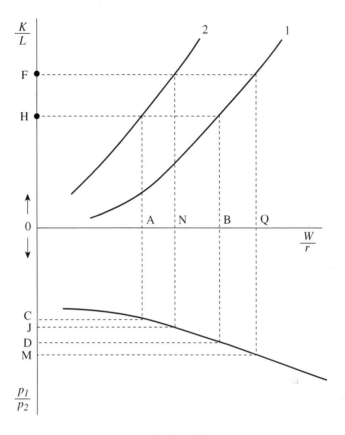

Figure 19.3.   Heckscher–Ohlin 2 × 2 Model

for any commonly faced factor price ratio.[9] Points H and F represent two possible endowment proportions, say in two different countries. If, say, Home has endowment ratio H, its wage/rental rate must lie in the range AB, while another country, Foreign, assumed here to share the same technological knowledge, must have the overlapping factor price ratio shown by the range NQ. The dependence of each country's wage/rental ratio on the commodity price ratio (e.g., as reflected in Eq. (19.15)) is illustrated

---

[9]This rules out the possibility of *factor-intensity reversal*, which might occur if the two loci in the top part of Fig. 19.3 crossed each other. A word of warning: in later diagrams that illustrate growth possibilities in an economy capable of producing more than two commodities the axes are reversed to emphasize how factor endowment proportions help to determine factor price ratios.

in the lower part of Fig. 19.3 by the downward-sloping locus, drawn in order to illustrate two important points. First, any increase in the relative price of the first commodity must, if the country is actively producing both commodities, serve to increase the relative wage rate because the first commodity is assumed to be labor-intensive. Second, there is the *magnification effect* formally shown in Eq. (19.15) by the (positive) *fractional* value for $|\theta|$ or by the ranking shown in Eq. (19.16). Finally, note that in the (2×2) Heckscher–Ohlin model the transformation curve in either country is not that much different from a downward sloping line (as in the Ricardian model). For Home the transformation schedule, whose slope reflects the commodity price ratio, allows incomplete specialization *only* for the price range CD, while for Foreign both commodities can be produced only if the commodity price ratio is in range JM.[10] The famous factor-price equalization theorem (see Samuelson, 1948, 1949) for these two countries would hold only if commodity prices allow *both* countries to be incompletely specialized by lying in the JD range.

Note that the lower dimensional version of the Specific-Factors model has dimension (3×2), while the lower dimensional version of the Heckscher–Ohlin model has dimension (2×2). With reference once again to Fig. 19.3 suppose, for the Home country, that the relative price of the first commodity should increase beyond $0D$ (in the lower quadrant of Fig. 19.3). Then this country becomes completely specialized in producing the first commodity, and the dimension passes from (2×2) to a (2×1) model. This latter model can be referred to as a *degenerative* case of the Specific-Factors model, and such a change provides a basic example of *a blending of* two types of model. (The dependence of the w/r ratio on the commodity price ratio in cases in which Home is completely specialized would be captured in Fig. 19.3 by adding, in the lower quadrant, a vertical cord connecting point

---

[10]Wolfgang Mayer (1974) provides a well-cited treatment of the specific-factor setting as a short-run model and the (2×2) model as a long-run model, and illustrates the connection between transformation schedules in the two models, with the (2×2) schedule being an envelope of the various (3×2) curves as one kind of capital is over time converted to the other kind as output patterns differ. The surprise that I find with his illustration in figure 1 (p. 959) is in the range of slopes of the long-run (2×2) model (almost the entire range of relative price from zero to infinity) compared with the limited CD range in Fig. 19.3 in this chapter. (Such a large range appears also in Krugman *et al.* (2012, p. 88).) Neary (1978) also emphasizes the short-run and long-run interpretation.

A to the curve in the lower quadrant corresponding to price ratio *C*, as well as a cord from this curve for the price ratio *D* to higher values of p_1/p_2.)

19.5   The Multi-commodity International Trade Scenario

In a Heckscher–Ohlin setting, the move to higher dimensions is difficult in one direction but easy in another. The difficulty arises in situations in which more than two inputs are involved in any production process.[11] Until later, I will assume that activities in the Heckscher–Ohlin setting use only labor and capital, both of which are mobile among sectors. I concentrate here on the case in which many commodities can be produced and many countries engaged in trade. This is useful in two principle ways. First, it allows a much more realistic setting than does the two-commodity version by revealing how much the move from autarky to international trade allows a great degree of *concentration* of productive activities, whereas discussions for the basic 2 × 2 model mostly emphasize that trade can allow different *proportions* of the two commodities produced than the ratio in which they are consumed. (This point is made more obviously in Ricardian models of trade in which the concept of comparative advantage in production for trade makes its first appearance.) Second, it is a setting in which the peculiar characteristics of growth and development in an economy open to trade are exposed: if a country can greatly limit what it produces without sacrificing its consumption desires, at various stages of growth it may make different decisions as to which commodity to produce. For open developing economies the vision of fairly balanced growth among productive sectors of the economy makes little sense if consumers can obtain their needs more economically by importing, and pay for these by concentrating on producing those commodities in which the country has the greatest comparative advantage. The answer to the question of which commodities to produce will systematically change as capital/labor endowment proportions are altered with development.

---

[11] Later I emphasize that the difficulty is not in having a large number of inputs in the economy. This will become obvious in general higher dimensional models of the specific-factors type, where every activity uses labor plus an input used only in that activity. By contrast, the plethora of different degrees of substitution among factors if many are used in a single activity, and of the possibility of complementarity among some factors if more than two are involved in production, are not discussed here, but are mentioned briefly later.

Figure 19.2 illustrates such systematic changes. With the capital/labor endowment ratio shown by the slope of a ray from the origin, development at the given set of commodity prices would involve producing only the first commodity if such a ray (not drawn) is flatter than 0A, and with further increases in the endowment proportions at these prices the country would produce commodities 1 and 2 (e.g., with a dollar's worth produced with input point G), and then produce only the second commodity with further growth until some of commodity 4 can be produced as well. How many commodities need it produce? If all commodities are traded, the answer is no more than the number of productive inputs. The earlier discussion of the Hicksian composite unit-value isoquant, the convex hull of the unit-value isoquants (at world prices) in Fig. 19.2, shows the tangent cords where two commodities are produced, as well as the strictly bowed-in sections along which full employment of both productive factors can be obtained by producing only a single commodity. As long as world prices do not mirror the details of technology in any single country, it would be accidental for more than two unit-value isoquants to be tangent to any single cord.[12] Thus, a country need not produce more commodities than the number of its productive factors. Could it produce fewer? Of course it can, as Ricardian models loudly proclaim, as well as in the (2 × 2) Heckscher–Ohlin setting whenever prices are such that the economy is driven to complete specialization. For example, the Home country in Fig. 19.3 could not produce any of the first commodity if its relative price should be lower than 0C.

Figure 19.4 is like a five-commodity version of the top diagram in Fig. 19.3, but the axes have been reversed, to highlight that with growth the equilibrium relative wage rate becomes endogenous.[13] More has been changed: other commodities have been added, and the technological relationship between wage/rental ratios and the capital/labor ratios that would

---

[12] An exception would have to be made for a country large enough in world trade that even in a two-factor setting world prices would have to allow such a country to produce at least some of the other commodities. Of course here I do not include an important and realistic possibility, one in which obstacles to international trade (natural or man-made) result in a set of "non-tradeables" being locally produced because otherwise local demands could not be met. The issue of producing many commodities when nontradeables are also produced is discussed later, and also in Jones and Marjit (1992) as well as Jones (2012).

[13] An early use of this kind of diagram is found in Jones (1974).

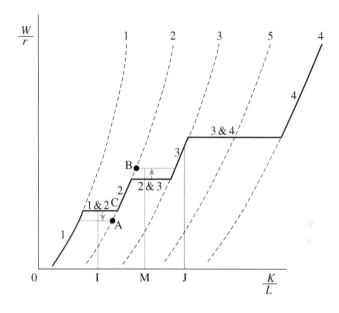

Figure 19.4.   Factor Endowments and Factor Prices

be adopted if each commodity were produced are illustrated by the upward-sloping dashed curves. The solid sections along these curves as well as the horizontal solid sections between curves illustrate the pattern of production that would take place for any given endowment proportions if world prices are given and unchanged. The horizontal lines are relevant if the economy produces a pair of commodities, such as commodities 1 and 2 along the cord at point G in Fig. 19.2 if, in Fig. 19.4, the endowment proportions are at point I. Along these flats in Fig. 19.4 an economy produces a pair of commodities and, as a consequence, the given commodity prices determine the factor prices (and their ratio). In a sense, the solid locus shows how even though the wage/rental ratio is often improved (at given commodity prices) by growth in the capital/labor endowment ratio, there are also regions in which such growth leaves factor prices unchanged. If two countries share the same technology and world prices, but have different endowments that, nonetheless, allow them to produce the same pair of commodities, their wages and rents on capital will be the same, reflecting the Samuelson factor-price equalization theorem.

In this setting with many commodities, the sets of endowments for which a pair of commodities is produced are interposed with regions in which only a single commodity is produced.[14] This represents the *degenerate* case of the specific-factors setting referred to earlier, with the (3 × 2) dimensions replaced by the (2 × 1) dimensions. (Of course, with only a single commodity produced, there is no distinction between mobile and specific factors.) Not only is the diagram useful in comparing the situation between two countries that share a common technology but differ in endowment capital/labor ratios, it also reveals how, if a country develops and its K/L ratio rises, both the Heckscher–Ohlin model (2 × 2) and the degenerate case of the Specific-Factors model can be blended to reveal how the bundle of a pair of commodities produced can change over time, with always an intermediate step of complete specialization. Furthermore, Fig. 19.4 is useful in revealing possible reactions to an increase in the world price of the second commodity. What happens to factor returns? This depends upon whether the country has endowment proportions such that it initially produces commodities 1 and 2 (such as for an economy with endowments given by point I), in which case the second commodity is relatively the more capital-intensive of the pair of commodities produced and the wage/rental ratio would fall. Alternatively, an economy producing both commodities 2 and 3 would, because commodity 2 is relatively labor-intensive, experience a magnified increase in the wage rate and the return to capital would fall. In this setting it would be incorrect to rule out "Heckscher–Ohlin behavior" if a pair of countries sharing the same technology and both producing the commodity whose price has increased respond in one country with a wage fall and in the other with a wage increase. Indeed, this kind of "factor-intensity reversal" is seen to be quite possible even if the technologies by themselves have rising curves (in a Fig. 19.4 scenario) that do not intersect.

In Fig. 19.4, an increase in p_2 enlarges the range of endowments for which a country is specialized to the second commodity (to region AB along the technology curve for the second commodity after the price increase). If an economy's factor endowment has it specialized to producing only commodity 2 before and (of course) after the price increase, both the wage

---

[14]The exception to this remark would be found in the extreme case in which all isoquants are right-angled (i.e., do not allow smooth substitution between labor and capital). In such an event, the positively-sloped dashed lines depicting technology in Fig. 19.4 would be vertical.

rate and the return to capital would increase by the same relative amount as the commodity price, so that the wage/rental rate does not change (unless the K/L ratio changes). The standard (2×2) Heckscher–Ohlin model describes the consequences on the internal distribution of income for a developing country as it grows by increasing its capital/labor endowment: of course factor prices do not change if commodity prices are constant (and the country remains incompletely specialized to the same pair of commodities). As Fig. 19.4 emphasizes, increased endowments of capital relative to labor only serve to increase the relative wage rate when a country changes its *pattern* of production by becoming completely specialized in what was its capital-intensive commodity before growth. Of course, changes in the relative price of a commodity that is produced always change factor returns, but in a manner highlighted in the (2×2) version of the model only if the economy is incompletely specialized.

19.6 Specific-factors: An Extended Version Blending with Heckscher–Ohlin

So far, the specific-factors scenario has envisaged each specific factor engaged in a single activity. This vision can be expanded by imagining a sector that consists of a number of activities or industries, all using the same kind of capital, a kind, however, that is not used in other sectors. In other words, each type of capital is sector-specific, not specific to just one industry. This is the kind of idea used in a special interpretation of a (3×3) model introduced some years ago by Fred Gruen and Max Corden (1970) to capture some features of the Australian economy. Theirs was a two-sector model consisting of manufacturing and agriculture. Manufacturing was represented by a single industry, textiles, produced by labor and capital. Agriculture, by contrast, was a sector consisting of a pair of industrial activities: wheat and wool. Whereas labor was used in (and was mobile among) all three industries, agriculture used a specific kind of sector specific "capital" (land), mobile only between industries (wheat and wool) in the agricultural sector. This kind of structure was generalized to higher dimensions in Jones and Marjit (1992) and is used here as another example of blending the basic ideas of the Specific-Factors model and the Heckscher–Ohlin model (see also Jones, 2013, pp. 565–566).

To introduce these ideas the present study starts not with a free-trade situation but, instead, with an economy initially in autarky, cut off from a world market in which different technologies and taste patterns have supported an array of commodity prices different from those in the autarkic equilibrium. Production in the autarkic economy is undertaken in many sectors, each of which has a number of industries all using labor (used throughout the economy) as well as a kind of capital specific to that sector. Diagrammatically, in the autarky equilibrium each sector can be visualized by a separate kind of capital on the vertical axis, labor on the horizontal and a set of unit-value isoquants for all industries in that sector. Unlike the Hicksian composite unit-value isoquant depicted in Fig. 19.2, market prices in autarky have adjusted such that all the unit-value isoquants in each sector are tangent to a common "budget line," whose slope is given by $-w/r_j$ for this, the jth sector. Commodity prices are brought into equilibrium by matching up local demand and supply for each industry, with additional balance between aggregate labor demand and supply determining the wage rate. This value for w, along with equilibrium prices, p_j^i, for the price of each industry, i, in the jth sector, determines the various specific-factor rentals, r_j. (For a commodity to be produced in autarky, its price must allow for the same positive return to sector-specific capital in that industry as for other industries in that sector.)

This setting provides a more robust example than found in the previous settings of how opening an economy to international trade can greatly reduce the number of goods in production compared with autarky. Each sector now faces world competitive markets for each of its industries, and the kind of comparison typically made in Ricardian models (the search for the item with the greatest comparative advantage) yields, let us assume, a "winner" in each sector: the commodity that yields the highest return to sector-specific capital. If such were the case, the economy would end up with an $[(n + 1) \times n]$ specific-factors setting, n commodities produced with a specific capital and mobile labor. However, this need not be the outcome! Think back to the Gruen/Corden setting: The agricultural sector supported a pair of industries, wheat and wool, and, indeed, the dimensions of the model were 3 (inputs) and 3 (commodities). So also in this case there may exist a single sector that has two industries surviving, making this economy have what we call a "Heckscher–Ohlin nugget" (i.e., with trade the sector collapses to a (2×2) Heckscher–Ohlin setting), and the economy, with trade, has the same number of industries as it does factors of production, $n + 1$.

Consider, now, a diagrammatic illustration for an economy engaged in free trade and having a number of "sector-specific" forms of capital. The procedure leading to Fig. 19.4 is no longer available, because there is no overall unit for "K": each sector has a different kind of capital. Nonetheless, all sectors face the same wage rate in equilibrium, and with commodity prices and the endowments of all specific factors given, all the separate "rents" earned by the various types of sector-specific capital would be determined. Therefore concentrate, first, on each sector's demand curve for labor. This is not a smooth negatively-sloped locus. Instead, it is a step-function of a type illustrated in Fig. 19.5.[15] Note that at a sufficiently high wage rate, any rate higher than point A, no industry in sector j would survive. The reason? With commodity prices determined in world markets, local demand for all industries in this sector could be supplied by

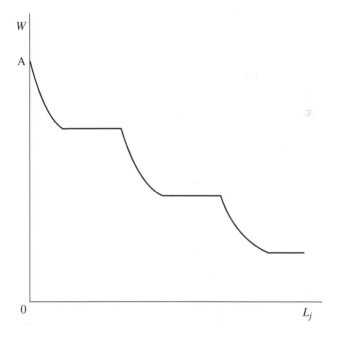

Figure 19.5. Labor Demand in Sector j

---

[15]This kind of diagram has previously been utilized by Deardorff (1984).

imports, because at such a high wage rate the specific factor used in sector j would, if employed, yield a negative rate of return.[16] For a wage rate slightly lower than shown by point A, there emerges a single "best" industry in sector j, and as the wage rate falls (with a concomitant increase in r_j), substitution possibilities for producing this best industry encourage more labor-intensive means of production, much as in Fig. 19.4's depiction for an economy with only one type of specific capital.[17] However, at a lower wage rate a more labor-intensive industry might join the previous "best" industry, and a range of labor demanded in this sector can support the same wage rate, corresponding, in Fig. 19.4, with a leftward movement along a flat segment (which would be a rightward movement in Fig. 19.5). When one "best" industry finally yields completely to a more labor-intensive one, a further lowering of the wage rate is associated with a greater demand for labor in this new single industry until an even newer (more labor-intensive) industry joins the previous industry, with a new flat segment appearing in the labor demand schedule. Thus, open trade does, indeed, lead to a great degree of specialization in each sector, but not necessarily to the extreme of a single surviving industry. Which single industry or which pair of industries survives after trade depends upon the value of the wage rate in equilibrium.

The kind of demand curve for labor in the jth sector illustrated in Fig. 19.5 can be visualized for all other sectors. The equilibrium value of the wage rate depends upon the summation of labor demands from all sectors, and this aggregate demand locus for labor is shown in Fig. 19.6. I have assumed that although there may be a number of flat segments for each sector (with its given amount of sector-specific capital), these occur at different wage rates from those for any other sectors. In Fig. 19.6, two possible vertical aggregate supply curves for labor are illustrated. If the labor supply is L', the equilibrium wage rate is shown at point A, implying that for this economy there is some single sector in which there is a *nugget* of two

---

[16]In the event that some commodities are nontradeable, there could be one or more such industries that could command a commodity price sufficiently high that sector-specific capital in sector j would earn a positive return. Later I discuss the issues involved if nontradeables are allowed in this model.

[17]A downward move in the wage rate (with a given quantity of capital but an increase in the labor supply) is, in Fig. 19.4, associated with a leftward movement along the horizontal axis (i.e., a reduction in K/L).

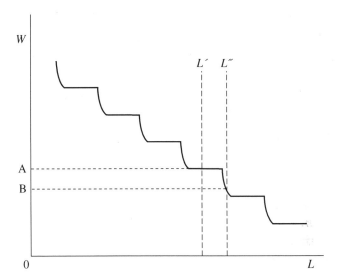

Figure 19.6. Aggregate Demand and Supply of Labor

industries that survive competition (as in the Gruen/Corden agricultural sector with wheat and wool). The economy as a whole has $(n + 1)$ factors of production, and is producing, with trade, an equal $(n + 1)$ number of commodities, a version of a Heckscher–Ohlin model.[18]

However, if the labor supply curve were to expand to L'', the equilibrium wage rate would fall (as shown by point B), but there would only be a single industry in every sector that survives competition. The economy would be characterized by an $[(n + 1) \times n]$ Specific-Factors model. That is, this economy exhibits either a Heckscher–Ohlin structure or a Specific-Factors structure. It all depends upon the particular technology for all commodities in all sectors as well as on the endowment of labor and of every type of specific capital. With growth of endowments and/or changes in world prices the model type is endogenous. Furthermore, even if the economy exhibits a producing nugget before and after change (i.e., it is Heckscher–Ohlin before and after) the particular industries that are producing as well as the sector in which the nugget operates may differ. The visualization of a *flat segment* along which factor prices stay the same is captured both in diagram like Fig. 19.4 for a Heckscher–Ohlin ($2 \times n$) setting as well as in a

---

[18]I assume that rates of return to all specific capitals are now positive.

multi-commodity model in which a number of sectors have their own type of capital but all use a homogeneous kind of mobile labor so that, as in Fig. 19.6, a diagram relating aggregate demand for labor with total supply can depict the economy's equilibrium.

There is a question that is at the core of general equilibrium models, especially for economies engaged in trade: If one industry in an economy experiences a price increase (or perhaps a technological improvement), how are other industries affected? In the international trade literature the phrase introduced to reveal that, given the importance of relative ranking embodied in the theory of comparative advantage, a price rise for one industry could easily spell trouble for other industries in the economy is the *Dutch disease.*[19] The two variants discussed above, the $[(n+1) \times n]$ version of the Specific-Factors model and the $[(n+1) \times (n+1)]$ version of the Heckscher–Ohlin model, allow radically different responses to a world increase in the price of a traded commodity. In the Specific-Factors version a price rise for any commodity produced would result in a wage increase (less than proportionate), and this spreads to all other sectors of the economy, resulting in a loss of labor and reduction in the return to capital in these sectors. The favored industry, as a consequence, expands at the expense of all other producing industries. This is the Dutch disease writ large. A radically different outcome is a possibility in the Heckscher–Ohlin version in which one sector of the economy contains a (2×2) nugget. Suppose the commodity whose price increases is produced in some other sector, not containing the nugget. Production of that commodity expands with the inflow of labor released by the nugget. No other industry outside the nugget is affected because the wage rate and all returns to capital (other than in the sector in which there has been a price rise) do not change because the wage rate is determined only by the prices in the pair of industries produced in the nugget. The labor-intensive commodity that is produced in the nugget is the loser. The other (capital-intensive) commodity produced in the nugget actually expands: an expression of the famed Rybczynski effect (1955) whereby an economy (here the nugget) that experiences a loss of labor at constant commodity prices (in the nugget) will suffer a

---

[19]See, for example, the discussion in Corden and Neary (1982) and Neary and van Wijnbergen (1986).

loss in output of the labor-intensive industry and an actual expansion of output in the capital-intensive industry in the nugget. The labor-intensive industry in the nugget is the only industry adversely affected in Dutch-disease fashion.[20] This example illustrates, via the capital-intensive industry in the nugget, that a price rise in one industry (outside the nugget) can result in a complementary expansion in another industry.

To round out this discussion of the differences between these two versions of higher dimensional cases, suppose that the externally-provided price increase (in the Heckscher–Ohlin version) is for one of the industries in the nugget. If the favored industry is the labor-intensive industry in the nugget, the wage rate increases and all other industries contract: once again, a scenario in which the Dutch disease is extreme. However, if the favored industry is the capital-intensive one in the nugget, the wage rate falls, thus allowing all industries outside the nugget to expand, with consequent enormously-spread complementary effects outside the nugget, with the single labor-intensive industry in the nugget supplying labor to all other industries in the economy.

These possibilities can be summarized as follows. First, strong Dutch disease results, with many industries that have not benefitted from a price increase suffering an output fall, are most likely to exist if the price rise is for the labor-intensive industry in the nugget in the Heckscher–Ohlin $[(n+1) \times (n+1)]$ scenario. Second, a less extreme version (in terms of outputs) of the Dutch disease is that found in the Specific-Factor model, the $[(n+1) \times n]$ case, in which any producing industry's price rise has a dampened effect in raising the wage rate, which nonetheless hurts all other sectors. Second, the weakest Dutch disease result is found in the Heckscher–Ohlin version if the price rise is for the capital-intensive industry in the nugget, where only the nugget's labor-intensive industry suffers and all other producing industries expand: a strong example of complementarity. First, if the price rise does

---

[20]In the Gruen/Corden (3 × 3) model, if the price of textiles in the manufacturing sector increases, the agricultural sector loses labor, and this actually results in an *expansion* in the less labor-intensive activity in agriculture; namely, wool production. In their case, the domestic price of textiles increases because of a tariff on imports of textiles, and, because Australia is a large producer of wool on world markets, such a tariff serves to worsen Australia's terms of trade. Such a result seemed paradoxical in the literature on tariff theory, where a country, large enough to have an influence on world prices, would benefit by an *improvement* in its terms of trade when it levies a tariff.

not take place in the nugget of the Heckscher–Ohlin version, factor prices are unaffected, as are outputs in all other industries except for those in the nugget. The labor-intensive industry in the nugget contracts, while the capital-intensive industry actually expands in a complementary fashion.

19.7   The Produced Mobile Factor Structure

One of the advantages of the Specific-Factors structure is the ease with which it can be generalized to any number of sectors. As in the earlier treatment of the (3×2) case, the focus can rest upon the market-clearing equation of change for the single mobile factor, say labor. The multi-commodity version of the equilibrium change in the wage rate, caused either by commodity-price changes or endowment changes, is the n-commodity version of Eq. (19.11), as well as to the form for each coefficient for price changes exhibited in Eq. (19.12). The n-dimensional structure is as easy to manipulate and understand as is the two-commodity case. Such a remark cannot be made of an n-commodity version of the Heckscher–Ohlin model without severe conditions being imposed on the production structure. One set of conditions that has been explored leads to an $(n \times n)$ structure that shows how similar a version of the Heckscher–Ohlin model can be made.[21] Indeed, one single modification in the multi-commodity Specific-Factors setting is sufficient to convert the model to a Heckscher–Ohlin setting in which the *strong form* of the Stolper–Samuelson (1941) theorem is obtained for any commodity price change: Any commodity price rise will increase by a magnified amount the reward to the single factor used most intensively in the industry whose price has increased and, as well, lower the return to all other factors. The modification: Suppose that instead of raw labor serving as the single mobile factor in a multi-commodity Specific-Factors model, the mobile factor is, instead, produced by all of the "specific" factors, in any of the normal ways assumed for constant-returns-to-scale production functions. This, in effect, reduces the number of independent inputs to n, the same as the number of produced commodities.

The proof of this kind of result for the produced mobile factor structure involves only a simple but intensive use of all the competitive profit Eqs.

---

[21] Details of the model are provided in Jones and Marjit (1985). A discussion of ways of generalizing the Stolper–Samuelson result can be found in Jones (2006).

of change (such as those for the (2×2) Heckscher–Ohlin case illustrated in Eqs. (19.13) and (19.14)). Let the first commodity experience a price increase, with all other commodity prices constant, and start with the $(n-1)$ equations of change for all commodities, $j \neq 1$:

$$\theta_{jj}\hat{w}_j + \theta_{Mj}\hat{w}_M = 0 \quad j = 2 \ldots n. \tag{19.17}$$

where M refers to the mobile factor and j to the specific factor used in the jth sector. From these one can conclude that $\hat{w}_M$ has a sign that is opposite to $\hat{w}_j$ for all $j \neq 1$. Next, consider the competitive profit equation of change for the activity that uses all "specific" factors in producing the mobile factor:

$$\theta_{1M}\hat{w}_1 + \Sigma_i\theta_{iM}\hat{w}_i = \hat{w}_M, \quad \text{for } i = 2 \text{ through } n. \tag{19.18}$$

From this equation one can conclude that $\hat{w}_1$ and $\hat{w}_M$ have the same sign and, furthermore, that in absolute value $\hat{w}_1$ exceeds $\hat{w}_M$. Finally, consider the remaining competitive profit equation of change, which refers to changes in the activity producing the first commodity:

$$\theta_{11}\hat{w}_1 + \theta_{M1}\hat{w}_M = \hat{p}_1. \tag{19.19}$$

Because $\hat{p}_1$ is positive by assumption, and because $\hat{w}_1$ and $\hat{w}_M$ have the same sign, they must both be positive, with $\hat{w}_1$ the greater of the two. Summing up,

$$\hat{w}_1 > \hat{p}_1 > \hat{w}_M > 0 > \hat{w}_j \quad \text{for all } j \neq 1. \tag{19.20}$$

Concentrating just on the "specific" factors, the so-called strong Stolper–Samuelson results hold: An increase in any single commodity price raises by a magnified amount the return to the factor used most intensively in producing the commodity and lowers the return to all other factors (except the mobile factor, which is now a produced factor).

The *produced mobile factor structure* is, indeed, a special case of the Heckscher–Ohlin model, and it does satisfy the strong Stolper–Samuelson condition, which many $(n \times n)$ models do not.[22]

---

[22]The argument presented here leads to the following mathematical result: Suppose **A** represents a positive diagonal matrix and **B** is a nonnegative matrix of rank 1 (of the same dimension as **A**). Add these two matrices and take the inverse. The result is that $(\mathbf{A}+\mathbf{B})^{-1}$ is a matrix, **C**, with strong Stolper–Samuelson properties. That is, **C** is a matrix of positive diagonal elements all greater than unity and negative off-diagonal elements.

19.8   More on the Multi-commodity Model: The Ruffin-Ricardo Model

By making use of the Ricardian-based model introduced by Roy Ruffin (1988) there is another scenario that leads to an easy-to-handle multi-commodity and multi-factor model. Ricardo's model envisaged a number of different labor types, but each type resided in a different country. While maintaining the notion that the world's labor supply was, indeed, heterogeneous, Ruffin assumed that residing in each country was a mix-ture of various labor types.[23] Each type of labor has a given productiv-ity in producing each commodity, as in Ricardo. However, and this is crucial, as in Ricardo each laborer on its own can produce any com-modity. That is, it is assumed that there is no joint production on the input side. Any commodity can be produced by a single type of labor; there is no necessity of having a proper balance among factors produc-ing a commodity because each works on its own. Furthermore, not only is labor of different types possessive of different levels of productivity, countries differ from each other in their relative endowments of different types. What emerges is a clean blend of Ricardian models with Heckscher–Ohlin models. Even in the (2 × 2) Heckscher–Ohlin model no commodity can be produced with a single input: A combination of the two types of input is required, although the particular intensities depend upon factor prices.

In the Ruffin–Ricardo model, free trade ensures factor-price equaliza-tion. It does not matter where each labor type lives, its productivity is the same in any country, and if commodity prices are equalized by trade so also will be the array of factor returns in different countries. As for produc-tion, the transformation schedule in any country, say in a two-commodity setting, will look much like that of a world transformation surface in the original Ricardian model, exemplified by a broken line along each seg-ment of which a single country's labor is shifting from the production of one commodity towards that of the other.[24] The resulting shape of the

---

[23]In this model there is *not* assumed to be any movement between countries of any labor type.

[24]This is illustrated in the Ruffin (1988) article. The higher dimensional three-commodity case is discussed in McKenzie (1954) and Jones (1961).

transformation schedule (or surface) depends both upon the productivity of each type of labor in each commodity as well as a country's relative endowment of each kind of labor. If each country hosts a complete variety of labor types, with free trade their transformation surfaces would exhibit the same allocation of commodity production to each type of labor, so that any labor type will be producing the same commodity (or commodities) in all countries for any given set of world commodity prices. The difficulties in analyzing production scenarios in the general case of many factors and commodities are removed in the Ruffin setting in which any factor can produce any commodity without the cooperation of any other factor or factors. Once a move to required joint production on the input side with three factors is made, a pair of factors might be complements and/or different pairs of factors may differ greatly in their substitutability with each other. The Ruffin–Ricardo model frees up the multi-factor models from these possible difficulties.

19.9   How Concentrated does Trade Make Production?
A Hybrid Model

Throughout this discussion of various competitive trade models a major generalization emerges: international trade allows consumption of a wide selection of commodities while permitting a great concentration of production for export. However, the extent of concentration in Ricardian models (especially) and in the two-factor Heckscher–Ohlin model seems realistically too drastic: the country can concentrate its production of tradeables to one or two commodities. Although a general model of production with many commodities and many productive factors can be developed (and it would, indeed, expand the number of commodities that might be producible in a competitive equilibrium), it would not be of much use if the comparative static solutions of output and factor price changes when the economy is subject to shocks are difficult to ascertain without detailed information on the structure of the economy. However, it is possible to create a simple hybrid model, a blend of the many-commodity, two-factor (labor and capital) Heckscher–Ohlin model with the easier-to-analyze specific-factor setting.[25]

---

[25]This model is developed in Jones (2007).

In the two-factor, many-commodity Heckscher–Ohlin model described in previous sections, it was assumed that capital as well as labor could (costlessly) become mobile from sector to sector should conditions in the market (such as the array of commodity prices) change to suggest an alteration in what becomes the "best" single or pair of commodities to produce. Although retaining the assumption that labor is homogeneous and mobile, suppose now that once capital is created, it is specific in its use, so that the commodity that was the previous year's best choice may no longer be the same in the current period. If so, current production of the previous period's winner can, nonetheless, take place, even if it were no longer to be the recipient of new capital formation. New capital takes specific forms once the choice of best locale for returns for this period's investment is made, and such capital then becomes useful in current and future periods as an input factor to the productive process for a particular commodity.

The setting of this model is useful in describing possible patterns of production over time. Thus, suppose that echoes of the past are present in an initial setting in which there exists positive production of a set of commodities in which currently there would not be any new capital formation because the return to capital there is exceeded by that in some other sector or a pair of sectors. Given a fresh set of commodity prices in the current period, if new capital formation is to take place, which sectors of the economy should be the recipients? The optimal answer to this query depends upon: (i) how much new capital formation takes place; and (ii) how much labor is allocated to join with this new investment. (The analogy is with Fig. 19.2, where the endowment ray determines the pattern of production. Here it is the ratio of investment to the amount of labor working with it that determines the pattern of new capital formation.) As to the first question I shall be completely simplistic and assume that there is a given amount of labor that is used every period to produce new capital.[26] This sidesteps the very important macroeconomic question concerning the determinants of the aggregate value of new net investment. To answer the second question it is necessary to balance two further sources of demand for labor, above and beyond the quantity used to produce new investment. First, all sectors that have in the past been recipients of specific capital will continue to produce

---

[26]Further to simplify, assume new capital requires only labor in its production.

(as long as the rental on that type of specific capital is positive), and, of course, will require current labor as well. How much labor each such sector demands depends upon the wage rate (with all commodity prices set on world markets). For each wage rate it is possible to add up the quantity of labor required in each such sector (call the total L_S, for specific labor demand). The L_S curve is downward sloping with respect to the wage rate. Second, as well, labor is demanded in order to join new investment in producing the best type of good (s) at this year's prices. This labor demand (call it L_I for labor used with new investment) is locally downward sloping with respect to the wage rate only if new capital is all used in a single sector. However, if new capital is to be used in a pair of industries, the demand for labor to accompany new capital formation lies anywhere on a flat segment where both these goods are produced. That is, at that wage/rental ratio, the demand curve for labor is horizontal along a flat segment.

These two sources of demand are brought together in Fig. 19.7. This should remind you of Fig. 19.1 for wage rate determination in the specific-factors model. Here the total labor supply is net of the predetermined amount used to produce new capital. In Fig. 19.7, the equilibrium wage rate (w_E) shows the allocation of labor (at point A) between the sectors that have specific capital from the past $(L_S)^{27}$ and the new sector receiving all current investment. If the L_S curve had intersected the L_I curve along a flat segment, new investment would be poured into a pair of industries, in the form of capital appropriate to the specific needs of each such sector.

One important characteristic revealed in this analysis is that new investment could take place in a sector that in an earlier period had been the recipient of capital formation. In addition, if there have been improvements over time in the efficiency of capital in this sector, the newer type of capital could receive a higher rental than capital of older vintage. Eventually, some types of specific capital could not earn any positive rents, and would be scrapped.[28] Furthermore, this period's winner might be an import-competing sector as opposed to an export sector, depending upon

---

[27] This includes the labor used with preexisting capital in this period's best sector.

[28] There is an older literature in economic theory dealing with capital of different "vintages" and distinguishing between "putty" type capital and "clay" type capital. The "clay" type of capital in our treatment is sector-specific, after determination of the sector to receive general "putty" type capital. See Johansen (1959) and Solow (1962).

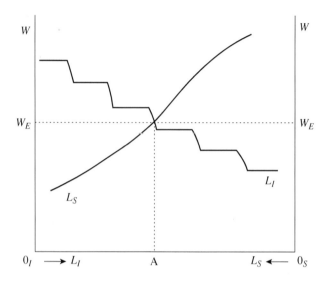

Figure 19.7. **Labor Allocation between New Best Sectors (*I*) and Older Producing Sectors (*S*)**

the past accumulation of capital in that sector as well as new capital formation. This hybrid model provides a useful base for describing the passage over time of investments, the growth or decline in separate sectors, and the impact of commodity price changes on the wage rate and, thus, on the rents that can be obtained by the type of capital specific in each sector. Such rentals on specific capital represent, in competitive models, the amounts left over from total revenues after labor has been paid. This is a model in which history matters.

19.10   Middle Products

A further example of ways in which Heckscher–Ohlin models have been blended with those of specific factors is provided by the work of Sanyal and Jones (1982), in which all productive activity in an economy is undertaken either in what is termed the *input tier* or the *output tier*. The input tier is one in which factors of production (labor and certain specific factors) produce items that can be traded on world markets. Such trade allows items that are available in world markets to be used as inputs along with labor to produce commodities in the output tier of the economy, and these represent final local consumption. In this scenario, international trade takes place in the

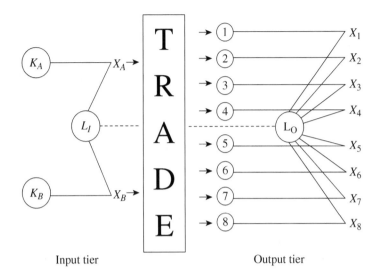

Figure 19.8.   Trade in Middle Products

middle of a country's production spectrum, as illustrated in Fig. 19.8, and all consumption items appear as outputs in the output tier.[29] There are two specific factors in the input tier, denoted K_A and K_B (and many more could easily be added), and each works with labor assigned to the input tier (L_I) to produce a pair of outputs called *middle products*, some of which are used as further inputs at home, and the rest are traded on world markets for a different array of inputs (goods in process or intermediate goods). Items taken from the world market (items 1 through 8) are specific inputs that are combined with labor in the output tier (L_O) to produce final consumer goods (labelled X_1 through X_8). These consumer goods have local prices determined by the wage rate and world prices for all middle products used in the output tier. Commodities X_1 through X_8 comprise the set of nontradeables. Note that the production structure in the output tier is of the specific-factors type, with each consumer good produced with one of eight different middle products and labor. However, with given prices for traded middle products, international trade in effect transforms the eight specific middle products into a single aggregate, thus turning the output tier into a Heckscher–Ohlin model with two factors (labor and this aggregate of

---

[29]This diagram appears as Fig. 19.3 in Jones and Marjit (2009).

middle products) and, in the case shown in Fig. 19.8, eight commodities. Whereas Peter Neary (1978) relied on time and depreciation to convert specific capital into a single mobile input, a similar conversion is made more rapidly in the middle products scenario with the use of international trade.

This description, how international trade helps to convert the original specific-factors structure of the output tier into a Heckscher–Ohlin structure with only two basic inputs (i.e., labor and traded middle products) differs somewhat from our earlier description (as illustrated in Fig. 19.4). In Fig. 19.4's depiction, with only two basic inputs (labor and capital), the number of commodities produced may be limited to a single commodity (along the rising portions of the dark locus) or, at most, a pair of commodities. By contrast, in Fig. 19.8, I show in the output tier that eight commodities are produced. The difference is that in the middle products scenario, all commodities produced in the output tier serve as final *nontraded* consumption commodities. All international trade takes the form of converting the input tier's output of middle products into a variety of specific inputs required to produce nontradeables that are consumed. Indeed, a further transformation could be developed. The labor used as inputs in the output tier are assigned to eight different tasks, and the different technologies that may be used in each could lead to a differentiated set of skills learned by labor in the output tier. That is, whereas originally the output tier could be described as a Specific-Factors model with many specific factors and labor, which by trade is converted into a Heckscher–Ohlin model, the further differentiated experience of the labor force might be described as converting a Heckscher–Ohlin model back into a specific-factors setting, a setting that now has a single aggregate mobile factor (because of trade leading to imports of middle products for items 1 through 8 at given world prices) and a collection of eight *specific* types of labor.[30]

19.11   Nontraded Goods

This discussion of Middle Products assumes that all commodities that are consumed represent value added in the output tier as local labor converts traded goods (middle products) into nontraded final consumption items.

---

[30]More details can be found in Jones and Marjit (2009).

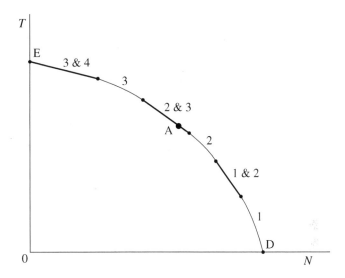

Figure 19.9. Transformation Curve: Traded and Nontraded Goods

Return now to the previous discussions of blends of Specific-Factors models and Heckscher–Ohlin models to investigate new issues that arise if some of the produced products do not enter international trade but instead are protected from the international markets by the existence of trade barriers that are natural (e.g., high transport costs) or man-made (e.g., prohibitive barriers to trade such as high tariffs). Focus attention on the situation faced by a small open economy that faces given prices for all traded commodities. Local demand and supply considerations nonetheless affect the prices of commodities that are not traded on world markets. Figure 19.9 illustrates a possibility for the transformation curve of an economy with given technology and endowment base facing given world prices for traded commodities 1–4, as well as producing a single nontraded good, N. Assume that N is more labor-intensive than any of the producible traded goods. The transformation curve reflects the supply side of the market. (Note, for example, that if there were no resources used to produce nontradeables, the country would produce both commodities 3 and 4. Because I have assumed the nontradeable commodity N is more labor-intensive than any of tradeables 1–4, as they descend from good 4 to good 1 the move is to higher ratios of labor intensity.) Local demand could be illustrated by an indifference curve

(not drawn) tangent, say, at point A, in which case the economy would produce traded goods 2 and 3 as well as the amount of the nontraded good, N.
The transformation curve has *flat segments* for regions such as point A at
which a pair of traded goods is locally produced, which determines the pair
of input prices (wages and rentals), thus establishing, as well, the price of
the nontraded commodity, N. For regions in which only a single traded
good is produced, demand factors help to determine the relative price of the
nontraded commodity given world prices for all the traded commodities
(and, thus, to determine factor prices as well).

Now consider a case in which there is a change in the price of one of the
traded commodities. To simplify, suppose this represents an improvement
in the country's terms of trade reflected in a price decrease in a commodity imported, but not of a commodity the country produces or would
produce even if the country's endowment were different; that is, a price
drop for a commodity in which the country's technology is sufficiently
inferior to that in the producing country abroad that Home competition
is impossible. Such a setting is helpful for exposing the basic property
of demand relationships: such a price change in world markets has both
an income effect and a substitution effect on all commodities consumed
at Home. Although all other prices for traded commodities are assumed
to remain unchanged, the price of nontradeable N might rise, or fall, or
remain unchanged. Figure 19.10 captures the possibilities. The supply curve
for N consists of rising sections as well as flat segments, and its shape is
consistent with that of the transformation schedule in Fig. 19.9.[31] With
the fall in the price of a tradeable commodity not produced at Home
(but imported), the substitution effect works to shift demand away from
all commodities that are substitutes in consumption with the tradeable
whose price falls, while the income effect works in the opposite direction
(assuming no commodities are inferior in demand behavior). For a finite
fall in the price of the tradeable item, Fig. 19.10 illustrates how the demand
curve for nontradeables shifts to the right (say to D_N') if income effects
are more powerful, and to the left (say to D_N'') if substitution effects outweigh income effects. The boundary value of demand elasticity leading to
no change (i.e., keeping the demand curve at D_N in Fig. 19.10) is, of course,

---

[31] This situation is discussed in more detail in Jones (2012).

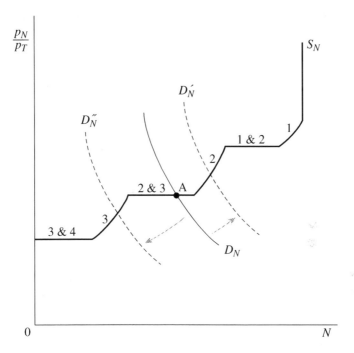

Figure 19.10.   The Market for Nontradeables

that showing unit elasticity, as in the Cobb–Douglas case. In Fig. 19.10, the possible shifts in the D_N curve are shown large enough to bring about a change in the price of nontradeable N. In general, the price of the non-tradeable does not change if the economy continues to produce the same pair of commodities.[32] A sufficiently large discrepancy between income and substitution effects may lead either to a fall or to an increase in the relative price of nontradeables, leading to changes as well in some produc-tion patterns as well as to changes in the amounts of various exports and imports.

This discussion of the role of nontradeables suggests that the demand relationships involved in the case in which the world price of one of the

---

[32]Note that the price change in any commodity that is tradeable and consumed has the effect of shifting the set of indifference curves between tradeables and the nontradeable, because it shifts the weights used in aggregating the various commodities composing the aggregate over all tradeables.

International Trade Theory and Competitive Models

(non–locally produced) tradeables goes down leads the nontradeable sector to act like a reservoir from which other sectors can extract labor if substitution effects in demand outweigh income effects (i.e., demand is elastic) or as a sponge soaking up labor from other sectors if income effects dominate. Alternatively, if the price of a locally produced and exported tradeable commodity increases (in a specific-factors setting), Corden and Neary (1982) point out that the rate of return to capital in the nontradeable sector may rise (if income effects are dominant), even possibly by a greater amount than in the favored export sector.

19.12 Fragmentation and Outsourcing

The earlier discussion of international trade in middle products focused on the use of international trade to alter the availability of inputs in the production process. The literature of the past couple of decades has focused in more detail on the possibility that all of the factors that are used in the production process of a given commodity need not be found in one locale. In particular, some parts or components might be produced in several different countries before being assembled perhaps in a different country in final form and then made available to consumers throughout the global market.[33] In an early contribution, Henryk Kierzkowski and Jones (1990) emphasized the important role played by various types of service activities, such as transport, communication, obtaining information and coordination, in allowing a widespread location of inputs involved in producing the various *production blocks* that need to be joined to obtain the final commodity. We labeled these service activities *service links*. Of critical importance in our treatment of such fragmentation is that even though the cost of such links might indeed increase the larger the scale of production of various production blocks, they would not generally increase step by step with output in a constant-returns-to-scale manner. Some types of these service link costs could be treated as constant cost elements, even if other parts may increase in proportion to the scale of outputs. As a consequence, the relationship between total costs and final output when such outsourcing takes place will exhibit increasing returns to scale, and

---

[33] It is often remarked that a traded final commodity that says "made in China" may have less than 10% value added by the work done in China.

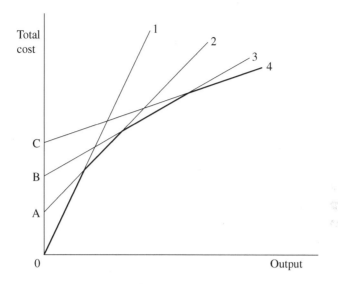

Figure 19.11. Fragmentation, Outsourcing and Increasing Returns to Scale

this, we argued, was the important reason why, as the level of production increases, the average costs of production would tend to fall as more and more output gets produced, a change that would tend to favor relatively large producers in making use of trade to aid in production, whether or not such production is in large part aimed at world markets.

This phenomenon can be conveyed by the extremely simple scenario depicted in Fig. 19.11. The cost schedule labeled "*1*" reveals constant returns to scale and reflects a production process in which all inputs (or "production blocks") are produced locally by a firm at home. An alternative schedule of total costs involves some fragmentation of the production process whereby some required input is obtained elsewhere: perhaps in the same country but different locale or perhaps from a foreign source. The outsourced fragment might be produced within the firm, or perhaps obtained by purchases from a different firm. In either case, outsourcing the fragment can be fit into the production process only by incurring "service link" costs involved with coordinating the various fragments together. As already emphasized, the costs of service links (such as obtaining information, insuring against delays, even transportation) in general do not increase proportionally to the scale of output. Such costs are partly indicated by distance 0A (like fixed costs), whereas those service link items that do increase with the scale of output are reflected in the slope of cost schedule "2", which on net shows the reduction in overall marginal costs compared with that of cost schedule "1", a reduction that is achieved by fragmentation and outsourcing. Further outsourcing may take place, e.g., outsourcing that would reduce marginal costs of production to those shown by the slope of "3", although entailing as well the added service link costs overall, shown by 0B. There are many more possibilities. For example, the cost structure illustrated by curve "4" may reflect a switch in the locale of a previously supplied production fragment, a switch not made at lower levels of output because its acknowledged lowering of the marginal costs of production is not sufficient to offset the increase in service link costs represented by the move upwards from 0B to 0C.

The heavy broken line in Fig. 19.11 reveals by its shape that once the possibility of fragmenting the various "inputs" in the production process to other locales (that have a lower cost pattern but do involve expenses to co-ordinate them into the process), the average costs of production tend to be reduced with the scale of output. This is one reason why international outsourcing of fragments of the production process has been such a growing activity in recent years: outsourcing becomes more prevalent once the scale of outputs increases as global incomes rise. However, perhaps a more important phenomenon has been the great advance in the past several decades in the costs of "service link," activities such as communication and transportation. Putting together these two more recent changes (higher incomes and lower service link costs) helps to explain the fact that international trade in "parts and components" is now one of the most rapidly growing types of trade. Furthermore, note that if, in some industry, there exists an array of firms that differ in size, it is the larger firms that engage in greater use of outsourcing, perhaps aided by undertaking foreign investment as well.

Worth emphasizing in discussions of fragmentation and outsourcing is the source of the increases in real income that accommodates such fragmentation. The basic gains are explained in a manner familiar from the basic Ricardian model of trade: the finer the division of items that can be traded, the greater the gains that accrue based upon the existence of differences between countries in the pool of resources (labor in the Ricardian scenario) that cannot be moved directly to other countries. This is the rationale for the doctrine of *comparative advantage*. If all resources were perfectly mobile between countries they would re-allocate to areas (and uses) in which their absolute returns would be maximized. If such mobility is not available, comparative advantage still supports gains. Of course, some productivity differences among countries in their labor forces depend as well upon the presumed lack of mobility of other inputs such as real capital and the proportions in which such internationally immobile resources are found. The importance of the fact that what has been referred to here as *service link activities* have costs that do not necessarily increase in proportion to the level of productive activity is that increasing returns to scale will appear as the level of total output expands. Such service link activities (such as transportation) could be found, of course, in more standard versions of trade in which only final commodities are exported and imported, but have been assumed away in previous sections of this chapter.

19.13   Concluding Remarks[34]

In pursuit of competitive models appropriate for comparative statics in open-economy development scenarios, I have illustrated examples that blend certain aspects of the three basic competitive international trade models: the Specific-Factors model, the Heckscher–Ohlin model and the basic (and earlier) Ricardian model. Blends of these models become appropriate when *finite* changes are considered, because one consequence of international trade is that the production array in a trading equilibrium encourages a great deal of concentration, with the result being that production *patterns* may change with alternating changes in the rankings by comparative advantage. Such finite changes can often be identified and analyzed using diagrammatic techniques when the calculus (so useful in trade theory when small shocks are analyzed) no longer proves sufficient to capture changes in equilibrium patterns of production. This chapter has discussed a number of different ways in which

---

[34]Much of the recent work on trade theory has made use of the Dornbusch, Fischer, and Samuelson (1977) so-called *continuum* model in which continuity (essential in using the calculus) is established by assuming that an infinite number of goods are produced and consumed, each good, of course, bearing infinitesimal weight. In our own work, Kierzkowski and I have instead retained the classical view of a finite number of separate activities, with changes in prices, output levels and technology leading to finite switches of production sites as fragmentation allows greater degrees of outsourcing.

blends of the standard neoclassical competitive models are useful for the purpose, especially for questions important in growth and development theory.

In discussing how blends of these basic models are important when considering finite changes, primary attention was given to the effects on the pattern of outputs when a country grows with increases in endowment capital/labor ratios. However, attention was also given to the situation in which a country is faced with finite changes in the prices of commodities that are traded in global markets. Such price changes not only affect the internal distribution of income among productive factors but also require changes in the composition of outputs, leading to a blend of the basic trade models. Indeed, even if price changes originating in world markets do not include those of any global commodities produced within a country, they may nonetheless cause changes (via income and substitution effects in demand for nontradeables) in which global commodities the country produces. Furthermore, the question of which commodities a country produces is in more recent times matched by the question of which parts or components of a fragmented production process are outsourced (or, indeed, insourced from) abroad.

The theory of international trade often emphasizes the remark attributed to Alfred Marshall that the forces of demand and supply are like two blades of a pair of scissors as both are required to determine whether commodities that enter trade are exported or imported. Trade theory clearly has made extensive use of the demand side for pursuing normative issues as well as emphasizing that certain questions that arise, such as in the question of the stability of equilibrium in a trade setting, are issues in which it is the demand side of the market in which characteristics are found that may lead to instability. Difficulties for such questions are not apt to be found on the supply side. However, it is the supply side of the market that dominates the question of the *pattern of trade*. In my view, the most important aspect of trade theory is not that consumption patterns differ from production patterns, thus leading to vectors of exports and imports in equilibrium, but instead it is the characteristic of trade that arises naturally in the Ricardian model: trade allows a country greatly to concentrate production. Unfortunately, the development of theory, in making extensive use of scenarios with small numbers of commodities (two being the most frequently used number, such as in the Heckscher–Ohlin (2×2) model) has most often illustrated equilibria in which trade indeed takes place, but in which both commodities are produced as well as consumed, with the focus directed on which of the two commodities gets exported and which imported. Left out of these exercises is the important question of which commodity or commodities get produced and which do not, because international trade opens up the possibility that some commodities that are consumed need not be produced at home. In a sense the important question concerns the greater extent to which production is affected by trade as compared with consumption. In addition, in considering the question of the political forces that are often arrayed against free international trade, much is often made of the plethora of home producers that are negatively affected by competition from abroad. This is the flip side of the argument promoting the gains from trade: such gains often depend upon taking resources away from production of commodities locally, perhaps production that represented important local export industries in the recent past; that is, before endowments, technology and price changes at home or abroad altered the patterns of comparative advantage.

The final remark that is perhaps justified in thinking of the importance of demand features and supply features is highlighted in the phenomenon of fragmentation and outsourcing. Think of the concept of *demand*. This typically brings to mind the reaction of consumers to price changes of commodities that they consume. However, producers also have demands: choices to be made as to where to obtain inputs into their production process. These issues of choice in production become increasingly important as input markets become evermore globalized. Furthermore, although the emphasis here is on local producers obtaining the use of some production blocks that are produced abroad, there are other local producers who are active in allowing foreign firms to outsource part of their production needs. Many of the gains in the developing globalization activities originate from the greater fragmentation of vast numbers of productive activities, allowing a greater number of different production blocks to enter global markets because of rising income levels and significant drops in the costs of service link activities. This reflects the heritage of a wider use of the Ricardian concept of comparative advantage, in which the finer division of items that can be traded leads to further gains from trade. A country may produce and export a commodity in which an important share comes from the contribution of foreign labor: not by the international movement of such labor but by the international trade in parts and components contained in the final product.

References

Caves, R.E., Frankel, J.A., and Jones, R.W. (2007). *World Trade and Payments* (10th edn.). Boston, MA: Addison Wesley.

Corden, W.M. and Neary, J.P. (1982). Booming Sector and De-industrialization in a Small Open Economy. *Economic Journal*, 92, 825–848.

Deardorff, A. (1984). An Exposition and Exploration of Krueger's Trade Model. *Canadian Journal of Economics*, 17, 731–746.

Dornbusch, R., Fischer, S., and Samuelson, P.A. (1977). Comparative Advantage, Trade and Payments in a Ricardian Model with a Continuum of Goods. *American Economic Review*, 67, 823–839.

Gruen, F. and Corden, W.M. (1970). A Tariff that Worsens the Terms of Trade. In: I. McDougall and R. Snape (Eds.), *Studies in International Economics: Monash Conference Papers*. Amsterdam: North-Holland.

Haberler, G. (1936). *The Theory of International Trade*. London: William Hodge & Co.

Johansen, L. (1959). Substitution versus Fixed Production Coefficients in the Theory of Economic Growth: A Synthesis. *Econometrica*, 27, 157–176.

Jones, R.W. (1961). Comparative Advantage and the Theory of Tariffs: A Multi-Country Multi-Commodity Model. *Review of Economic Studies*, 28, 161–175.

Jones, R.W. (1965). The Structure of Simple General Equilibrium Models. *Journal of Political Economy*, 73, 557–572.

Jones, R.W. (1971). A Three-Factor Model in Theory, Trade and History. In: J. Bhagwati, R. Jones, R. Mundell and J. Vanek (Eds.), *Trade, Balance of Payments and Growth*. Amsterdam: North-Holland.

Jones, R.W. (1974). The Small Country in a Many Commodity World. *Australian Economic Papers*, 13, 225–226.

Jones, R.W. (2006). 'Protection and Real Wages': The History of an Idea. *Japanese Economic Review*, 57, 457–466.

Jones, R.W. (2007). Specific Factors and Heckscher–Ohlin: An Intertemporal Blend. *The Singapore Economic Review*, 52, 1–6.

Jones, R.W. (2008). Key International Trade Theorems and Large Shocks. *International Review of Economics and Finance*, 17, 103–112.

Jones, R.W. (2012). Real Wages and Non-Traded Goods. *International Review of Economics and Finance*, 21, 177–185.

Jones, R.W. (2013). Bubble Diagrams in Trade Theory. *Pacific Economic Review*, 18, 561–573.

Jones, R.W. and Kierzkowski, H. (1990). The Role of Services in Production and International Trade: A Theoretical Framework. In: R. Jones and A. Krueger (Eds.), *The Political Economy if International Trade* (Ch. 3, pp. 31–48). Hoboken, NJ: Wiley-Blackwell.

Jones, R.W. and Marjit, S. (1985). A Simple Production Model with Stolper–Samuelson Properties. *International Economic Review*, 19, 565–567.

Jones, R.W. and Marjit, S. (1992). International Trade and Endogenous Production Structures. In: W. Neufeind and R. Riezman (Eds.), *Economic Theory and International Trade: Essays in Memoriam J. Trout Rader.* New York: Springer-Verlag.

Jones, R.W. and Marjit, S. (2009). Competitive Trade Models and Real World Features. *Economic Theory*, 41, 163–174.

Krugman, P., Obstfeld, M., and Meltiz, M. (2012). *International Economics* (10th edn.) Boston, MA: Addison-Wesley.

Mayer, W. (1974). Short-run and Long-run Equilibrium for a Small Open Economy. *Journal of Political Economy*, 82, 955–967.

McKenzie, L.W. (1954). Specialization and Efficiency in World Production. *Review of Economic Studies*, 21, 165–180.

Neary, J.P. (1978). Short-run Capital Specificity and the Pure Theory of International Trade. *Journal of Political Economy*, 88, 488–510.

Neary, J.P. and van Wijnbergen, S. (1986). *Natural Resources and the Macroeconomy.* Boston, MA: MIT Press.

Ruffin, R. (1988). The Missing Link: The Ricardian Approach to the Factor Endowments Theory of Trade. *American Economic Review*, 78, 759–772.

Rybczynski, T.M. (1955). Factor Endowments and Relative Commodity Prices. *Economica*, 22, 336–341.

Samuelson, P.A. (1948). International Trade and the Equalisation of Factor Prices. *Economic Journal*, 58, 63–84.

Samuelson, P.A. (1949). International Factor-Price Equalization Once Again. *Economic Journal*, 59, 181–197.

Samuelson, P.A. (1971). Ohlin was Right. *The Swedish Journal of Economics*, 73, 365–384.

Sanyal, K. and Jones, R.W. (1982). The Theory of Trade in Middle Products. *American Economic Review*, 72, 16–31.

Solow, R.M. (1962). Substitution and Fixed Proportions in the Theory of Capital. *Review of Economic Studies*, 29, 207–218.

Stolper, W. and Samuelson, P.A. (1941). Protection and Real Wages. *Review of Economic Studies*, 9, 58–73.